# INTRODUCING GENDER AND WOMEN'S STUDIES

# Introducing Gender and Women's Studies

## Third Edition

Edited by

Diane Richardson
and
Victoria Robinson

First edition published 1993
Second edition published 1997
Third edition published 2008 by
PALGRAVE MACMILLAN
Houndmills, Basingstoke, Hampshire RG21 6XS and
175 Fifth Avenue, New York, N. Y. 10010
Companies and representatives throughout the world

PALGRAVE MACMILLAN is the global academic imprint of the Palgrave Macmillan division of St. Martin's Press, LLC and of Palgrave Macmillan Ltd. Macmillan® is a registered trademark in the United States, United Kingdom and other countries. Palgrave is a registered trademark in the European Union and other countries.

ISBN-13: 978–0230–54300–3     paperback
ISBN-10: 0230–54300–6     paperback
ISBN-13: 978–0230–54299–0     hardback
ISBN-10: 0230–54299–9     hardback

This book is printed on paper suitable for recycling and made from fully managed and sustained forest sources. Logging, pulping and manufacturing processes are expected to conform to the environmental regulations of the country of origin.

A catalogue record for this book is available from the British Library.

A catalog record for this book is available from the Library of Congress.

9   8   7   6   5   4   3   2   1
16   15   14   13   12   11   10   09   08

Transferred to Digital Printing in 2009

*For my mother and father and in memory*
*of my grandmother Fannie Hinchliffe*
Diane Richardson

*For my mother, Sandra Robinson, my nana, Nellie Robinson,*
*and in memory of my grandmother, Winifred Thompson,*
*for their strength and dignity*
Victoria Robinson

# Contents

# List of Tables and Figures

## Tables

## Figures

# Acknowledgements

We would like to thank all those involved in the preparation of this book. Special thanks go to Sally Hines, who worked with me at Newcastle developing the Sexualities Interdisciplinary Network (SIN), for the mammoth task of sorting out the bibliography. Thanks also to Sue Tatah in the School of Geography, Politics and Sociology for her help with boxing! We would also like to thank our publishing editor Catherine Gray and the production staff at Palgrave Macmillan. Sadly, since the last edition Jo Campling, who was consultant editor, and Anne Witz, who contributed an excellent chapter on Women and Work, have both died. We would like to remember them here, and also acknowledge the contribution to women's and gender studies of other feminist scholars who have died since the publication of the second edition, but whose work continues to inform many of the debates discussed in this book, including Sue Lees, Meg Stacey and Tamsin Wilton. I am also (yes, still) grateful to Vicki Robinson, who originally had the idea of writing this book, for asking me to co-edit it with her. A great deal has changed since then, but our friendship endures as does our sharing of ideas, colour charts and chocolate. My thanks to family and friends for their support, in particular Jackie Davis, Nina Laurie and Hazel May. Lastly, to my dad, who died in the final stages of production of this book, and who taught me so much.

*Newcastle*                                         DIANE RICHARDSON

It may be something of a (feminist) record not to have one cross word over editing three editions of this book, but working with Diane continues to be a pleasure. We are both immensely proud of being associated with a textbook which continues to inform different generations of students interested in feminist theories and research. Students at different institutions have contributed to the ideas in this book, and for many reasons, it was a fortunate thing that Colin Gibberd turned up at the very first women's studies course I ever taught. Jenny Hockey, with whom I now work at the University of Sheffield, and who has been associated with both the first and second editions of this book, continues to be a very valued friend and colleague. I want to thank family and others for bearing with me over the course of the book, including longtime friends Maggie Murdoch, Heather Symonds, Rod Pollard and Eleanor Ingram. I also want to thank my friends Sarah Pickles and Rose Crawley for all the help they have given me with child care whilst this book was in progress. A special thankyou to Joe Picalli and, as usual, my son Eddie Joe Robinson now aged 12 and whose patience with me never ceases to amaze.

*Sheffield*                                         VICTORIA ROBINSON

# Notes on the Contributors

**Nickie Charles** is Professor and Director of the Centre for the Study of Women and Gender at the University of Warwick. She is currently working on an ESRC-funded project, Gender and Political Processes in the Context of Devolution, with colleagues in Swansea University and writing a book, *Families in Transition* (The Policy Press). The book is based on a restudy of the classic research into the family and social change undertaken in the early 1960s by Colin Rosser and Chris Harris at Swansea. She has published widely on gender, her most recent book being *Gender in Modern Britain* (2002), and has a particular interest in feminist social movements and their influence on policy change.

**Debbie Epstein** is Professor of Education at Cardiff School of Social Sciences. She has published widely on sexuality, gender and 'race' and is interested in how these and other 'differences that make a difference' are produced and sustained in sites of cultural struggle like educational institutions, the media (especially television) and in legislative discourse. Her books on these issues include *Silenced Sexualities in Schools and Universities* (2003), co-authored with Sarah O'Flynn and David Telford, *Schooling Sexualities* (1998), co-authored with Richard Johnson and *Border Patrols: Policing the Boundaries of Sexuality* (1997), co-edited with Richard Johnson and Deborah Lynn Steinberg, and *Failing Boys? Issues in Gender and Education* (1998), co-edited with Jannette Elwood, Valerie Hey and Janet Maw. She has also written the *Academic's Support Kit* (2005), six books to support early-career academics and their mentors, with Rebecca Boden and Jane Kenway. She is currently working on a book about gender and sexuality in the context of HIV/AIDS in South Africa with Robert Morrell, Deevia Bhana, Relebohile Moletsane and Elaine Unterhalter.

**Stacy Gillis** is Lecturer in Modern and Contemporary Literature at Newcastle University. She has published widely on contemporary feminist theory, cybertheory and twentieth century literature and film. The editor of *The Matrix Trilogy: Cyberpunk Reloaded* (2005) and *Third Wave Feminism: A Critical Exploration* (rev. edn, 2007), her forthcoming work includes *Feminism and Popular Culture: Explorations in Post-Feminism* (2008), *The Edinburgh Critical Guide to Crime Fiction* (2008) and a collection on the First World War in popular culture.

**Sally Hines** is a lecturer in the School of Sociology and Social Policy at the University of Leeds. Her research interests fall within the areas of identity, gender, sexuality, the body and citizenship. Her work is particularly concerned with transformations in gendered, sexual and embodied identities. Her current work addresses recent legislative shifts around sexuality and gender in relation to gendered, sexual and embodied diversities and citizenship debates. She has published a number of journal articles and book chapters on gendered and sexual transformations, and a sole authored book, *TransForming Gender: Transgender Practices of Identity, Intimacy and Care* (2007).

**Ruth Holliday** is Professor of Gender and Culture and Director of the Centre for Interdisciplinary Gender Studies at the University of Leeds. Her research interests are primarily located in contemporary social and cultural theories of intersectionalities, the body and popular culture. In particular she is currently applying these issues to two substantive areas: 'elective' cosmetic surgery (published in *Feminist Theory* and the *Journal of Consumer Culture*), and material culture – through her forthcoming book (co-written with Tracey Potts) *Kitsch: A Cultural Politics of Taste*. In the past she has carried out research on identity performances and sexualities through the use of video diaries, which has been published in *Sexualities, American Behavioral Scientist* and *Sociological Review* and she has edited a number of books on work, organizations and the body.

**Zoe Irving** is Lecturer in Comparative Social Policy in the Department of Sociological Studies, University of Sheffield. Her research interests focus on the relationship between social policy and the labour market, particularly the impact of changing employment practices on gender relations. She has published on women's self-employment in Denmark, France and the UK and male part-time employment in OECD countries. She has also undertaken pedagogical research in association with the UK Higher Education Academy's subject centre for Social Policy and Social Work (SWAP) and published work addressing the internationalization of the Social Policy curriculum.

**Stevi Jackson** is Professor of Women's Studies and Director of the Centre for Women's Studies at the University of York. Her main research interests are feminist theory and sexuality, with a particular emphasis on heterosexuality. She is author of *Childhood and Sexuality* (1982, 1996), *Heterosexuality in Question* (1999) and *Theorizing Sexuality* (forthcoming, with Sue Scott), as well as numerous articles on sexuality and intimacy, including 'Gender, Sexuality and Heterosexuality: The Complexity (and Limits) of Heteronormativity', *Feminist Theory*, 7 (1) (2006); 'Faking Like a Woman: Towards an Interpretive Theorization of Sexual Pleasure, *Body and Society*, 13 (2) (2007) (with Sue Scott); and 'The Appalling Appeal of Nature: The Popular Influence of

Evolutionary Psychology as a Problem for Sociology', *Sociology*, 41 (5) (2007) (with Amanda Rees). She has co-edited, with Sue Scott, *Feminism and Sexuality* (1997) and *Gender: A Sociological Reader* (2002).

**Kate Reed** is a lecturer in Sociology at the University of Sheffield. She has published broadly in the area of race, gender, social theory and the sociology of health and illness. She is the author of *Worlds of Health* (2003) and *New Directions in Social Theory: Race, Gender and the Canon* (2006).

**Diane Richardson** is Professor of Sociology in the School of Geography, Politics and Sociology, and Director of the Centre for Gender and Women's Studies at Newcastle University. She has written extensively about feminism, gender and sexuality, including work on HIV/AIDS, sexuality and citizenship, sexual politics and social change, and feminism and queer theory. She is author of *Theorising Heterosexuality* (1996), *Rethinking Sexuality* (2000) and, co-edited with Steven Seidman, *The Handbook of Lesbian and Gay Studies* (2002). In 2006 she published *Intersections Between Feminist and Queer Theory* (co-edited with Janice McLaughlin and Mark E. Casey).

**Jessica Ringrose** is a lecturer in the Sociology of Gender and Education, at the Institute of Education, University of London. Her writing on femininity, neo-liberalism, class, gender and educational achievement can be found in *Gender and Education* (2007) and *The Gender and Education Handbook* (2006). Her current research focuses on girls and bullying and the pathologization of girls' aggression in popular culture and schooling, and she has published on this theme in *Feminism and Psychology* (2006). She is also interested in race, class and gender inclusive feminist pedagogies and has published in these areas in *Women's Studies International Forum* (2007), *Race, Ethnicity and Education* (2007), *Resources for Feminist Research* (2003), and *Working through Whiteness: International Perspectives* (2002).

**Victoria Robinson** is Senior Lecturer in Sociology at the University of Sheffield. She has published widely in the areas of masculinities, heterosexualities and debates in women's, gender and masculinity studies. Her publications include: with Jenny Hockey and Angela Meah *Mundane Heterosexualities: From Theory to Practices* (2007) and *Everyday Masculinities and Extreme Sport: Male Identity and Rock Climbing* (2008). With Jenny Hockey, she has held two ESRC grants. One was for the first major study of heterosexuality across the generations in the UK. The other was on masculinities in transition across public and private spheres. She has been European and Middle Eastern editor for *Women's Studies International Forum*. She is currently working on a new book, with Jenny Hockey, on masculinities in transition in different occupations.

**Liz Stanley** is Professor of Sociology at the University of Edinburgh. A feminist theorist, Liz has written extensively on (feminist and other) methodology and epistemology, including in relation to auto/biography and representations of self and other, and also on a range of historical topics, including Mass-Observation and its diaries, sex surveys from the 1940s on, the suffragette movement, and the work of the feminist writer and social theorist Olive Schreiner. Her most recent book is *Mourning Becomes... Post/Memory, Commemoration & the Concentration Camps of the South African War* (2006), while work in progress includes preparing the complete Olive Schreiner letters for publication.

**Yvette Taylor** is Lecturer in Sociology, School of Geography, Politics and Sociology, Newcastle University where she teaches on class, gender and sexuality. Recent publications include: '"If your face doesn't fit...": the misrecognition of working-class lesbians in scene space', *Leisure Studies* 26: 161–78 (2007); 'Going Up Without Going Away: Working-class women in Higher Education', *Youth and Policy*, 94: 35–50 (2007); *Working Class Lesbian Life: Classed Outsiders*, Basingstoke: Palgrave Macmillan (2007). She is currently conducting a British Academy funded study: 'What the Parents Say: Lesbian and gay parents, social and educational capitals' and an ESRC funded study: 'From the Coal Face to the Car Park? Intersections of class and gender in the North East'.

**Kath Woodward** is Senior Lecturer in Sociology at the Open University and a member of the ESRC Centre for Research into Socio-cultural Change (CRESC), working on gendered, racialized identifications in sport and the policies and politics of diversity, 'New Footballing Identities?', *Cultural Studies* (2007 Special Edition, 4/5). She is currently working on sport across diasporas on the BBC World Service for the AHRC Diasporas, Migration, Identities programme. Her most recent book, *Boxing, Masculinity and Identity, the "I" of the Tiger*, uses feminist critiques of embodiment to explore discourses of masculinity in boxing.

**Sue Wise** is Professor of Social Justice and Social Work at Lancaster University. She is interested in all aspects of social justice and teaches and writes on social divisions and social diversity. She has written extensively on feminist epistemology and ontology with Liz Stanley, including in *Breaking Out Again* (1993).

# Introduction

## *Women's and Gender Studies*

The first edition of this book was published in 1993, the second edition in 1997, and the third in 2007. In that period, it is something of an understatement to state that much has happened to gender studies and women's studies in the UK, and worldwide, due to political, economic, social and intellectual changes. What is clear, given the continued demand for material on feminism and gender around the world, is that (despite variations in different countries) women's and gender studies, either as separate areas of study or integrated into the disciplines, continues to be a vibrant, dynamic, innovative and influential area of study. This continues to be at both undergraduate and postgraduate levels. For example, recent collections on gender and women's studies include Grewal and Kaplan, 2001; Essen, Goldberg and Kobayashi, 2004; Davis, Evans and Lorber, 2006; Marchbank and Letherby, 2007.

It is still encouraging that such a diversity of books on research on gender and women is available, especially as no one book can do justice to the variety of concepts and ideas which make up the field of gender and women's studies. But, as with previous editions, we feel that this volume is unique in terms of the subjects covered, the mix of authors contributing to the book, (which includes established theorists and those new to the field), the comprehensive and up to date nature of the collection, as well as its accessibility, which is still important to us if a new generation of scholars are to be inspired and enthused by feminist debates. Further, the third edition of Introducing Gender and Women's Studies, like the previous two, has chapters written by a specialist in that area, which give an overview of key themes and issues in the field. Each chapter highlights differences between different feminist writers, gives a summary of debates in particular areas, and includes relevant critiques. As well, chapters are grouped into sections, which are preceded by a helpful summary of what each chapter will contain and which emphasizes links between chapters. The chapters themselves contain boxes and bullet points to enable key points to be highlighted, for ease of reading, and the suggestions for further reading at the end of each chapter recommend texts which are very useful overviews or summaries, and allow the reader to follow up debates raised in each chapter in more depth.

To place this volume in a historical context, the institutionalization of women's studies began at the same time and, in part, grew out what has been termed 'second wave feminism'. It was primarily women academics who fought to set up the first women's then gender studies courses, and it was mainly women students who took these classes. This is no longer the case, as in a period of 'third wave feminism' (Gillis, Howie and Munford, 2007), and its concerns with postcolonialism, globalization and the fluidity of identity, for instance, we have increasingly seen men as both staff and students interested and involved with gender.

In earlier editions of this volume, we argued that at the very start of the 1990s the general mood regarding both women's studies and gender studies in the UK was still an optimistic one, and undergraduate and postgraduate women's studies/gender studies courses had been established in many universities and higher education institutions. The old debate about whether women's studies/gender studies should enter the 'malestream/mainstream' no longer existed and, in general, their establishment in the higher education system was seen as a positive move, bringing feminist theoretical ideas and pedagogical practices to a wider audience, transforming the disciplines and the academy more generally from 'within'.

However, an important change since the 1990s has been the increasing use of the term 'gender studies' rather than 'women's studies', as well as the naming of research centres and degrees. Though this shift has caused much debate, without doubt it can be argued that gender has now fundamentally informed many disciplines in the social sciences and humanities, both in the UK, the US, Australia, and Western and Eastern Europe, amongst other countries.

Now, more students than ever are taking courses with feminist content and which deal with gender issues. The reason for this is that over the last decade there has been a shift towards mainstreaming gender/women's studies as a core part of the teaching of traditional disciplines such as, for example, Sociology, Education, History and English. In this sense we can say that over the last thirty years women's/gender studies has changed the established canon of the social science and arts and humanities disciplines, as well as the teaching of research methods, by becoming assimilated into traditional disciplines, often as a compulsory element. Gender issues are therefore a key aspect of many undergraduate and postgraduate students' education. So whilst work and research on gender is widespread and feminist research is extensive, it is no longer necessarily associated with women's/gender studies degrees.

## Changing practices

A changing theoretical landscape has seen innovative work emerge, for example on gender as a concept, queer theory and critical theorizing on masculinity, and this new edition reflects many of those changes.

In the first edition of this volume, there were fourteen chapters including women's studies as a field of study, race, feminist theory, sexuality, violence, popular culture and film, literature, family, motherhood, reproduction, health, work, history and education. The second edition also contained entirely new chapters on methodology, science and technology and social policy, reflecting areas and perspectives which came to prominence during the 1990s. This third edition sees more changes, again reflecting shifts in women's and gender studies. We now have new chapters on masculinity, sexuality and queer theory, cyber technologies, gender and politics, and the concept of gender, for example.

These shifts are not without criticisms. For example, another important development has been the rapid institutional growth of queer theory, associated with postmodernism, since the 1990s. One of the implications this has had for research and teaching on both gender and sexuality is that there has been a shift in content, to a focus on cultural practices rather than on material inequalities. This is something that many feminists are critical of (for discussion see Richardson et al., 2006). The move to theorizing masculinities too has not been without criticism (see Robinson, 2003) nor has the embracing of 'post feminism' by some, which continues to inform media representations of both feminism and women's lives. Such a concept denies the inequalities and oppressions women still face worldwide.

We are aware that having to grapple with publishing the third edition of a text which has achieved a 'cultural hegemony' in the UK and the US may seem like a luxury more likely to be had by Western European feminists than those in other parts of the world, who may well have to deal with the dual burden of a hostile institutional climate and having to develop teaching and research materials, as well as major political upheavals.

But these shifts, which have lead to our highlighting gender in the title of this volume and in the chapters, if seen in a wider international context, are interesting in other ways. For instance, an issue to consider, is whether the shift to gender is seen in the same way or even makes intellectual 'sense' to all concerned in gender and women's studies. What, for example, of those countries which do not have a tradition of women studies and/or do not utilize the category 'woman'?

One immediate question that arises from this is raised by Braidotti (2000) of whether the term women's studies, in itself a North American invention, can be applied systematically across Latin, Catholic, Southern and Eastern Europe. This is very debatable because of such different cultural, religious, political and educational practices. Is, therefore, the women' studies (and gender studies) concept respectful of cultural diversity today? Temkina and Zdravomyslova (2006) point out that, in post-1990s Russia, gender studies has been connected with grass roots organizations, whilst 'Feminology' which they define as women's studies was connected to the Russian political movement 'Women of Russia' which follows a social protectionist policy. Also, in Slovenia, it has been suggested that the Slovene word for women's studies, should be replaced by the safer, more neutral term, 'studies of the sexes' (Bahovic, 2000).

It is still important to acknowledge linguistic differences but it is also crucial to avoid any straightforward cultural relativism raised by considering differences in terminology. As we also argued in Robinson and Richardson (1994), supposedly simple linguistic issues are not in themselves inconsequential but reflect complex, and sometimes controversial political, practical and cultural issues, which impact on whether and in what form women's studies and gender studies exist. As well, it is necessary to note that to avoid a simplistic and homogenizing east/west and north/south dichotomy, it should be acknowledged that in countries such as the UK and elsewhere in Europe, Australia and the US the debate about whether the category 'woman' or the concept of gender is best suited for feminist theoretical purposes continues. Gender itself is debated as a suitable category of analysis both inside and outside of Western European contexts, however, the question needs to be asked if gender as a concept both survives translation, and if it serves as an illuminating concept which is capable of being challenged and transformed through discourse with feminists outside of Western Europe.

## The Future

The important contribution that gender and women's studies has made in its young history is undeniable. Over the last 30 years gender research has enabled us to develop frameworks to identify and theorize the specific problems that women face at both local and global levels and, very importantly, begin to develop strategies to deal with them. We need also to recognize the wider contribution it has made within the academy. Indeed, one of the most important successes of gender and women's studies has been the new approaches to knowledge it has brought to the traditional disciplines. Not only, as Gamble (2001) states, by addressing the gaps that existed by focusing on women's interests, but in doing this rethinking the conceptual frameworks for thinking about and understanding the worlds we live in.

There is a positive relation between a high degree of institutionalization of gender/women's studies education in universities and equal opportunities (Griffin, 2005). We can think about this connection at intersecting levels; in terms of how researching and teaching about gender is important to understanding and challenging inequalities at work and in the home, and in developing wider understanding and respect for social diversity, something that is central to contemporary notions of good citizenship. Gender and women's studies provides students with knowledge of the social processes that produce gender discrimination and inequality in their own country and elsewhere in the world. Analyzing different gender cultures or 'regimes' helps to broaden students' thinking and open up questions about social change and how to develop strategies to deal with gender inequalities, as well as a better understanding of social diversity more generally. In this way, the feminist and gendered academy can be seen as connected to both our understandings of the world and possibilities for changing it. We remain confident that this will continue, albeit in new and diverse ways across the world, and look forward to the next decade of feminist theorizing and action.

VICTORIA ROBINSON and DIANE RICHARDSON

# SECTION ONE
## THEORY AND POLITICS

---

This book is divided into five sections. In the first section we address some key issues and concepts. In Chapter 1, **Conceptualizing Gender**, we begin by asking a question that is fundamental to feminist theory and gender and women's studies: What do we mean by gender? As later chapters go on to illustrate, gender is a key organizing concept of institutions and practices in culture and society. However, as you will come to understand by reading this section, understandings of gender differ. In considering a number of different ways of thinking about gender, Chapter 1 discusses the important contribution that feminism has made to the study of gender. It focuses on three main areas: gender as a social construction, the binary divide between sex and gender, and the relationship between gender and sexuality. This is a starting point for reading the next chapter on **Feminist Theories**, which goes on to examine some of these issues in more detail. As well as this, Chapter 2 provides a summary of the main theoretical approaches that have informed the development of gender and women's studies, both in the past and more recently. It discusses the influence of poststructuralism and postmodernism, including debates between feminism and queer theory, and uses the example of transgender studies to highlight some of the challenges to feminist theories in recent years. Within feminism, theory and politics are inherently connected. Just as feminist theories have reconceptualized gender, they have also redefined what we mean by 'politics'. Chapter 3, **Feminism, Social Movements and the Gendering of Politics**, discusses how feminists have not limited understandings of politics to participation in government or 'party politics', but have expanded definitions of the political to include personal relations, for instance at work, in the family and in sexual relationships. This is reflected in the feminist slogan 'the personal is the political'. As well as examining women's participation in politics, this chapter illustrates the connection between theory and politics by pointing out how the development of gender and women's studies grew out of feminism. The last chapter in the first section, **Men, Masculinities and Feminism,** looks at the growth in areas of research into men and masculinities. In addition to discussing the contribution of masculinity studies to understandings of gender, in particular the notion of hegemonic masculinity, this chapter considers the broader implications of these trends for the study of gender. These developments have led to the establishment of 'men's studies' or what some prefer to call 'critical studies of masculinity'. The difference between these two approaches, and their relationship with gender and women's studies, is examined.

CHAPTER ONE

# Conceptualizing Gender

DIANE RICHARDSON

## Introduction

Why begin this book with a chapter on conceptualizing gender? After all, feminist theory is not just about gender as reading this book will demonstrate. In many ways, however, it is an obvious place to start. Gender is a key organizing concept of institutions and practices in culture and society. It is central to feminist theory and to the teaching of gender and women's studies. So before we can introduce some of the broader debates in gender and women's studies it is important that we ask: what do we mean by gender?

The meaning of the terms sex and gender, and the ways that writers have theorized the relationship between the two, have changed considerably over the last fifty years. Prior to the 1960s, gender referred primarily to what is coded in language as masculine or feminine. Gender has subsequently been variously theorized as personality traits and behaviours that are specifically associated either with women or men (for example women are caring, men are aggressive), to any social construction having to do with the male–female distinction, including those which distinguish female bodies from male bodies; to being thought of as the existence of two different social groups 'men' and 'women' that are the product of unequal relationships (Alsop et al., 2002; Connell, 2002; Beasley, 2005). In this latter sense, gender is understood as a hierarchy that exists in society, where one group of people (men) have power and privilege over another group of people (women) (Delphy, 1993). More recent postmodern approaches, associated with the work of Judith Butler (1990, 1997) in particular, conceptualize gender as performance; where gender is understood to be continuously produced through everyday practices and social interactions.

We need to understand these theoretical changes around the concept of gender, not only in a historical sense but also in terms of cultural context. In other words, it is important that we ask whether gender as a concept translates in different countries and cultures in a manner that is analytically useful. As Robinson and I argue in the Introduction to this book (see also Richardson and Robinson, 1994), differences of terminology and translation have existed, and clearly still exist. For instance, 'in Scandanavia there are no separate words that cohere with the Anglo/American sex/gender distinction (Lempiainen, 2000). In Slavic languages, the same word is used for both terms (Bahovic, 2000). In Germany, the term gender has several meanings including grammatical and as a biological/social category (Wischermann, 2000)' (Robinson, 2006:224). So we must not assume that gender as a concept is universal. Rather, as Walby (2004) argues, we need to develop understandings of gender that allow us to theorize both cultural variation and historical changes in understanding gender relations.

This chapter outlines the major changes that have taken place in how we define gender. It begins with an examination of the use of the terms gender and sex and the distinction made between them, what is commonly called the sex/gender binary. In this discussion, I will illustrate how feminist gender theory has played an important role in developing our understandings of sex and gender. The chapter then goes on to discuss the development of theories of gender within feminism, as well as the contribution to understandings of gender made by queer theory. In this section, I will look at how different theoretical approaches have led to different understandings of gender. The final section of the chapter examines the relationship between gender and sexuality. This is important because, as I shall demonstrate, our understandings of gender are closely connected with the concept of sexuality as well as sex. Also, this is identified as a key area for future feminist and queer theorizing.

## The sex/gender binary

During the late nineteenth century and the first half of the twentieth, it was the theories put forward by biologists, medical researchers and psychologists that dominated understandings of gender. These early accounts were mainly concerned with establishing 'natural' or 'biological' explanations for human behaviour. Researchers sought to discover underlying 'sex differences' which they believed produced different psychological and behavioural dispositions in males and females. They spoke of sex not gender and did not distinguish between the two as we often do today. Within these *naturalistic* approaches sex is conceptualized in terms of *binaries*: male/female; man/woman; masculine/feminine. In this binary thinking male and female are understood as 'opposites', who, despite their differences, compliment one another. This pairing of 'opposite sexes' is seen as natural. Gender here is understood to be a biological 'fact' that is pre-given and located in the body. Although, as I shall go on to discuss, its precise location in the body (for example gonads, chromosomes, or nerve centres in the brain) has been the subject of considerable debate.

At the time, few within the social sciences questioned these 'scientific' theories about sexual difference. As Seidman (1997) has argued, classical sociology both drew on and contributed to understandings of sex, gender and sexuality as binary categories ordained by nature. However, this was to change dramatically in the second part of the twentieth century as debates about how we conceptualize gender steadily grew. In the 1960s and 1970s a new way of thinking about gender began to emerge that critiqued earlier 'essentialist' frameworks, signalling a shift away from biologically based accounts of gender to social analysis. This shift from naturalizing to social constructionist accounts, although not necessarily denying the role of biology, emphasized the importance of social and cultural factors in defining gender.

At the same time as social scientists and historians were beginning to challenge the assumption that gender was rooted in 'nature', more and more people were beginning to question dominant ideas about gender roles. The late 1960s and early 1970s saw the emergence of both women's and gay and lesbian liberation movements in the US and Europe. An important contribution to the study of gender at that time was the distinction that many of those involved in sexual politics – along with some sociologists, psychiatrists and psychologists – sought to make between the terms sex and gender. Sex referred to the biological differences between females and males defined in terms of the anatomy and physiology of the body; gender to the social meanings and value attached to being female or male in any given society, expressed in terms of the concepts femininity and masculinity (see also Hines and Woodward in this volume). This distinction between sex (biological) and gender (cultural) is what is termed the sex/gender binary. A number of key assumptions associated with the sex/gender binary are summarised below.

---

### The Sex/Gender Binary

- A distinction can be made between sex (biology) and gender (culture)
- Sex is biologically given and universal
- Gender is historically and culturally variable
- Sex consists of two – and only two – types of human being
- This two-sex model of sexual difference (the distinction between females and males) is a natural 'fact of life'
- One sex in every body
- Identities develop as either one or other of these two sexes/genders

---

Studies of transsexuality were also very important to the differentiation between sex and gender. The sex/gender binary made it possible to imagine that a person could feel themselves to be a particular gender trapped in the 'wrong' sex, for instance a person who felt themselves to be a woman and feminine (their gender identity) but who had a male body (their sex). This was difficult to account for without allowing for a separation of body (sex) and gender (identity). (See also Hines in this volume.)

The sex/gender binary was also an important aspect of early feminist work and has since provided an important foundation for much feminist theory and politics (Hird, 2000). Feminists have used the sex/gender binary to argue for social change on the grounds that although there may exist certain biological differences between females and males, societies superimpose different norms of personality and behaviour that produce 'women' and 'men' as social categories. It is this reasoning that led Simone de Beauvoir (1953) in the feminist classic *The Second Sex* to famously remark 'One is not born, but rather becomes a woman'. We cannot, de Beaviour argues, understand womanhood or manhood as fixed by nature, rather this is something that is acquired through the social process of *becoming gendered.*

During the late 1960s and early 1970s feminist writers expressed similar views in developing the idea of the sex/gender binary. Ann Oakley, for instance, argued that it was important to distinguish between two separate processes that, at that time, she claimed were often confused. That is:

> ... the tendency to differentiate by sex, and the tendency to differentiate in a particular way by sex. The first is genuinely a *constant* feature of human society but the second is not, and its inconstancy marks the division between 'sex' and 'gender': sex differences may be 'natural', but gender differences have their source in culture, not nature (Oakley, 1972: 189, emphasis added).

Oakley takes sex for granted in assuming that we all 'have a sex', sex is not something we acquire it is a constant, part of being human. Gender, by contrast, she understands to be the cultural interpretation of our biologically given sex. It is important to acknowledge that, at the time, this distinction between sex and gender was hailed as a conceptual breakthrough and 'became one of the most fundamental assumptions in feminist gender theory from the 1970s on' (Alsop et al., 2002: 26). It was also very important to feminist politics as it supported the argument that the social roles men and women occupy are not fixed by nature and are open to change. This view was also facilitated by anthropological studies such as Margaret Mead's work on gender which, although it was first published in the 1930s, was reprinted and gained considerable attention in the 1960s (Mead, 1935, 1963).

## Sex as a construction?

More recently, a new understanding of sex and its relationship to gender has emerged. The distinction between sex and gender has been challenged by arguments that sex is just as much a social construction as gender. Rather than thinking about sex and gender as separate from one another, sex being the foundation upon which gender is superimposed, gender has increasingly been used to refer to any social construction to do with the female/male binary, including male and female bodies. This has led to debates about whether it is useful any more to differentiate between sex and gender. On this basis, many feminist writers have questioned the usefulness of the sex/gender binary that twenty years earlier had seemed such a conceptual breakthrough (Hird, 2000).

For example, both Christine Delphy (1984) and Judith Butler (1990) have argued that the body is not free from social interpretation, but is itself a socially constructed phenomenon. It is through understandings of gender that we interpret and establish meanings for bodily differences that are termed sexual difference (see also Butler, 1993; Nicholson, 1994; Hood-Williams, 1996). In this model, sex is not something that one 'has' or a description of what someone is. Without the concept of gender we could not read bodies as differently sexed. It is gender that provides the categories of meaning for us to interpret how a body appears to us as 'sexed'. In other words, gender creates sex.

## *The variability of sex*

Historical research supports the argument that understandings of the body are socially constructed. In *Making Sex*, for example, Laqueur (1990) argues that the idea that human bodies divide into two different sexes – male and female – only became commonplace during the nineteenth century. Prior to then, it was thought that male and female bodies developed out of one type of body. The idea of two distinct biological sexes is associated with the development of science and medicine (Colebrook, 2004). Historical studies also show that what biological 'facts' determine sex has been the subject of much debate. Chromosomes, hormones, gonads (ovaries/testes), internal reproductive structures and genitalia have variously been seen as the basis for defining a person's sex. For instance, studies of medical responses to cases of 'doubtful sex', – people who in the past were often referred to as third sex or hermaphrodites or more commonly nowadays intersex – suggest that definitions of what constitutes a male and a female body have changed. People born with a mixture of sexual markers, for example with both an ovary and a testis present in their body, challenged the idea that there is one 'true sex' in every human body and often resulted in disagreements between doctors over whether someone was 'truly' a male or a female (Foucault, 1980a).

In analyzing such cases writers such as Dreger (2000) and Fausto-Sterling (2000) show how definitions of 'sex' have changed over time. What this demonstrates, they argue, is that the meanings of bodies and the assumptions made about the relationship between bodies and identities have varied from one historical period to the next (see also Woodward's chapter on the body in this volume). During the nineteenth century, for instance, doctors believed reproductive capacity – the presence in the body of ovaries or testes – characterized the sex of a person. This led in some cases to individuals being diagnosed a different sex to the one they felt themselves to be. For example, in one case a woman who had lived all her life as female was 'diagnosed' as male because of the discovery of testes in the abdomen (Dreger, 2000). Here, the truth of a person's character is sought in the body, not in terms of how the person identifies. This is in stark contrast with medical opinion from the mid twentieth century, as illustrated by studies both of intersex (Money and Erhardt, 1972) and transsexuality (Stoller, 1968) which stated that sex and gender were not always one and the same. Such studies were not only supportive of the development of the sex/gender (body/identity) binary, as I suggested earlier, they also led to a privileging of identity over body (see also Woodward in this volume).

The continuing concern to resolve bodily ambiguity in cases of 'doubtful sex', despite the fact that medical knowledge has demonstrated that there are many variations of sex and that human bodies are not fully dimorphic (always one thing or the other), demonstrates the *social* importance of sex and gender. It suggests that there are strong reasons for wanting to sort people into two different groups and to maintain the idea of two separate sexes. In the nineteenth century, according to Dreger (2000), the main concern was the fear of social disorder that doctors believed could result from 'misdiagnosed sex'. They thought that this would encourage both divorce and homosexuality. It is important to ask, then, why doctors have been so concerned to 'resolve' cases of 'doubtful sex'. If intersex people lived in a world where sex/gender was not socially important then arguably being of 'doubtful sex' would not matter in the way it does. In recent years an intersex movement has emerged, which objects to the idea that human bodies should have to be defined as male or female and instead claims an identity as intersex rather than as man or woman.

There may then be two sexes but what I am suggesting here is that this is not a naturally occurring 'fact of life', rather it is socially produced because of the significance placed on defining bodies as either male or female. This is what Dreger (2000) refers to as the 'medical invention of sex', where bodies are literally shaped to fit the categories of sex and gender. By doing this medicine constructs a single believable sex for each ambiguous body, removing any challenge to ideas about sex.

In this section I have described how understandings of the relationship between sex and gender have gone through three important phases over the last fifty years:

- First, sex (male/female) defines gender (masculine/feminine).
- Second, a distinction is made between sex and gender (the sex/gender binary), with gender understood as a construction and sex as a biological given.
- Third, sex is viewed as a construction (gender creates sex).

I will now go on to consider theories of gender and the specific contribution made by feminist writers. In so doing, I will illustrate how the idea of gender has also undergone significant change.

## Feminist gender theory

Feminists have critiqued essentialist understandings of gender and sex, and have played an important role in establishing a body of research and theory that supports social constructionist approaches. However, the main concern in feminist theories of gender is not simply to describe the ways in which gender is socially and culturally defined in any given society. For instance, whether 'being a woman' is associated with having the responsibility of childcare or whether 'being a man' is associated with being the principal breadwinner in a family structure. It is to develop understandings of how gender is connected to social, economic and cultural status and power in society. In this sense, *gender is theorised not as difference but as a social division*; that is, in order to illuminate how the social reproduction of gender difference is connected to gender inequality.

### *Gender role*

The main focus of work on gender carried out during the 1970s and 1980s was on exploring the production of masculinity and femininity. Many feminist writers, as I stated in the previous section, argued that gender is culturally determined and that we become differently gendered through socialization into gender roles, or as it was often termed then 'sex roles'. Sex role theory, drawing on the principles of social learning theory, claimed that through various learning processes (for example observation, imitation, modelling, differential reinforcement) and agencies of socialization (for example parents, teachers, peers, the media) children learn the social meanings, values, norms and expectations associated with 'being a girl' or 'being a boy' and thereby learn to develop ways of behaving and personality characteristics considered appropriate (or not) for being a woman or man. Gender is here defined as the learning of a culturally and historically specific social role associated with women or men, and used to describe a person's identity as masculine or feminine. This is what we

---

**Becoming Gendered**

▧ Gender labelling
Attribute terms boy, girl, woman, man to self and others

▧ Gender knowledge
Culturally specific knowledge about gender

▧ Universality of gender
The idea that all human beings 'have' a gender

▧ Gender constancy
The idea that gender is unchanging

might refer to nowadays as the process of becoming gendered, involving learning a number of specific ideas, practices and values associated with gender.

As Connell (2002) points out, a great deal of research, by social psychologists and anthropologists in particular, sought to explain the development of gender roles. That is, what the mechanisms of acquisition and the key sites of learning gender roles were, as well as documenting variation in gender roles in different cultures. However, feminist theories of gender, as I indicated above, are not interested in simply describing how girls and boys grow up differently and become gendered, but how a key aspect of that difference is understanding that girls and boys, women and men have different social status and value. This focus on gender inequality was on how gender role expectations, in particular the expectation that a woman's primary role was to be a good wife and mother, were limiting girls in a myriad of ways as they grew up, especially in terms of their educational aspirations and the types of job they might end up doing.

## Gender as hierarchy

These early social theories of gender appear to us now as rather naïve. From thinking about gender roles in terms of either masculinity or femininity, we now recognize that there are *multiple* genders and many patterns of masculinities and femininities. At the time, feminists were among those who critiqued sex role theory, in particular pointing out that it was a highly mechanistic and static account of gender that attributed little agency to subjects who were assumed to acquire a certain gender role by simply internalizing what they had been taught. Feminists argued that such theories of gender were oversimplified as many young people reject what they are taught and resist social norms and cultural assumptions about gendered roles. This was clearly in keeping with the feminist political goal of challenging gender role expectations and norms which were seen as restricting women's lives.

By the end of the 1970s feminist theories of gender were becoming increasingly sophisticated. Some writers took Oakley's and other feminist critiques of essentialist understandings of gender a step further by questioning the existence of the category of gender itself. The development of such an analysis of gender is particularly associated with the work of materialist feminists such as Christine Delphy (1984) and Monique Wittig (1981/1992). Although Delphy and Wittig recognized the importance of demonstrating that the *meaning* of 'gender' is historically and culturally specific, they argued that the *concept* of gender should not be taken for granted. In other words, they questioned the idea that gender is a universal category, which it can be assumed will always exist in some form or other in all times and places. Instead, they defined gender as a *socially constructed product* of patriarchal hierarchies (Jackson, 1999a). Gender here is understood to be the result of gendered power differences. For example, in her paper 'One is Not Born a Woman', echoing Simone de Beauvoir whose work I mentioned earlier, Wittig (1981/1992) argues that gender is an imaginary foundation, the outcome of a social hierarchy where one class of people (men) have power and privilege over another class of people (women). The categories 'woman' and 'man' are relative, defined by a specific social and economic position in society. Gender is commonly thought to be the cause of one's social and economic position (a). Here gender derives from one's place in the social hierarchies that exist in society (b). In other words, gender is the mark of one's subordination as a woman, rather than its basis:

(a) One's gender as 'Woman' leads to social subordination;
(b) Patriarchal hierarchies define one as a 'Woman'.

For those feminists who agree with such analyses of gender relations, the political goal of challenging gendered power differences will, as a consequence, lead to the elimination of the idea of gender. Gender categories would not exist if social divisions did not exist.

## 'Doing' gender: gender as performativity

New conceptualizations of gender associated with postmodernism and the rise of queer theory emerged in the 1990s, and shifted the emphasis away from definitions of gender as fixed, coherent and stable, towards seeing gender categories as plural, provisional and situated. In part this grew out of a partial shift in the 1980s from a focus on divisions between women and men to theorizing difference between women, in particular those of class, race, ethnicity and sexuality, and the associated problematization of the category 'woman' (Bhavnani, 1997). At the same time, poststructural models of power, influenced by Foucault's work (1979), demanded a more complex account of gender than as hierarchy.

It is the work of Judith Butler (1990, 1993) in particular that is associated with this theoretical shift and which has had a profound influence on theorizing gender. (See also Hines, Woodward and Stanley in this volume.) Butler's work, especially her book *Gender Trouble*, has been highly influential in the development of *queer theory*. In *Gender Trouble* Butler:

- proposes a new understanding of gender as performance;
- questions the usefulness of the sex/gender binary;
- suggests heterosexuality is an effect of gender.

Butler argues that gender is *performatively* enacted. In her early work she used drag to convey what she means. Typically drag is understood as impersonation: a drag queen is a 'real' man giving a performance as a woman. Butler argues that there are parallels between drag and the performance of gender in everyday life: gender is a kind of impersonation that passes for real. Gender is constituted out of attempts to compel belief in others that we are 'really' a woman or a man. For Butler, there is no 'real' gender of which drag is an impersonation. She claims 'there is no gender identity behind the expressions of gender', arguing instead that identity is constituted by 'the very "expressions" that are said to be its results' (Butler, 1990:25). What she means by this is that we assume that a person performed in a certain way *because* that person is a man or a woman. In this sense Butler's notion of gender performance is different from how the term performance is usually used; that is, to refer to a subject (the doer) who is formed prior to the acts s/he chooses to perform (do). For Butler, performances are *performative* in that they bring into being gendered subjects. The act of performance is productive rather than expressive of gender. It is through 'doing gender' that we produce the effect that there was some gendered person who preceded the performance: 'the doer'. This, for Butler, is a continual process. So while it might seem to us certain that a person is a woman, Butler is suggesting that this is not fixed or stable. Gender identities, it is argued, are momentary and need to be re-performed. Gender is a process of continuous construction that produces the effect (an illusion) of being natural and stable through gender performances that make us 'women' and 'men'. A person might seem to have a particular identity, but this is only because we keep doing things that maintain the appearance of us 'being the same'. Theories of performativity, then, challenge the idea that gender identities are simply 'always there', claiming instead we are constantly *becoming gendered* through performances that constitute us as women or men in a variety of ways.

One of the criticisms made of poststructuralist/postmodern accounts of gender is that they appear to have little interest in discussing material inequalities between women and men (Hennessey, 2006). This is seen as having serious consequences for feminist politics. For example, Martha Nussbaum has been highly critical of Butler's queer approach because she claims it is an individualized approach that is not concerned with social change (Nussbaum, 1999).

Butler also challenges the idea that heterosexuality is natural. She argues that heterosexuality is 'unstable', dependent on ongoing, continuous and repeated performances of normative gender identities, which produce the illusion of stability. There is no 'real' or 'natural' sexuality to be copied or imitated: heterosexuality is itself continually in the process of being re-produced. As well as *denaturalizing* gender and heterosexuality, Butler also questions biological understandings of sex in arguing that sex is as culturally constructed as gender. As a consequence, as I pointed out earlier in the chapter, she questions the usefulness of making a distinction between sex and gender. This disruption of the sex/gender binary has been identified by some feminist writers as being one of the most important contributions of *queer* theorists to feminist theory (Martin, 1998a). However, it is important to recognize similar arguments in the work of social psychologists (Kessler and McKenna, 1978, 2000) and feminists (Delphy, 1993; Nicholson, 1994). Some of these preceded postmodern/

queer accounts of 'doing gender' such as those put forward by Butler. For instance, as early as 1978 Kessler and McKenna used transsexuality (rather than drag) as illustrative of the everyday 'doing of gender' in order to show how people are rendered intelligible to us as either 'male' or 'female' through the successful (or not) performance of bodily appearance and characteristics, behaviours, and language that we expect from men and women, and that we then interpret as a valid expression (or not) of their 'real' sex. Sex, in this sense, is constructed through everyday social interactions that are reliant upon gender norms, which enable us to make sense of a person as 'male' or 'female'

In this section I have described how the concept of gender has developed in a number of important ways to a point where:

● Rather than a binary we now understand gender to be multiple and context specific;
● There is a shift towards a more materialist and embodied account of gender;
● Greater attention is given to develop understandings of gender as a site of agency as well as inequality.

The first part of this chapter looked at how understandings of gender rely on particular understandings of the relationship sex has to gender. In the final section I will go on to examine the question of how the relationship between gender and sexuality has been theorized. This is necessary because our ideas about gender are also connected to assumptions about sexuality and its relation to gender. Indeed, in the majority of feminist theories of gender it has been assumed that 'gender and sexuality have to be examined together' (McLaughlin et al., 2006:1).

## Gender and sexuality

Five broad approaches can be identified that have structured the study of gender and sexuality and ways of understanding their relationship.

### *Naturalist approaches*

As I stated in the first part of this chapter, from the middle of the nineteenth century to the second half of the twentieth century naturalist approaches dominated understandings of gender (sex) and sexuality. The relationship between the two was understood as an expression of something natural, a universal order that was *heterosexual* and where 'it is assumed that sex-gender-sexuality relate in a hierarchical, congruent and coherent manner' (Richardson, 2007:460). For instance, using this principle it was expected that a biological female should naturally grow up to experience herself as a female and have a feminine gender identity, and that her sexual practices and sexual identity should be heterosexual. This is what is meant by the principle of sexual and gender coherence. This helps us to understand why 'cross gender identity' (for example feminine men or masculine women) has been central to theories of homosexuality. Within this approach sexuality is understood to be a property of gender, a gender that is pregiven and located in the gendered/sexed body. Thus, the masculinization of lesbians and the feminization of male homosexuals is also associated with understanding the lesbian and homosexual body as 'cross gendered.' For example, descriptions of lesbians as boyish, with narrow hips, flat chests and 'spectacular clitorises' capable of vaginal penetration and male homosexuals having 'feminized' bodies, including the idea that gay men have 'feminized brains' (see Byne, 1995; Terry, 1999).

## Feminist approaches

Feminist writers, as I discussed earlier in the chapter, were among the first to challenge the essentialist frameworks for understanding gender and sexuality. However what they did not do, in the main, was suggest that these two concepts should be de-coupled from one another.

Feminist theories of gender offer the second and third broad approaches to understanding the relationship between gender and sexuality. In the first of these:

- *Gender is prioritized over sexuality*

In most feminist accounts it is assumed that gender and sexuality need to be examined together and, also, that gender takes precedence over sexuality. That is, concepts of sexuality are understood to be largely founded upon notions of gender. This tradition is associated with the work of earlier materialist feminists such as Wittig (1981/1992) and Delphy (1984), whose work I mentioned earlier, as well as more contemporary feminist writers. For example, Stevi Jackson (1996, 2006) argues for the logical priority of gender over sexuality. She claims that '...without gender categories we could not categorize sexual desires and identities along the axis of same-gender or other-gender relationships, as heterosexual, bisexual or homosexual/lesbian' (Jackson, 2006:62). In other words, our understanding of sexual categories like 'gay' or 'straight' depend on knowing the gender of a person.

In the second approach that I have identified in feminist work on gender:

- *Sexuality is prioritized over gender*

Here, sexuality is understood to be constitutive of gender. Traditionally this is an underlying assumption in psychoanalytic accounts, as well as informing the work of some feminists. For example, Catherine MacKinnon (1982) suggested that it is through the experience of sexuality, as it is currently constructed, that women learn about gender; learn what 'being a woman' means. As well as constituting our gendered subjectivities, MacKinnon argues that sexuality

(heterosexuality in particular) is the cause of gender inequali
men are divided by gender, made into the sexes as we kno\
social requirements of heterosexuality, which institutionaliz
dominance and female sexual submission' (MacKinnon, 198
this perspective, understandings of gender are located in terms
of how sexuality both reflects and constitutes patriarchal values and practices
(Walby, 1990; Richardson, 1997). More recent feminist work has developed
the argument that gender is an effect of sexuality. For example, Chrys Ingraham (1996, 2005) raises the question of whether, without institutionalized
heterosexuality, gender would even exist.

In these debates, feminist theories have extended definitions of gender and
sexuality in going beyond considerations of how the link between them is socially constructed, to viewing their relationship as one of the key mechanisms
by which gender inequalities are (re)produced (Richardson, 1997).

## Queer distinctions

The assumption that gender and sexuality need to be examined together remained relatively unchallenged until the emergence of queer theory in the
1990s. Queer theory is associated with poststructuralist/postmodern approaches to sexuality and gender, and a critique of feminist theories of sexuality that are seen as limited by an emphasis on gender (Jagose, 1996; Sullivan,
2003). (Equally, some feminists argue that queer theory risks paying insufficient attention to gender in its analyses of sexuality (Walters, 2005; Richardson, 2006).) It rejects the idea of stable and unified gender and sexual categories and emphasizes the fluidity, instability and fragmentation of identities and
a multiplicity of sexuality and gender categories. Associated with this is a shift
in 'definitions of gender away from social division towards an understanding
of gender as cultural distinction' (McLaughlin et al., 2006:18). Queer theory
also questions the assumption that there are specific connections between sex,
gender and sexuality (Martin, 1998a), what I referred to above as the principle
of sexual and gender 'coherence'. In queer accounts the relationship between
sexuality and gender is not seen as fixed and static, but as highly complex and
unstable.

Various writers associated with queer theory have put forward arguments
for theorizing sexuality independently from gender. Rubin's work has been
influential in the development of such arguments. In the early 1980s Gayle
Rubin argued that, although connected, gender and sexuality 'are not the
same thing' (Rubin, 1984:308). Rubin is highly critical of the approach of
feminist writers like MacKinnon (Rubin with Butler, 1998). Opposed to the
view that sexuality can be adequately understood as causing gender, Rubin
instead offered an account of what she termed a 'sex/gender system' in which
she separates out sexuality and gender. Queer writers have subsequently drawn
on these ideas in developing their theories of gender. For example, in the
*Epistemology of the Closet* Eve Sedgwick (1990) calls for a radical separation of

..uer and sexuality. Doing this, Sedgwick argues, opens up our understand-
ngs of gender and sexuality, as well the links between them, allowing more
complex and diverse understandings. This means that new sexual and gender
stories may begin to be told, heard and experienced. For instance, it allows the
possibility of thinking about 'sexualities without genders' (Martin, 1998a),
where sexual desires, practices and identities do not depend on a person's
gender for their meaning. Similarly, it enables recognition of the existence of
multiple genders as illustrated, for example, by studies of female masculinities
(Halberstam, 1994) and transgender (Hines, 2006).

---

**Queer v Feminism?**

The distinction between sexuality and gender is at the heart of debates about
queer theory and its relationship to feminist thought. According to Merck et al.
(1998:1) queer and feminism are now 'widely understood to be two fields of
study' with the investigation of sexuality seen as the 'proper subject' of queer
theory and the analysis of gender that of feminism. While some agree with this
position (see, for example, Halperin, 1995), many writers prefer instead to think
about how feminist and queer theories are interconnected and can enrich each
other (Martin, 1998a; Richardson et al., 2006).

---

## Conflated categories

The fifth and final approach to thinking about the relationship between gender and sexuality that I have identified, rather than arguing for the logical
priority of one over the other (gender over sexuality/sexuality over gender) or
separating out the two, conflates these categories. Here, the assumption is that
sexuality and gender are mutually dependent to the extent that they cannot
be disentangled. For example, in her work on heterosexuality Tamsin Wilton
appears to take this view when she says that 'discourses of gender and sexuality
are inextricably interwoven' (Wilton, 1996:125).

## New imaginings: patterned fluidities

As I have indicated above, modernist understandings of gender and sexuality
as fixed, coherent and stable have been challenged by queer, postmodern and
poststructuralist accounts that conceptualize these categories as plural, provisional and situated. And if there are multiple genders and multiple sexualities,
then it is also likely that there will be multiple relationships between these categories. This means we need to consider how different sexual categories relate
to different genders. A challenge for future theories of gender and sexuality,
therefore, is to develop frameworks that allow more complex accounts of how
gender and sexuality are related to each other. According to Butler (1997),
this is one of the main tasks facing both feminist and queer theory.

To achieve this we need to consider the question of the relationship of gender and sexuality at a number of levels. This opens up the possibility that rather than thinking of gender and sexuality as separate areas of analysis, as do many queer theorists, or as interrelated, as do many feminist writers, they can be conceptualized as *both* depending on the level of analysis and the social context. Jackson (2005) identifies four levels of social construction of the relations between gender and sexuality:

- the structural;
- the level of social and cultural meaning;
- the level of everyday interactions and routine practices;
- the level of subjectivity.

At any one of these intersecting levels Jackson suggests that the relationship between gender and sexuality may be different. Like Jackson, I agree that we need to conceptualize gender at these different levels to enable 'new ways of articulating and understanding the diversity of contemporary gender and sexual categories and the complexities of their relationship with one another' (Richardson, 2007: 458). In attempting to represent the connections between gender and sexuality a number of writers have used the metaphor of a theoretical 'knot' (Alsop et al., 2002) or a 'tangled web' (Jackson, 2005). However, I would argue that these metaphors are too static to aid understandings of the relationship between gender and sexuality as a dynamic, historically and socially specific multilayered process. For this we need a different metaphor. Elsewhere I have outlined what might help us in this re-imagining (Richardson, 2007). This is the metaphor of the shoreline: a boundary in motion between land (configured as gender) and sea (configured as sexuality) where, like the connections between genders and sexualities, there are 'patterned fluidities'.

As well as the development of frameworks that allow more complex accounts of how gender and sexuality are related to each other and, by implication, how feminist and queer theory intersect, there have been a number of other important developments in theorizing gender since the 1990s. There is not the space to discuss these here, but other chapters do address some of these developments. These include: examinations of the interconnections between gender, race and class (see Reed and Taylor); work on gender and 'the body' and the use of the notion of embodiment (see Hines and Woodward); and potential changes in understandings of gender arising from shifts in technology and in cyberspace (see Gillis).

## Conclusion

This chapter has provided a brief overview of some of the different ways in which we can theorize gender and the contribution that feminist work in particular has made. The references it contains and the suggestions for further reading given below will help you to develop your understanding and recognize the complexities of many of the ideas I have touched on. Examining theories of gender is important not only in an academic sense, but also because it is through analysing different ways of theorizing that we are able 'to interrogate the processes whereby people generally become divided into the two categories male and female' (Alsop et al., 2002:2). This is a process of categorization that, as the remainder of this book will demonstrate, has important social, economic and personal implications. Moreover, it is important to acknowledge that the theories that we use to make sense of gender are part of this process and the meanings that derive from gender categorization. Theories of gender are not simply descriptions of 'what is', they actively structure the social worlds we inhabit. In the past, theories that assumed biology had a determining role in how we develop as women and men were used not merely to explain 'sex differences', but also to justify certain social arrangements as natural (Alsop et al., 2002). For instance, the idea that it was natural for women to want to have children and to care for them, and unnatural for men to feel the same, has often been used to both explain *and* justify why women have primary responsibility for childcare. In theorizing gender we are, then, actively engaged in a political process, an assumption that is central to the project of feminist gender theory. As McLaughlin et al. (2006:18) state: 'If feminism has one legacy to take forward...it is the legitimacy of using political criteria as the marker for the validity of social theorising.' That is: the pursuit of knowledge not just for its own sake, but for social change. It is this that has inspired much of the research you will read about in this book and which motivates many teachers and students of gender and women's studies.

## Further reading

R. Alsop, A. Fitzsimons and K. Lennon (2002) *theorizing gender*, Oxford, Polity
This is a good overview of the important debates in theories of gender. The book discusses the major theories concerned with the way we 'become gendered'. There are chapters on the body, men and masculinities, gender politics, and the relation between gender and sexuality, as well as discussion of transgender and queer approaches to understanding gender.

C. Beasley (2005) *Gender and Sexuality: Critical Theories, Critical Thinkers*, London, Sage
This book draws on the work of key theorists and offers an overview of the literature and debates in feminism, sexuality studies and masculinity studies. A central aim of the book is to link the important strands of both gender and sexuality theory.

H. Bradley (2007) *Gender,* Oxford, Polity
This is an accessible introduction to the concept of gender and the different theoretical approaches that have developed within women's and gender studies over the last thirty years. It explores contemporary relations of masculinity and femininity and highlights how our thinking about gender is influenced by changing political contexts. It uses life narratives to help contextualize the theory.

C. Colebrook (2004) *Gender*, Basingstoke, Palgrave Macmillan
This text provides an overview of the concept of gender and places the term in historical context, from the Enlightenment to the present. Colebrook discusses the development of theories of gender within feminism, as well as exploring recent developments in queer theory and 'post-feminism'. As a literary theorist, she also provides analyses of a number of key literary texts to demonstrate how specific styles of literature enable different understandings of gender.

R.W. Connell (2002) *Gender*, Oxford, Polity
This is a good introduction to the sociological study of gender. Written in a highly readable and accessible style, Connell traces the history of western ideas about gender, discusses the processes by which individuals become gendered as well as studies on gender differences. The book also examines gender inequalities and patterns in modern society, and considers whether these are changing under globalization. It also discusses gender politics and how these arise in personal life, showing how 'the personal is political.'

# CHAPTER TWO

# Feminist Theories

SALLY HINES

## Introduction

Women's studies developed in the late 1970s with the political goal of rectifying the marginalization of women's experiences and interests within academia. In seeking to theorize gender inequalities, and thereby help to end women's oppression, women's studies mirrored the prevailing link between feminist theory and activism. As Stacey outlined in the previous edition of *Introducing Women's Studies*: 'The aim was to explain the problems in order to transform the patriarchal relations of all spheres of social, cultural and economic life...' (Stacey, 1997:54). In the 1980s, then, feminist theory and the politics of feminist activism went hand in hand. Yet, by the 1990s, this connection had become troubled by debates within women's and gender studies and feminism more broadly concerning whose interests were being represented and by whom.

Through the 1990s, and over the past decade, there have been numerous shifts in feminist theory, which are captured in other chapters of this book. Significant developments have occurred around the theorizing of gender (see Richardson in this volume); 'race' and ethnicity (see Reed in this volume) and sexuality (see Taylor in this volume). Moreover, running through these developments has been the importance placed upon global social positionings and inequalities. It is not possible to encapsulate all of the developments in feminist theory in this chapter. Rather, I focus upon three areas which, I believe, have posed distinct challenges and represent key shifts within feminist theory:

- the development of poststructuralist and postmodern theory;
- debates between queer theory and feminism;
- the development of transgender studies.

The development of *deconstructionist analyses* – poststructuralism, postmodernism, queer theory and transgender studies – have presented key challenges to feminist theory over the past decade. Moreover, debates within these areas are important to the ways in which feminist theory is presently being rethought. Central to these developments is the sex/gender distinction, as discussed in the last chapter, and the troubling of unitary gender categories. Whilst the relationship between feminism and deconstructionist theory has frequently been contentious, there are also important areas of overlap. These are especially evident in the recent material 'turn' within deconstructionist theory, and in debates about embodiment (see Woodward and Gillis in this volume). It is these areas that I will move on to explore; firstly to reflect upon the challenges for feminist theory, and secondly to consider the intersections between deconstructionist theory and feminist theory.

The first section of this chapter addresses how feminist theory has diversified from the earlier dominant frameworks of radical, Marxist and liberal feminism. The next section explores the ways in which the development of poststructuralist and postmodern theories of gender both challenges, and connects with, feminist theory. The chapter then moves on to look in similar ways at dialogues between feminism and queer theory. The last section of the chapter addresses the development of transgender studies; highlighting significant debates between feminist and transgender scholars and examining work within transgender theory around the body. Such studies are important because they inform a number of key issues and debates in women's and gender studies including:

- the construction of the category gender;
- the relationship between sex and gender;
- the relationship between 'the body' and identity;
- feminist politics and who can claim a feminist identity.

## Beyond the 'Big Three': developments in feminist theory

From a feminist perspective, gender is a socially constructed concept which gives rise to distinct gender identities and gender roles. Feminist scholars have analysed the operation of power at both a micro and a macro level in order to investigate the ways in which gender inequalities are constructed. Different feminist perspectives have foregrounded particular social sites as central to the construction, maintenance and reproduction of gender inequalities. Feminist perspectives have accounted for gender inequalities in different ways and have offered competing solutions to unequal power relations between women and men. During the 1970s and 1980s, feminist perspectives can be loosely summarized as falling within a radical, Marxist or liberal school of thought. These main points of argument are outlined in the box overleaf.

It is important to note, however, that the divisions between these three feminist perspectives were not wholly demarcated. For example, radical feminism emerged in the 1970s in the US alongside the civil rights movements and many radical feminist activists had been involved in working-class politics and anti-racism campaigns in the 1960s. Yet by the 1990s each of these schools of feminist thought were critiqued for neglecting the positioning and experience of

## Radical Feminism

The concept of 'patriarchy' – systematic male dominance of women – was central to radical feminism. Patriarchy was seen to be universal in that it existed across all cultures and historical periods, if in different forms. Radical feminists highlighted the nuclear family as a key site of women's oppression, whereby men exploited women through unpaid domestic labour in the home, which, in turn, restricted their ability to gain positions of power in society. Reproduction was identified as central to these processes of inequality; whereby women become materially dependent upon men. Shulamith Firestone (1971), for example, argued that the abolition of the family was intrinsic to women's liberation. Other radical feminists highlighted sexual violence – rape, domestic violence, sexual harassment and pornography – as part of the patriarchal system of male oppression of women. From a radical feminist perspective, women's liberation is only achievable if patriarchy is overthrown.

## Marxist Feminism

While radical feminism positioned patriarchy as an over-arching structure of women's oppression, Marxist feminists argued that the system of capitalism structured gender inequality. From this perspective, economic class relations lay at the root of the subordination of women. The oppression of women is maintained through domestic labour and as a result of women's unequal position in the labour market. Gender inequality is therefore a system of class inequality, which is maintained to serve the interests of the ruling class. From a Marxist feminist perspective, women's freedom from oppression is only achievable if capitalism is overthrown.

## Liberal Feminism

Rather than focus upon an over-riding cause of women's inequality (for example, patriarchy or capitalism), liberal feminists tended to highlight issues such as cultural gender stereotyping and gender divisions in the home and employment. These aspects of gender inequality, liberal feminists argued, can be ended through equal opportunities legislation and other democratic measures. From this perspective, equality for women is achieved through gradual processes of social and legal reform.

non-white non-middle-class women. Working-class, black and lesbian feminists in particular argued that traditional feminism centred on the interests of middle-class, white, heterosexual women. As Robinson outlines:

> Reflecting debates and divisions within the women's movement, the most fundamental dilemma of Women's Studies has concerned the marginalisation of Black, working-class and lesbian perspectives amongst others, and often in opposition, it has been argued to the prioritising of the needs and experiences of white, middle-class Western women.
>
> (Robinson, 1997: 18)

Radical feminism's positioning of patriarchy as universal attracted much criticism from other feminists and, particularly, from black feminists who argued that the concept neglected cultural and historical specificities. The notion of patriarchy was therefore challenged for not accounting for how 'race' and ethnicity impact upon women's experiences. In this way, hooks (1981) argued that radical feminism takes white women's experiences as the norm; failing to recognize the distinct experiences of non-white women. Similar points of argument have been made in relation to the ways in which 'patriarchy' fails to account for the ways in which social class intersects with gender relations and processes of power. Criticisms were also brought to bear on Marxist and liberal feminism by radical feminists who argued that these schools of thought failed to account for the ways in which women's oppression is structured by practices and understandings of sexuality (Rubin, 1975).

As the recognition of 'difference' led to more complex models of feminist analysis, work fitting under the broad church of 'feminist theory' spread across academic disciplines and the need for women's studies as a discrete field was questioned (see Chapter 3 for further reflection on these debates).

Accordingly, as the category of 'woman' came unstuck within the broader politics of feminism, so feminist theory diversified. Whilst politically it became appropriate to talk about a diversity of feminisms, within the academy feminist perspectives developed in increasingly extensive and interdisciplinary ways (see Richardson in this volume for discussion of how feminist theory has diversified in relation to theorizing gender; Robinson in this volume for discussion of the relationship of masculinity to feminist theory; Reed in this volume for discussion of developments in feminist theory in relation to 'race' and ethnicity). Moreover, during the past decade the scope of feminist analysis and the breadth of feminist concerns have continued to widen. The chapter will now turn to address how developments within poststructuralist, postmodern, queer and transgender theory have reflected recent conceptual and substantive shifts in feminist theory.

## Poststructuralist and postmodern theory

### Challenges for feminism

The central premise of poststructuralism is that discourse constructs meaning. Judith Butler (1990) defines discourse as 'the limits of acceptable speech'. Discourse, then, structures what can, or what cannot, be said about a certain subject. From a poststructuralist perspective, identity is produced *through* discourse. Poststructuralist feminist analyses take the discursive formations of gender and sexuality as their starting point to examine how gender and sexuality are constructed through language and institutionalized ways of thinking.

Early feminist writers differentiated between 'sex' and 'gender'. Within this binary framework, 'sex' referred to the biological body and gender to the social roles and cultural understandings that were attached to male or female bodies. Conceptually separating 'sex' and 'gender' was politically significant for feminism as it followed that gender roles were socially and culturally, rather than 'naturally', constructed. During the 1990s, however, feminist scholars developed alternative ways of theorizing the relationship between sex and gender. Significantly, 'sex' became to be seen as socially and culturally constructed, as was gender (see Richardson in this volume).

From this perspective, Butler shows how the binary categories of 'sex' and 'gender' have restricted feminist understandings. As Richardson also points out, she argues that the way in which feminists have understood 'sex' as constituting the biological male or female body and 'gender' as referring to the social meanings attached to such bodies, has limited understanding of gender as distinct from sex:

> When the constructed status of gender is theorized as radically independent of sex, gender itself becomes a free-floating artifice, with the consequence that *man* and *masculine* might just as easily signify a female body as a male one, and *woman* and *feminine* a male body as easily as a female one.
>
> (Butler, 1990:6, italics in original)

An understanding of gender as separate from sex thus holds the potential for a greater diversity of masculinities and femininities, which, in turn, allows for the recognition of *differently* embodied gendered identities and expressions, or of different ways of being women and men. Further, Butler argues that we should be wary of seeing 'sex' as a purely biological characteristic. Rather, 'sex' is socially and culturally determined.

Alongside poststructuralism, postmodernism has been influential on the way in which strands of feminist thinking have reconfigured the sex/gender binary. In challenging the idea of unified identity categories (for example, of 'woman' or 'man') feminist postmodern writers have troubled the notion of shared identity and experience. Subsequently, the belief that feminism is able to speak on behalf of women per se was questioned. Yet in rejecting the notion of common experience, postmodernism has appeared as politically divisive to some feminists. There has existed a contentious relationship between feminist and postmodernist theory and for many feminist scholars a postmodern framework is at odds with feminism. The arguments of feminist writers who are critical of postmodernism can be summarized as follows:

- Postmodernism conflicts with a politics of identity that is central to feminist politics. This is because in deconstructing the category 'woman' it threatens the idea of organizing politically around this category. From this perspective Benhabib states:

> The postmodern position(s) thought through to their conclusions may not only eliminate the specificity of feminist theory but place into question the very emancipatory ideals of the women's movements altogether.
>
> (Benhabib, 1994:78–9)

Stefano (1990) has also been concerned about how feminism can articulate and organize around the interests of women if the identity category of 'woman' itself is abandoned.

● Postmodernism neglects the material, which is central to women's experiences. From this perspective, scholars such as Walby (1997) argue that postmodernism's focus on the discursive formations of gender is at the expense of a structural analysis necessary to examine the social and economic forces that affect the lived experiences of gender.

In different ways, then, many feminist writers and activists have argued that poststructuralism and postmodernism are incompatible with feminism. Others, however, disagree and look at their areas of overlap; these arguments will be outlined in the next section.

## Common ground

Rather than viewing postmodernism as oppositional to feminism, other feminist writers have traced the common ground between the two. Flax (1997), for example, argues that postmodernism's deconstruction of gender categories complements feminism's problematizing of gender relations. However, she proposes that it is necessary for feminism to extend its deconstructive analysis in order to think more carefully about the relationship between sex and gender. Whilst talking about women's experiences is of continued importance, Flax believes that such accounts are invariably partial, since 'none of us can speak for "woman" because no such person exists except within a specific set of (already gendered) relations-to "man" and to many concrete and different women' (Flax, 1997:78). Rather, she proposes that the way forward lies in the recognition and acceptance of multiple gendered experiences and identities.

As well as usefully highlighting the common ground between feminism and postmodernism, these types of argument indicate the benefits postmodernism may hold for feminism. For instance, Wright suggests that: 'postmodernist theory provides feminism with an additional framework, enabling it to articulate the diversity and contradictions that spring up not only between various positions but also within various positions' (1997:179). In this way, a postmodern framework may be used to move on from the concept of a unitary gender identity (of 'woman' or 'man') to recognize differences across and between gender categories.

Braidotti's (1994) work is important in signposting a feminist incorporation of postmodernism. This approach enables political allegiances whilst recognizing that unitary identity categories are unstable. A postmodern feminist approach can also be seen in the work of Spivak (1990), Butler (1992), Ahmed (1996), Heckman (2000) and Roseneil (2000a) who variously illustrate how the deconstruction of identity categories can be followed through with an analysis of how identities and gender politics are continually shaped and re-shaped anew. Very similar themes and points of debate to those that have been discussed here can be seen in the dialogue between feminism and queer theory.

## Debating queer and feminism

Like poststructuralist and postmodern debates about identity, queer theory has posed a challenge to feminism's theorization of gender and sexual identity formation. Moreover, queer theory has, both positively and negatively, been seen to have taken centre stage within sexuality studies in recent years (see also Taylor's chapter in this volume). Queer theory draws on poststructuralist and postmodern deconstructions of identity categories, and sees gender and sexual identities as potentially fluid. In arguing for the importance of analyzing how gender and sexual identities are constructed and localized in the everyday, this has provided '...increased space for exploring how sexual and gender identities are the product of local situations and contexts within which such identities have meaning and value' (Richardson et al., 2006:8). A micro-analysis of identity formations has shed light upon the factors that interweave within and between identity categories. This has brought greater attention to the ways in which under-theorized aspects of identity, such as race and ethnicity (for example, Anzaldua, 1999); geographical and cultural location (for example, Bell and Binnie, 2000) and gender variance (for example, Halberstam, 2005; Hines, 2007), intersect with gender and sexuality to impact upon power relations and subjective identifications. Further, a queer analysis has illuminated the ways in which the cultural realm acts as a site of identity construction and resistance.

In viewing all gendered or sexual identities as socially constructed, queer theory aims to challenge the naturalization of normative gender and sexual categories. Yet, as Seidman notes, queer theory's rebuttal of identity may para-doxically lead to the denial of difference:

> This very refusal to anchor experience in identifications ends up, ironically, denying differences by either submerging them in an undifferentiated oppositional mass or by blocking the development of individual and social differences through the disci-plining compulsory imperative to remain undifferentiated.
>
> (Seidman, 1993:133)

As with poststructuralist and postmodern analyses, then, queer theory pres-ents the dilemma of how to deconstruct identity categories and positively ac-count for difference, without losing sight of the experiences that constitute difference. Thus, very similar criticisms are levelled at queer theory as those previously discussed in relation to postmodernism, i.e. it runs the risk of ob-scuring gender divisions and inequalities.

One of the central critiques by feminist scholars of queer theory is that cultural analyses of gender and sexual transgressions have been developed at the expense of political theories (Hennessy, 1995; Fraser, 1997a; Jackson, 1999b). Yet, recently, a number of writers have stressed the importance of bringing a social and economic analysis to the deconstruction of gender. These developments, which will be outlined below, also provide methods through which to navigate the analytical dilemmas for feminism of postmodernism, as previously discussed.

- *Queer sociology*
  Writers such as Seidman (1996), Roseneil (1999) and Hines (2007) have called for a 'queer sociology'. Queer sociology examines how power is produced and resisted in relation to both discourse and material factors. A queer sociological approach is helpful in allowing feminism to positively recognize gendered differences, whilst exploring the lived experiences and competing forms of difference. This model also develops deconstructive approaches to gender by grounding analyses of gender plurality within a social and economic framework.

- *Material queer studies*
  Alongside proposals for a queer sociology, recent work by feminist scholars has brought a social analysis to deconstructive gender theory. In theorizing the intersections of sexuality and social class, Taylor (2005a), for example, explores women's material positioning alongside their subjective identifications. Hennessy (2006) has termed the convergence of material feminism and queer theory as 'material queer studies'.

- *Intersections of feminism and queer theory*
  As some postmodern writers have examined the commonalities between postmodernism and feminism, others have traced the connections between feminism and queer theory (Butler, 1994; Martin, 1998a; McLaughlin, 2006). Significantly Warner (1993) and Richardson (2000, 2006) have stressed the ways in which feminism has been instrumental in the development of queer theory. Warner argues that: 'feminism has made gender a primary category of the social in a way that makes queer social theory newly imaginable' (Warner, 1993: viii). For Warner, feminism as a method of analysis has much to offer queer theory in relation to developing further distinctions between the categories of gender and sexuality. In turn, this would enable a more detailed analysis of the ways in which sexuality is gendered. Richardson et al. (2006) suggest that the juncture between feminist and queer theory reflects 'the wish to bring global and local dynamics together and the role a fusion of queer and feminist ideas can play within this, revolves around a desire to see material and cultural issues examined together' (Richardson et al., 2006: 11). In attempting to forge stronger links between feminism and queer theory, Richardson (2006) identifies several ways in which queer theory can enhance feminist theory:

1. Queer theory is helpful in focusing attention upon how sexuality affects social relations.

2. Queer theory has been important in developing critiques of normative assumptions about gender and sexuality.

3. Queer theory has the potential to offer feminism further tools through which to theorize the relationship between gender and sexuality.

4. Queer theory's emphasis on 'difference' may enable feminist theory to analyze power across and between identity categories.

5. Queer theory offers feminism theoretical tools through which to understand the sex/gender binary.

The theoretical developments within feminist theory discussed so far have troubled conceptualizations of unitary gender categories and have facilitated a more careful theorization of the sex/ gender distinction. These tendencies are also evident through the development of transgender studies, which the chapter will consequently now move on to explore.

# Transgender studies

## Transgender and feminism

The term 'transgender' relates to a diversity of practices that call into question traditional ways of seeing gender and its relationship with sex and sexuality (see also Richardson in this volume). Used broadly, the concept of transgender is extensive – incorporating practices and identities such as transvestism, transsexuality, intersex, gender queer, female and male drag, cross-dressing and some butch/femme practices. Transgender may refer to individuals who have undergone hormone treatment or surgery to reconstruct their bodies or to those who cross gender in ways that are less permanent.

Second wave feminism was one of the first academic fields to respond to the growing public awareness of modern western transgender practices (Hird, 2002). However, feminism has traditionally been hostile to transgender practices (Raymond, 1980; Jeffreys, 1997a). The publication of Janice Raymond's book *The Transsexual Empire* (1980) established an anti-transgender feminist perspective that was to significantly affect the dominant feminist position for successive decades. There are two central strands to Raymond's position. I will address these in turn and summarize the key points of argument in relation to each. First, from a biological position, she argues that it is impossible to separate 'sex' and gender:

● 'Sex' is chromosomally dependent and thus secured at birth.
● 'Gender' is the coherent expression of biological 'sex'.

- The categories of 'sex' and 'gender' are inherently co-dependent.
- Transsexuality (male to female) is a genetic male practice that is created by a patriarchal medical system to construct servile women.

Raymond argues that transgender women are not, nor can they ever be, 'real' women:

> It is biologically impossible to change *chromosomal* sex. If chromosomal sex is taken to be the fundamental basis for maleness and femaleness, the man who undergoes sex conversion is *not* female.
>
> (Raymond, 1980: 10, italics in original)

The second strand of Raymond's argument is that transgender practices are oppositional to the values and politics of feminism:

- Transgender women are men who reinforce a stereotypical model of femininity;
- Transgender men are women who seek to acquire male power and privilege.

Raymond's book was widely read and created the dominant feminist perspective on transsexuality throughout the 1980s in both the US and Britain. Riddell (1996) documents how transgender feminists and/or lesbians were frequently excluded from feminist and lesbian communities, and argues that Raymond's work had personally and politically damaging consequences:

> My living space is threatened by this book. Although I have had to challenge its attacks on transsexual women, its dogmatic approach and its denial that female experience is our basic starting point are a danger signal of trends emerging in the whole women's movement.
>
> (Riddell, 1996: 189)

More recently, Jeffreys (1997a) has rekindled the radical feminist tradition of positioning transgender practices as anti-feminist: 'Transsexualism opposes feminism by maintaining and reinforcing false and constructed notions of correct femininity and masculinity' (1997a: 57). Such feminist approaches to transgender show how a binary understanding of gender is unable to incorporate transgender into feminist theory and politics. Although some feminist writers (Hausman, 1995; Wilton, 2000) continue to reflect Raymond and Jeffreys' critique, other feminist writers have adopted more progressive approaches to transgender. Here it is possible to see the ways in which a feminist framework can be used to theorize diverse gendered identities and expressions that are unfixed to the 'sexed' body.

Rubin's (1996) work is useful in examining the intersections of feminism and transgender. In contrast to an essentializing insistence that 'one must inhabit a female body to have the experiences that makes one a feminist' (Adu-Poku, 2001:157), Rubin calls for an understanding that feminist identity arises out of political commitment rather than female biology. She states: '"Woman-hood" is no longer a necessary, nor sufficient qualification for feminist identity. A feminist is one who acts in concert with feminist ideals' (Rubin, 1996:308). Thus, political practice, rather than gender or sex, lies at the heart of femi-nist identity. Koyama's (2003) discussion of 'transfeminism' also shows how transgender politics may enable contemporary feminism to reconfigure the relationship between sex and gender. Koyama writes: '[Transfeminism] is not merely about merging trans politics with feminism, but it is a critique of the second wave feminism from third wave perspectives' (Koyama, 2003:244). Here, Koyama uses the term 'third wave' to refer to feminist perspectives de-veloped through the 1990s. She argues that, in addition to enabling stronger links between feminist and transgender theory and politics, closer attention to gender diversity may enable a collective arena in which gender differences pro-duce a more extensive feminist knowledge. As I will now move on to explore, a focus upon embodiment within feminism and transgender studies indicates further how material concerns are being debated and developed.

## Embodying gender

In taking the formations of gender and sexuality as their starting point, queer feminist analyses have engaged directly with transgender. For Butler, gender does not exist outside of discourse. She develops the concept of 'performa-tivity' to address the ways in which the rules of gender are compulsively and repetitively acted out to reinforce the idea of gender as natural. The practices of cross-dressing and drag are employed as examples of how the naturalization of gender can be challenged through parody – to signpost 'gender trouble'. (See Richardson in this volume for a fuller discussion.)

Yet many transgender theorists have argued that queer analyses of transgen-der have neglected the centrality of the body within transsexual experiences. Prosser (1998) argues that Butler's focus on drag presents a selective analysis of transgender, which neglects the role of embodiment within gendered expe-riences and expressions. For Prosser, transsexualism is the outcome of being born in the 'wrong body'. Transsexuality, then, is a state whereby self-gender identity and the body are at odds. Gender reconstructive surgery thus enables the two to correlate. Although as Halberstam (1998) and Heyes (2000) point out, and, indeed, as has been the focus of feminist work around women's bodily image and experience (for example, Woolf, 1991), it is not only trans-sexuals who express disharmony between the imagined and the material body. (See also Woodward in this volume.)

Rather than focusing upon transsexuality as synonymous of the 'wrong body', and surgery as a means of constructing the 'right' body, other transgender writers have drawn attention to identities that are consciously constructed on the borderlands of gender. Bornstein (1994), for example, blows apart any categorization of sex as defined by biological genitalia:

> Most folks would define a man by the presence of a penis or some form of penis. Some would define a woman by the presence of a vagina or some form of vagina. It's not that simple though. I know several women in San Francisco who have penises. Many wonderful men in my life have vaginas. And there are quite a few people whose genitals fall somewhere between penises and vaginas. What are *they*?
>
> (Bornstein, 1994: 56–7, italics in original)

Bornstein uses queer theory's deconstruction of gender identity categories: 'I know I'm not a man – about that much I'm very clear, and I've come to the conclusion that I'm probably not a woman either, at least not according to a lot of people's rules on this sort of thing' (1994: 8). In articulating herself not in the 'wrong body' but as a 'gender outlaw', Bornstein explicitly challenges a sex/gender binary and troubles presumptions of fixed gender categories.

Over the last decade transgender writers have articulated their personal gender trajectories, and have engaged with the theoretical debates of feminism, postmodernism and queer theory. Transgender studies brings varied meanings to understandings of gender and reflects a diversity of theoretical positions. Whilst some writers have continued to articulate a transsexual narrative (Prosser, 1998), others have worked to reshape the meanings of transgender and to problematize normative understandings of gender and sexuality more broadly (Stone, 1991; Halberstam, 1998). Thus the key question in transgender studies has become 'what is the "right" body?' (Halberstam, 1998).

Transgender studies incorporates a body of work that is autobiographical in its style and content, and includes political commentary aligned with transgender community activism. In common with much feminist work, there is no strict demarcation between these areas, leading many writers to move between the theoretical, the autobiographical and the political. A mix of deconstructive gender analysis, social critique and autobiography is employed to explore a diversity of gender and sexual identities. In line with the feminist influenced postmodern and queer work I discussed earlier, much work from transgender studies argues for the importance of bringing a social and material framework to analyses of transgender.

MacDonald's (1998) emphasis upon gender as socially relational as well as peformatively constructed is helpful in overcoming the theoretical problems for feminism of deconstructionist perspectives. Whilst acknowledging that the focus on difference within deconstructive analyses is useful, she argues that postmodern and queer theory has a tendency to ignore the specific subject positions under analysis. In a similar way to Prosser (1998), MacDonald argues that 'It [queer theory] does so at the expense of investigating the actual lives, political demands, or feelings expressed by transgendered people of having an identity that is often experienced as "authentic" or "integral" and that it is considered to be neither "chosen" originally nor "performed" strategically' (MacDonald, 1998:4). She proposes that the celebration of difference be accompanied by an analysis of the social experiences of difference: 'to postmodern theory, transgender argues, then, for the reality of difference, and the need to investigate the social structures which enforce sex/gender incongruity and stability at every level' (MacDonald, 1998:10). MacDonald's ideas mirror the aims of the feminist scholars previously discussed who attempt to analyze how gender is constructed at the level of discourse *and* at the level of the material. This framework enables the theorization of differences within and between gender cultures and identity positions, as well as accounting for subjective and embodied experiences.

Work from transgender studies provides a complex analysis of the sex/gender binary, and further troubles the positioning of gender categories as either authentic or unified.

To feminism, transgender studies offers a further model through which to account for gender difference. This is not only relevant to theorizing the social positioning and subjective identifications of transgender people, but, importantly, sheds further light upon the construction of the category of gender itself. This enables a richer understanding of the constructions, social positionings and subjective experiences of *all* genders.

## Conclusion

I began this chapter by addressing how the diversification of feminist knowledge and politics over the past two decades has brought particular challenges for feminist theory. I suggested that the development of poststructuralist, postmodern, queer and transgender theory has been especially contentious within feminism. Key issues at stake here concern understanding of 'sex' and gender, and their relationship to each other, and the constitution of gender categories. Moreover, these questions stand as important issues for feminist theory. In order to explore developments around these issues, I have focused my attention in this chapter upon debates within poststructuralism, postmodernism, queer theory and transgender studies. I have sought to examine the ways in which the relationship between 'sex' and gender has been theorized within these fields and to explore what such dialogues say about understandings of gender categories. I have attempted to think through these questions in two ways. First, by reflecting upon the challenges these developments have brought to feminist theory. Second, by considering how common ground between poststructuralism, postmodernism, queer theory, transgender studies and feminist theory may be mapped out.

Postmodern and queer feminist approaches provide an understanding of gender that is able to account for non-normative identities and practices. In theorizing gender as distinct from biological 'sex', these approaches present an analysis of divergent gender expressions that are unfixed to the 'sexed' body. I have explored how some aspects of postmodernism and queer theory, however, have posed problems for feminist theory. In particular, there has been a tendency to neglect material conditions. Moreover, these perspectives have been inclined to focus upon gender transgressions as symbolic sites of gender deconstruction. This has left questions of embodiment under-theorized. Recent developments within poststructuralism and postmodernism, however, indicate the emergence of a deconstructive framework that situates the material alongside the cultural. This provides a model through which to analyze how social structures impact upon distinct gender identity formations. Such a line of enquiry is valuable in its understanding of gender as socially relational *and* performatively constructed. These developments convey useful tools for feminist theory to account for diversity and difference.

In addressing debates between feminism and queer theory, I have again attempted to map out the areas of intersection and to consider what queer theory may offer contemporary feminist theory. Queer theorists have challenged the correlation of 'sex' and gender, and have sought to untie these features. Yet, I have argued that queer theory has had a tendency to neglect social structures. This limitation is being overcome, however, by a queer sociological framework and through material queer studies, which examine how gender and sexuality are constructed through both discourse and social structures.

I moved on to suggest that work from transgender studies has much to bring to both deconstructive analysis and to feminist theory. Transgender studies articulates the importance of a grounded theory that not only celebrates the deconstruction of gender categories, but also attends to the material and bodily formations and experiences of gender. Moreover, the intervention by transgender theorists has shown that a queer imaginary does not have to run counter to social analysis.

In conclusion, I suggest that the intersections of poststructuralism, postmodernism, queer theory, transgender studies and feminist theory offer a space in which to develop new understandings and more nuanced analyses of contemporary gender formations and identifications. Dialogues within and between these theoretical fields indicate how understandings of gender, sex and embodiment continue to be reconfigured. Moreover, the intersections between these fields enable an arena in which gender difference and diversity can be productively retheorized across the next decade.

## Further reading

C. Beasley (1999) *What is Feminism?: An Introduction to Feminist Theory,* London, Sage
This is an accessible introduction to feminist theory. The first part of the book presents an analysis of feminist critiques of traditional social and political theory. Later chapters address early feminist theories and perspectives as well as more recent feminist debates; including poststructuralist, postmodern and postcolonialist feminisms.

V. Bryson (2003) *Feminist Political Theory: An Introduction*, 2nd edn, Basingstoke, Palgrave Macmillan
This book provides an accessible and wide-ranging history of feminist thought. Additionally, it examines a range of contemporary feminist perspectives and debates; including black and postmodern feminisms. Feminist theories and concepts are usefully applied to empirical issues such as political representations of women, sexual violence and the family.

S. Hines (2007) *TransForming Gender: Transgender Practices of Identity, Intimacy and Care*, Abingdon and Portland, Policy Press
This text provides a detailed discussion of debates within the social sciences, and particularly within feminism and gender theory, around transgender. It examines the relationship between the disciplines of feminism, lesbian and gay studies, poststructuralism, postmodernism, queer theory and transgender, and calls for a queer sociology, which is able to account for gender diversity. Drawing on data from empirical research with transgender people, the book also provides accounts of the different ways in which gender may be lived.

J. McLaughlin (2003) *Feminist Social and Political Theory: Contemporary Debates and Dialogues*, Basingstoke, Palgrave Macmillan
This book explores central debates within contemporary feminist theory and addresses how these relate to social and political thought. Drawing on a range of theoretical and political perspectives, and key figures, it provides an accessible and broad-ranging discussion of feminist theory, which includes transnational feminism, queer and postmodern feminisms, and feminist engagements with new technology.

D. Richardson, J. McLaughlin and M.E. Casey (2006) *Intersections between Feminist and Queer Theory*, Basingstoke, Palgrave Macmillan
This collection discusses both the areas of disagreement and connections between feminist and queer theory. As well as illustrating the ways in which queer theory has been influenced by feminism, the book considers how a queer feminist approach may be developed. Rather than existing in opposition, this book points to the number of ways in which feminist theory and queer theory intersect and complement each other. With chapters on early feminist theories, women and the labour market, same-sex partnerships, and debates around transgender, this book brings together cultural and material concerns to provide an interdisciplinary overview of the dialogue between feminism and queer.

# CHAPTER THREE

# Feminism, Social Movements and the Gendering of Politics

NICKIE CHARLES

## Introduction

Women's and gender studies grew out of the women's liberation movements of the 1960s and 1970s. These movements – which were known as second wave feminism and emerged across Europe and North America and, later, in Latin America, Africa and Asia – mobilized hundreds of thousands of women and were associated with significant cultural shifts and policy change. They challenged the state and raised demands for gender equality, for reproductive rights, for the right to define one's own sexuality and to be free from the threat of violence. Those involved demanded resources from the state and that society recognize their rights as women and as citizens. Second wave feminism was political from the word 'go'. It challenged male-dominated institutions like universities, trade unions and political parties. Women campaigned for an end to sex discrimination in the public sphere and an end to the abuse of women by men that went on in the private sphere of the home. One of the outcomes of the women's movement was the establishment of women's studies courses and departments in universities (and later gender studies). Another was the engagement of a new generation of feminists with the formal political process. Women joined political parties in order to make sure that they took 'women's issues' seriously. And now, over 30 years later, we are beginning to see what a massive transformation has been wrought in the world of politics by second wave feminism.

In this chapter I explore some of these changes, looking at how feminism has influenced both the way politics is understood and the way it is practised. I look first at the women's movement and how it gave rise to feminist activity within the academy and within the political sphere; I then explore the challenge to male definitions of politics that emerged from the women's movement and feminists' critique of political theory; thirdly I explore women's engagement with formal politics; and finally I look at women's political participation and the difference it is making to political processes and policy development.

## Women and social movements

### *The women's liberation movement*

The women's liberation movement emerged in the late 1960s and 1970s and campaigned around issues of equal pay, equal opportunities, violence against women, sexual orientation, discrimination in the social security and tax systems, child care and fertility control. Women in the movement rejected conventional politics and undertook forms of direct action and campaigning. Their activism was loosely coordinated at a national level, but existed primarily in local women's groups, which were both consciousness raising and involved in political activity (Lovenduski and Randall, 1993; Charles, 2000). They assumed that all women were united by similar experiences and a shared identity and that this gave them interests in common that could be encapsulated as 'women's interests'. The women's liberation movement was one of a wave of social movements that emerged in the 1960s and 1970s – others were the peace movement, the students' movement, lesbian and gay liberation and the green movement – and in all of them women's participation was relatively high (Stephenson, 1998). These have come to be known as 'new social movements' because of their engagement in the cultural as well as the political realm and because they are seen as moving away from the class-based politics which had previously characterized advanced western societies. As we shall see, however, there is disagreement as to whether it is accurate to describe the women's liberation movement as a new social movement.

---

**The Demands of the Women's Liberation Movement**

- Equal pay

- Equal education and job opportunities

- Free contraception and abortion on demand

- Free 24-hour nurseries

- Financial and legal independence

- An end to all discrimination against lesbians and a woman's right to define her own sexuality

- Freedom from intimidation by threat or use of violence or sexual coercion, regardless of marital status

- An end to all laws, assumptions and institutions which perpetuate male dominance and men's aggression towards women

---

Towards the end of the 1970s differences between women in the movement emerged and it began to fragment. Black women, lesbians, disabled women, older women and working-class women argued that the women's movement was based on a specific identity – that of young, white, middle-class, highly-educated women – that it excluded women who did not share this identity and that there could be no automatic assumption that all women had the same political interests (Lovenduski and Randall, 1992). Although this marked the end of a particular manifestation of second wave feminism, the fragmentation of the women's movement meant that its ideas and practices spread much more widely throughout society. Thus, the UN decade for women (1975–85) raised the issue of women's integration into the development process, triggering 'the formation of thousands of women's organisations' on a global scale (Inglehart and Norris, 2003: 3) while, in Britain, feminist activists moved into political parties, trade unions and academia.

## The birth of women's and gender studies

Many women who had been active in the women's liberation movement took their activism into higher education and, during the 1970s and 1980s, women's studies courses and programmes were set up in universities. Feminists argued both that gender was central to disciplines such as sociology, history and english and that there ought to be a particular area of study called women's studies. This movement within education was spearheaded in the US but feminists in higher education elsewhere were soon involved and the number of women's studies courses and degree programmes increased. This eventually resulted in women's studies being recognized as an interdisciplinary area of study in its own right and, subsequently, departments and centres of women's studies were established in many institutions of higher education. This development can be seen as an important outcome of the women's movement and studying gender is now a central part of the curriculum in many arts and social science disciplines. Since the 1990s, there has been a shift from women's to gender studies. Men's studies and the critical study of masculinities also became established (see also Robinson in this volume).

## Women's support groups

Women also continued their involvement in social movements, sometimes in ways which seemed to reproduce existing gender divisions of labour and sometimes in ways which overtly challenged them. Here, I look at two examples of such involvement, women's support groups during the 1984–5 miners' strike in the UK and the women's peace camp at Greenham Common.

### 1984–5 miners' strike

During the 1984–5 miners' strike women set up support groups which fulfilled a welfare function for mining communities. This form of activity can be seen as an extension of women's caring role within the family but, at the same time, it involved them in activities which went beyond this role, such as speaking at demonstrations and being present on picket lines. This was claimed by some to be evidence of the influence of feminism in working-class women's lives and an indication that gender relations in mining communities were being transformed (see for example Stead, 1987). This, however, is a romanticized picture (Spence and Stephenson, 2007). In fact many of the women who were active in women's support groups had been engaged in community or political activism prior to the strike and, in many ways, the activity of the support groups 'reinforced the traditional gendered division of labour' (Spence and Stephenson, 2007:7). Also, once the strike was over, the feminist movement was unable 'to integrate the class concerns of the women' (Spence and Stephenson, 2007:10) and most of the women who remained active after the strike were involved in local politics and/or were active in the Labour Party. Thus, although the strike brought about significant changes for individual women, for most, whether or not they had been active during the strike, things reverted to 'normal' once the strike was over (Waddington et al., 1991). This normality included a class and community based political consciousness and the gender divisions of labour existing prior to the strike (Spence and Stephenson, 2007).

### Greenham Common

A contrasting example is the women's peace camp at Greenham that was set up in opposition to the presence of US nuclear missiles at airbases in Britain, which challenged gender relations and led to the emergence of a feminist political consciousness (Roseneil, 1995). The women's peace camp began with a march from Cardiff in south Wales which included men as well as women; it was established in 1981 and quickly became women-only (Charles, 1996). In Sasha Roseneil's words:

> Greenham was not a pressure group, concerned to be integrated into the political process, but rather sought to undermine from outside the legitimacy of a political order which promoted militarism and excluded women.
>
> (Roseneil, 1995:170)

It was a movement which profoundly challenged the 'established routines of "doing politics"' (Eyerman and Jamison, 1991:149) and confronted, with unconventional forms of direct action, the armed might of the state. It also challenged patriarchy by operating at a symbolic level and 'conveying messages about women's independence, autonomy and agency' (Roseneil, 1995:171). It challenged and transformed gender relations by refusing 'men's power to control women's actions' and 'women's confinement by domestic responsibilities' even when those men were armed by the state and were acting in its name (Roseneil, 1995:171).

> Greenham women refused to perform gender as they should, above all resisting the heterorelational imperative of patriarchy which demands that women exist first and

foremost for men. Many challenged this as lesbians...But, lesbian or heterosexual, Greenham women in their thousands symbolically and practically put women first in their political and daily lives.

(Roseneil, 1995:171)

These two examples, women's support groups during the miners' strike and the women's peace movement, show that women are active in trade union struggles such as strikes as well as in alternative politics such as the women's movement. In the first, they organize on the basis of existing gender divisions of labour albeit challenging gender boundaries in the process, in the second, they both challenge gender divisions of labour and transgress gender boundaries.

## *Recognition and redistribution*

These forms of political activity are conceptualized as social movements; the peace movement and (more contentiously) the women's liberation movement being seen as 'new' social movements in contrast to 'old' social movements such as the labour movement.

- New social movements aim primarily to bring about cultural change, their politics is a politics of recognition.
- 'Old' social movements aim to bring about political and economic change and their politics is a politics of redistribution.

This distinction has, however, been contested, particularly in the light of the women's liberation movement which aimed to transform the structures underpinning gender inequalities, as well as the cultural valuation of women (Roseneil, 1995, 2000a; Charles, 2000).

Nancy Fraser (2003) argues that claims for redistributive justice relate to structural inequalities within society. In capitalist societies these have been thought of as class inequalities which determine an unequal distribution of rewards. Claims for recognition relate to cultural patterns of misrecognition, domination and disrespect, patterns which marginalize and devalue certain social groups. She argues that in these two conceptions of injustice the groups involved are defined differently. In the first they are 'classes or class-like collectivities' defined by their relation to the means of production; a Marxist definition. In the second, they are 'more like Weberian status groups' defined 'by the relations of recognition' and 'distinguished by the lesser respect, esteem, and prestige they enjoy relative to other groups in society' (Fraser, 2003:14). The need for redistribution therefore relates to the 'economic structure of capitalist society' while the need for recognition relates to 'the status order of society' (Fraser, 2003:17). Furthermore 'gender is a hybrid category rooted simultaneously in the economic structure and the status order of society' and therefore gender politics is at one and the same time a politics of redistribution *and* recognition, it is both political *and* cultural (Fraser, 2003:19).

This bringing together of culture and politics in the political practice of the women's movement created new understandings of the world. Politics was shown to be gendered. It was not only about who people vote for in general elections but also about the distribution of resources and power in society and about cultural meanings and values. The feminist critique of how politics is defined can be seen as part of the challenge to our ways of understanding the world which arises from new social movements (Eyerman and Jamison, 1991).

## Redefining politics

These shifts in the way that we understand and know the world arising from feminist social movements have challenged 'the very basis of politics and in-terrogated the conventions of knowing and studying political life' (Mackay, 2004:99). Despite this, gender has not yet 'been fully integrated into political science' and similarly, the work of 'feminist scholars in political science [has not]...been fully integrated into women's studies' (Sapiro, 1998:68; Randall, 2002). This last comment is supported by the fact that it is only with the third edition of this book that a chapter on women and politics is being included and perhaps reflects the reluctance of some sections of the women's move-ment to engage with formal politics and the state. Despite this reluctance many have done precisely this, both practically and academically, and here I wish to explore the feminist critique of 'malestream' politics before moving on to women's engagement with formal politics.

### *Public and private*

Feminists developed a critique of the way the political is theorized, focusing particularly on the division between the public and the private. This division is crucial to Western political thought and structures, not only in the way politics is defined, but also the way gendered differences in political participa-tion are explained. Feminists pointed out that the distinction between public and private was gendered, men being associated with the public and women with the private. Carol Pateman argues that 'the patriarchal division between public and private is also a sexual division' (Pateman, 1989:183). She argues further that the public world of politics rests on a sexual contract which is prior to the social contract binding free (male) individuals to the state. The sexual contract refers to the fact that, within liberal political thought, the free individuals recognized by the state as citizens were men. The state conferred upon them, as heads of households, the rights and duties of citizenship. These rights and duties were denied to women and children who were dependent on male heads of households and confined to the domestic sphere. And it is a sexual contract, one based on gender and sexuality, that subordinates women to men within the domestic sphere and gives men power over them. The public world of politics is also based on a 'racial contract' which underpinned the development of liberal democracy (Murray, 1997). Thus, the story of the original social contract in the modern world excludes women and blacks from political obligation as well as from the rights of negative liberty, and so from the rights of citizenship (Bogues, 2001).

The feminist argument that 'the personal is political' alerts us to the fact that by recognizing the family's right to privacy the state is actually upholding men's right to control other members of their households. The very definition of privacy is gendered and has serious implications for those who are subordinate within the domestic sphere. This is evident in regulations which relate to women as 'wives and mothers' and religious law which applies to the domestic sphere and to women within it. In many societies the public–private divide enables the state to 'delegate control of the family and women's sexuality to communal or religious authorities and/or to male heads of household' (Charles and Hintjens, 1998:9). Such regulations govern marriage, divorce, child custody and inheritance and affect millions of women world wide (Helie-Lucas, 1994). They are legitimated by the separation of the private, domestic sphere from the public sphere and infringe women's citizenship rights and, it is argued, their right to privacy. An important way of defending women's rights is therefore to argue for women's rights to privacy in contradistinction to the right to privacy of 'the family' or 'the community' (Okin, 1998). Politics is not therefore only about what men do in the public sphere but also about how the private sphere is constructed and the power relations which operate within it.

## Politics is a man's world

Until the emergence of the feminist critique of 'malestream' politics, however, politics was seen as what men do in the public sphere. Bourque and Grossholtz, in their critique of political science, argue that:

> in the choice of data to be analysed and in the interpretation of that data, the discipline insists upon a narrow and exclusive definition of politics which limits political activity to a set of roles which are in this society, and many others, stereotyped as male.
>
> (Bourque and Grossholtz, 1998:23)

Because politics is defined as male, women 'can never be full participants' (Bourque and Grossholtz, 1998:24). Prior to the emergence of the feminist critique, studies of political behaviour stressed women's lack of political activity, their different political attitudes and values and their failure to put themselves forward as candidates in the formal political process. Feminist critiques pointed to the functionalist view of sex roles underlying such studies with men being defined as instrumental and engaging in the public world of work (defined as paid employment) and politics (defined as party politics and voting) and women as being emotional and engaged in the domestic sphere with little independent experience which would be relevant to the formation of their own political views. Political allegiances were often explained by socialization theory which alleged that fathers' political affiliation determined both mothers' and children's because of men's greater power and authority within the family (Goot and Reid, 1975). Feminists pointed out that such explanations are based on stereotypical assumptions about gendered behaviour rather than on evidence collected from both women and men (unsurprisingly since studies tended to focus on men). Goot and Reid (1975) suggest that women's alleged lack of interest in politics may be due to the failure of political parties to concern themselves with issues that are important to women such as abortion reform and child care, and to recognize that women as well as men work, whether inside or outside the home, rather than to women's essentially non-political nature. Politics was, therefore, studied as if it was quintessentially male and women's different behaviour was somehow to be explained as deviation from the norm. It is women's role in the private domain of the family that is advanced to explain the nature of their political participation rather than their distinct work situations. Further, the private realm is by definition apolitical; thus women's association with it marginalizes them from politics and is used to explain gender differences in political behaviour.

The central message of feminist critiques was to demonstrate that gender differences were not as significant as they were being made out to be and that, where women did not have child care and domestic responsibilities, they were just as involved politically as were men (Siltanen and Stanworth, 1984). They also showed that conventional politics, whether in the political parties or trade unions, sidelined issues that were important to women and were organized in such a way as to make it difficult for women to participate (Charles, 1983). Such studies began to highlight the fact that the problem lay not with women, but with the way organizations operated and the issues which they prioritized.

## Women's political participation

### *The gender gap*

Students of politics had long assumed that women's political participation was lower than men's, and that if women did engage in politics they would tend to be more conservative than men. This is known as the traditional gender gap (Norris, 1999). However, during the 1980s and 1990s the modern gender gap emerged which describes a situation where women are more likely to support parties of the left than of the right. This modern gender gap in voting patterns first emerged in the US where women's support for the Republicans was replaced by support for the Democrats. This shift from a traditional to a modern gender gap is found in all advanced capitalist societies and is associated with the emergence of post-material values. In such societies a greater proportion of the population believe in gender equality and have liberal views on issues of sexual and reproductive politics. This shift in cultural values is associated with socio-economic change, specifically the increase in women's employment and the emergence of welfare states, and is apparent in younger rather than older generations (Inglehart and Norris, 2003). Thus, the gender gap in voting, when broken down by age, is traditional amongst older generations and modern amongst younger, post-war generations.

There are similar changes occurring in levels of political activism although it remains the case that women are still less politically active than men. As far as involvement in conventional politics is concerned women are more likely than men to vote. For instance, in the 1997 general election in Britain, 17.7 million women voted compared with 15.8 million men (Inglehart and Norris, 2003:105). Men are slightly more likely than women to be members of political parties, although there is a left–right split here with parties of the left showing less of a gender gap (Inglehart and Norris, 2003). Most women, however, like most men, are not involved in party politics and there is evidence that this is affected by age and ethnicity. In Britain, for instance, 76 per cent of women are not involved in any form of political activity and those who are 'young, black and female are significantly less likely to be politically active than the middle-aged, the white and the male' (Squires, 1999b:169).

Involvement in voluntary organizations, community politics and new social movements is another important form of political engagement and women tend to be more involved in this sort of activity than they are in formal party politics. However, although there are organizations where women outnumber men – such as the women's movement and those relating to 'women's issues' – there is 'no support for the popular assumption that more women than men are engaged in new social movements' (Inglehart and Norris, 2003:113). Even though men's involvement is higher, however, the gender gap is being reduced and, in some cases, has been reversed. Similarly, women are slightly less likely than men to be involved in political protests such as demonstrations or direct action. However, once other factors have been taken into account, such as 'levels of democratisation, education, class, age, union membership, and religiosity – then the effect of gender on protest activism becomes insignificant' (Inglehart and Norris, 2003:123). It is therefore social characteristics other than gender which explain the apparent gender gap in the propensity to protest.

As well as a gender gap there is also an 'ethnic gap' in voting patterns with ethnic minorities showing consistently high support for Labour in Britain and, in the US, for the Democrats. What we do not have, however, is any systematic analysis of the way gender and ethnicity interact and 'scholarly work located at the intersections of "race" and gender ... has remained largely underdeveloped in the theoretical literature as well as in more substantive empirical research' (Puwar, 2004:69).

## Political elites

The other dimension of political involvement that has been traditionally studied by students of politics is participation in political elites. Globally women are in a minority amongst political elites, although there is considerable regional variation (see Table 3.1) with women's political representation highest in the Nordic countries and lowest in the Arab States. If we look at women's representation in national parliaments for the end of February 2007, the UK is ranked equal 53rd with the Dominican Republic out of the 189 countries listed by the Inter Parliamentary Union (www.ipu.org/wmn-e/world.htm, consulted 2 April 2007). There are different ways of explaining the lack of women and minority ethnic representatives. Some focus on the highly masculinized cultures operating within political parties and legislative assemblies, others explore the way parties select potential candidates. Here I look at:

- organizational cultures;
- selection processes.

I use research on political parties in Britain to illustrate the theoretical argument.

**Table 3.1**    Regional averages of women in national parliaments
(28 February 2007)

| Region | Single house or lower house (%) | Upper house or senate (%) | Both houses combined (%) |
|---|---|---|---|
| Nordic countries | 40.8 | — | 40.8 |
| Americas | 20.0 | 19.3 | 19.9 |
| Europe – OSCE member countries including Nordic countries | 19.7 | 17.5 | 19.2 |
| Europe – OSCE member countries excluding Nordic countries | 17.6 | 17.5 | 17.6 |
| Sub-Saharan Africa | 16.8 | 18.2 | 17.0 |
| Asia | 16.5 | 15.7 | 16.4 |
| Pacific | 12.4 | 31.8 | 14.5 |
| Arab states | 9.5 | 6.3 | 8.8 |

*Note*: Regions are classified by descending order of the percentage of women in the lower or single house.

*Source*: www.ipu.org/wmn-e/world.htm, consulted 2 April 2007.

## Political parties as organizations

Within women's and gender studies it has long been recognized that organizational structures and cultures are gendered and that this operates to the disadvantage of women (Acker, 1990). In organizational hierarchies men occupy the highest and most powerful positions and women the lowest and least powerful. Thus, in all the organizations which are central to the political process it is men who occupy the positions of power. This is also true of organizations of the state such as the civil service, the judiciary, the police and the army where men are overwhelmingly at the top of organizational hierarchies (Connell, 1987). The picture is not, however, static and there is evidence that the proportion of women in political elites is increasing, albeit at an excruciatingly slow pace. How slow is suggested by the fact that 'there were about 5500 women in parliament worldwide in spring 2002, representing 14.3 of all members, up from 9 in 1987. If growth at this level is maintained (0.36 per annum), a simple linear projection predicts that women parliamentarians will achieve parity with men at the turn of the twenty second century' (Inglehart and Norris, 2003:129). Since 2002 there has been a 2.9 percentage point increase in the proportion of women in parliament which represents a slightly increased growth rate of 0.58 percentage points per annum (www.ipu.org/wmn-e/world.htm, consulted 2 April 2007).

An analysis of organizations as gendered has been used to explore the processes internal to parties, which work against the selection of women as candidates. Such studies highlight both the ways in which the masculine culture of political parties operates to exclude women and the cultural and social backgrounds of prospective MPs. In this way attention has turned away from the domestic circumstances of women as explanation for women's underrepresentation towards the structure and culture of political parties. The culture of the British Labour party for instance was 'rooted in the experience of male trade unionists' and 'extremely conservative in its attitudes towards women members':

> [It] reflected a traditional, familial and paternalistic gender order in society in which men and women occupy different spheres. The model of the political activist, central to both party ideology and its ethos, was the male unionised worker.
>
> (Perrigo, 1996:120)

Further, the party 'was ruled by a coalition of parliamentary and trade union elites' who were overwhelmingly male (Perrigo, 1996:120). Perrigo argues that Labour's way of organizing began to change during the 1970s and that this accelerated with the influx of feminist activists at the end of the 1970s (Perrigo, 1996; see also Lovenduski, 1996). The campaigns of women within trade unions for better representation and changes in policy which date from the 1960s, combined with the fall in union membership associated with the decline of heavy industry, meant that unions had to begin to take women workers, who were concentrated in the service sector of the economy, more seriously. The shift in the power base of the unions meant that women's voices were louder both within the trade union movement and within the Labour party. In the 1980s women's committees were set up as part of local government and in 1986 a Women's Ministry was proposed by Jo Richardson (Perrigo, 1996). These developments can all be seen as part of the modernization process and attempts to feminize the party's image in the face of repeated election defeats. They can also be understood as an important outcome of the women's liberation movement and of gender politics within organizations.

The existence of this masculine culture is used to explain resistance to moves towards greater gender parity, resistance which has been particularly strong in the old Labour heartlands, 'the declining manufacturing and mining areas', where men's jobs in heavy industry were disappearing (Lovenduski, 1996:5, 14). There is a feeling in such areas that a woman's place is most definitely not in politics and most certainly not as a parliamentary candidate instead of a man. Unlike the Labour Party with its masculine image, the Tories' image is more feminine. Despite this, their record on selecting women MPs lags far behind that of Labour (Lovenduski, 1996). Thus political parties are characterized by male-dominated hierarchies and a masculine organizational culture.

## Selection processes

The other way in which the masculine organizational bias of political parties is apparent is in the process of candidate selection. Norris and Lovenduski (1995) suggest that the lack of women is due to supply factors, i.e. women not putting themselves forward, and/or to demand factors, i.e. even when they put themselves forward they are not selected. They explored selection processes within three of the main political parties in Britain; the Labour, Conservative and Liberal Democratic parties. They found that both supply and demand factors were apparent in the Conservative party but that in the Labour and Liberal Democratic parties demand factors were more important (Norris and Lovenduski, 1995). This failure to select is explained by institutional sexism and the masculinist culture that is evident within political parties (Lovenduski, 2005a). In a recent study, Lovenduski interviewed women who had experienced the selection process within political parties in Britain and found that they faced overt sexism and what has to be called sexual harassment during the selection process. One woman in the Labour party told her:

> They are absolutely adamant they will not consider a woman ... it was said to me ... 'we do enjoy watching you speak, we always imagine what your knickers are like'. It is that basic. 'We picture you in your underwear when you are speaking.' That is what you are dealing with.

(Lovenduski, 2005a:77)

There are certain characteristics which parliamentary candidates share – they have often had experience in local government or trade unions or are barristers, journalists, lecturers or trade union officials. These are, of course, all jobs and positions which are more likely to be filled by men than women and, unsurprisingly, the typical parliamentary candidate is 'a well-educated, professional, white male in early middle age' (Norris and Lovenduski, 1995:87). Coming from a political family is also an advantage in seeking selection and may be critical in making standing for election seem within the realm of possibility for women rather than being something that is unthinkable. Therefore, the background which is deemed appropriate for prospective candidates is far more likely to be achieved by men than women because of the gendered structure of society.

Research has shown that similar processes can be found around the world. Globally political parties are resistant to selecting women as candidates and women have less access to the resources and experiences which are deemed appropriate for political representatives (Stokes, 2005:63).

The supply and demand model has been criticized because it does not take into account the way supply and demand interact (Childs, 2004). An alternative explanation analyzes the difference between white, middle-class male candidates and others in terms of their 'entitlement to power', both as prospective candidates subjectively experience it and as others (the selectorate in this case) perceive it (Liddle and Michielsens, 2007). This type of analysis theorizes the gendering of power in terms of both 'the recognition by others of a person's legitimacy to exercise power' and the 'self-confidence one feels in oneself to exercise power' (Liddle and Michielsens, 2000:129). Using these concepts, Liddle and Michielsens provide an answer to the question of why it is that women in positions of power tend to come from more privileged backgrounds than their male peers. They suggest that elite women's higher class position is associated with greater access to symbolic capital and an 'entitlement to power' which together 'challenge the gendered power deficits attached to their femininity' (Liddle and Michielsens, 2000:127). Thus, class position provides upper-class women with a view of themselves as entitled to represent others and to exercise political power which is normally the preserve of men. In this way, they can overcome the gender deficit they experience as women. This suggests that the way gendered, classed and racialized subjectivities are constructed contributes to an explanation of why women and minority ethnic groups are under-represented in parliament. Men assume they are entitled to exercise power and this entitlement is seen as legitimate by party selectors. Women are less likely to make such an assumption and if they do it is not always seen as legitimate. Although Liddle and Michielsens do not explicitly address the significance of sexualized subjectivities there are hints in their analysis that a heterosexual identity can advantage prospective candidates. In discussing a male candidate who was originally working class they comment that '[h]is embodiment of heterosexual respectability and his commitment to marriage and family values helped his candidature' (Liddle and Michielsens,

2007). In other parts of the world, such as Zimbabwe where male homosexuality remains outlawed, it is likely that sexualized subjectivities much more overtly disadvantage those seeking selection as political candidates.

## Women making a difference

### Representation

It is clear that women are under-represented in political elites but there is considerable debate about whether the social characteristics of our political representatives matter and, if they do, what, if anything, should be done about it. There are several grounds for arguing that the proportion of women representatives should be increased. These include (Phillips, 1998a):

- that it is unjust for men to monopolize political representation;
- that if there are no women representatives then 'women's interests' will not be taken into account;
- the idea that women politicians provide a role model;
- that an increase in women's representation would contribute to a revitalization of democracy;
- that the presence of women is symbolically important as it gives legitimacy to the political system.

Here, I focus on the first and second questions of gender justice and 'women's interests'.

The justice argument is based on the idea that all things being equal you would expect political representatives to be drawn randomly from the population and to reflect its gender and ethnic composition. That this is not the case suggests that barriers are being put in the way of women and other minority groups which, in the name of justice, should be removed. These barriers deny women and minority ethnic groups the right to political participation. This desire that the proportion of women representatives should somehow mirror their distribution in the general population has come to be known as the *politics of presence*.

The second major argument is that if women are not present as political representatives their interests will not be represented adequately. This argument begs the question of whether we can talk in terms of women's interests. Given the postmodern deconstruction of woman as subject and the acknowledgement of differences between women, it is no longer possible to assume that all women share interests simply because of their gender. Other identities crosscut with that of gender and challenge the idea of unitary women's interests arising from their common experiences. However, Phillips counters this by arguing that the more varied and the harder to define are women's interests, the more important it is to have a variety of women as representatives (Phillips, 1998a: 235).

These two dimensions of representation – (a) reflecting the distribution of women and other minority groups in the population and (b) representing their interests – are referred to respectively as *descriptive* and *substantive* representation.

## Quotas

Political practitioners have been quicker to accept the case for increased representation of women than have political theorists, and many political parties have adopted quota systems to this end. It was as early as the 1970s that political parties in Norway adopted quotas and since then their use has spread, growing particularly rapidly during the 1990s. By 2003 there were 75 countries around the world where quotas were or had been used. These included not only countries like Norway, France and Britain, but also Mexico, Nicaragua and South Africa (Stokes, 2005). Indeed, in South Africa 'after the 1994 elections, just over one quarter (27 per cent) of members of Parliament were women' (Albertyn, 2003:99). This was largely achieved through women's activism in developing the new constitution and through the African National Congress (ANC) adopting 'a 30 per cent quota on the ANC party list' (Albertyn, 2003:102). These elections marked the transition from apartheid to democracy in South Africa and, at the time, meant that the level of women's political representation there ranked 7th highest in the world.

---

**What are quotas?**

'Political quotas are regulations that a certain number or proportion of women (in this case) must be present in a representative forum or institution. They may operate at different stages of the selection process, with political parties, at the nomination stage, or as a requirement for the composition of a legislature, assembly, council or government.'

(Lovenduski, 2005a:93–4)

---

In Britain, the proportion of women MPs doubled in the 1997 election which was almost entirely due to the fact that the Labour party had adopted all-women shortlists. They were used in half the vacant and winnable seats and resulted in an increase in the number of women MPs at Westminster from 60 to 120 (Charles, 2002:153). However, the idea of quotas received considerable and hostile press coverage once it began to be implemented. It was opposed on a number of grounds, among them being that women should fight on an even playing field. Such arguments of course fail to recognize that the playing field is not, and never has been, even and that it advantages men. Despite this, the policy was challenged by two 'wannabe' male candidates who used the Sex Discrimination Act to argue that all-women shortlists discriminated against them because they were being denied the right to be considered

for employment. They were successful despite the fact that the Sex Discrimination Act was not applicable to political parties (Lovenduski, 1999:205). This judgment was not contested by the Labour party but since then the Sex Discrimination (Electoral Candidates) Act 2002 has been passed which allows political parties to use positive discrimination in selecting candidates. As a result all-women shortlists have been reintroduced although not without opposition (see for example Lovenduski, 2005a). In the first general election since the legislation was passed 128 women MPs were elected which was 19.8 per cent of the total (http://www.fawcettsociety.org.uk, consulted 30 March 2007).

---

**Case Study – The National Assembly for Wales**

In new institutions, like the South African parliament in 1994, it is easier to ensure more equal representation of women because there are no male incumbents to feel threatened by positive discrimination. The elections for the National Assembly for Wales provide an illustration of this. In Wales feminists and women's organizations had been actively involved in drawing up the constitution which specified the nature of the political institutions; their goal was a legislature characterized by gender parity and, as in South Africa, quotas were used very successfully to ensure that this was achieved (Chaney et al., 2007/8). In order to increase women's representation the Labour Party 'twinned' constituencies. Twinning meant that there was a single selection committee for two constituencies, this selection committee selected two candidates, a woman and a man, one for each constituency (Stephenson, 1999). This resulted in their fielding an equal number of women and men in the first Assembly elections. Plaid Cymru/the Party of Wales also introduced measures to increase the number of women representatives by placing women at the top of their regional lists. This, together with a system of proportional representation (which is more favourable to the election of women and other minority groups than a first past the post system) led, in 1999, to 40 of National Assembly for Wales Members being women (Feld, 2000). In the 2003 elections the proportion of women Assembly Members increased to 50 and, before the 2007 elections stood at 52 which, for a legislative assembly, was the highest in the world. The 2007 elections mean that women now constitute 47 of Assembly Members and, for the first time, there is a minority ethnic representative (male) in the Assembly.

---

## Changing politics

For a long time it has been accepted wisdom that for women to be able to make a difference they need to be present in relatively high proportions. If they are in a small minority they are unlikely to be effective in an overwhelmingly male environment. This idea is known as 'critical mass' and derives from organizational theory (Mackay, 2004). Despite its wide acceptance in practical politics, it is not without its critics (Dahlerup, 2006). It has been pointed out that the idea of 'critical acts' as well as 'critical mass' may be more fruitful for understanding the conditions under which women are able to make a difference (Dahlerup, 1988). Furthermore, there are two dimensions of making a

difference which need to be explored separately. Women can make a difference in terms of policy development and they can make a difference to their working environment (Dahlerup, 2006). Here, I look at these two aspects of women making a difference.

## Policy change

Individual women in positions of power within parties and governments are sometimes critical in taking forward a progressive gender agenda. In Britain this was apparent in Barbara Castle's support for equal pay legislation when she was Minister of Labour in 1968 and, more recently, in Clare Short's support for quotas (both women were Labour MPs). It was also evident in the work of mostly Labour women MPs in the 1970s on the Select Committee on Violence in the Family and in opposing attempts to restrict the 1967 abortion act (Hills, 1981:26). The presence of women in political elites, even in small numbers, means that the claims of women's organizations and feminist social movements are more likely to be heard. Now, however, the proportion of women representatives in Britain and in other parts of the world, has increased significantly (Lovenduski, 2005b). It is therefore possible to investigate whether women's descriptive representation is linked to their substantive representation and to explore the difference they make to the working environment of political institutions.

There has been evidence for some time that women and men political representatives have different attitudes which are likely to be linked to different choices. In the US, for example, women representatives were more likely than their male colleagues to support the Civil Rights Act (1964) and the Equal Rights Amendment. Also, research that looked at the attitudes of women and men in Congress between 1987 and 1992 found that Democrat women were the most liberal, Democrat men came next followed by Republican women with Republican men being the least liberal (Burrell, 1994). In the UK, if the attitudes of women and men MPs are compared, those of women are found to be more left-wing than those of men and women are 'consistently more strongly in favour of women's rights' (Norris, 1996:95). And although party remains 'the best predictor of attitudes' there is a 'modest gender difference' on most issues with women MPs tending to be more unilateralist than men and more left-wing or liberal on almost all issues (Norris, 1996:98). In sum:

> Women tended to give stronger support for issues of women's rights, they express greater concern about social policy issues, and they give higher priority to constituency casework.
>
> (Norris, 1996:103)

Women representatives also appear to regard themselves as representing women and feel that it is important to maintain links with women's organizations in civil society (Stokes, 2005). This is supported, for example, by evidence from a range of countries including Scandinavia and the US. At the same time, however, women understand themselves as representating the whole population within the geographical boundaries of a constituency. Research on the 1997 intake of new Labour women MPs shows that they regard themselves as representing women but that they also feel under pressure to prove themselves as MPs. This entails distancing themselves from too close an identification with either women's issues or feminism, and has led to a questioning of any automatic link between descriptive and substantive representation (Childs, 2004). There is evidence, however, from this and other research that women feel that they have a special responsibility to act on behalf of women, that they have more contact with women's organizations than do men, and that there is a connection between the election of women and the development of pro-women policies.

## Working environment

Women representatives may also have an impact on the working environment. One dimension of this is that they tend to have a different political style from men, being less adversarial and confrontational and more interested in a consensual style of politics (Stokes, 2005). This is something that many women politicians claim for themselves and further research is needed to explore the extent to which this relates to gender or to other factors such as generational change or political culture.

Women have also been involved in attempts to introduce 'family-friendly' working hours. In Britain, the new devolved institutions in Scotland and Wales have operated 'family-friendly' hours since their inception in 1999. These are seen as having great symbolic significance by many women representatives but are continually under threat. In contrast, attempts to modernize working practices at Westminster after the Labour party was elected into government in 1997 met with considerable resistance and hostility from the media as well as from many politicians of both genders. Much of this hostility was directed against the new women Labour MPs who were accused of only being interested 'in improving their own working conditions' rather than with getting on with the tough and difficult job of being a representative (Lovenduski, 2005a: 170). Lovenduski notes that 'women MPs were enjoined by reform advocates not to make their case in feminist terms' as this would court the danger of losing support (2005a). These sorts of changes are likely to have an impact on the organizational culture of political institutions and the way in which politics is done, eventually influencing the working environment and behaviour of all political representatives, men as well as women.

As well as affecting policy and the working environment, it is argued that women and minority ethnic representatives are bringing about cultural change in spaces which are defined culturally as masculine. Women and minority ethnic representatives entering the world of Westminster, for instance, are regarded as 'space invaders' – they are out of place and their legitimacy is questioned, even by themselves (Childs, 2004; Puwar, 2004). However, they make a difference simply by being in 'an institution that has for centuries been overwhelmingly male and white' and this is part of what is meant by the politics of presence (Puwar, 2004:66). This suggests that their presence is symbolically important, that it 'disrupts and highlights how this institution ... is "built by men and shaped by men, in men's image"' (Puwar, 2004:66). It is of course not only Westminster but the whole institution of politics that is 'shaped by men, in men's image' (Puwar, 2004:66).

## Conclusion

The indebtedness of research such as this, which views politics 'as a social and cultural space' (Puwar, 2004), to feminist definitions of politics is evident and more of this kind of research is now emerging. This suggests that at last the issue of women, gender and politics is attracting the attention, not only of political scientists, but of those working broadly within the interdisciplinary field of gender and women's studies. It also suggests that feminist political scientists are looking outside the boundaries of their discipline and drawing on theories and methods more usually associated with sociology, anthropology, cultural studies and gender studies. Moreover, there is a new generation of feminist activists within academia, setting up feminist student societies and renewing the feminist challenge to the continuing gender blindness of many disciplines (see for example WASS, 2007). This third wave of feminism is building on the achievements of the second wave. The demands raised by the women's liberation movement are now central to the political agenda. As we have seen, this has come about by feminists working within and outside political parties to develop policies which address the demands of the women's movement, and within universities to create the knowledge on which these policies are based. In Britain there is now a national child care policy and a domestic violence policy, same sex couples can register their union in civil partnerships and lesbian mothers are no longer denied custody of their children because of their sexuality. Reproductive rights are still highly contested, however, not only in Britain but around the world, and abortion is a critical electoral issue in both the US and Poland, for example. In Britain there is pressure for religious law to apply within Muslim communities, ceding to men's control over women's sexuality and reproduction, a pressure which is being resisted by organizations such as Women Living under Muslim Laws. Such grassroots women's organizations are vital in ensuring that women's rights are recognized and that any threats to them are resisted.

This chapter has shown that the women's movement and feminist political engagement have had a major impact on the gendering of politics, and it is now accepted that women's issues (however they are defined) are a political matter, and political power, whether at the level of government or the community, still resides in the hands of men. We have come a long way since the early days of second wave feminism, but there is still a long way to go before women and men enjoy equal access to political power, and all women are freed from men's exercise of global power over them in the most public and private areas of their lives.

## Further reading

J. Lovenduski (2005) *Feminizing Politics*, Cambridge, Polity Press
This provides a good discussion of the difference that is being made by women to conventional politics. It draws on international material but is mostly based on empirical research that she carried out on British political parties.

M. Marx Ferree and C. Mueller (2004) 'Feminism and the Women's Movement: A Global Perspective', in D.A. Snow, S.A. Soule and H. Kriesi (eds), *The Blackwell Companion to Social Movements*, Oxford, Blackwell
This is a chapter-length discussion of the women's movement internationally. Together with the following reference it provides an international perspective on women's political activism.

B.J. Nelson and N. Chowdhury (eds) (1994) *Women and Politics Worldwide*, Yale University Press
This book provides an international perspective on 43 countries which represent different political systems, levels of economic development and regions and, although dated, is the only work which includes such an international range of material.

W. Stokes (2005) *Women in Contemporary Politics*, Cambridge, Polity Press
This is a useful overview of women's involvement in conventional politics that explores developments globally, providing a wealth of case study material.

# CHAPTER FOUR

# Men, Masculinities and Feminism

VICTORIA ROBINSON

## Introduction

This chapter is fundamentally concerned with the connection of masculinity to gender relations and feminism. As Whitehead (2000) notes, since the mid 1980s research on men and masculinities has grown quickly, citing as evidence the enormous number of books, websites and courses as evidence of this phenomenon. Initially, some feminists were sceptical about such developments (Canaan and Griffin, 1990), but now these developments show no sign of abating. Indeed, interest in the study of men and masculinity across the disciplines has increased in different countries worldwide, especially in the UK, the US, Australia and Europe, for instance, in the Nordic countries. This has manifested itself in courses on men's studies, as in the US, or, in an increasing number of countries, courses on masculinity in disciplines such as sociology, history and education.

In this chapter, the following will be discussed:

- A historical context to the study of men and masculinity;
- The institutionalization of masculinity studies;
- Some fundamental concepts and ideas which inform this theorizing on masculinity;
- A case study of hegemonic masculinity and heterosexuality, in relation to education, in particular;
- A case study of men and sport, especially extreme sports;
- Feminist and other critiques of theorizing on masculinity;
- Future directions.

## The historical context

It should initially be noted that feminists, and others, have constantly maintained that the study of masculinity has always been, and remains, part of the feminist agenda (see Hanmer, 1990; Evans, 1997). As early as 1978, in *About Men*, Phyllis Chesler wrote about men and patriarchy, men's relationships with other men and relationships with women. She considered, amongst other issues, men and sex, pornography, fantasies and male violence:

I wrote this book in order to understand men. First, I turned to books already written by men, about men. I found them of limited usefulness. Only some men, mainly poets and novelists, spoke about themselves in a personally authentic voice; only some men wrote about the male condition with an awareness that is different from the female condition.

(Chesler, 1978: xv)

Feminists in different countries have also commented on and critiqued masculinity theorists' attempts to theorize gender in relation to feminism (see Wetherell and Griffin, 1991; Robinson and Richardson, 1994 and Bartky, 1998 for diverse views on this); so too have gay men (Edwards, 1994) and those concerned with issues of race and ethnicity (Abdel-Shehid, 2005). Such critiques will also be considered later in the chapter. However, even prominent feminist criticisms of the 1990s, such as Canaan and Griffin (1990) and Cornwall and Lindisfarne (1994), were cautiously optimistic about such developments.

As we will see later in this chapter, the theories and concepts used by masculinity theorists have developed and become more sophisticated. However, theorists writing about masculinity have been reflective, from the 1980s, about the methodologies they have employed when engaging in such theorizing. For instance, there have been various criticisms of the sex-role paradigm used in the early days within men's studies. The sex role concept originally developed by Talcott Parsons, which sees masculinity as a fixed and easily defined set of behavioural norms into which all men fit, has been criticized by feminists and those involved in men's studies. Key criticisms have been that masculinity, and indeed femininity, are seen in singular, not plural, terms. As well, power relations between women and men, and between men themselves can be ignored and cultural or historical differences can be downplayed, within the sex role theoretical framework (see Brod, 1987 and Kimmell, 1990 for further discussion of this topic).

As well as functionalist concepts like sex roles coming under scrutiny, some have also criticized the biological determinism which has underpinned some thinking on male behaviour and identity (Whitehead, 2002). The general theoretical consensus, as with feminism, being that social constructionist theories are best suited to explain mens' behaviour in a contemporary, historical and cross-cultural context. But within a broad, and increasingly problematized social constructionist viewpoint on masculine identity, subjectivity and behaviour, there are diverse perspectives, viewpoints and issues covered, some of which this chapter will go on to explore.

Therefore, out of these earlier critiques of initial concepts such as sex role theory and biological determinism, came some key contemporary concerns:

- the notion that masculinities are multiple;
- the need to study men and masculinities in historical and cross-cultural contexts;
- the idea expressed by the term 'hegemonic masculinity' that power relations are involved in men's relationships with women and with other men.

# The institutionalization of the study of men and masculinities

Both women and men have theorized masculinity, and masculinity studies has been institutionalized, especially in the US, in the guise of 'men's studies'. I have previously argued (Robinson, 2001) that men's studies as a field of study was a recent development in higher education, mainly in North America and Europe. The so far limited institutionalization of men's studies can be seen as having its origins in the 'men's movement' (particularly in the US) or in other western countries in the context of diverse groupings of 'men against sexism'.

Generally, men's studies has been defined as 'the study of masculinities and experiences as specific and varying social-historical-cultural formations' (Brod, 1987:40). The need for such an interdisciplinary subject area has been based on the idea that, whilst seemingly about men, traditional scholarship precludes the study of masculinity as a specific male experience. Men's studies like women's studies/gender studies is opposed to patriarchal ideology's masquerade as knowledge, as well as raising new questions whilst simultaneously revealing the inadequacy of established frameworks of knowledge in answering old ones (Brod, 1987).

Others have preferred the term 'critical studies of men and masculinities', for political and theoretical reasons (Hearn and Morgan, 1990), or more recently 'the critical studies of men' (Hearn, 2004). This perspective has been seen to be more sensitive to earlier feminist scepticism and fears of the de-politicization of gendered power relations through a 'complementary' approach to the study of masculinities, ie 'men's studies'. Such simplistic typologizing obscures differences and similarities within and between such positions. Further, many theorists writing on masculinity outside of these two positions, across the disciplines, may not align themselves with either position but may well use the theoretical insights of both perspectives, sometimes combined under the broad term of 'masculinity studies'. Within these broad perspectives, those theorists writing about men and masculinities do so on a growing number of different topics, which include the body, globalization, intimacy and the emotions, fatherhood, sport, violence, aging and the life course and feminism, amongst others.

However, it is important in looking at the growing and diverse critical positions on masculinity to recognize theoretical and methodological differences both between and within the groups and perspectives that characterize this body of writing. For instance, those interested in both theorizing men and masculinities and in men's position in society have ranged from the North American Robert Bly's movement which sought to heal men's deep psychological wounds by them becoming 'wild men', in touch with each others' feelings as men and sometimes defined as the mytho-poetic men's movement; the Jungian perspective, which sees masculinity and femininity as connected intimately to psychic truths; the gay men's movement; the pro-feminists who would align themselves with the feminist cause; and those men who are simply 'anti-women', and who argue that the women's movement and feminism have emasculated men, with women now having the advantage, in the world of work, for example.

Edwards (2006) sums up some of these shifts and argues that the study of men and masculinity can be divided into three main 'waves':

- The 'first wave', in the 1970s, refers to the development of the 'sex role' model in relation to questions surrounding masculinity.
- The 'second wave', in the 1980s, was based on the notion that the model of a white, western and middle-class account of masculinity was not adequate to explore the multi-faceted nature of men's diverse experiences. Further, working-class, black and gay men were now viewed as subordinate to this hegemonic model, and importantly, the main emphasis in the study of masculinity was now on power, and its very complex meanings and operations.
- The 'third wave' since the 1990s is very much influenced by poststructuralist theory, in so much as it relates to performativity, normativity and sexuality. In this phase, Edwards argues, we see a much more interdisciplinary body of work occuring, for instance, with work across literary, cultural and media studies, as well as the social sciences. Here, the emphasis is now on masculinity as contingent, open to change and in flux.

Having given both a brief historical context and an institutional context, this chapter will now go on to examine some of these key conceptual developments in the study of masculinity in more depth.

## Conceptual developments in the study of masculinity

---

### Multiple Masculinities

Mac an Ghaill summed up developments in the mid 1990s thus:

> A fragmentary literature has begun to suggest a more complex conceptualization of masculinity. Most specifically there has been a shift to the notions of hegemonic masculinity and multiple masculinities (Brittan 1989). Clatterbaugh (1990: 2), in his book written within the context of contemporary North American society, identifies six major perspectives that dominate discussion of men and masculinity: the conservative, pro-feminist, men's rights, spiritualist, socialist and group specific perspectives. In Britain during the 1980s, particularly, as a result of feminist, gay and lesbian writing, and AIDS activism, the changing nature of men's lives and their experiences were much debated within a range of literatures, drawing upon sex-role, psychoanalysis and gender and power theories.
>
> (Mac an Ghaill, 1996:2)

---

As already stated, amongst masculinity writers generally there has been, in the 1990s especially, an acceptance of masculinity as a social construction which, as such, sees masculinity as fluid and open to both contestation and change:

> This has led to a recognition that the dominant forms of men and masculinities are themselves not merely 'natural' and unchangeable...
>
> Thus men and masculinities are not seen as problematic, but as social constructions which need to be explored, analysed and indeed in certain respects, such as the use of violence, changed.
>
> (Morgan, 1992: vii)

There has also been a move away from the notion of a singular masculinity to the idea of 'masculinities'. As Whitehead (2002) notes, masculinities are multiple and plural, differing over time, space and context and they are enmeshed with variables such as race and ethnicity, class and age. He also warns against seeing 'truths' of masculinity in the behaviours, attitudes and practices of men and boys. He argues that theorists such as Freud, Jung and Talcott Parsons have fallen into this tendency.

R.W. Connell (2000) makes the point in relation to the concept of multiple masculinities, that in multicultural societies there are also multiple definitions and dynamics of masculinity. As well, such diversity between men exists both in different settings, and in the same setting. Men enact manhood in different ways, depending on whether the context is work, school or home based, for example. He gives the instance of a 'transnational business masculinity', which he defines as a form of masculinity marked by egocentricism, conditional loyalties, even to corporations, and a declining sense of responsibility to others. Such men have power in multinational corporations and operate in global markets. However, it is important to recognize that this group is not a homogenous one. For instance, in East Asia, there is more of a tendency for this group of men to be involved in business by a commitment to hierarchical relations and a social consensus. By contrast, for men operating in business in North America, there is a tendency to display hedonism, individualism and more social conflict. He concludes:

> Though the hierarchy of masculinities is part of the problem in gender relations, the fact that there are different masculinities is in itself an asset. At the lowest level, it is established that masculinity itself is not a single fixed pattern. More positively, multiple masculinities represent complexity of interests and purposes which open possibilities for change.
>
> (Connell, 2000: 226)

In this way, by seeing masculinities as different across and between contexts, we can envisage change occurring through the dynamic and multi-faceted experiences of men, in a global context.

## The 'crisis of masculinity'

The idea of a 'crisis of masculinity' has had much purchase for some of the theorists writing on masculinity, and in popular culture and the media. Therefore, due to changes in the economic structures which have impacted on occupational roles for men, and subsequent changes in their family position as head of the household, as well as the rise of feminism, some have claimed that men no longer have a stable identity and an existential state of crisis has thus ensued (see Faludi, 1999). Whitehead (2002) argues we need to be wary of insisting that men are in crisis. In his view:

- Firstly, men are not a homogenous group and therefore all men cannot be in crisis.
- As well, the notion of a crisis justifies a backlash against women's interests in general and feminism in particular.

Alternatively, Edwards (2006) asserts that the very concept of a crisis itself is unclear in terms of what it actually means. He argues that it is important to neither dismiss the concept, nor fully accept the validity of it. Are men, he asks, actually in crisis, but not in ways which are most popularly thought of? If, as he further argues, it can be seen that such a crisis stems from both 'inside' and 'outside' for men, that is outside in relation to men's position in the family and work for instance, and inside, in relation to men's experiences and any perceived shifts in these experiences of actually 'being men', then we can perhaps start to narrow down what the concept might mean for different men. He concludes:

- Through an examination of specific areas such as work, crime, family and sexuality, amongst others, it can be seen that, geographically, some men have 'crisis tendencies', that is, for example, some men indeed have been affected by wider economic trends leading to increased unemployment and deprivation in inner city or rural areas, for instance.
- However, he feels there is very little evidence to support the thesis of an 'overall crisis' in masculinity.

Connell (2005), on the other hand, sees the crisis as dual edged, in that he notes that masculinities have been configured around a 'crisis tendency': 'both through conflict over strategies of legitimation and through men's divergent responses to feminism.... While the tension leads some men to the cults of masculinity....it leads others to support feminist reforms' (Connell, 2005:85). Out of such 'crisis' then, can emerge, at least potentially, positive changes to gendered power relations. (See also Ringrose and Epstein in this volume on the 'crisis in masculinity'.)

## Hegemonic masculinity

The most debated, discussed and influential concept in masculinity studies has been the concept of 'hegemonic masculinities'. Historically, there has been a move to recognizing 'hegemonic masculinities', that is, asking how 'particular groups of men inhabit positions of power and wealth and how they legitimate and reproduce the social relationships that generate their dominance' (Brod, 1987:92). It is also argued that most men do not correspond to the hegemonic model, but that many men are complicit in sustaining it. The hegemonic model of masculinity is also seen as heterosexual (see Carrigan et al., 1985), a claim I go into more detail on later in the chapter.

The Australian R.W. Connell, already referred to (1987, 1995, 2000, 2005), is one of the theorists writing on masculinity to reach a wider audience outside of the field of masculinity studies. His work on a 'critique of hegemonic masculinity' has been very influential in shaping the terms of the debate on masculinity. In 1987, he speculated on the reasons for the persistence of men's involvement in sustaining patriarchy:

---

'What reasons for change have enough weight, against this entrenched interest, to detach heterosexual men from the defence of patriarchy? There are, in my experience, five:

1. Even the beneficiaries of an oppressive system can come to see its oppressiveness, especially the way it poisons areas of life they share.
2. Heterosexual men are often committed in important ways to women – their wives and lovers, mothers and sisters, daughters and nieces, co-workers – and may desire better lives for them. Especially they may see the point of creating more civilized and peaceable sexual arrangements for their children, even at the cost of their own privileges.
3. Heterosexual men are not all the same or all united, and many do suffer some injury from the present system. The oppression of gays, for instance, has a back-wash damaging to effeminate or unassertive heterosexuals.
4. Change in gender relations is happening anyway, and on a large scale. A good many heterosexual men recognize that they cannot cling to the past and want some new directions.
5. Heterosexual men are not excluded from the basic human capacity to share experiences, feelings and hopes. This ability is often blunted, but the capacity for caring and identification is not necessarily killed. The question is what circumstances might call it out. Being a father often does; some political movements, notably the environmental and peace movements, seem to; sexual politics may do so too.'

(Connell, 1987: xiii)

---

Connell's definition and analysis of hegemonic masculinity saw heterosexual men as entrenched in the system of patriarchy, but he also finds reasons for men to want to change this system, even though they are the main beneficiaries of such an oppressive structure. He asserts that not all men are the same, and some groups such as 'effeminate or unassertive heterosexuals' may not be part of the dominant masculinity.

For these theorists writing in the 'second wave': hegemonic masculinity is one which is 'white, heterosexist, middle class, Anglophone, and so on' (Hearn and Morgan, 1990:11). This model allows us, they claimed, to look at the various subordinations, stigmatizations and marginalizations men may experience because of their sexuality, ethnicity, class, religion or marital status, within patriarchal societies.

Feminists, for instance Cornwall and Lindisfarne (1994), have also explored the concept of a hegemonic masculinity. They noted that masculinity varies over time and setting, and also argue that:

> Hegemonic versions of masculinity frame relations of inequality. However, hegemonic forms are never totally comprehensive, nor do they ever completely control subordinates. That is, there is always some space for subordinate versions of masculinity – as alternative gendered identities which validate self-worth and encourage resistance.
>
> (Cornwall and Lindisfarne, 1994:5)

The concept of change in relation to different groups of men is a prevalent one in recent literature on masculinity. In his later work, Connell (1995) further examines the concept of hegemonic masculinity by stressing multiple masculinities and by exploring groups of men undergoing different experiences of change. Some are seen to be wanting to transform gender relations, and others are resisting these transformations. Connell's general theoretical construct is to combine, in his analysis, both men's personal life and social structures. So a notion of compulsory heterosexuality for men, for example, is seen to reveal both the complexity of changes in masculinity and also the diverse possibilities of real change.

The concept of hegemonic masculinity is one which has attracted, in more recent years, some criticism of it as a concept which can explain the experiences of all men, in different cultures and historical periods, and I will raise some of these criticisms later in the chapter. It is worth now considering the idea of hegemonic masculinity in relation to heterosexuality more closely, given the number of issues it raises for feminists and others. A case study on this aspect of theorizing about masculinity illustrates some of the key areas to which masculinity theorists have turned their attention, specifically here, education. Another case study, on men and sports, serves to further illustrate some of the key concepts already discussed.

## Case study: hegemonic masculinities and heterosexuality

As I have argued (Robinson, 2007), there have been a number of theorists who have closely linked hegemonic masculinities to heterosexuality which is seen to have consequences for diverse groups of women and men in different ways. One such theorist, Mac an Ghaill (1996), has argued that theorists have explored the ways in which dominant definitions of heterosexual masculinity are affirmed and authenticated within social and cultural arenas, where ideologies, discourses, representations and material practices, for instance, systematically privilege men and boys. Further to this, in the late 1970s and early 1980s, the focus on men's violence as systematic and central to male domination, and a growing critique of normative heterosexuality and masculine sexuality as fundamentally implicated in this, was developed (see Hearn, 1998a). More recently, there has been a growing complexity in feminist accounts of power and violence in heterosexuality, as exemplified, for instance, in the work of feminist theorists such as Jackson (1999c) and Richardson (2000). As well, heterosexual men have been seen to be entrenched in a defence of patriarchy, but some, such as Connell (2000), as noted in the previous section of this chapter, have also found a number of reasons why it is in men's interests to question the institution of heterosexuality and their part in upholding this and patriarchal relations.

The specific concept of 'masculism' recognizes hierarchical forms of masculinity as powerful and privileged in different settings and contexts, including the way heterosexual men are advantaged (see Carrigan et al., 1985 and Whitehead, 2002). Further, hegemonic masculinity can be viewed as how dominant male sexual practices are used to generate a naturalized view of the world that is so ingrained in dominant culture that it appears as natural or as 'common sense'. Indeed, hegemonic masculinities are premised on masculinity being defined as femininity's opposite and within this context, heterosexuality is the unchallenged, often essentialized norm which upholds this hegemony (see Connell, 2000 and 2005). Connell also asserts that men have different relationships to heterosexuality. For instance, subordinate masculinities, such as the categories of effeminate or unassertive heterosexuals, may not be part of a dominant masculinity.

A number of diverse topics and areas have sustained critical attention in the context of hegemonic masculinities and heterosexuality. These have been, for instance: sport, intimacy, the emotions, embodiment, violence, education, fatherhood and relationships.

In education, for example, where hegemonic forms of masculinity cultivated in a school environment are implicated with regimes of compulsory heterosexuality, masculinity has been seen to be constructed as the necessary counterpart to heterosexuality and so anything that does not fit into this pairing up of masculinity and heterosexuality becomes understood as being different. In environments where young, straight males are exploring and testing the boundaries of their sexuality, it becomes necessary to assert their masculinity, and so their heteronormativity (see Mac an Ghaill, 1996 and Haywood and Mac an Ghaill, 2003).

Haywood and Mac an Ghaill (2003) further argue that there are a number of elements that form the identities of heterosexual male students in secondary schools. These include:

- contradictory forms of compulsory heterosexuality;
- misogyny;
- homophobia.

Such elements combine, they found in their studies, to form institutionally specific forms of gendered and sexual power. This was evidenced in their findings that many heterosexual male students were involved in a 'double relationship' where they both put down the 'other', i.e. women and gays, and, simultaneously, got rid of any femininity and homosexuality from within themselves. They conclude that:

> Hence in structuring the attributes of maleness, the various forms of masculinity that are hegemonic in English schools can all be argued to be crucially involved in policing the boundaries of heterosexuality as much as the boundaries of 'proper masculinity'.
>
> (Haywood and Mac an Ghaill, 2003: 78)

Indeed, Connell (2005) goes so far as to argue that when it is safe for boys at school to come out as gay, we will then have made progress in relation to challenging hegemonic masculinities themselves.

## Case study: men and sport

Heterosexual, homophobic, hegemonic masculinities have been looked at in relation to sport. These issues have been theorized and problematized in the context of wrestling, athletics, nationalism, sport and sexuality, football, and more non-traditional, extreme sports, amongst others (see McKay, Messner and Sabo, 2000). Traditional sport, in particular, has been seen as the site where a globalized and dominant heterosexual, hegemonic masculinity is constructed.

There have been a number of studies on men, masculinities and identities in relation to sport (see for instance Messner and Sabo, 1994 and McKay, Messner and Sabo, 2000). Connell argues that '[i]n western countries... images of ideal masculinity are constructed and promoted most systematically through competitive sport' (Connell, 1987: 85), though this homogenous conception of an ideal masculinity has started to be critiqued. For example, Messner (1992), in an attempt to problematize the construction of a dominant, hegemonic masculinity in sport, outlines three reasons why sport does not construct a single dominant masculinity:

- One is the costs of sport to men.
- The second is men's different experiences of class, race and sexuality in athletic careers.

- The third is the challenges to sport and heterosexual masculinity posed by the rise of women athletes.

Messner asks if dominant conceptions of sex and gender are challenged in any of these three contexts and states that individual men in relationships with women can challenge the gender order. Though such relationships are ambivalent, he also found that some men elevate relationships above winning in some sporting activities. Men, he also argues, have had to change their attitudes because of women's increasing participation in sport. Some, for instance, have questioned the myth of female frailty. (See also Woodward in this volume.) Thus, theorists have argued that some men's behaviour, in specific sites, can be seen to challenge dominant conceptions of a heterosexual, hegemonic masculinity. There has also been a recognition that the construction of a sporting, hegemonic and heterosexual masculinity can change across the lifecourse, in that men's attitudes to competition with other men, and the achievement of a glorified and powerful sporting, heterosexual body shifts as they get older, and often more reflective (Robinson, 2008).

## Masculinities and extreme sports

The social significance of sport at both local and global levels has become apparent since the 1980s through recent theoretical concern with sporting identities. More recently, an interest in extreme sports has also been put on the sporting theoretical agenda, informed by an investigation of shifting, flexible and multiple hegemonic masculine identities (Wheaton, 2004). These sports are, arguably, less about competition, status, bravado and are supposedly more individualistic, potentially less gendered and more about cooperation.

However, if sport is used by a diversity of people to express and negotiate their identities, as well as to challenge the way they are identified by others, and to assist in the creation of new social identities (MacClancy, 1996), it is also crucial in the maintenance and reproduction of a specifically masculine identity. Elaborating on this idea, Dunning (1999) sees sport simultaneously as one of the most significant sites of resistance against, and challenge to, but also of production and reproduction of, traditional masculinity.

However, Gardiner's (2000:8) view that '[i]ncreasingly, the "everyday" is evoked in a gestural sense as a bulwark of creativity and resistance, regardless of the question of asymmetries of power, class relations, or increasingly globalized market forces' needs to be borne in mind if gendered [sporting] relations are also to be seen as sites of power and dominance in the context of feminist and other criticisms (see Creedon, 1994). This point is also important to bear in mind for any critical examination of the fluidity and possibilities of change in hegemonic masculinities, so that any shifts identified in sporting masculinites are seen in the continuing context of gendered and other power relations.

The studies by Beal (1995, 1999), Wheaton (2000) and Robinson (2004, 2008) look at newer, less traditional sporting environments to examine men's attitudes to women participants. Beal's (1999) findings that of the 41 skaters interviewed in a study of male skateboarders, only 4 were women and other women associated with the sport were 'skate betties', women who were there primarily to enhance the men's egos, stands in interesting comparison to Wheaton's 'surf babes' or, Robinson's climbing 'belay bunnies', women who don't often climb but who hold the ropes of their boyfriends to ensure that they can climb safely.

In the framework of her identification of the specific sport of windsurfing as a 'male heterosexual arena', through men's attitudes to both female participants and those labelled ' beach babes', Wheaton's (2000) findings on female and male windsurfers revealed diverse attitudes to women windsurfers ranging from respect and acceptance to negative attitudes. Borden (2001) found that skaters are mostly young men in their teens and twenties, with 'broadly accommodating dispositions towards skaters of different classes and ethnicity' (p. 263), but here too, gender relations are problematic, with female skaters being discouraged by convention and including sexist objectification. Older skaters were also seen to face prejudice whilst homophobic attitudes and homosocial masculinity were created in a skateboarding environment. Thus, whilst there is evidence, from different sports, of changes in traditional masculine identities, especially where women are entering sports in greater numbers and achieving at a high level, there is also evidence of continuing patterns of gendered and other inequality.

To sum up this case study of men and sport, McKay, Messner and Sabo (2000) state that there is now a need to develop critical relational studies of gender and sport so that analysis takes into account unequal power relations between women and men. The sporting studies considered here have, as I have stated, underlined how, along with the recognition that masculinities are shifting, an emphasis on power in its different dimensions is important to studies of sporting masculinities and gendered relations, and also must be central to the masculinity studies agenda more broadly. I go on to consider this aspect in the conclusion to this chapter,.

## Critiques of theorizing on men and masculinities

There have been both general critiques by feminists and others of theorizing on masculinities and more specific interrogations of key concepts such as 'hegemonic masculinities'. I will discuss both these elements in this section.

In their diverse responses to theorizing masculinity, theorists have varied in their relation to feminist theory and feminism as a political movement. Some theorists have acknowledged the debt male theorists owe to feminism, while others have rejected feminist insights or stereotyped particular feminist positions such as radical feminism (Robinson, 2003).

Further, there has been an over-riding concern that the current notion of emphasizing changing masculinities should not ignore or minimize men's continuing power at both a structural and personal level. Putting such critiques in a historical context, the feminist Jalna Hanmer (1990) has asserted that there are aspects of the approaches to the study of men which worry her, particularly the US role theory and socialization theory. She saw this as limiting the study to the individual, or else attempting to explain social formation and processes purely at the level of the individual. As already noted in the chapter, some masculinity theorists themselves have criticized this approach (see Whitehead, 2002).

Victor Seidler (1994), when discussing 'men's studies' as it has developed in the US, has put forward the argument that its development has left behind 'difficult personal terrain' for theoretical engagement. This suspicion is connected to the strength of a positivist social science methodology in men's studies, which Seidler feels is related to the disciplinary strength of psychology, and leads to his criticism of a behaviourist approach. This is seen to be a simplistic explanation for the connection between empirical research and feminist theory: for example, in the relationship of pornography's effects on men and their behaviour and relationships with partners.

Other writers, for example Harry Christian (1994), are more concerned to dislocate the idea of hegemonic masculinity. He has argued that, though a common conception of heterosexual men's experiences of sex is one of domination and control, his personal experience has been that sex is about shared physical enjoyment. So, he argues against general statements about heterosexual men, based on limited empirical evidence, which ignore variations amongst straight men, and concludes: 'The non-gay identity needs to be distinguished' (Christian, 1994: 188).

Edwards (1994, 2006), writing on the issue of gay studies and masculinity, has further argued: 'In addition, men's studies of masculinity added some insights into masculinity and male experience though frequently excluded full consideration of sexual orientation and heterosexuality as a component of masculine identity' (Edwards, 1994: 1).

Whether masculinity studies has fully discussed or theorized these differences, which a focus on hegemonic masculinities reveals, is doubtful. Some would disagree, and moreover would argue that men's studies has recognized that it 'owes a lot to those voices proclaiming the legitimacy of experience and the need for recognition of the inherent dignity of other marginalised groups (gays, lesbians and people of colour)' (see Doyle, 1994). Thus, it is claimed that the early works of men's studies practitioners, where masculinity was constructed by generalizing from white, heterosexual and middle-class experience, do not now inform and limit the analyses of masculinity. Other scholars may not agree that men's studies, or other masculinity theorists in general, have theoretically embraced diversity and difference fully.

## Race and Masculinities

Gamal Abdel-Shehid (2005) is concerned with exploring how black sporting masculinities have been both constructed and interpreted within critical masculinity studies which he terms 'Good Boy Feminism'. He illustrates this by the use of Michael Messner's work on sport, which he critiques as being too simplistic in its conflation of sport and patriarchy. Here, Good Boy Feminism's notions of masculinity are seen to incorporate a hierarchical and essentialized notion of maleness. Further, black men are presumed to be 'written out of text of male participation in feminism by virtue of their placement within the "state of the nature"' (Abdel-Shehid, 2005:53). He claims that 'Good Boy Feminism' is a heterosexist, as well as racist, paradigm because of an inherent inability to theorize desire and how it works for men in the making and unmaking of masculinity. Men, by virtue of their essential maleness, can only be either masculine or emasculated, and, therefore, Abdel-Shehid sees no theoretical middle ground is available.

A more general critique of hegemonic masculinities is offered by White-head who argues, on one hand, that the concept 'achieves what patriarchy fails to achieve: it offers a nuanced account of femininity-male power while staying loyal to the notions of gender and sexual ideology, and male dominance' (Whitehead, 2002:90). But, he also argues that, as a concept, hegemonic masculinity is as reductionist a category as patriarchy, its fundamental inconsistency being that, while it recognizes difference and resistance, its primary underpinning is seen to be its notion of a fixed male structure. Ultimately, he argues: 'Hegemonic masculinity is a useful shorthand descriptor of dominant masculinities, but its overuse results in obfuscation, in the conflation of fluid masculinities with overarching structure and, ultimately, in "abstract structural dynamics"' (Whitehead, 2002:9).

Seidler (2006) further critiques Connell's notion of hegemonic masculinities for making it difficult to understand the relationship of diverse masculinities within particular cultures, as cultures have been reduced to relationships of power and so we have not been able to theorize the ways in which culture relates to emotional life and power, for example. For his part, Hearn (2004) calls for a shift from masculinity to men and a focus on 'the hegemony of men'. In this way he seeks to address the double complexity that men are both a social category formed by the gender system as well as being collective and individual agents, and often dominant collective and individual agents, of social practices. However, Connell (2005) argues that the concept of 'hegemonic masculinities' is still essential to theorize gendered power relations. He also states that though it is time to consider the use of the concept and how it has been utilized in masculinity studies, whether it is time to reject the category, or re-affirm it, is still very much debated. For Connell, then, it is still of great use in theorizing power relations between men and looking at masculinity in relation to how gender orders are legitimated.

## Future directions

Kegan Gardiner (2002) sees academic masculinity studies as an independent field, informed by queer theory, 'race' studies, poststructuralisms and the full range of feminisms. As she asserts, masculinity studies can help feminist theories break free from theoretical impasses, whilst a feminist focus on the institutionalization of power can guard against simplistic theorizing about gender.

However, her argument that '[c]urrent masculinity studies focus less on men's power over women and more on relationships between men, as these are regulated by regimes of masculinity' (Gardiner, 2002:14) indicates that the field of masculinity studies has not yet reached a state of (critical) consensus on its relatively embryonic, though certainly now more developed, relationship with feminism.

In his book *The Men and the Boys* (2000), Connell outlines a useful and overarching framework within which to reflect on the concepts and ideas that have captured the imagination of masculinity theorists. The key concerns of research on masculinity for him have been:

- The ideas of multiple and diverse masculinities;
- Men's hierarchical and hegemonic social relations;
- Collective masculinities in culture and institutions;
- Bodies;
- Men's construction of their own and others masculinities;
- The idea of complexity, contradiction and change in different contexts and different countries.

He argues that, for strategic reasons, the most compelling issues masculinity theorists face now are to rethink masculinities and 'gendered politics of men' in a much more global context and that the body still needs to be centre stage. His view that social-scientific research on masculinity needs to be 'driven by practical concerns' through a concern with boys' education and men's health and violence, reveals the importance of grounding emerging theories on boys and men in empirical data. Thus, a focus on the everyday, mundane, lived complexities of different men's lives is of continuing importance. (See Robinson, Hockey and Hall, 2007.)

Connell's views are also that we need a deeper understanding of change in masculinities, and in relation to race, ethnicity and class, as well as to explore what he defines as 'the patriarchal dividend' which men receive. In later work (2005), he is positive about the amount of work already done on masculinities in the context of globalization and international work on men and masculinities and of the amount of applied work, policy work and professional practice now available in the field.

Furthermore, as I have argued with Hockey and Hall (2007), theoretical and empirical issues of men and masculinities in relation to space, intimacy, the emotions and the body are now being addressed within a variety of disciplines. However, such theorizing starts from assumptions about fluid and multiple masculinities, but tends to assume a static framework within which to explore men's experiences. Men are treated as if they inhabit and perform masculinities in one space alone, for example, either the workplace or domestic sphere. Little consideration has been given to how men exist in different spaces, sometimes simultaneously and at various stages of the life course, and how they manage transitions between work and home life, between being a colleague, friend, father and partner. Focusing on men's mobility and experiences, their strategies and performances of 'being' a man, can speak not only about masculinities, but also to gendered, classed and aged relationships across and beyond separate life spheres.

## Conclusion

Although it is still debatable how much the theories and concepts of masculinity studies have informed social theory more generally (Hearn, 1998b) and, it could be argued, feminism, it is indisputable that there is now a body of critical work on masculinity which spans many (but not yet all) of the disciplines in the academy. Though, importantly, as Whitehead points out:

> However, in undertaking any critical examination of men, it is important not to lose sight of the material consequences and political dimensions to masculinities and their associated myths and ideologies ... it is evident that, while masculinities may be illusory, the material consequences of many men's practices are quite real enough.
> (Whitehead, 2002: 43)

This chapter has discussed the historical context in which the study of men and masculinity has taken place, including the institutionalization of masculinity studies.

As well, a number of fundamental concepts and ideas which have characterized this theorizing on masculinity have been explored. A case study of hegemonic masculinity and heterosexuality especially in the area of education, and a case study of men and sport have been introduced and feminist and other critiques of theorizing on masculinity, as well as of the concept of hegemonic masculinity, have been considered. I ended by briefly outlining future directions for the field.

Lynne Segal (2007), in her new edition of the classic text on masculinity, *Slow Motion: Changing Masculinities, Changing Men*, first published in 1990, writes:

> We can learn from the discursive contradictions and fluidities of a falsely homogenized and universalized 'masculinity'. But we still need concrete programmes for

modifying everyday gender practices, once we have taken on board the multiplicity of subject positions women and men actually occupy, and the manifold complexities of the lives they lead.

(Segal, 2007:xxxi)

The challenge for those involved with theorizing masculinity lies in this need to consider the everyday realities of gendered lives along with a continuing theorization of shifting female and male subjectivities, whilst recognizing the importance of making such connections in a global context.

## Further reading

R.W. Connell (2005) *Masculinities*, Cambridge, Polity
An updated version of his earlier (1995) work which has become a classic piece of work on the construction and nature of masculinities. Connell looks especially at global masculinity, multiple masculinities and the politics of masculinity.

T. Edwards (2006) *Cultures of Masculinities*, London, Routledge
A nuanced survey of social, cultural and political issues around masculinities. Especially thoughtful on the idea of a 'masculinity in crisis' and on marginalized masculinities, such as black and gay masculinities.

C. Haywood and M. Mac an Ghaill (2003) *Men and Masculinities*, Buckingham, Open University Press
This accessible book reviews and provides an overview of central theories, concepts and empirical research in the field of masculinity studies. Topics covered include fatherhood, work and education.

V.J. Seidler (2006) *Transforming Masculinities*, London, Routledge
A multi-disciplinary approach which discusses male identities, bodies, sexualities and emotional lives across diverse histories, cultures and traditions. It explores men's power in relation to particular traditions and cultures.

S.M. Whitehead (2002) *Men and Masculinities*, Cambridge, Polity
A very useful and comprehensive collection on theories of masculinity, as well as key issues such as families, sexualities, intimacy and the emotions and the relationship of men and masculinities to feminism.

# SECTION TWO
# BODIES–IDENTITIES

---

This section explores the importance of 'the body' in gender and women's studies and, also, the concept of identity. A key question is: How are bodies and identities linked? The body has been a major concern of feminist theory and politics. This is because the ways in which women and men have often been treated, reproducing gendered inequalities, have been justified by their having different bodies. The first chapter, **Gendered Bodies, Gendered Lives**, summarizes some of the key debates in thinking about bodies developed out of gender and women's studies, including binaries such as nature/culture; sex/gender; mind/body and woman/man. It asks 'What is a body?', and looks at the meanings we give to bodies and how these meanings are connected to understandings of 'difference'. Two different approaches to understanding the body are considered in detail: feminist phenomenological and postmodernist theories. The notion of embodiment, linking bodies and selves, has superseded that of 'the body' in many areas of gender and women's studies. **Gendered Bodies, Gendered Lives** provides a basis for reading the next two chapters in this section. Bodies are important markers of difference, not only for gender but also for race and sexuality. Chapter 6, **Racing the Feminist Agenda: Exploring the Intersections Between Race, Ethnicity and Gender**, outlines the relationship between feminism, race and ethnicity and examines how this has changed over time. In particular, it explores how the influence of black feminism, as well as postmodernism, on feminist agendas has led to greater emphasis on diversity. New agendas in the study of race and ethnicity have emerged in gender and women's studies, including issues such as identity, whiteness, masculinity, race and ethnicity and postcolonial feminism. While Chapter 6 looks at the intersections between gender, race and ethnicity; Chapter 7, **Sexuality**, examines the interconnections between gender, sexuality and class. Sexuality can be linked to a range of issues and has long been an important aspect of feminist theory and politics. Like race, sexuality is a central aspect of contemporary identities, as well as our understandings of bodies. This chapter provides a discussion of the social construction of sexuality using feminist and queer theory. Much of this work is central to debates about how we understand identity, in particular whether gendered and sexual identities are increasingly multiple, fluid and fragmented rather than fixed, static and unitary. It asks how sexuality connects to globalization, understandings of 'space and place' and whether or not we are seeing a 'transformation of intimacy'. The final part of the chapter, and this section, looks at how sexuality has been a central concern for social movements concerned with 'sexual politics'. More recent campaigns have drawn on the language of citizenship, and the chapter looks at some of the claims and 'successes' of these rights based campaigns, including civil partnerships for lesbians and gay men.

# CHAPTER FIVE

# Gendered Bodies: Gendered Lives

KATH WOODWARD

## Introduction

Over the last twenty years, 'the body' has become a major concern of academic study. This chapter explores the importance of 'the body' and bodies in gender and women's studies. Bodies have also been central to activists' campaigns, especially those associated with 'identity politics', many of which have focused on claiming rights over one's own body. People sought to take control over their own sexuality, reproductive rights and to gain freedom from harassment and acts of racism and aggression. Therefore, theory and the politics of experience are inextricably linked. This chapter demonstrates that feminist critiques present significant challenges to the idea that it is possible to talk about 'the body' without acknowledging how bodies are treated and valued differently, and often unequally, and what sort of explanations can be offered for inequalities that are based on bodily differences. Firstly, the chapter looks at why bodies are important, especially in being seen as marking what makes people different from each other as well as, of course, being what is common about human experience. How are bodies experienced in the contemporary world? What are the meanings which are attached to having different kinds of bodies? Secondly, the chapter maps out some of the problems about thinking about bodies, which have developed in women's and gender studies. In particular, the problem of binaries such as, for example, nature/culture, sex/gender, mind/body and women/men, where women have often been associated with the less valued element in these dualisms. What are the problems presented by these opposing categories and by recognizing the importance of the body in everyday life? Thirdly, the chapter addresses the question of bodies and selves. How are identities shaped by the bodies we have? This section discusses some of the problems raised by thinking about bodies; sex and gender, and mind and body, as oppositions which have been linked to nature and culture. Lastly, the chapter makes two different attempts to re-think bodies:

- feminist phenomenological analyses of 'lived bodies' (see p. 84 for a definition of phenomenology), which explore the links between gendered bodies and gendered lives; and
- postmodernist approaches which address changes in the world, including those made possible through technological developments.

The body, although it was for some time ignored in academic work, has become central to much of contemporary debate and it is thanks in large part to the insistence by theorists of gender studies such as R.W. Connell (1995) and feminists, from Ann Oakley (1972) to postmodernist writers like Judith Butler (1993) and Elizabeth Grosz (1994), that the relevance of bodies in people's lives has to be addressed. Bodies matter and they matter in specific ways. But what do we mean by 'bodies'?

## Bodies

What is a body? It is an assemblage of breathing, eating, sleeping, reproducing functions; a collection of body parts. However, some body parts, especially those linked to the reproductive process and visible differences of racialized characteristics, seem to be accorded more social and political significance than others in the organization of society and social relations. Bodies come in different shapes and sizes, but bodies are also marked by gender, class, 'race', 'ethnicity', generation, ability, disability and sexuality, to mention but some of their distinguishing characteristics. Bodies are, however, classified in particular ways. Londa Schiebinger (1993), in her studies of the history of science outlining Linnaeus's taxonomy of animals and plants, argues that this is the result of his controversial attempt to classify human beings as part of the animal world, when human bodies were classified against the norm of the European, white male. Schiebinger demonstrates how reproductive capacities were central to the system of classification adopted by Linnaeus in 1735 (and still used today) with all creatures which give birth to live young and have mammary glands to feed them being called *mammals* (Schiebinger, 1993), thus reducing women to their reproductive role and presenting this as a universal class. The bodies we have are used as a means of ordering people, through attributing particular significance to aspects of those bodies. Racialized characteristics, sexual difference, increasingly as measured by DNA rather than visible, external features, have all been used to create categories of person, regardless of the capacities and capabilities of those persons. The gendered bodies of women have historically played a key role in the politics through which women have been excluded from public life and the visibility of gender has made it the focus of much of the differentiation that has been based on bodies and their attributes and characteristics. For women, the claim that 'we are our bodies' has often meant being *reduced* to our bodies and feminists (for example, Birke, 1986; Fausto-Sterling, 1992) have sought both to understand and explain the thinking behind this phenomenon, and to suggest strategies for dealing with the injustices that are based upon gendered embodiment. However, bodies change; through life experiences, health and ill health and through aging, and through the interventions of science and technology and transforming cultural practices. A key question in gender and women's studies concerns finding ways of talking about the body without fixing it as a naturally determined object which exists outside politics, culture or social change, for example (Fausto-Sterling, 2005), whilst also holding on to the materiality of living bodies. Bodies are always in the world and those bodies and the world are also changing.

## Bodies in the contemporary world: targets of intervention

Bodies are everywhere in western societies; images of bodies, beautiful bodies, damaged bodies, bodies that can be transformed by medical, technological and pharmaceutical interventions and training regimes. The contemporary western focus upon the body means that people are routinely exhorted to look after their bodies, for example through healthy eating, keeping fit and looking good. Increasingly, the promotion of a healthy body through exercise and healthy eating has become a regulatory strategy of the neo-liberal state; good citizens have healthy bodies and look after themselves. Participation in sport is encouraged to further social inclusion and diversity (Woodward, 2006). The body is targeted by the state as a site at which good citizens can be made, suggesting that there is a causal link between the healthy body and the healthy mind (K. Woodward, 2005); a link based on the idea that mind and body are separate and distinct. The proliferation of 'body projects' in western societies (Giddens, 1991), whereby people are expected to take control of their bodies and thus their lives, presupposes that bodies can be shaped and modified by active agency, sometimes expressed in the everyday phrase 'mind over matter'.

However, the disciplining of bodies involves varying degrees of control and constraint. Bodies are regulated through the subtle wishes of government as well as through legislation, whereby strategies operate to construct good citizens who conform to norms of sexuality, appropriate behaviour and good health and regulate themselves (Rose, 1996). Magazine articles, television programmes and internet sites provide vast amounts of guidance on how to have a better body and thus attain greater happiness. This is a gendered citizenship (Richardson, 1998) where assumptions are made about what constitutes the 'good' citizen. Citizenship has been institutionalized as white, male and heterosexual. The athletic rather than intellectual capacities of young black men are encouraged, for example through participation in sport. Women have often been criticized for body practices deemed to be inappropriate or unacceptable, for example young women who smoke, drink alcohol and engage freely in sexual activity, especially if this leads to lone motherhood. Bodies are differentiated, with women's bodies being subjected to moral as well as practical interventions. Policies and practices which are directed at the promotion of healthy, fit bodies include health care, which may be denied to those who are outside the boundaries of acceptability: smokers, drinkers, overweight people. Bodies are classified in ways that have material consequences for the recipients of care and interventions. For example, the assistance of reproductive technologies may be denied to lesbians, older women, women in some ethnic groups and those who are judged to be in the wrong sort of relationship or too poor (Steinberg, 1997).

Women are expected not only to look after their own bodies, but also those of others such as children or partners. Women are also often the target of state campaigns, especially those which focus upon the body, for example to promote lower cholesterol and fat consumption, higher intake of fruit and vegetables, and increased exercise. Body practices include body projects through which the body can be enhanced, toned and beautified, as well as the interventions of modern medicine. Through technoscience the external surfaces and internal cavities of bodies become visualized in the common currency of popular culture, as, for example, in television programmes which show extreme 'make-overs', including cosmetic surgery, as well as raising expectations about overcoming ill health and the frailties of the flesh, and creating new reproductive possibilities. The body images and practices which saturate contemporary western cultures seem to endorse Bourdieu and Wacquant's (1992) claim that we *are* our bodies and to suggest that we might be able to control and shape our own bodies.

Bodies are constantly subject to exposure to the scrutiny, not only of the state, but also of the mass audiences of popular culture. From the bodily intimacy and emphasis upon physical tasks and encounters of Reality TV, to contemporary versions of the 'perfection' of supermodels, the body is everywhere in culture and this invokes the desire to take control of the body and, thus, the self. Body projects offer the promise of agency, but depend upon the fear of failure. The body images of popular western culture embrace the celebration of the exceptionally, almost impossibly, thin body of the prepubescent supermodel or pop star, which occupies an uneasy space with repeated warnings of the dangers of obesity (Orbach, 2006) and the representations of malnutrition and starvation in large parts of the developing world.

All these body projects suggest that:

- Bodies are targets of intervention, which assumes the possibility of *agency*, that is, that people could change themselves by changing their bodies.
- *Difference* is crucial because bodies are seen as the markers of difference.

## Feminist critiques of the body

Bodies have been both subjects of theoretical analyses in gender and women's studies and central to political campaigns of the women's movement, which has striven to enable women to reclaim control over our own bodies in aspects of life such as health, reproduction and sexuality. For a long time feminist theorists have seen the project of feminism as intimately connected to the body. They have acknowledged not only the importance of the body as a vital dimension of social relations and of the interrelationship between individuals and the societies in which they live, but also one in which relations of inequality are deeply invested. The body, or more specifically women's embodied experience, has been a major concern of feminist activism, as well as being of enormous interest to critical thinkers in gender and women's studies, because the social, political and cultural differences in the ways women and men have been treated have been attributed and even justified by their having different bodies which bear some anatomical differences. Feminist critiques (Martin, 1988; Battersby, 1998) have shown how the body in western thought has often been either denied or dismissed with the mind or the soul occupying a position of superiority over the women's embodied experiences, such as those of menstruation, birth, lactation and the menopause. Motherhood has been an absent presence (Woodward, 1997) both in the systems of representation that make up culture and in critical analyses (Irigaray, in Whitford, 1991). In contrast to this, as Iris Marian Young argues, women's and gender studies have taken as their starting point: 'the sociohistorical fact that women's bodily differences from men have grounded or served as excuses for structural inequalities' (Young, 2005:4).

Feminist activism of the late 1960s and 1970s addressed women's bodies as the site of experience and developed a body politics which engaged with campaigns over sexuality, reproductive rights, combating the constraints of patriarchy and its objectification of women's bodies, for example, through pornography and sexual violence against women (Dworkin, 1981; MacKinnon, 1987; Hanmer, 1997; Phillips, 1998b).

The body and ways of thinking about the body have an unsettled history in feminist thought. At times it might have appeared that, by focusing on the gendered body, feminists were falling into the trap of associating women with 'nature' and, by implication, linking men to 'culture', with all its connotations of superiority. Feminist critiques have been haunted by the ghost of biological essentialism and the unrealistic binary of nature and culture. For example, this was present in early second wave feminism in the work of Shulamith Firestone (1970) who argued that the only release from the constraints of the female body would come from technological advances that would free women from the tyranny of childbirth. In this dualism, women's bodies have been associated with a devalued nature, which has to be overcome by a superior (male) culture. More recently however, feminist accounts have drawn attention to the necessity of foregrounding the body and embodiment by adopting a range of different approaches which I will go on to explore (Butler, 1993; Grosz, 1994).

Later work, which has provided both more complex theories of the body and broadened the scope of analysis to include literary and philosophical texts (Butler, 1990, 1993; Gatens, 1991; Grosz, 1994, 1995), might be seen to so emphasize the primacy of social and cultural construction, that bodies are seen as disembodied and disassociated from everyday 'real life' experience and material structures. This is what Michele Barrett (1992) has called the move from 'things' to 'words', represented by Foucauldian theory in which the body might be read as text. Foucault's work has been immensely important in highlighting the historical processes through which bodies are constituted and re-created and it has informed many feminist analyses (for example, Butler, 1990; Grosz, 1994). The body here in poststructuralist and postmodern accounts might be construed as a textual conceptual space rather than the material location of experience and everyday practice and subject of substantive enquiry, which has been perceived as a problem in poststructuralist views. For example, Foucault's work may claim to be primarily concerned with bodies, but they are inscribed bodies that are the product of social, cultural regimes and practices rather than material, living breathing bodies. The legacy of binary thinking has led some feminist critics to be reluctant to embrace the body as a key component in the formation of identity because of its associations with essentialist or reductionist accounts. Luce Irigaray (1985a, 1985b; in Whitford, 1991), whose work partially draws upon and challenges Lacanian psychoanalysis, has most positively presented the centrality of the gendered, sexed body in a politics of difference. Her work has been subject to criticism (for example Crossley, 2001) as fixed and essentialist, but she argues for the centrality of the body and its experience in the construction of cultural and social gender differences, highlighting the absence of the cultural importance of women's bodies in western thought. Women's bodies are largely absent from western cultural traditions except in the more negative images, for example, in religious discourse through associations with the sins of the flesh. Criticism of Irigaray's work arises partly from the assumptions of dualistic thinking that focus on the body as an entity which is devoid of agency and intentionality, and is separate and distinct from gendered identity which is *embodied*.

The recognition that bodies are important has also created problems. There is a long history of women's bodies being seen as the cause and justification for their exclusion from public life. If feminist theorists claim that women's bodies are different from men's, could it suggest that biology determines who we are and could be used to justify inequality? Women's and gender studies theorists have grappled with the problems of biological determinism and what is 'natural', in order to resolve such problems which have been framed by the binary of sex and gender (see Richardson in this volume). Such oppositions between agency and constraint and between nature and culture have presented problems, especially for feminism. If all difference is socially constructed, where is the experience of the lived material body? However, on the other hand to claim that the body is the key marker of gendered difference might be seen to suggest an approach that reduces differences between women and men to biology and naturalizes and potentially marginalizes social inequality.

## Sex/Gender

Some second wave feminists, notably Ann Oakley (1972), argued that sex and gender were frequently collapsed to women's disadvantage, whereby cultural expectations of what was appropriate or possible for women was attributed to some biological law. The notion that women should be relegated to second class citizenship, or even accorded no citizenship status, because of anatomical difference from men, in particular, the possession of a uterus, has a long history. Women have been excluded from activities ranging from sport (Hargreaves, 1994), to membership of the professions and posts in the military, because of their 'sex', which was claimed to be the cause of dire outcomes such as, for example, hysteria. Women have been barred from participating in sports and continue to run shorter distances, play bouts of less duration and comply with different regimes from men in sport, such as playing off different tees in golf or fighting fewer rounds in boxing, on the basis of physical difference (Woodward, 2006). (See also Robinson in this volume.) Women's role in societies, unlike men's, was seen to be determined by their biological sex. Feminists sought to make a distinction between the biological characteristics of the body, the anatomical body and gender as a cultural construct.

Debates about the sex/gender relationship within feminist theory and the social sciences have addressed this very problem, namely the hierarchical nature of that relationship when the two are presented as separate concepts. In the sex/gender debate, embodied sex has greater weighting as a determinant of gender. Liz Stanley (1984) described the argument as being one between biological essentialism, which prioritizes biological sex as the determinant of femininity or of masculinity, and social constructionism, which focuses on gender as a social, cultural category. Stanley's argument suggests a separation between the two concepts, with sex being associated with biology and embodiment and gender with social and cultural practices. There are two issues here. Firstly, sex and gender have been combined, but there is still the assumption that sex as a biological classification, is privileged over gender as covering social attributes. Secondly, where the two have been explicitly disentangled, the influence of sex upon gender has been awarded priority and higher status than any influence gender as a cultural and social construct might have over sex. There is also a normative claim involved in this hierarchy, namely that sex *should* determine gender. (See also Richardson and Hines in this volume for a discussion of the sex/gender binary.)

The idea of an oppositional distinction between sex and gender has been challenged, most powerfully by postmodernist feminists such as Judith Butler (1990, 1993), and for many the term 'gender' is largely preferred. The meaning of 'sex' is strongly mediated by cultural understandings that, it is argued, make it impossible to differentiate between sex and gender (see Price and Shildrick, 1999).

## Embodied identities: body and self

At one level, especially in common sense terms, the relationship between the body and identity might appear relatively simple: 'One body, one self' (Fraser and Greco, 2005: 12). However, as Mariam Fraser and Monica Greco (2005) argue, the relationship between body and identity occupies a contested terrain. The idea of the uniqueness of the self has a very specific history that goes back to the eighteenth century and the development of the notion of an autonomous individual, based, for example, on the distinction between mind and body in western culture. This might be expressed in everyday language as the possibility of exercising 'mind over matter', with the primacy of thought and cognition over the flesh that is subject to the will. This most famous *Cartesian dualism* of mind/body (see Gillis in this volume) has not only held enormous sway in shaping common sense understandings of the self and of identity, but also has informed academic discourse. As Steven Rose (1998) has pointed out, the mind/body dualism and the marginalization and devaluation of the body arose from the association of the body with 'biology' in an understanding which posits biology as the opposite of the social. It is this body which eats, breathes, gives birth, bleeds, feels pain and dies; these are the attributes of the body, which may seem so routine that they are not central to social investigation or so 'biological' that they can only be addressed by medical and biological sciences. This has implications for the configuration of 'who we are'. As Moira Gatens argues, whilst the male subject is:

> constructed as self-contained and as an owner of his person and his capacities, one who relates to other men as free competitors, with whom he shares politico-economic rights...[t]he female subject is constructed as prone to disorder and passion, as economically and politically dependent on men...justified by reference to women's nature.
>
> (Gatens, 1991:5)

There is, however, a need to engage with the biological dimensions of the body and with what Judith Butler calls the 'anatomical body' (1993), not only because of the importance of the body in shaping experience, but also because of materiality and the diversity of bodies and the embodiment of difference across class, 'race', 'ethnicity', disability, generation and gender, to name but a few aspects of these differences.

The body might seem to offer a source of security and present a bounded self, demarcating one embodied self from another. Thus, the body might offer some fixity in locating a sense of identity. As Pierre Bourdieu (1986) argued, the body is the only tangible manifestation of the person. Sex and gender, as shaped by the physical, largely observable characteristics of the body are seen as key sources of identity. The visible difference of gender is both a key dimension of classification and a source of troubling anxiety when the classificatory system breaks down, for example, when a person cannot be neatly slotted in one of two genders (Woodward, 2002). At birth, babies are ascribed a gender. This is often the first observation of parents and birth attendants and is part of the process of registration as a citizen and recorded on the birth certificate. Not only are established, orthodox sources of identity confirmed by categories of sex, people seek the security and certainty of an identity – as a woman and as a man – which is rooted in some corporeal, grounded, material certainty.

The body, and in particular the sexed body, may be the source of such certainty, although ambiguity about gender identity can be a challenge to certainty, a source of insecurity or a subversion of the fixity of identity. For example, surgical interventions have been carried out so that the gender identities of intersex infants are consistent and conform to social and cultural external, visible expectations (see also Richardson and Hines in this volume). Gender may precede sex, given that expectations of what it is to be a woman or a man are there before any external, bodily characteristics are noted. As Susanne Kessler (1998) argues, although it is largely on the basis of the social implications of uncertainty about gender categories, the initial observation is made on the basis of features that are visible in the infant body.

People's bodies clearly offer limitations to what is possible, to the identities to which they might like to lay claim. Physical disabilities, the impact of ageing and the limits to the physical powers and competence of our bodies clearly restrict our potential in the routine of everyday life and in the aspirations which shape identity. These are the constraints of the material body, which constantly remind us that human beings are embodied subjects.

The body does also offer more positive aspects of security and certainty about who we are. All societies and cultures have a series of gendered attributes and expectations and practices that are associated with women and with men. These cultural associations vary across societies and across time and space, but they are almost always linked to the properties of the body. The physical features which create the categories of female or male are connected to social, cultural expectations, practices and, since categories and their embodiment change over time, behaviour (Fausto-Sterling, 1992). Thus, being assigned to a specific gender provides a set of ground rules that govern our behaviour, establishing a cornerstone of identity. This is not to deny or underplay the materiality of the body and reduce difference to what is visible. Embodied identity is closely enmeshed with the materiality of clothing which at many points cannot be disentangled from the gendered body (S. Woodward, 2005). Similarly, ethnicity is often characterized by visible difference, whether of physical features such as skin colour, or clothes that are specific to particular cultures. For example, clothing has a material impact upon the body as exemplified by corsets, tight trousers and narrow pointed-toed shoes. Disability is not always a visible difference; for example, deafness is not immediately apparent, although other disabilities may be more visible. However, along with 'race' and some disabilities, gender is the most notable visible difference which may have led to the dominance of visibility (and invisibility) and of the visual at the expense of other senses (Sobchack, 2004).

Feminist critics (for example, Gatens, 1991; Braidotti, 1994) have challenged the notion of a 'disembodied' somehow gender neutral (for which read male) person by stressing that the person, and thus the self, is necessarily *embodied*. The traditional universalizing of the self involved the idea of an abstract, rational self which has largely been associated with a masculine person. Feminists' renewed emphasis on embodiment reinstates gender differentiation.

## Embodied Selves

The notion of embodiment has superseded that of 'the body' in many areas of gender and women's studies:

▓ Because of the concept of embodiment, we can break out of the dualism of the Cartesian legacy, phenomenologically appreciating the intimate and necessary relationship between my sense of myself, my awareness of the integrity of my body and the experience of illness as not simply an attack on my instrumental body but as a radical intrusion into my embodied selfhood (Turner, 1992: 167)

▓ The notion of *embodiment* challenges the Cartesian dualism which suggests that mind and body are separate

▓ Embodiment means that our bodies are who we are and are inextricably linked to an understanding of the self

▓ Sexual difference is an important part of identity, whatever form it takes and embodiment stresses the relevance of gender in making up the self

# Phenomenology: embodiment and experience

Phenomenlogy, according to Merleau-Ponty, 'tries to give a direct description of our experience as it is, without taking account of its psychological origin and the causal explanation which the scientist, the historian or the sociologist may be able to provide' (1962: vii).

## Phenomenology

Phenomenology is a philosophical approach drawing on the work of the German philosopher Edmund Husserl (1859–1938), which attempts to describe experience directly in terms of what is happening and how people describe themselves and their actions. It is a systematic investigation of consciousness. It is direct because it is not mediated by origins, history or psychology.
   Merleau-Ponty's (1962) phenomenological approach has been especially useful in gender and women's studies because of his discussion of the links between bodies, consciousness and the outside world. His use of embodiment is relevant because it brings together minds, bodies and the social world.

Merleau-Ponty's work has been very influential in the development of theories of 'the body', especially in incorporating agency into a critique of the body. Bourdieu and those who have developed aspects of his work (for example Crossley, 2001) have used the notion of embodiment to locate body practices within material, economic circumstances. The notion of embodiment, especially as developed in phenomenological accounts, is a radically material condition of human beings, which involves:

> body and consciousness, objectivity and subjectivity in an irreducible ensemble. Thus we matter and we mean through processes and logics of sense-making that owe as much to our carnal existence as they do to our conscious thought.
>
> (Sobchack, 2004: 4)

This does not, of course, mean that there is necessarily harmony in this inter-relationship. It may never work perfectly and, as with so many other current theories of embodiment, the process is unfinished and incomplete. There are moments in this alliance when we are more preoccupied with the body and others when consciousness takes us up. The idea of embodiment opens up another possibility for avoiding the binary logic of mind and body. Even in those situations where the body might seem to 'take over' and deny the possibility of agency, the notion of embodiment can permit an understanding of what constitutes agency. For instance, in a situation in which the body (or at least two bodies) might seem to be the prime determinant of experience such as childbirth, labouring women are more likely to perceive themselves as in control when they do 'go with the body', rather than attempting to resist its demands, whether this involves making the decision to receive pharmaceutical or technological intervention or to take a non-interventionist, unassisted route (Akrich and Pasveer, 2004). Childbirth not only involves the bodies of the mother and infant, but also those of attendants, as well as the interventions of technologies, that become inseparable from the body from which the baby is emerging.

Toril Moi (1999) suggests the concept of the 'lived body' as an alternative to the categories of sex and gender, drawing on the work both of the phenomenologist Maurice Merleau-Ponty (1962), mentioned above, and the feminist philosopher Simone de Beauvoir. The body is located in a given environment so that, as de Beauvoir (1953/1997) argued, the body is a 'situation' incorporating the physical facts of its materiality, such as size, age, health, reproductive capacity, skin, hair and the social context. Moi's 'lived body' is not biologistic, that is, it is not reducible to its corporeal parts, subject only to laws of physiology and divided into two categories of gender. This eliminates the constraints of other binaries too, such as nature/culture. Here, the body is always part of culture, inculcated with habits, acting according to social and cultural rules:

> To consider the body as a situation...is to consider both the fact of being a specific kind of body and the meaning that concrete body has for the situated individual. This is not the equivalent of either sex or gender. The same is true of 'lived experience' which encompasses our experience of all kinds of situations (race, class, nationality etc) and is a far more wide-ranging concept than the highly psychologizing concept of gender identity.
>
> (Moi, 1999: 81)

---

**Lived Bodies: Bodies as Situations**

Simone de Beauvoir's exploration of sexual difference and the status of women in her famous book, *The Second Sex* (1953), rejects the two categories of sex and gender and includes the following:

▨ Body as object

▨ Body as situation

▨ Lived experience (subjectivity)

▨ Myths of femininity (ideology; norms)

▨ Sex (the fact of being a man or a woman)

(See Moi, 1999)
    Bodies are not only *in* a situation, for example a social context, they are *themselves* the situation of our experience

---

The idea of the 'lived body' clearly has strong advantages in the field of women's and gender studies and for exploration of the lives of those who have been marginalized or excluded, not the least because of its focus upon experience. However, as Iris Marion Young (2005) points out, although the lived body avoids the binary logic of sex/gender and even nature/culture, it may pay insufficient attention to the structural constraints which shape experience. Consequently, she argues for the retention of the concept of gender.

Gendered, racialized differences and body practices in sport have often been attributed to bodily inequalities, relating to size, anatomy, muscle power and stamina and often elided with psychological aspects of competition. The exclusion of women from many sports has often been based on the claim that women's bodies are smaller and weaker. Being 'weaker' may be translated as being less aggressive, for example, less prone to tackle assertively in football or rugby, or less competitive in contact sports like boxing (Woodward, 2006). These are bodily dispositions and practices. Young (2005) has combined the phenomenological concept of embodiment with Simone de Beauvoir's (1949/1982) notion of the body as a situation to explain the apparent 'remarkable differences' between masculine and feminine body comportment and style of movement and uses the example of 'throwing like a girl' (Young, 2005) to demonstrate how gendered embodiment is constituted through routine and repeated bodily practices. She examines the practices through which women and girls experience the world through their movement and orientation in spaces by developing specific body competences:

> The young girl acquires many subtle habits of feminine body comportment – walking like a girl, tilting her head like a girl...the girl learns actively to hamper her movements...thus she develops bodily timidity that increases with age. In assuming herself to be a girl, she takes herself to be fragile.
>
> (Young, 2005:43)

The body is here subject, not object and as such affords the possibility of transformation and of a reconfiguration, for example, through different sets of bodily practices. Femininity is understood in de Beauvoir's (1953) sense of a typical situation of being a woman in a particular society and is thus not fixed, or inherent, or in any sense biological.

## What's normal? Technoscience and the promise of cyborgs

Much of the discussion so far has been concerned with breaking down boundaries such as those between mind and body and between nature and culture. These binaries are often underpinned by notions of normality and the 'normal' body, which has frequently been encoded as male, white, able-bodied, heterosexual and middle class. A fluidity of gender roles in much of the contemporary world upsets traditional ideas of there being only two sexes. The myriad ways of living in transgendered identities, including intersexuality and transsexuality, challenge notions that sex and gender are separate and distinct (Chanter, 2006; see also Hines in this volume). Some of the challenges to assumed norms have been framed within analyses of the developments in science and technology, which have subverted ideas of normality and of what is natural. Some of the most exciting recent work has been carried out by feminist technologists and scientists, like the biologist Anne Fausto-Sterling (2001) who argues that, not only do sexed categories and sexologists change over time, but bodies are gendered in different ways. For example, in later work (2005), she considers the gendered constitution of the bones which make up the skeleton, to demonstrate the interconnections between what could be called 'natural' (our bones) and the social world we inhabit, which impacts upon even our skeletons.

The interventions of medical science have broken down the boundaries between humans and machines and between humans and animals; the 'certainty' of genetic inheritance and of parenthood are abandoned in situations where one woman carries and delivers a baby conceived by donor egg and donor sperm and cloning raises questions about the whole reproductive process. As Donna Haraway has argued, following her ground-breaking 'Cyborg Manifesto' (1985) and in her development of cyborg thinking (1989), the body is 'mixed up' with other things, including technology, or more broadly what she calls technoscience. The body is not free from social meanings, including the practices and interventions of science and technology, through which it is constituted. It is not possible to conceive of a 'pure' or authentic identity based on the body. Haraway argues that there is never a separate human, or animal, body entity. Human and machine, human and animal are just two of the distinctions challenged by cyborg thinking. Haraway takes Simone de Beauvoir's famous dictum that 'one is not born a woman' and translates it into 'bodies are not born; they are made' (1989:7). Thus, bodies are made in myriad ways, including the merging of humans and machines and of animals and humans. (See also Gillis in this volume for a discussion of cyborgs and feminism.)

Bio-technology and technoscience do not only challenge 'normality' and transform bodies by overcoming their limitations, (for example, by permitting Adrianna Illescu, a Romanian woman of 66 to carry to term and give birth to a baby in 2005), they also challenge the dualisms through which nature and culture and mind and body are constructed. Such practices as reproductive technologies divide up categories that were previously united in single identities, birth mother, egg donor, social mother, genetic mother/father, sperm donor, familial father. Contemporary societies abound with such practices and technologies of the body, such as plastic surgery and transgender realignment. Technoscience may confuse the notion of a bounded body that is a 'natural' object, but it does not demonstrate clear technological, scientific or any other body-based roots or determinants of identity:

> Ideas about biological, biomedical and genetic identity will certainly infuse, interact, combine and contest with other identity claims; we doubt that they will supplant them.
>
> (Novas and Rose, 2000:513)

## Conclusion

In exploring some of the different ways in which theorists of gender have sought both to theorize 'the body' and to reinstate the material body into analyses of power and difference, one of the major continuing features of the discussion has been the challenge to inflexible, rigid categories and, especially to those which are characterized by a binary logic. Feminists have sought to reinstate living breathing material bodies into the analysis through specific empirical work and through theorizing material bodies in more fluid and dynamic ways. 'Thinking the body' has extended to incorporate both the situations in which bodies are located (indeed the body itself has been construed as a 'situation') and the living, breathing, material body. The impetus for development of theories of embodiment has in part, particularly in the case of feminist and women's and gender studies' contributions, arisen from the call for action, especially to combat inequalities, many of which have been justified in relation to embodied differences. Gender inequalities articulate with other inequalities that are also embodied, such as those based on disability, racialization, sexuality and class.

New explanatory frameworks are also required to meet the needs of technological and material transformation and the body has been a significant site for some of the advances of technoscience, especially medical technologies and scientific advances. Although Haraway's work has often focused upon such technologies, her approaches have much wider application especially in deconstructing the binaries that are associated with that of sex/gender and extend to categories of flesh, body, biology, 'race' and nature, all of which she seeks to recognize are characterized by diversity and fluidity. Bodies may, however, be very vulnerable to this process and there may be moments when cyborgification may not provide such a rosy future and fail to deliver its promises. The unsettling of stabilities and certainties may be more troubling than anticipated. Much theorizing, such as that of Haraway (1985, 1989), Butler (1990, 1993) and Grosz (1994), has been directed at challenging gender as well as sex, and there is also a case for reinstating diverse bodies that are nonetheless gendered and to seek to accommodate the articulation of 'race', 'ethnicity', disability, sexuality and generation into an explanatory framework that retains the concept of gender. Retaining a focus upon gender differentiation remains a major challenge for theorists of embodiment.

Phenomenological accounts with a focus on gender and difference have been most useful in highlighting both the inseparability of mind and body, and the need to focus on practice and experience. This allows an acknowledgement of agency, bringing together what happens to bodies and what is done to them and what bodies do. One of the problems identified by early second wave feminists was the objectification of women's bodies which has parallels among diverse groups of people who are also constituted as 'other'. The process of making the body and thus, the person, an object, drew attention to structural constraints, notably as manifest in patriarchal societies, also characterized by different inequalities. However, explanations which theorize the body as an object have difficulty in accommodating change and action. If the body is an object then the world acts upon it rather than the body being implicated in action. Some notion of agency is necessary to effect change. If mind and body are one and the body subject as well as object, transformation and active engagement with the world become possible through 'doing'.

The 'lived body' provides a useful redress to the limitations of the concepts of sex and gender. The demand to include empirical material and to listen to the voices of everyday experience importantly counterbalances a surfeit of theory and abstraction. However, as I have suggested, to retain the term gender is also important, because bodies and embodiment have histories as well as current practice and it is only through an acknowledgement of histories of the body that power relations and inequalities can be addressed. There are continuities in the ways in which bodies are defined and disadvantaged, but there are also transformations which have to be acknowledged and explained, especially within the framework of feminist political positions. For example, as argued by Ariel Levy (2005), the supposed 'post-feminist' body practices and representations of bodies, which might suggest that the participation of some women in the sex industry and in its peripheral practices are liberatory, rather than exploitative, is an area that demands fuller explanation as well as activism. Such explanations demand, not only recognition of the fluidity and diversity of experience, but also a focus upon the continuities and specificities of gendered embodiment.

# Further reading

M. Fraser and M. Greco (2005) (eds) *The Body: A Reader*, London, Routledge
This reader has an extensive introduction and covers a very wide range of texts through which the body has been theorized across different disciplines and positions, as well as discussions of 'the body' and embodiment in relation to social concerns and ethical questions. It addresses matters of identity, health and disease, technologies and technoscience.

A. Howson (2005) *Embodying Gender*, London, Sage
This is a more theoretical book, which develops in greater detail some of the ideas and debates introduced in this chapter, tracing the progress of feminist theories of the body.

J. Price and M. Shildrick (1999) *Feminist Theory and the Body. A Reader*, Edinburgh, Edinburgh University Press
This text provides a useful selection of extracts from 'classic' and contemporary texts organized around different themes including 'Women as Body', 'Sexy Bodies' and 'Bodies in Science and Biomedicine'. This book also offers short extracts which you could follow up.

I.M. Young (2005) *On Female Body Experience: 'Throwing Like a Girl' and Other Essays*, Oxford, Oxford University Press
This book covers diverse aspects of women's lived bodies from sport to aging from a phenomenological position. The first essay offers a useful re-thinking of the category of gender.

# CHAPTER SIX

# Racing the Feminist Agenda: Exploring the Intersections Between Race, Ethnicity and Gender

KATE REED

## Introduction

This chapter seeks to outline and evaluate the historical relationship between feminism, race and ethnicity in order to explore the ways in which this relationship has been transformed over time. It will begin by exploring the ways in which issues of race and ethnicity have historically been excluded from feminist agendas. Drawing on a selection of examples from across the globe, the chapter will move on to explore and evaluate the impact of black feminist challenges, highlighting the ways in which black feminism has introduced debates on race and diversity into the feminist agenda. The chapter will also explore the ways that postmodernism and disciplinary shifts in the fields of women's studies and ethnic and racial studies also underpinned this emphasis on diversity. It will be argued that, as a result of these changes, new agendas in the study of race and gender have emerged within contemporary feminism. Some of these new agendas will be explored within the chapter, including research on issues such as identity, whiteness, masculinity and postcolonial feminism. The chapter ends with a note of caution. While black feminist agendas have been acknowledged by existing feminism, these agendas still fail to be fully centred within the feminist 'canon' and continue to be placed on the fringes of feminist debates.

It is important to be clear about what is meant here by race and ethnicity. Race and ethnicity are both contentious concepts and ideas that refer to social and political distinctions made between people and groups of people (Knowles, 2003). The concepts of race and ethnicity have different meanings despite often being used interchangeably in academic research. The idea of 'race' as a discrete biological entity has been undermined by modern science and genetics. However, while race as a fixed biological entity has long been disputed, social scientists acknowledge the continuing significance of assumptions based on a belief in the existence of 'races' (Parker and Song, 2001). As a result, most social scientists tend to describe 'race' as a social construction with potentially destructive consequences. However, it is also recognized that racialized identification can be a significant force for those struggling against discrimination and disadvantage (Parker and Song, 2001:4–5). The concept of ethnicity represents an attempt to replace an emphasis on physical difference with a stress on cultural variation and diversity. It emphasizes the social rather than the biological, and it is rooted in people's own self-definitions (Mason, 2003:11).

Within this chapter race and ethnicity will be viewed as socially constructed and fluid concepts which refer not only to issues relating to the experiences of black people but also include a focus on whiteness. In suggesting that these ideas and concepts are used discursively, it is important not to minimize their social and political reality but rather insist that their reality is social and political rather than natural or fixed (Frankenberg, 1993). These definitions of race and ethnicity will be adhered to throughout the chapter.

## Feminism, race and the invisible black woman

According to Bernard (1989), the 1970s and 1980s marked a significant era for feminist activism and writing. During this time a proliferation of feminist perspectives emerged including those that sought to adapt existing malestream theories. According to Shilling and Mellor (2001) for example, Marxist-feminism focused on gender, while sharing Marxism's emphasis on the economic superstructure. Other perspectives, including radical feminism, also emerged in the 1960s and became influential in the 1970s. Radical feminism examined the sexed nature of social action. It emphasizes the control men have over women's bodies through the institutions of marriage, motherhood and heterosexuality. Psychoanalytical feminism also arose during the 1970s and became popular during the 1980s (Shilling and Mellor, 2001).

Despite this proliferation of feminist perspectives, however, there was no real attempt to address issues of race and ethnicity, nor to recognize that women's experiences were mediated by race and ethnicity. Mirza (1997) argues that the desire for equality, the struggle for social justice, and the vision of universal sisterhood constituted the project of white feminism throughout the 1970s and early 1980s. According to her, a desire to expose patriarchal power and its manifestation in terms of female invisibility, along with the inevitable psychological, social and economic pressures it engendered across the globe, was the driving force of feminism. There have been attempts by feminists such as Walby (1989) to develop a more complex, culturally specific concept of patriarchy. However, racial power within the white feminist production of knowledge about gender was never directly challenged by much white western feminism. The irony was that feminism aimed to develop knowledge that was supposed to rest on inclusion and equality, but actually was itself excluding and inequitable (Mirza, 1997:9). Amos and Parmar (1984) further developed this argument in their article entitled 'Challenging Imperial Feminism'. This article argued that white, mainstream feminist theory, whether from a socialist feminist or radical feminist perspective, did not speak to the experience of black women. Further, where it attempted to do so it was often from a racist perspective. They argued that few white feminists in Britain placed the issue of racism at the top of their agendas. Mirza (1997) asserted that in feminist theory the focus was on women's silenced voice and the privileging of masculinity. Black women's experience was invisible or, if it was made visible, it was spoken in a white feminist voice.

However, while there was a lack of interest in issues of race in feminism during the 1970s and 1980s, there was a growing body of literature on race relations. According to Solomos and Back (1996) a number of early studies of what came in Britain to be called *race relations* were carried out in the 1950s, 1960s and 1970s by scholars such as Michael Banton, Ruth Glass, John Rex and Sheila Patterson. The majority of these studies focused on the interaction between minority and majority communities in employment, housing and other social contexts. Although gender was not a central concern of these studies, women's position in the migration process was given some consideration. For example, Patterson (1963), in her study on West Indians in London, examined marriage, migration and family. Despite the growth in the 'race relations' field, however, it could be argued that western feminism failed to explore ethnic and racial differences among women and, in the main, continued to develop its theoretical framework from a perspective of universalism. Such universalism had no space for difference and diversity and so race was either ignored within feminist analysis or marginalized from the core focuses of women's studies. As Bhattacharyya argues (1999), discussions of race in many disciplines and fields has often come at the tail end of more established discussions of gender. However, with regard to women's studies all this was about to change with the emergence of black and other feminist literature on race.

## Black feminist challenges

During the 1980s white women could no longer fail to notice the critique of white feminist racism by black feminists (Frankenberg, 1993). From the 1980s onwards, black women have critiqued and transformed feminist analysis, urging existing feminism to recognize difference and diversity between women. Such an emphasis on difference has been further enhanced by postmodernism and by shifts in the fields of women's and gender studies and ethnic and racial studies themselves.

According to Mirza (1997:20–1), while a diverse body of thought that incorporates a variety of perspectives, black feminism is a political project with a single purpose: 'to excavate the silences and pathological appearances of a collectivity of women assigned as the "other" and produced in gendered, sexualized, wholly racialized discourse' (Mirza, 1997:20–1). The term 'women of color' is used most often in North America to refer to black women and all women who do not consider themselves to be white (see Moraga and Anzaldúa, 1983). In Britain and Europe the term 'black women' has often been the term used to discuss issues relating to women of color including black and Asian women (see Mirza, 1997). Within this chapter, in order to avoid confusion, the terms 'black feminism' and 'black women' will be used to refer to all women who identify as non-white women. According to Amos and Parmar (1984), during the 1980s there was a proliferation of books by black women documenting black women's experiences (for example, Moraga and Anzaldúa, 1983). This marked the beginning of a systematic documentation of black women's individual and collective histories (Amos and Parmar, 1984). Many of these critiques within Britain came from women of Afro-Caribbean descent (for example, Carby, 2000), although Asian women also spoke out about their experiences of gendered and racial oppression (Wilson, 1978).

Black feminists drew attention to the white-centeredness of much white feminism, and also to its false universalizing claims. Black feminists pointed to the limitations of existing feminist analysis in relation to the experience of black communities and the history of slavery and racial discrimination (Carby, 2000; hooks, 2000). Black feminists such as hooks also made a heartfelt plea for racism to be removed from feminist analysis in order for sisterhood to prosper. Black feminists, as well, drew attention to the race blind nature of areas of feminist analysis such as the family and reproductive health (Amos and Parmar, 1984). Existing feminist work which focused on families of ethnic minorities tended to stick to stereotypes, portraying Asian women for example as helpless victims in forced marriages. Black and Asian feminists such as Bhopal (1997) have since provided challenges to such accounts by conducting studies exploring the interconnections of ethnicity and gender in the context of the family, marriage and domestic labour (see also Jackson in this volume). Another key area of contention was sexuality and reproduction. Sexuality and sexual oppression has been a key issue in debates on white feminism. Amos and Parmar (1984) argued that black feminists have been peripheral to these debates. Black women, however, have since made important advances in these areas. They campaigned against issues of forced sterilization and the use of contraceptives such as Depo Provera which were routinely aimed at black women and women in developing countries, and it was campaigning on such issues that brought about a broadening of the National Abortion Campaign in Britain in 1983.

Black feminists also developed theoretical frameworks which took into account intersecting variables of women's lives. As Hill-Collins (1998) argues, black feminist thought confronts the differing variables of oppression of race, gender and class. According to her, black feminist thought offers two significant contributions towards developing an understanding of the important connections between knowledge, consciousness and the politics of empowerment. She argues that, first, black feminist thought fosters a key paradigm shift in how we theorize oppression. By embracing a paradigm which focuses on the interactions between class, race and gender as interlocking systems of oppression, she argues that black feminist thought reconceptualizes the social relations of domination and resistance. Second, she argues that black feminist thought addresses and contributes to ongoing debates in feminist theory. In so doing, black feminist theory unveils new ways of knowing that enable oppressed groups to define their own reality.

Bhattacharyya (1999) argues that the development of a distinctive arena of black women's thought and politics within the boundaries of the western world has been complemented by a heightened awareness of the range of women's experiences across the globe. This has lead to recognition of the complicit nature of white women's position in the uneven relations of the global world. During the 1980s and early 1990s postcolonial feminist critics like Sara Suleri (1992) and Chandra Taplade Mohanty (1988) began to argue that western feminism was situated in bourgeois, Eurocentric rhetoric which had to be challenged in order to avoid the continued neglect of women from low income countries.

---

**Postcolonial Feminism**

Postcolonial feminism is a form of feminist thought which criticizes western feminism for its tendency to generalize about women's oppression from a western perspective. Postcolonial feminism is a diverse body of thought, with a variety of perspectives. However, generally speaking postcolonial feminists relate women's oppression and marginalization in low income countries to their experience of colonialism. Postcolonial feminism is part of the broader project of Postcolonial Studies. See p. 97 for a definition of Postcolonial Studies.

---

Mohanty (1988), argued that in many western radical and liberal feminist writings there is a 'so-called colonialist move'. This consists of presenting women from developing countries as a singular subject. White western feminist texts, according to Mohanty (1988), make three assumptions. First, there is an assumption that women from developing countries are a single category of people with the same experiences and goals. Secondly, white western feminists assume that one type of patriarchy fits all, that women in developing countries suffer the same types of oppression and for the same reasons as those in the developed nations. Thirdly, she argues that their methodology is too simple and too monolithic, failing to account for diversity in women's experiences. In making these critiques the concept of universal sisterhood is also contested and the importance of diversity in women's experiences recognized.

The importance of recognizing difference between women was reinforced by other feminists writing at this time, for example Trin T. Minh-ha (1988) and other authors who argued for the need to situate women's experience in a politics of location (Mani, 1989). The differences in women's positions across the globe have continued to be highlighted, focusing in recent years on such issues as sex trafficking (Sullivan, 2003), and female genital mutilation (Nnaemeka, 2005).

## Black feminism, postmodernism and difference

Black feminism then emerged during the 1980s in both the *North* and *South* – that is in nations and communities that are privileged, and also nations and communities that are economically and politically marginalized (Mohanty, 2003). As I have pointed out, black feminism served to critique the universalism inherent in much feminism. It placed black women's experiences on the feminist agenda and pushed for the need to recognize difference and diversity in feminism. It also contributed to the development of feminist thought through recognizing the need to explore the multiple sites of oppression, not just focusing on gender relations. This undoubtedly had an impact on white hegemonic feminism. According to Bhattacharyya (1999), against white feminist exclusion, black feminism has attempted to develop an analysis of gender, which can encompass the differences among and between women (Mirza, 1997). This acknowledgment of diversity was taken on board by existing white western feminists and has since become the orthodoxy in feminist inquiry (Bhattacharyya, 1999).

This shift towards diversity and difference and the recognition of the importance of multiple sites of oppression by feminism was further enhanced by postmodernism. Postmodernism challenges universalism and emphasizes difference, diversity and relativism instead.

According to Mason (1999), the emphasis on the significance of difference by postmodernism has given rise to greater sensitivity to the gendering of ethnic boundaries. Views on whether the impact of postmodernism on feminism, race and ethnicity has been positive remain somewhat mixed. For example, there are those who argue that postmodernism has been invaluable to feminist academics because it provides feminism with theoretical legitimacy (Evans, 2003a). On the other hand there is the fear that postmodernism undermines the importance of material factors and hinders the potential for radical social change both in terms of gender (see Smith, 1999) and race (Smith, 1993). Furthermore, despite the advances made by postmodernism to the study of race and ethnicity, some black feminists argue that little has really changed on a practical level for black women who remain subject to racial and gendered discrimination and exclusion (Mirza, 1997). There are black feminists such as hooks (1990) who outline the benefits of postmodernism for black women. hooks argues that postmodernism calls attention to those sensibilities that are shared across the boundaries of class, gender and race and that could be fertile ground for the development of solidarity and coalition.

The increased sensitivity to diversity and the intersection of gender, race and ethnicity in feminism also reflects wider academic changes. In particular changes in the fields of women's and gender studies and ethnic and racial studies themselves have impacted on such shifts towards the recognition of diversity. There has been a shift in recent years from *women's studies* that focused particularly on women's positions to *gender studies* which includes a more complex analysis of gender relations including a focus on the positions of men and masculinity. (See also Robinson, this volume.) It has been recognized that this shift is not necessarily a wholly positive one. For example, some have argued that in moving towards an inclusion of men and men's positions within feminist analysis, there is the potential to neglect women and their positions (Robinson and Richardson, 1994). However, by drawing attention away from a focus on women's positions to include a focus on men and masculinity, feminist universalism has been further challenged. Furthermore, there has been an expansion and growth in the area of ethnic and racial studies whose reach and influence has come to span several disciplines and fields, including gender studies. According to Banton (2001), ethnic and racial studies have recently flourished; more students attend courses on the subject and publishers continue to market books. Consequently, the study of race, ethnicity and post-colonial studies has moved from the margins of academic life to the very core of teaching and research in a diverse range of disciplines from sociology to literary theory (Bulmer and Solomos, 1999).

---

### Postcolonial Studies

During the 1970s Postcolonial Studies became a prominent field of study. It is a diverse body of thought including a range of themes and perspectives. However, generally speaking postcolonial studies focuses on critically interrogating interactions between European nations and their former colonies. In recent modern history European empires were the dominant players. After the Second World War this dominance disintegrated and by the end of the twentieth century the great European colonies of the past had collapsed. Postcolonial Studies focuses on this disintegration, exploring and critiquing colonial and postcolonial encounters through a wide variety of approaches from literature to film.

---

The black feminist challenge, the impact of postmodernism and shifts in the fields of women's studies and ethnic and racial studies has had a great impact on the position of black women and the study of race within feminism. The black feminist voice once excluded from the white western feminist agenda now stands alongside it. Furthermore, the current emphasis in the humanities and social sciences on difference and diversity, along with the increasing popularity of ethnic and racial studies, now means that race is taken seriously in feminism. Differences between women along ethnic and racial lines can no longer be overlooked by feminism. As a result there has been a move to incorporate multiple axes of diversity into feminist theorizing. The race-blind feminism of the 1970s has been replaced by a feminism at the heart of which is the concept of diversity. There are of course problems associated with this move to diversity within feminism, for example, some argue that it restricts the development of solidarity between women. The limitations associated with an emphasis on difference and diversity will be discussed in more detail in the conclusion of this chapter. In the next section I will go on to discuss the ways in which this emphasis on diversity has moved research on gender and race into new areas.

In recent years, there has been a growth in new work that focuses on exploring the interactions between race, ethnicity and gender. This body of work has emerged from black and white feminists working in the realm of gender studies along with those working more specifically in the area of race and ethnicity. In the next section I want to explore some of these new directions in research.

## Race, ethnicity and gender – new agendas

As work acknowledging the intersections between race and gender grows, research is being taken in new directions on issues such as, for instance, anti-racism, identity, masculinity and sexuality, some of which I will explore in this section. In particular, I will consider some of the feminist work being conducted on gender, ethnicity and identity. In recent years there has been a proliferation of work in this area. We have also seen recently the emergence and development of critical whiteness studies. This includes a body of work that integrates or critiques, rather than justifies, the hegemony of whiteness. Feminists such as Frankenberg (1993) and Byrne (2006) have joined in this critical exploration of whiteness and this will also be explored within the chapter. Furthermore, the academic changes that have taken place over the past few years, in particular the shift from women's studies to gender studies, have sparked the growth of feminist work in the area of masculinity. Within academic debates on masculinity some new work in the area of race and ethnicity has emerged, in particular that which focuses on black and Asian masculinity. The last section of the chapter will explore some of this work. Finally, in recent years postcolonial feminism has continued to develop, expanding on its earlier focus on difference. Examples of work in this area will also be examined.

In exploring these bodies of work I want to show that, as a result of black feminist challenges, postmodernism and the changes in fields such as women's studies, a number of changes in the study of feminism and race have also taken place. Firstly, race and ethnicity as concepts of analysis are now incorporated into current agendas and debates in gender studies and feminism. Secondly, feminism now incorporates multiple axes of diversity into its analysis. Thirdly, white western feminism not only recognizes differences between women, but can also interrogate and critique its own raced position of whiteness. Thus, as we shall see, the white hegemonic feminism that was discussed in the first part of this chapter has been transformed. It is important to note that the material chosen in is this section will be necessarily selective due to the breadth of new research in the area of race and gender.

## Race, ethnicity and identity

According to Kershen (1998), at the cusp of the 21st century debates about identity, its construction and meaning took centre stage within academia. The emergence of postmodernism during the 1970s emphasized the importance of studying identity. While initially identity was seen as something that was fixed, in recent years identity has been increasingly understood as fluid and fragmented. An interest in identity has spanned the areas of class, race, ethnicity, sexuality and gender (to name but a few) (Bradley, 1996). In the area of race and ethnicity, the focus has mostly been on exploring the nature of black and white identities (Frankenberg, 1993; Alexander, 1996). More recently work has been carried out on Asian identities (C. Alexander, 2000), and on hybrid identities, which employ a mix of differing cultures in their construction (Gilroy, 1993; Bhabha, 1994; Reed, 2003). There is also a burgeoning literature on studies on mixed race identity (Parker and Song, 2001). Most studies of ethnic identity have aimed to show that identity is in a constant state of flux and will never be static. They have attempted to explore how identity is multifaceted, exploring the ways in which ethnicity interacts with other factors such as social class and gender to form identity construction.

Feminists have also contributed much to these debates on ethnicity and identity, in particular highlighting the ways in which identity is fluid and multifaceted. A great deal of feminist work has focused on exploring the position of Diaspora women throughout the globe. In particular, there has been a growth in feminist work exploring the identity of British-born ethnic minority women whose parents migrated from the Indian subcontinent, Africa and the Caribbean. The aim of such work has been to move away from earlier work which has viewed the identity of British-born ethnic minorities as caught between two cultures (for example, Watson, 1977). It has attempted to explore the fluid nature of the identities of ethnic minority groups, identities which include hybrid mixes of both British and parent culture (Parker, 1995; Reed, 2000, 2003). Woollett et al. (1994) for example, conducted a study on gender, ethnicity and identity among south Asian women in London. They explored the effects of British culture and those of the parent culture on women's identity. They argue that women's identity is an ongoing process, changing developmentally in terms of transitions in women's lives, particularly if they marry or become mothers. In recent years others have continued this work on gender, hybridity and Diasporic identities. Hussain (2005), for example, explores issues of generation, gender and ethnicity in the identity of south Asian women through literature and film.

Feminists have also contributed to the ongoing debates on mixed race identity. Work has been conducted on gender and paradoxical representations of 'race', nation, culture and generation among metisse (mixed race) women (Ifekwunigwe, 1997). Research has also focused on issues such as mixed race relationships (Alibhai-Brown and Montague, 1992) on mixed race parentage and children (Ali, 2003), and on the identity of Anglo-Indians in the context of debates on mixed race identity (Blunt, 2005). Studies such as these highlight the ways in which mixed race identities transgress multiple boundaries and challenge essentialized constructions of identities, place and belonging.

These are just some examples of feminist work on race, ethnicity and identity. They offer contributions both to debates within feminism on gendered identity and also to those in the area of race, ethnicity and identity. The studies noted here challenge the notion that identity is fixed. They highlight instead the ways in which it is both fluid and multi-faceted and also explore the interactions between race, gender and other facets of identity.

## Women and whiteness

Another area in which there have been new developments in the study of gender and race is that of critical whiteness studies. In recent years there has been a shift by those studying race and ethnicity away from a focus on minority ethnic groups towards a focus on whiteness. According to Dyer (1997), whiteness has a central, yet undeclared, position. It is a position that makes claims to universality. In critical white studies whiteness is named and acknowledged as a position of privilege (Knowles, 2003). It carries with it an acknowledgement of a history of exclusion, racial guilt and accountability, and recognition that an anti-racist future would require white people to move beyond their racial privilege (Cohen, 1997). As argued earlier, some white western feminists of the 1970s and 1980s focused on mobilizing against gender inequality from their own position as white women. Many white feminists developed their theories from a basis of white universalism, assuming that their experiences of oppression would be mirrored by everyone else's. Some differences between women were acknowledged by feminism, for example, differences in women's experiences of patriarchy or differences in terms of social class. However, difference along the lines of race and ethnicity often remained under-explored and women's position of privilege as white women mostly failed to be addressed. This privileging of whiteness within feminism can be seen to have parallels with the privileging of heterosexuality within mainstream feminist thought – a position that was subsequently challenged by lesbian feminists (see Rich, 1980; Richardson, 1996a). Within the context of debates on race and ethnicity, as a result of the challenges and changes already discussed in this chapter, white women started to question their own positions of privilege and started to recognize that whiteness was also a racialized category and that white people's lives were racially structured.

There have been several studies on women and whiteness. Vron Ware (1992), for example, explores the role of ideas about white women in the history of racism. In her book *Beyond the Pale: White Women, Racism and History* she focuses on two key themes relating to women and whiteness – the need to view femininity as a historically constructed category, and the importance of understanding how the political movement of feminism developed within racist societies. Her aim is to explore the political connections between black and white women by deconstructing the various meanings of femininity and womanhood. Ruth Frankenberg (1993) also conducted a landmark study on women and whiteness, based on interviews with white women in California. Her study maps out a discourse of race, sex and intimacy, and discusses issues of interracial relationships and parenting. She also focuses on white women's descriptions of their identities, through which she analyzes dominant conceptions of culture. Overall, Frankenberg considers the ways in which white women's experiences contribute to the reproduction of racism and at the same time also challenge it.

Studies such as these show that the position of white women is no longer taken for granted or taken as a universal standard from which all other women's positions can be generalized. The position of white women is now reflected upon and challenged. The ways in which their lives are racially structured is acknowledged and interrogated. White women are no longer placed outside debates on race, but race is now placed at the heart of their gendered identity.

## Masculinity, race and ethnicity

The transformation in women's studies is symbolized by a shift in focus from women's studies to gender studies. According to Evans (2003a), throughout the 1970s and 1980s the word 'gender' belonged to feminism. It focused mainly on the study of women's oppression, and was associated in the academy with the field of women's studies. In the 1990s, however, the term 'gender studies' was increasingly used, with greater acknowledgment that the study of gender was not just about women, but included a more complex analysis of a range of gendered identities (Robinson and Richardson, 1994). Evans (2003a) argues that to study gender now is to study the impact of the social world on constructions of masculinity and femininity. In recent years there has been an increase in more critical studies on men; those ranging from feminism to queer theory that critically address men's position in the context of gendered power relations (Segal, 1990; Connell, 1995; Hearn, 2004). These have been important in questioning and exploring men's positions in society and 'men' as a social category. (See also Robinson in this volume.) This focus on 'gender' and the social relations between women and men has had a significant effect on studies in race and ethnicity with an emerging body of work in the area of race and masculinity.

Several studies have focused on constructions of masculinity among black communities in both the US and UK. In the US, Harper (1998) explores the representation of black masculinity in the mass media, focusing in particular on African-American identity. Drawing on examples from differing cultural contexts, from pop music and television to literature, Harper highlights the ways in which restricted definitions of black masculinity have neglected to recognize differences between African-American men. There have also been studies in the UK on black masculinity. Alexander (1996) conducted a study of black men in South London. She argued that black men have traditionally been viewed as emasculated by society and, as a consequence, they are widely seen to turn upon black women to create an artificial sense of masculine power through exploitation. Black women, in comparison, are viewed as financially and emotionally autonomous and comparatively successful. This has led to an image of black female-male relationships whereby men are characterized as weak and frustrated, and black women as strong and independent. According to Alexander however, in practice, the interactions between black women and men are far from cut and dried, and power relations between them are fluid and changing.

More recently, debates on race and masculinity have also included a focus on South Asian masculinity. C. Alexander (2000) explores the negative and stereotypical views that surround young Asian masculinities, through an ethnography of an all-male Bengali Muslim youth group in South East London. Using in-depth interviews and observation Alexander examined how such a group of young men are constructed as a 'gang'. It can be argued that the field of masculinity studies has always been concerned with the problematization of masculine identities, and that Asian men are simply the latest inheritors of a tradition that almost inherently places them as a problem. The notion of 'masculinity in crisis' and gang mythmaking has long been associated with white male identity and criminality, and so Alexander argues that for Muslim young men, the association with ethnicity and religion brings with it a further stereotyped identity. The result is that Asian masculinities become racialized through the media and placed as even more deviant and more dangerous than white men.

This work on masculinity broadens the scope of the study of gender and race. It expands on earlier debates in black feminism which focused on exploring women's experiences of gendered and racial oppression to include a more detailed focus on the position of black men and the construction of black masculinity. It also brings debates on diversity into the realm of masculinity studies, recognizing the need to acknowledge differences in men's positions.

## Postcolonial feminism

Finally, when we look at advances in the study of gender and race we can also see that these have occurred in the area of postcolonial feminism. During the 1980s postcolonial feminists critiqued western feminists for imposing their own brand of feminism on women from low income countries, generalizing about women's positions and failing to acknowledge diversity between women. Postcolonial feminists have continued to take these debates on difference further. Instead of focusing specifically on emphasizing difference between women across the globe, more attention has been paid by many feminists over the last fifteen years to developing *transnational* feminist practice. This is a feminism which is concerned with how nationhood, race, sexuality and gender, for instance, interact in global capitalism.

This desire to develop a transnational feminist practice can be found in the work of Grewal and Kaplan (1994) who explore the possibility of conducting feminist practice across cultural divides without ignoring differences or falling into cultural relativism. This move can also be found in the more recent work of Mohanty (2003) who argues that, while it is important to recognize difference and diversity between women, we must also see the connections and commonalities. She argues now that it is precisely the differences between women that allow us to explain the connections and 'border-crossings' between them. She argues that we need to see how specifying difference actually allows us to theorize universal concerns more fully. According to Mohanty (2003), this move allows women of different communities and identities to build coalitions and solidarities across borders, rather than just to subside into multiple difference. While Eurocentric universalist approaches continue to exist and flourish, she argues that it is important not to focus too much on the differences between women. Her central concern is rather to build connections between feminist scholarship and political organizing. She argues for what she calls an 'anti-capitalist transnational feminist practice', a feminist practice that explores the possibility of developing women's solidarity across nations. This cross-cultural feminist work must recognize the specific contexts in which women live their lives as well as the macro-politics of global economic and political systems and processes (Mohanty, 2003). In arguing for the development of transnational feminism Grewal and Kaplan (2000), however, emphasize the need for caution. They argue that there is no such thing as feminism which is free of asymmetrical power relations, and transnational feminism should not be celebrated as such.

While recognizing the importance of diversity between women, some postcolonial feminists have moved on to focus their attention more directly on developing feminist frameworks that build solidarity between women across difference. This again takes us beyond some of the earlier approaches to understanding the position of women which tended to either emphasize universalism or to collapse into difference.

## Conclusion

### *Race, ethnicity and feminism: the limitations of change*

As discussed at length in this chapter, over the past twenty years the study of race and ethnicity has been transformed through black feminist challenges, through postmodernism and shifts in disciplines such as ethnic and racial studies and women's studies. However, despite this success there are still some problems in suggesting that race and ethnicity now take centre stage on feminist agendas. While it can be argued that white feminists now take issues of race seriously, they still have a tendency to regard race as a secondary form of analysis to gender. For example, while undergraduate curricula in gender studies may include a focus on the intersection of race and gender, race is often subsumed under the main focus of gender. This can be illustrated by the position of race in many texts on feminism and gender. Thus, it is questionable as to how much race is really incorporated into the feminist agenda.

The same argument could be applied to the position of black women in the feminist canon. For example, while black feminists have critiqued and changed the white feminism of the past, are they viewed equally within the feminist canon with white women? To use the example of texts on feminism, mainstream feminist texts often only include one or two 'token' black women as contributors. When black women are included in such texts they are rarely incorporated into main sections of the text, for example, on the history and development of feminism (see Reed, 2006). They are instead normally confined to sections about women viewed as 'different' i.e. black women, lesbian feminisms (for example, Humm, 1992). As Afshar and Maynard (2000) state, while there has been a prolific and vibrant contribution by black and third world women to feminist debates, too often their position is delineated in terms of differing from a norm that is western and usually Anglophone. According to them, the global dominance of western feminism has meant that its views on women's issues has tended to be very narrowly defined (Afshar and Maynard, 2000: 809). As discussed throughout this chapter, this is something that is changing over time, as the feminist agenda has become more open to change through challenges from black feminists and others. Nevertheless, issues of race continue to remain on the sidelines of the feminist 'canon' and have yet to be given a more central place within it. Of course, it is important here not to suggest that issues of race and the position of black feminists should become 'mainstreamed' into feminist texts. While it is important to make sure that black feminists are not sidelined by existing feminism but centred in key debates, it is also important to make sure that black feminist voices don't just become subsumed by existing feminism. As well as being centred in feminist debates, black feminist voices must also continue to be heard in separation from other feminist debates, particularly when telling the history of exclusion.

The current relationship then between race, ethnicity and feminism, is a complex one. On the one hand the white universalizing feminism of old has given way to a newer version of feminism, at the heart of which is the concept of diversity. Black feminist critiques have been the catalyst for such changes. This transformation has been further supported by shifts in disciplines such as ethnic and racial studies and women's studies. In recent years these shifts have sparked a proliferation of new work in the area of race, ethnicity and feminism – some of which has been discussed in this chapter. This heralds a remarkable transformation in the feminist study of race and ethnicity. However, as discussed in this chapter a note of caution must be applied here. Despite significant changes in the study of race and ethnicity, in texts and curricula on gender and race, gender is still identified as the primary and most important variable of analysis. Thus, while there have been great advances in the study of race and ethnicity in feminism, a more careful inclusion of the concepts into a feminist agenda needs to be further developed and supported.

## Further reading

C. Alexander (2000) *The Asian Gang: Ethnicity, Identity and Masculinity*, Oxford, Berg
This is an excellent research monograph which explores issues of race, ethnicity, identity and masculinity. It is based on a lively and engaging ethnographic study with a group of young Bangladeshi men in South London.

L. Back and J. Solomos (2000) (eds) *Theories of Race and Racism: A Reader*, London, Routledge
This is a really useful text in ethnic and racial studies. It gives a solid background to debates on race and racism. It also includes an excellent collection of articles on race and feminism.

P. Hill-Collins (2000) *Black Feminist Thought: Knowledge, Consciousness and the Politics of Empowerment,* London and New York, Routledge
This excellent book engages with both personal and collective issues relating to black feminist thought. It provides an interpretative framework for the exploration of black feminists working both inside and outside of academia.

H. Mirza (1997) (ed.) *Black British Feminism*, London, Routledge
This is an engaging text which includes an interesting and diverse set of articles on debates and themes in black British feminism. It is an essential text for newcomers to the area of race and feminism.

C. Mohanty (2003) *Feminism Without Borders*, Durham, NC, Duke University Press
This is a good collection of the work of Chandra Taplade Mohanty. It includes a focus on issues such as the politics of difference and solidarity, cross-national feminist practice and the link between feminist knowledge and social movements.

# CHAPTER SEVEN

# Sexuality

YVETTE TAYLOR

## Introduction

As Richardson (1997) has noted, the growth of interest in sexuality continues across disciplines, as sexuality studies moves from the academic margins to the 'respectable' academic mainstream (Weeks, 2003). It is no longer a specialist and often silenced area, but one capable of linking an array of issues, from the globalization of sex and sexual citizenship (Hennessy, 2000), to the proliferation of 'queer tendencies' (Roseneil, 2000b, 2002) versus the continual reinforcement of heterosexuality (Jackson, 1999c; Richardson, 1996b, 2000). Although concerns with sexuality are not new to feminist agendas the range and shape of such concerns shifts across time and place (Whelehan, 1995). Yet the feminist focus on issues of power and inequality remains. Other social divisions, such as 'race', class and age, which intersect with and re/create sexual and gender inequalities, are receiving new consideration (see Reed in this volume). New times require new attention. This is not to suggest necessarily a tension between 'past' feminist struggles and 'present' issues, but rather a continuation in the ways in which gender and sexuality are produced, lived in and experienced in changing times.

There have been many changes and developments in the study of sexuality over the last decade or so, and not all of these will be captured in this chapter. Instead, the chapter focuses on what are considered to be important, new and enduring issues. The first section explores the rise of queer theory. Queer theory now sets much of the agenda on sexuality studies, yet its dominance and agenda setting does not go unquestioned, as I will go on to discuss. The next section looks at the material, embodied and subjective aspects of sexuality across different social spaces, from home space to 'scene' space, from the nation state to a globalized sense of place. Within feminism, there is a political point to interrogating constructions of sexuality. The final part of the chapter focuses on 'sexual politics', and examines recent demands and 'successes' in the field of sexual citizenship.

# Not quite queer? Sexuality, gender and 'the rest'

## *The social construction of sexuality*

Feminist theorizing has, for a long time, sought to challenge essentialist assumptions about gender and sexuality, proposing that both are socially constructed rather than innate traits to be read off fixed, biological and 'sexed' bodies, either female or male. Such notions of gender mapping onto biological bodies continue to be widespread and continually reproduced (McKenna and Kessler, 2000). Within this model, sexuality is assumed to be what follows 'naturally' from two 'opposite sexed' bodies and as such, heterosexuality is foregrounded and naturalized in this fixing equation and same-sex desire is marginalized, if not medicalized and demonized (Weeks, 2003). Academic research and popular understandings may have moved on somewhat from late nineteenth century conceptualizations of homosexuals as medical anomalies, biological mistakes, incapable of adhering to the equation between sex-gender-sexuality, yet the assumption of such a relationship steadily endures (Braun and Wilkinson, 2005).

The (disputed) linkages between sexuality and gender, including ways of knowing, thinking and speaking about sexuality and the privileging of het-erosexuality, continue to be focal points of feminist research and resistance. Queer theorists tend to privilege sexuality, analytically separating it out from gender. This untying represents a continuation of earlier feminist debates fuelled by the work of Rubin (1984), but also extends prior to this in second wave notions of the prime causes of women's oppression, variously debated by socialist and radical feminists (McLaughlin, 2003; Richardson, 2006; see also Richardson in this volume).

Sexuality, and indeed gender, may have moved away from biological binaries and imperatives; understood, perhaps, as less driven by procreative hetero-sex and more by the endless possibilities afforded by 'new' 'queer tendencies' (Roseneil, 2000b). Within postmodern feminism and queer theory, sexuality and gender are considered to be fluid and multiple, rather than discoverable, singular or natural essences, and cannot be straightforwardly read from fixed bodies. Such 'queer' approaches to sexuality do not necessarily depart from well established feminist theories of the socially constructed nature of sexuality and, in this respect, cannot claim to be breaking new ground, newly disrupting and contesting biological determinism (Jackson, 2001, 2006). Nonetheless, where many queer and feminist approaches differ, respectively, is in the conceptualization and highlighting of sexual differences and diversities as providing more fluid possibilities, as against a focus on gender and sexual inequalities and the real material limit to 'transgressing' or 'performing' sexuality (Hennessey, 2006; Richardson et al., 2006) (see boxed example overleaf).

Queer theory points towards increasingly multiple, shifting and fragmented sexual and gender identifications currently in existence, seeking to undermine sexual categorization based upon a heterosexual/homosexual divide

---

**Example: *The Vagina Monologues***

Speaking of the *Vagina Monologues* Bell and Reverby (2005) highlight the tension between the celebration of the pleasure of the body versus the body politic and ask just whose pleasures, whose bodies, are made visible and political? The power of the production is said to come 'from its transgressive and carnivalesque public stance' bringing 'private' experiences onto a public stage (Haaken, 1998, quoted in Bell and Reverby, 2005: 433). However, a warning is issued against the essentializing discourses of a 'globalized feminism', where pleasure and politics are collapsed rather than connected, echoing 1970s women's health politics, whereby a universal notion of celebratory sisterhood was invoked. In exploring the experiences of young women in Hong Kong, Ho and Tsang (2005) continue this argument, highlighting the prevalence of Western medical language even within *The Vagina Monologues*, which potentially silences other ways of speaking and reclaiming 'other' bodies. 'Women' may share similar, yet very different bodies, while whiteness – like maleness – has often denoted and signified *the* body, reinforcing hierarchical, binary categories.

---

(Roseneil, 2000b; Eves, 2004). Queer seeks to destabilize the assumed links between sex-gender-sexuality and draws on the notion of 'performativity' as a way of understanding how sexuality and gender are 'done' (Butler, 1990, 1993). If we 'do' gender and sexuality as we inhabit the world around us, by wearing, thinking, speaking and desiring in certain ways, then the potentiality of doing these in different ways, detached from any kind of biological base, are theoretically, if not actually, possible. In focusing on 'non-normative' forms of identities and practices, from same-sex and bisexual desire to gender ambiguity, from drag to 'gender-corrective' surgery, queer seeks to challenge established ideas that people are born, feel and remain either female or male, act in masculine or feminine ways and are solely attracted to the opposite sex.

Increasingly, in popular culture there are representations of individuals whose gender identity does not match with their apparent genitals (for example, the films *Boys Don't Cry, The Crying Game*). While such depictions make clear the potential mismatch between sexed bodies and gender identities, they also often draw upon sexual and gender binaries, reinforcing the idea that there are only two, dichotomous sexes (Braun and Wilkinson, 2005). Jeffreys (2006), for example, examines the labelling of gender identity disorder as a construction created by the medical profession, which she argues normalizes the phenomenon of sex reassignment and, thus, the choice of either a distinctly 'male' or 'female' body. That is, as opposed to being grounds for acknowledging, if not accepting, infinite gender possibilities. Moreover, Jeffreys (2006) proposes that sex reassignment has social consequences for same-sex desire, a desire which is potentially 'fixed' in sex reassignment. Similarly, Wilson's (2002) research claims that 'true' transsexuals were expected to rapidly claim and consolidate a gender certainty, with no room for ambiguity. Such studies point to the gap between theorizing the instability of gender and sexuality, in contrast to its perpetual reinforcement in lived lives, questioning attempts at eliminating, even 'outlawing', gender (Bornstein, 1994; Wilson, 2002; see also Hines in this volume).

What is considered to be 'properly' masculine and feminine behaviour, dress and demeanour regulates and proscribes sexualities. Such regulation and constraint applies across gender and sexuality and, arguably, no one can completely stand outside these divisions and distinctions, no matter what their sexual or gender identity. Browne (2004), for example, notes the way in which butchness amongst lesbians has been equated with and, misrecognized as, maleness. Such biological determinism serves to make invisible a myriad of gender expressions and identities (Feinburg, 1993; Halberstam, 1998). The binary of homo/hetero-sexuality is, then, reinforced in everyday social interactions and practices, assumed to be easily discoverable and obvious, yet in need of constant regulation and policing. Instability itself may well provoke a desire to fix and clarify the borders of woman/man. This is also revealed in Browne's (2004) research where lesbians, as gender ambiguous women, were a threatening presence in women only (female toilet) space. Reactions against their presence served to distance lesbians away from the category of 'real' woman, bolstering the notion of dichotomous sexes. If such a binary is essentially an illusion, yet a rigorously enforced material reality, how best to challenge the condemnation of certain identities and the everyday structuring of sexuality? This question has been debated amongst feminist and queer writers, who often differ in their conceptualization of gender and sexuality.

## Feminist and/or queer?

The 'future imaginings' (Butler, 1993) of queer theory may well lay in its ability to investigate 'all normative and non-normative acts, identities, desires, perceptions, and possibilities, for those not even (directly) related to gender and sexuality' (Giffney, 2004: 74). So to see queer theory as only concerned with cultural issues is, perhaps, an oversimplification of a body of work which seeks to broaden sexual theory beyond the spotlight on lesbian and gay identity, to a focus upon heterosexuality, its norms, regulatory power and institutional grip (Richardson et al., 2006). Nevertheless, the positioning of queer as anti-mainstream is itself problematic when considering the inclusions and exclusions such an agenda may foster.

This point is often emphasized by materialist feminist/sociological approaches, which previously held the foreground on theories of sexuality: a position that has increasingly been occupied by queer theory (Jeffreys, 1997b, 2003; Jackson, 1999b; Hennessy, 2000). A major criticism of queer theory from feminist approaches is that its social constructionist approach to sexualities is in fact not that new. A further criticism is a lack of attention in much queer theory to the material in negotiating (sexual) identities, as they intersect with other social identifications in everyday social life such as, for example, gender, race and class. The material has, indeed, often been absent from an overly cultural, and textual based queer agenda, where the main queered disciplines, as Seidman (1995) mentions, are those in the arts and humanities rather than in the social sciences. In taking sexuality as its primary focus, often via cultural texts rather than through empirical studies, queer theory has been accused of singling and separating out sexuality as the significant, disruptive and potential source of anti-mainstream subversions (Jackson, 1999b; Hennessy, 2000).

The cultural valorization of queer in popular culture, fashion, magazines and television is taken by Roseneil (2000b) as evidence of the 'aspirational status of queer', a new queer moment of undoing and unfixing gender and sexual identities. The ways that appearance is commodified has long been a feminist concern (Skeggs, 1997, 2004; see also Holliday in this volume). The 'latest fashion' is about more than choice alone, and queer debates on sexuality, lifestyles and appearances perhaps serve to simply recast old issues in new clothes, discarding and ignoring much feminist research on the interrelation between consumer 'choice' and capitalist and patriarchal power structures (Fraser, 1999).

## Sexuality, appearance and lifestyle

To the discontent of many feminists, theories of sexual identity are increasingly preoccupied with the (queer) subject of desire, rather than with material needs and constraints, representing a separation between gender and sexuality (Hennessy, 2000). The queer emphasis on identities as 'performative significations' rarely takes account of the material distribution of opportunities for such self-fashioning (Taylor, 2005a). Queerness may in fact only be accessible to those materially able to occupy the position, i.e. be seen as queer, in contrast to those excluded from both heterosexual privilege and the circles of the fashionably queer, 'lesbian chic' (Hennessy, 2000). Clearly, queer is not really for everyone, with the ability to be read as queer dependent upon displaying the correct style and inhabiting the appropriate space (Skeggs, 1999, 2001).

In 'Classing Queer' Fraser (1999) argues that queer's stance on visibility and recognition further marks a connection between identity and aesthetics, whereby queer becomes a brand name, an identity project assuming the form of aesthetic, consumer based lifestyles (see also Featherstone, 1991; Hennessy, 1995). In a UK lesbian lifestyle magazine ('Lesbians: Loaded and Loving It', *DIVA*, February 2005), lesbians were declared to be the 'new gay men', equally capable of matching gay men's income and spending power. This was followed by press attention in the UK mainstream broadsheet, *The Guardian*, which failed to question such middle-classification of lesbians and instead pointed out the historical lineage of lesbians' middle, even upper-class, backgrounds. While Binnie (2004) challenges the 'myth of the pink economy', arguing that it compounds the idea of a 'special', even privileged, group who can more than afford their 'rights', much feminist research continues to emphasize the gendering of finances, pink or otherwise. The politics of visibility, based around consumption and proliferating 'McPink' lifestyle options, is both gendered and classed (Fraser, 1999).

There are many aspects of popular culture that deal with issues of relationships, intimacy and identity (see Holliday in this volume). Whelehan (2004) claims that 'choice' 'control' and 'empowerment' are used seductively: young women, she argues, face a burden of 'having it all' whereby having it all – good career and good sex – becomes an imperative rather than a choice. Pick 'n' mix relationships, and 'identity umbrellas' become necessities in building an experienced, endlessly adaptable and refashioned self, and multisexualism becomes another sought after and purchasable commodity (Petchesky, 2000). For example, 'lesbian chic' is apparent and celebrated in the US series *The L Word* and the UK series *Sugar Rush*. Nonetheless, multiplicity does not translate into equality and such choices are not equally available or validated on the (sexual) market.

The body, from a queer perspective, is seen to bestow a political value (Butler, 1993). But within this model are important ramifications for escalating inequality, given that appearance can be another signifier upon which to denigrate working-class bodies and tastes, in which they (again) become 'flawed consumers' who cannot pay and display in 'proper', 'tasteful' ways (Skeggs, 1999, 2001). Identity constructed via consumption of cultural goods, may mark the self as tasteful, authentic and thus entitled (for example, to occupy queer space), or it may exclude and mark as wrong, unentitled and unauthentic (Taylor, 2007a, 2007b). In such ways, sexuality *and* class are written on the body and cannot easily be discarded or refashioned at will: not so much performative subversions as entrenched material dispositions – signs to be read, understood (and misunderstood) by those in 'the know', those with the social, cultural and economic resources to decode and decipher – and even degrade – these appearances. (See also Woodward in this volume.)

## Sexuality, femininity and class

Class has been particularly absent from queer theories and, it can be argued, trailing off sociological agendas (Skeggs, 1997; Crompton et al., 2000). Recent feminist work, however, has put class back on the agenda, teasing out the interconnections between class, gender and sexuality (Adkins and Skeggs, 2004). Skeggs' (1997) work on working-class heterosexual women revealed their positioning as 'wrong', as inhabiting an 'excessively' sexual femininity. For example, in the UK there is an increasing concern about 'teen mums' given the country's standing in Western European teenage pregnancy rates, and young women are often solely examined through this lens (Clavering, 2004). Romanticized representations that seek to reaffirm traditional femininity (Lawler, 2000) exist alongside representations which problematize and pathologize women's sexual behaviour and appearance in public, especially leisure space, and their uptake of a 'laddish' drinking culture, as 'unfeminine' (Harris, 2004a). Here, there is a classed polarization between new celebratory (white and middle-class) femininities and sorrowful, pitiful and excessive working-class sexuality, embodied in the pathological representations of the 'teen mum' (Carabine, 2004; Kidger, 2005). Conceptualizations of sexuality are also racialized, and black women have also been historically depicted as promiscuous and in need of control (Collins, 1996; hooks, 1996). Celebrations and denigrations of 'new' femininity may be challenged and resisted by the realization that gender, 'race', class and sexual inequalities remain embedded within economic and social structures, something that materialist feminist – rather than queer – approaches, have highlighted (Jackson, 1999b). Such contentions about inequality lie alongside debates on the supposed transformation of intimacy.

## The 'transformation of intimacy'?

In posing the question 'Young, Free and Single?', Heath and Cleaver (2003) introduce a series of debates and controversies, which point to people choosing to live the way they want to live. For example, choosing to create equal, what Giddens (1992) calls 'pure', relationships that are mutually entered into and exited from, breaks down traditional gendered obligations and inequalities. The possibility of sex without reproduction paves the way, in Giddens' (1992) view, for an increased 'plasticity' of sexuality. He defines plastic sexuality as 'decentred sexuality, freed from the needs of reproduction' (Giddens, 1992:2). Such a liberalization of sexuality supposedly allows for the pursuit of sexual possibilities and postmodern identities, as the (sexual) self becomes a *reflexive project*. Lesbians are represented as exemplars of the 'pure relationship', whereby 'sameness', defined as shared gender, becomes an equalizing, transformative force (Giddens, 1992; Dunne, 1997). Yet in privileging accounts of 'reciprocity' and 'accountability' in lesbian relationships, inequalities and challenges within lesbian relationships are smoothed over (Weeks et al., 2001).

Much feminist research argues that intimate relationships still do not transcend structural inequalities and so cannot be thought of as undergoing radical alterations (Jamieson, 1998). For example, in reviewing academic research on personal relationships, across Europe, North America, Australia and New Zealand, Jamieson's account suggests a rather more complex and conflicting tale of intimacy 'transformations'. As Jamieson notes, a major criticism against the work of Giddens is that much feminist scholarship on gender inequalities within intimate relations, and the ways these relate to wider societal inequalities, is sidelined.

While Giddens (1992) talks of sharing thoughts and feelings, a 'mutual disclosure' of talking and listening within intimate relationships, Jamieson argues that intimacy can only take on this form if participants can remove social barriers and transcend structural inequalities. Although she acknowledges that stories of equality and 'disclosing intimacy' may be popular, Jamieson suggests that these are 'easily matched by more conventional tales predicated on gender inequality and conventional heterosexual practices' (1998:134). Thus, reports of transformation of intimacy and increasing queer tendencies may be contrasted with the continued dominance of heterosexuality, as an 'invisible' and 'neutral' identity and practice, yet one which potentially consolidates gender inequalities, and structures 'other' outsider sexualities by their distance from its normative position.

In contrast, Roseneil (2000b, 2002) suggests an erosion of the heterosexual/homosexual binary is well under way, and that greater fluidity in 'postmodern', reflexive sexual identities actively undermines heterosexuality as an organizing principle of sexuality:

> we are currently witnessing a significant destabilization of the hetero/homo binary. The hierarchical relationship between the two sides of the binary, and its mapping onto an inside/out opposition, is undergoing intense challenge, and the normativity and naturalness of both heterosexuality and heterorelationality have come into question.
>
> (Roseneil, 2002:33)

This argument, put forward by Giddens (1992) and Roseneil (2000b, 2002) alike, takes as evidence liberal discourses of greater tolerance and recognition for lesbians and gays. However, as Johnson (2004) points out, 'liberalizing' discourses of sexuality and intimacy can co-exist with restrictive practices and, importantly, with an actual reproduction of the homosexual/heterosexual binary. Thus, while the social and political climate surrounding sexuality and intimacy may well have changed somewhat, the everyday experience of *doing* heterosexuality is founded through, and reinvents, rigid boundaries and borders. Both 'enlightened inclusiveness' and 'disgust' about homosexuality, voiced by Johnson's (2004) interviewees, served to highlight 'us' and 'them' approaches to sexuality, in often essentializing ways. This suggests that stories about 'fluidity', 'plasticity' and 'multiplicity' may, at best, be rather premature (Jamieson, 1998).

Heterosexuality relies upon – and creates – differences of gender and sex. However, other 'differences', such as social class, are also significant factors in heterosexual and same-sex relationships. Johnson and Lawler (2005) explore how class can become an obstacle to successful, heterosexual relationships and, in contrast with Giddens (1992), suggest that it is crucial in how people experience and enact intimacy. Within heterosexual relationships, class 'differences', unlike biological differences, are not viewed as positive, compatible forms of variation. Based on Johnson's PhD research in the UK with twenty-four heterosexual men and women between sixteen and eighty, Johnson and Lawler (2005) examined emotional, rather than purely material aspects of class, which affect how individuals feel about one another. They explore how people construct who are worthy compatibles, who know the 'right' things to do and say socially and conversationally, who can partake in 'proper' leisure practices, all the time being culturally tasteful as opposed to uneducated, brash and overly sexual ('tarty'). In considering aspects of classed in/compatibilities this research demonstrates that love really cannot conquer all. Although some working-class women could be the basis of desire and sexual attraction, they were most definitely not 'the type of women' to form lasting relationships with. While love may be thought of as deeply personal, once again the social organization of who we love, or feel 'at home' with, is revealed.

Seemingly individualistic 'pick and mix' relationships, unconfined to traditional family ties, may actually serve to reproduce other social divisions, and factors such as poverty and unemployment have an impact on 'picking and choosing'. In my research on self-identified working-class lesbians in the UK I found that, as well as material divisions within intimate relationships, there exist painful boundaries around class identifications, experiences and empathies, which can produce disassociations in intimacy (Taylor, 2007a). These points of intersection have not received sufficient attention in queer or feminist perspectives. Often theories 'abstract' class to the structures of capitalism, failing to consider how class is reproduced in individual, intimate lives (Taylor, 2005a). Class is often seen as challenged or compounded by globalization (Castells, 2000; Hennessey, 2000), yet it is the intersection between class and sexuality that highlights dual processes of 'fluidity' and 'fixing', as some people experience greater mobility under globalization whereas others are 'fixed' in localized space. This highlights a new spatialization of class and sexuality. Initial studies on sexuality and space mostly focused on (gay male) commercialized scene space. This has been challenged by feminist writers, such as Valentine (1993), who have highlighted the significance of both sexuality *and* gender in creating material inequalities and subjective tensions across various social spaces. From home space to scene space, from the nation state to a globalized sense of place, sexuality effects embodied and subjective positionings. The next section explores feminist investigations in researching sexuality and space.

## Sexuality, the self and the space in between

### *The globalization of sex*

Binnie (2004) unravels the links between sexuality, the nation state and globalization, critiquing previous studies for their *heteronormative* assumptions and attentions (while acknowledging existing feminist accounts such as Hennessy, 2000), and instead chooses to 'queer' globalization. Binnie (2004) and Hennessy (2000) link issues of sexuality and globalization with class inequalities, questioning the link between globalization and inevitable and progressive mobility, movement and liberation. Not only are there enduring citizenship and immigration restrictions, perhaps felt less by the monogamous, high earning couple, but the process of transnational movement is itself a highly gendered phenomenon. Who, for instance, can be a sex tourist? Binnie (2004) claims that tourism is a sexualized process, but there are inequalities within this. For instance, gay men's tourism is often problematized and pathologized as overtly and deviantly sexual, while feminists may want to question the benefits of sex tourism which rests upon the exploitation of women and children.

A global sense of place and a globalization of sexuality as dangerous and in need of containment – as well as a point of political activism and resistance – is evoked through the spread of HIV/AIDS and the formation of international HIV/AIDS campaigning groups (Chasin, 2000). Yet, in exploring the experiences of HIV positive women of colour in the US, Berger (2004) turns attention towards the often invisible and silenced 'new faces' of HIV; those living in wealthy western countries who have not been included in gay male activism around HIV/AIDS. Berger (2004) provides a timely insight into the increasing existence of HIV/AIDS in 'developed' countries, noting that the face of HIV/AIDS is increasingly a 'woman's face'. Her respondents were defined as 'deviant women', through their often disturbing experiences of drug use, sex work and, in many cases, childhood sexual abuse, where competing and cumulative hierarchies of race, class and gender were daily negotiated. State politics and practices actively excluded such women from obtaining material goods and services, given their exclusion from the category of 'respectable citizen'. Evidently socio-spatial sites (re)create entitlements, whereby sexed and gendered bodies are placed 'in', 'out' or somewhat in-between space (Valentine, 1999; Browne, 2004).

## Spatial entitlements

Bell and Valentine note the destabilizing potential of infiltrating straight space: 'By operating within a heterosexual index while at the same time being the "other" to heterosexuality, the "passing" lesbian challenges how spaces and identities become constructed and encoded, by being inside and outside simultaneously' (1995:156). While this challenges the notion of either being 'in' or 'out' of space, because space is understood as more complexly negotiated and people may at once be included and excluded, there are consequences in being unrecognisable and not everyone can 'pass'. While a queer take on this may highlight the subversive potential, the material consequences of disrupting the spatial relation between sexed bodies and 'proper' spaces needs to be recognized and challenges the 'playful' picture of gender transgression often associated with queer theory.

Nevertheless, commercialized 'scene spaces', often regarded as 'safe spaces' for lesbians and gay men, are becoming more tolerated, even promoted, as part of regenerating cities' cultural and economic capital, capable of generating global tourism (Casey, 2004). Binnie (2004:58) argues that 'without these commercialized territories, there would be far fewer possibilities for people to explore their sexuality and come-out' (Binnie, 2004:58). However, Bell and Binnie (2000) also note that lesbians and gay men on low incomes are excluded from such urban commercial scenes (Hennessy, 2000). In attempting to re-locate scene space within a class framework, Binnie (2000:173) argues that 'queer cosmopolitanism' is based on knowingness and sophistication: 'knowingness about the hippest destinations and urban sites for queer consumption becomes a self-reflective marker of their own sophistication...'. Similarly, Weston (1995) shows the connections between 'coming-out', developing a gay identity, and becoming a 'sophisticated' city dweller, which ultimately requires access, both culturally and economically, to these spaces. By including the experiences of classed individuals, the socio-economic inequalities operating in scene space can be grasped. These have been given attention in terms of the structuring of space, via commercialism, regeneration and 'sophistication', serving to produce upmarket and 'classy' scene space (Taylor, 2007a). But while the general 'structural' forces defining the trend of commodification have been well commented upon (Evans, 1993; Chasin, 2000; Hennessy, 2000), there has been little attempt to understand it from the perspective of the meaning that individual, classed, *women* find in commercialized scene spaces that are so often criticized.

In an earlier study of fifty-three working-class lesbians none of the respondents identified as queer, opting instead to define as 'lesbian', 'gay' or 'dyke'. Whilst not wanting to discount the difference between queer theory and the use of queer as an identity, this would seem to be significant (Taylor, 2007a). Respondents participated in scene space, felt excluded from it, criticized it as 'pretentious' and 'unreal' and, overall, expressed a sense of regret that despite its flaws something, some space, was 'better than nothing', given that they sought affirmation of their sexual identities. There was much criticism of scene space as 'pretentious', 'middle-class' and male, perhaps representing another aspect of what Casey (2004) calls the 'de-dyking' of queer space. Such responses combine critiques of 'queer cosmopolitanism' (Hennessy, 2000; Binnie, 2004) and problematize queers' focus on visibility via consumption and activism.

## Home spaces

Gabb (2005) charts another dimension of sexuality and space in focusing on lesbian mothers' management of their maternal-sexual identities. This is typically absent from studies into lesbian/queer spaces. The home, in Gabb's study, was found to be crucial in lesbians' consolidation of their (whole) selves, a space where lesbian and maternal identities could be reconciled. Nonetheless, Gabb's research, although highlighting that 'lesbians are everywhere', rather in special, queer spaces, at times glosses over the fact that, for some, home may be neither sweet nor safe. In examining the place of home in the lives of lone mothers, Head (2005) reveals the tensions between the home as a place of refuge, versus home as a place of isolation, generating a sense of captivity. While much research has focused on the demographics and employment patterns of lone mothers, Head's (2005) research represents an attempt to understand the everyday experiences of lone mothers on their own terms, whereby having an 'adequate' home was understood as an important part of being a good mother.

Clearly the home remains an important site in the lives of heterosexual and lesbian women. Robinson et al. (2004) unpack heterosexuality as an embodied, spatially located experience, examining its constitution in particular times and places, expanding upon studies which have covered the experience of lesbians and gays in everyday space (Valentine, 1993; Namaste, 1996). They consider space as neither rigidly straight or gay, but instead as constituted via a multiplicity of (hetero) sexualities, as well as by class, gender and age (Hockey, Meah and Robinson, 2007). In their analysis, home space is both a resource and a constraint. A place where knowledge is transmitted and resisted, even in the avoidance of explicit talk about sex, and gender and sexual identities 'performed', even as sexual practice is marked as illicit (see also Yip, 2004). Like Johnson and Lawler (2005), the significance of class within intimacy is foregrounded in creating a 'good match': 'Thus, while *differences* of gender are seen as integral to hegemonic heterosexuality, *similarity* of class or social background underpins what is seen as the purely emotional experience of "falling in love"' (Robinson et al., 2004: 427). Once again, the profoundly social nature of deeply personal emotions is highlighted.

## Sexual entitlement

Whilst some sexual stories are legitimated, easily circulated and heard, and the process of 'falling in love' affirmed and celebrated, others are not and are subject to criticism (Plummer, 1995; Jamieson, 1998). This happens in the denigration of queer sexuality, but it also profoundly applies to young 'teen' mothers, as Kidger (2005) makes apparent. Her analysis of young mothers in classroom sex education programmes highlights continued heterosexist moralizing discourses of 'improper' sexuality. In being encouraged to talk about risk, danger and poverty, young mothers in schools are often discouraged from discussing positive and pleasurable aspects of their sexualities, and in doing so, redeem themselves as 'good citizens'. This seems not so much of a queer celebration of choice and desire, but rather a restriction and reinforcement of a morally worthy female identity, via an official monitoring of the 'correct' ways of telling their sexual stories.

In her investigation of lifestyle magazines, McRobbie (1996) argues that contemporary femininity and masculinity are being reappraised with representations of sexuality now challenging traditional gendered boundaries of acceptance. Tyler (2004) claims such 'resources' bring managerial imperatives, such as efficiency and effectiveness, which must be incorporated into the self management of sexuality. With pre-nuptial contracts laying out joint financial relations, should couples now declare contractually how often they can reasonably expect to have sex? (Collinson, 1999 in Tyler, 2004). Tyler (2004) claims that the focus on 'good sex' deflects attention away from gendered inequalities, such as women's continued familial dependence and exploitation in family and work realms, potentially separating out interconnections between sexuality, gender and the household as emphasized in feminist research (Jamieson, 1998; see also Jackson in this volume).

The enterprising, self-improving self, as a product of neo-liberalism, is fundamentally classed, erasing structural explanations of inequalities and power with individualistic psychological ones (Hey, 2003; Walkerdine, 2003). In 'new' (sexual) times, this individualism ostensibly opens up 'new choices' and while this positions some women with agentic drive, carriers of a new middle-class individuality, others are 'fixed' in this process as simply unable to make the correct 'choices'. Rich (2005) explores how young women negotiate structured gender dynamics, while constructing a neo-liberal narrative of gender inequality as a thing of the past (see also Ringrose and Epstein in this volume), conflicting with their own (classed) sense of entitlement. Discourses of entitlement are both class and gendered. Oriel (2005), for example, vividly highlights the potential conflict between men's demands for sexual pleasure and women's rights against sexual exploitation, coercion and objectification (Klugman, 2000; WHO, 2003). The 'rights' of different sexualities can also be questioned, as lesbians and gays continue to make demands for inclusion into mainstreamed human rights agendas. This may not be regarded as a collective, equal and liberalizing 'coming out' but, rather, one which potentially perpetuates exclusions.

## Left of centre? The politics of sexuality

### *Feminist politics*

A key feature of feminist agendas is to link understandings of sexual and gender inequalities with political change. Yet what constitutes political activism and change is highly debated within feminism (McLaughlin, 2003). The queer emphasis on the politics of transgression, as a playful subversion of restricted gender and sexual identities and practices, produces an uneasiness amongst those who continue to highlight that hierarchies cannot be simply overturned by playfulness, especially when real harms and exploitations are apparent in, for example, pornography and prostitution. Such disputes resonate with and continue from the 'Sex Wars' debates of the 1980s, which manifested in divisions between those feminists who believed that analyses of sexuality and gender had to be concerned with issues of power, and those who sought to highlight sexual pleasure (Jackson and Scott, 1996). Issues of what is simply difference and diversity rather than inequality and oppression continue to be significant points of debate, further problematizing the link between person-hood, identity and politics, as one's notion of liberation may be another's idea of injustice.

Binnie (2004), following feminist writers such as Chasin (2000) and Hennessy (2000), problematizes the idea of a universal gay rights discourse, discussed in the context of international campaigning groups. The exclusion of working-class queers (and various de-legitimized heterosexualities may also be added here) who cannot be rightfully included in the nation state is demonstrated. This highlights Fraser's (1999) concerns about queer activism, which relies so heavily upon 'outness', voice and recognition, with no sense of the multiple misrecognitions suffered by those who are excluded from this political space and identity (Lawler, 2002). This is echoed more generally in feminist scepticism about the political – as well as theoretical – priorities of queer agendas. The idea of a universal (western) closet, and a universal movement/ desire to be 'out' of 'the closet', is explored and challenged. For so many this concept has little applicability or relevance. Nonetheless, there is increased, formalized and legitimized visibility, as lesbian and gay issues impact upon state agendas and policies. One example of this is civil partnerships.

## Civil partnerships

There has been increasing recognition of same-sex relationships across Western Europe and elsewhere, such as Canada, Australia and New Zealand, with the introduction of the Civil Partnership Act in the UK (December 2005) effectively mainstreaming same-sex rights and apparently 'mirroring' heterosexual marriage. With this Act has come new sexual stories, taking up much coverage in the lesbian and gay press and mainstream international media. Commentaries and controversies run from the celebration of (monogamous) coupledom that has been extended to same-sex partners, to partial mockery and ironic humour, to outright condemnation, where the featuring of 'homosexuality' as a 'sin' is endlessly repeated. While some evangelical Christian groups have disapproved of civil partnerships on the grounds that they supposedly parody and make a of mockery of traditional heterosexual marriage, others (including feminist and queer writers) question why lesbians and gays would want to adopt the conservative values of marriage in the first place, given that it places sexuality in its 'proper' place: within the private, monogamous, (tax-paying, dual-income) household (Richardson, 2004). There have been extensive feminist critiques of marriage as an institution which perpetuates gender and sexual inequalities (Jackson, 1999c; Maushart, 2001; see also Jackson in this volume), yet the Civil Partnership Act, in transferring this model of monogamous coupledom over to same-sex relationships, perhaps fails to 'un-do' hierarchies of intimacy, possibly aggravating the distinction between un/acceptable lifestyles.

Thus, entering a civil partnership may not constitute a queer erosion of the traditional version of coupledom. However, we might still ask whether the proliferation of commercial services, from 'bride and bride' attire to a 'gay' wedding cake represent what Roseneil (2000b) describes as the cultural valorising of the queer in popular culture, fashion and magazines. It is important to remember who is excluded from such 'aspirational' markers of queerness – just as not all heterosexualities are equally validated or legitimized (Head, 2005; Kidger, 2005). For example, for many working-class lesbians and gays, civil partnerships may mean little at best, given that extensions of pension rights are less likely to apply. Instead, the implications and consequences of civil partnerships may actually be restrictive and penalizing. When either partner in a same-sex couple applies for a means-tested state benefit, the income of both partners will be taken into account. This represents a change, as before such legislation same-sex couples were invisible to means testing; now they are not and this applies whether same-sex couples have a registered civil partnership or not. This has the air of suspicion and unease, potentially forcing a 'coming out' to local authorities in the uptake of services and a monitoring of who lives – and sleeps – where. Nonetheless, others point to the benefits which will apply once same-sex relationships are incorporated into a similar legalized framework. For example, domestic violence in same-sex couples may well receive more attention as couples can apply for a domestic interdict to ban a violent partner from the home they both live in. This gives voice and potential recourse to victims experiencing violence in same-sex relationships, an area which is currently under-researched (Lobel, 1986; Ohms, 2002).

Many commentators have revealed the ambiguities, tensions and contradictions in pressing for lesbian and gay rights within the existing heteronormative social order (Rahman, 2000, 2004; Brickell, 2001). Following Smith's (1997) distinction between 'good homosexuals' and 'dangerous queers', Richardson (2004; 2005a) points to the potential to further recreate a binary between good (long-term, monogamous, middle-class) and bad (non-monogamous, working-class) homosexuals. Viewing sexuality as intersecting with other social inequalities offers an understanding of who can, and cannot, occupy the category of sexual citizenship – or, indeed, citizenship more generally. While lesbian and gay activist groups have demanded, and continue to demand, equal rights, they have often done so, for pragmatic reasons perhaps, on a platform of essentializing, homogenizing discourses (Rahman, 2000, 2004). In prioritizing sexuality as the focal point of resistance, other social inequalities affecting lesbians and gays have often been sidelined. While the sectioning off of identity categories, against a notion of universal (white, middle-class) sisterhood proved divisive, yet necessary, to second wave feminism (Whelehan, 1995), the concept of intersectionality now allows for exploration of the relations between various social categories and experiences. Elsewhere I have explored working-class lesbians' political awareness and activism within a changing political climate that promotes notions of 'classless', yet in which classed conflict remains apparent (Taylor, 2005b, 2005c). In emphasizing the daily politicization of their lives, inequalities of class and sexuality in the sphere of citizenship are interconnected. Just as pro- and anti-repeal protesters in the UK's Section 28/2a debates, as potential and actual sexual citizens, were able to occupy and argue for social positions legitimated as 'normal' as 'respectable', this arguably continues in the Civil Partnership debates. Working-class lesbians have opinions and beliefs to express, especially around 'past' *and* present class, gender and sexual struggles, but rarely have these achieved political credibility; rarely were their concerns easily assimilable or respectably mainstream (Taylor, 2005c, 2007a).

## Conclusion

In this chapter, I have tried to point to the continual disruption and reinforcement of the linkages between sex-sexuality-gender, which many recent studies now demonstrate. While queer approaches tend to point to the fluidity and multiplicity of gender and sexuality in (post)modern times other, feminist, writers highlight the reinforcement of heterosexuality, not just as a sexual identity, but as a structuring, institutionalized force. To acknowledge the structuring presence of heterosexism, should not mask the plurality of – and variously de/legitimized – heterosexualities. The linkages between space, sexuality and gender has typically been researched in relation to non-normative genders and sexualities, yet it is important to remember that heterosexuality is also spatialized and embodied, as is the lived intersection of gender, sexuality, 'race' and class. Feminism has long argued for a politics of sexuality. Taking account of the trend of neo-liberalism in western countries means unpacking the discourses of individualism and entitlement to sexual citizenship, where sexuality becomes a matter of human rights. In taking account of class and 'race', the divisions within, without and beyond western feminist agendas can be made more explicit, serving to resist a globalized feminism of sexuality (Bell and Reverby, 2005).

## Further reading

J. Binnie (2004) *The Globalization of Sexuality*, London, Sage
This book unpicks the links between sexuality, the nation state and globalization. It asks important questions. Why have mainstream sociological and cultural studies (even lesbian and gay studies) ignored questions of sexuality in relation to globalization? What are the links between sexuality, national and global concerns? Binnie's analysis, while thorough, lacks empirical detail and sometimes foregrounds sexuality at the expense of detailed attention towards gender.

A. Chasin (2000) *Selling Out: The Gay And Lesbian Movement Goes To Market*, Basingstoke, Palgrave
This text uncovers the linkage between the development of the 'lesbian and gay movement' in the US and the growth of lesbian and gay 'niche markets'. Chasin suggests that lesbians and gays are integrated, even assimilated, as consumers rather than as citizens, with money representing the prerequisite for social inclusion.

J. Hockey, A. Meah, and V. Robinson (2007) *Mundane Heterosexualities: From Theory to Practices*, Basingstoke, Palgrave Macmillan
This text provides a useful overview of feminist theorizing around heterosexuality. Based on the first major empirical study of heterosexuality across the generations in the UK, it covers key issues in relation to gender and sexuality, including the body, masculinity, emotions and intimacy.

L. Jamieson (1998) *Intimacy: Personal Relationships in Modern Societies*, Cambridge, Polity Press
In reviewing research on personal relationships, across Europe, North America, Australia and New Zealand, this book suggests a rather more complex account of intimacy 'transformations' than that suggested by Giddens (1992). Drawing on empirically based feminist research, Jamieson focuses on relationships between parents and children, families, sexual partners, couples and friends.

J. Weeks (2003) *Sexuality*, London, Routledge
This 2nd edition discusses the construction and regulation of sexuality, as well as points of struggle and resistance. It examines how talking about sex, using terminology to describe and categorize sexual pleasures, dangers and identities is deeply problematic. While Weeks continues the contributions of many feminist scholars, their absence is rather surprising.

# SECTION THREE

## INSTITUTIONS

This section looks at social institutions that are key to understanding gender in contemporary societies. The first of these is 'the family'. In Chapter 8, **Families, Domesticity and Intimacy: Changing Relationships in Changing Times**, the concept of 'the family' is discussed and feminist theories of the family are explored. Feminists have identified the development of the nuclear family as key to understanding inequalities between women and men. This chapter explains why this is the case and asks whether this might be changing with the increasing diversity of family forms existing today. This is often referred to as the idea of 'postmodern families'. The next chapter in this section, **Gender and Schooling: Contemporary Issues in Gender Equality and Educational Achievement**, focuses on gender and education. It examines how issues of educational equality and achievement are related to gender as well as to issues of class, race, ethnicity, religion, citizenship and location. A key issue is the discourse of 'girl power' and the rise of the 'successful girl' contrasted with the discourse of 'failing boys', which has come to dominate debates on gender and education. The chapter explores these debates and shows why claiming a 'feminist victory' is far too simplistic and premature. Educational opportunities and experiences shape a person's life in numerous ways, including their position in the labour market. In Chapter 10, **Gender and Work**, women's and men's experiences of work, both paid and unpaid, is described, including the type and status of jobs women and men do; the financial rewards they receive and their relative contribution to unpaid work in the home. It examines different explanations for gender divisions in work and employment, and looks at full-time and part-time work; unemployment rates and the notion of work–life balance. Finally, it considers the claim that in the twenty-first century gendered patterns in work may be changing, with a shift away from the traditional breadwinner model.

# CHAPTER EIGHT

# Families, Domesticity and Intimacy: Changing Relationships in Changing Times

STEVI JACKSON

## Introduction

The early twenty-first century is a time of uncertainty and much public debate about the meaning and consequences of changes in family life. With falling rates of marriage and rising rates of divorce, families are seen as less stable, more fluid and more diverse, a diversity increased by the greater acceptability of alternative lifestyles from living alone to forming families based on gay and lesbian relationships. These trends are much debated: they are variously understood as heralding 'the end of patriarchalism' (Castells, 2004), the rise of 'postmodern families' (Stacey, 1996), a democratizing 'transformation of intimacy' (Giddens, 1992) or a shift from 'communities of need' to individualized 'elective affinities' (Beck and Beck-Gernsheim, 2002). However, there is a general agreement that new forms of family life are associated with shifts in relations between men and women. Historically families in most of the world have been in some sense patriarchal, dominated by men – and this dominance is now in question. How far it has been eroded is, however, disputed.

In this chapter I will map out this contested terrain, charting the major changes taking place in late modern family life and feminists' efforts to make sense of them. I will begin by exploring feminist engagements with 'the family', concentrating on the period since the 1970s and explain how and why the concept of 'the family' came to be seen as problematic. I will then move on to assess the state of family, and especially couple, relationships in the early 21st century in order to evaluate the claims currently being made about the trajectory of social and cultural change.

## Feminism and the family

Family relationships have historically been central to women's lives, but also a locus of major inequalities between women and men. In the late 1960s and early 1970s, second wave feminists identified 'the family' as a key site of women's subordination. Feminist concerns of the time reflected their location in the 'west' (a short-hand term denoting Western Europe and other wealthy nations dominated by those of European descent such as the US, Canada, Australia and New Zealand). Their critique was focused on a very particular family: the heterosexual couple of breadwinning husband and home-making wife with their dependent children. In the mid twentieth century, this was seen as the 'normal' family and, by many sociologists, as functionally adapted to the needs of advanced industrial societies (see for example Parsons, 1951). Even in the 1950s and 1960s, however, researchers began to expose the boredom and isolation felt by full-time housewives (Friedan, 1965; Gavron, 1966), the strains between 'two roles' experienced by women in paid work (Myrdal and Klein, 1956) and women's unhappiness with the lack of companionship in their marriages (Komarovsky, 1962). By the early 1970s sufficient evidence had accumulated to substantiate Jessie Bernard's claim that there 'are two marriages in every marital union' and that 'his...is better than hers' (Bernard, 1972, 1982: 14).

Feminist critiques gathered pace in the 1970s and into the 1980s, radically transforming approaches to family life. They highlighted previously hidden problems, such as domestic violence (Hanmer, 1978; Dobash and Dobash, 1980), and exposed more routine injustices, such as unequal divisions of labour and resources within families (Comer, 1974; Allen and Leonard Barker, 1976; Delphy, 1984). Increasing attention was also paid to marriage and families as heterosexual institutions, reinforcing both women's subordination and the marginalization of lesbian and gay lifestyles (Bunch, 1975; Rich, 1980; Wittig, 1992). For some, however, critique was tempered with a degree of ambivalence, the recognition that, whatever inequities are associated with family life, it is also frequently the source of women's most meaningful and supportive relationships. Middle-class feminist and gay activists who sought to escape the constraints of 'the family' were often insufficiently attuned to the benefits family relationships might provide for women who did not share their material and social privileges. Black feminists argued that families could be sites of resistance to, and protection from, racism rather than a source of oppression (hooks, 1981; Carby, 1982; Bhavnani and Coulson, 1986). They exposed the ethnocentric assumptions underpinning white feminists' emphasis on women's dependence in families when African American women and African Caribbean women in Britain were frequently the main family breadwinners and had little opportunity to be dependent housewives (Somerville, 2000). They highlighted the intersections between racism and sexism whereby black women were pathologized as irresponsible single mothers and Asian women as 'passive victims' of overly 'controlling' extended families (Parmar, 1988: 199).

Feminists did, however, problematize and denaturalize 'the family', pointing out that what was deemed normal and 'natural' in western societies was culturally and historically specific. Soon some feminists began to question the concept of 'the family' (Barrett and McIntosh, 1982; Thorne, 1982), presaging a shift in the social sciences from the concept of 'the family' as a singular noun, to pluralizing it in order to emphasize the diversity of 'families' (Stacey, 1996) or treating it as an adjective, denoting varied 'family practices' (Morgan, 1996).

## Bringing the family into question

Some of the difficulties inherent in the concept of 'the family' are evident if we consider the multiple meanings it can have in everyday life. It can be used to refer to close relatives who live together or it can include wider kin, as when we say 'the whole family' attended a wedding or funeral. When we talk of a possession that has been 'in the family' for generations, we think of the family as existing through time, including long-dead forebears. When a couple talk of 'starting a family' they imply that a family comes into being with the arrival of children. Terms such as 'the typical family' may still conjure up a heteronormative image of mother, father and children, but a diversity of families – step-families, lone parent families, and lesbian and gay families – now populate the social landscape. Those living outside conventional heterosexual families, whether in lesbian or gay 'families of choice' (Weeks et al., 2001) or as single people, may regard networks of friends as 'family' (Weston, 1991; Roseneil and Budgeon, 2004). Feminist and other scholars have raised three interrelated objections to the concept of 'the family':

- it conceals inequalities within families;
- it is essentialist and universalist;
- it masks the diversity of family forms existing today.

### *Differences and inequalities*

Families are constituted through a complex set of relationships and practices; their individual members are differently located within them and a single family unit comprises multiple family lives. The term 'the family' can mask such differences. Feminists were particularly concerned with gender differences (Comer 1974; Allen and Leonard Barker, 1976; Delphy 1984), although some considered the subordinate position of children within families (Jackson 1982; Thorne, 1982). Throughout the 1970s and 1980s detailed feminist research uncovered economic inequalities within families produced by women's dependence on men suggesting, for example, that 'while sharing a common address, family members do not always share the same standard of living' (Graham, 1987:221). While this has become less of a focus with the decline of the male breadwinner family, inequalities persist and remain important in understanding the gendered consequences of socio-economic change. More recently feminists have given attention to the emotional and sexual aspects of heterosexual couple relationships (for example Langford, 1999) and have engaged critically with recent debates on the supposed late modern 'transformation of intimacy' (Giddens, 1992; Jamieson, 1999). They have also explored the possibility of forging alternative, more equitable domestic relationships (VanEvery, 1995; Dunne, 1999).

## Essentialism and universalism

To talk of 'the family' can give the impression of an essential, natural unit that exists outside society. Families are, however, embedded in wider patterns of social and economic relations which they are shaped by and which, conversely, they affect. For example, feminists drew attention to the essentialist assumption that women as wives and mothers were 'naturally' dependent on men, which historically justified their limited access to employment and low pay, which in turn reduced their economic opportunities and reinforced their dependence (Hartmann, 1976; Walby, 1986). Locating families in social context also entails recognizing the impact of class, race and nationality that shape experiences of family life, as well as cross-cultural and historical variations.

Feminist anthropologists were among the first to point out that there is no single entity that can be defined as 'the family' and compared across cultures. What we think of as 'a family' is a complex set of relationships and practices all of which can vary (see for example Edholm, 1982; Moore, 1988): there are differences in kinship, in who counts as related to whom; in who can marry whom; in what marriage entails; in how children are raised and by whom and in who does what work for which kin. While drawing attention to this variability, feminists also noted regularities – that all societies, albeit in diverse ways, had some means of ordering relations between women and men in terms of both divisions of labour and sexual and reproductive relationships (Rubin, 1975; Thorne, 1982). However, it is clear that 'the family' as a bounded unit of parents and children cannot be thought of as a trans-cultural phenomenon.

Of course, many of the societies documented by anthropologists have changed and are changing under the impact of imperialism and globalized capitalism, though variations persist (Therborn, 2004). In the west, too, family life has changed and continues to change. Family history is by no means as straightforward as was imagined by mid twentieth century sociologists – as a shift from extended to nuclear families brought about by industrialization. During the late twentieth century historians revealed that the extended family, though widespread in Eastern Europe and Asia, was never common in most of Western Europe. Moreover, European families varied by class, occupation and region, as well as over the life-cycle: 'there is not, nor ever has there been, a single family system' in the west (Anderson, 1980:14). Moreover, 'the family' did not always mean co-resident kin, but all those under the authority of a male head of household, whether kin or servants (Davidoff et al., 1999). Western families may have been diverse, but they were always patriarchal.

Recent changes are usually measured against a supposed 'traditional' family form where couples stayed married for life, where husbands worked and women presided over the home and cared for the children. But this 'traditional' family 'is not all that traditional' (Nicholson, 1997: 27). It emerged in western societies in the nineteenth century, was initially a middle-class phenomenon and only became widespread among the working classes after the Second World War (Stacey, 1996; Nicholson, 1997). It was the product of complex and gradual changes accompanying industrialization whereby most forms of production were removed from households and waged work – previously characteristic only of particular occupations (Davidoff et al., 1999) – became the norm. Among the rising bourgeoisie a new lifestyle developed based on a 'domestic ideology', which separated the male world of work and commerce from women's sphere in the home (Davidoff and Hall, 1987; Hall, 1992). This ideology subsequently spread to other classes, creating the ideal of a male 'family wage' sufficient to sustain a domesticated wife and children, which became the norm by the mid twentieth century. Even then, however, it was barely attainable among poorer sections of the working class (Stacey, 1996). And while, in the period from 1950 to 1970, a higher proportion of the western population were married than ever before, the male breadwinner model was already changing as more women were drawn into the paid labour force (Lewis, 2001). The 'traditional' family, then, was an historically short-lived product of particular social circumstances. As an idea, however, it retains a strong hold on the collective imagination of late modern societies and has left a legacy that still shapes the lives of many women today.

## *Diversity*

While diversity among families is not new, it became more apparent from the late 1970s leading to a more radical questioning of the concept of 'the family'. In the early 1980s, Michèle Barrett and Mary McIntosh (1982), noting that less than half the population then lived in households comprising married couples and children, argued that 'the family' was an ideological construct – but one with real effects. It marginalizes those living outside families, encourages us to expect our families to satisfy all our personal and emotional needs and acts as a perpetual excuse for the paucity of public services: 'It is as if the family has drawn comfort and security into itself and left the outside world bereft. As a bastion against a bleak society it has made that society bleak' (1982: 30). The view of 'the family' as a construct that conceals the diversity of families has since become widespread in the social sciences (see for example Bernardes, 1997), but without the critical edge of Barrett and McIntosh's analysis. Feminist opinion has changed too. Where Barrett and McIntosh hoped 'to transform not the family – but the society that needs it' (1982: 159), feminists are now more inclined to celebrate family diversity. For Judith Stacey, for example, a critique of traditional 'family values need not be anti-family': we should, she says, 'acknowledge and support the diversity of family patterns, preferences and relationships in which we actually live' (1996:51).

Two main sources of family diversity feature in accounts of contemporary social life:

- those based on cultural and ethnic differences;
- those associated with fluidity and change in families and the emergence of new lifestyles.

The prevailing image of the 'typical' family' is a white family, yet western societies are now increasingly ethnically diverse as a result of postcolonial patterns of migration. These varied cultures and their histories lead to differences in family formation. In Britain, women of African descent, like African-American women, are far more likely to head households as lone parents: 57 per cent of 'Black Caribbean' and 47 per cent of Black African families with children are headed by a lone parent (generally a mother); in both groups at least twice the proportion found among white families with children (ONS, 2006a: 25). British Asian families (Pakistani, Indian, Bangladeshi and Chinese), on the other hand, are the least likely to be headed by lone parents, for example, 85 per cent of Indian families with children were headed by a married couple (ONS, 2006a: 24–5).

---

**THE DISAPPEARING FAMILY?**
**British Households in 2005**

▨ 22% of households comprised (heterosexual) couples* with dependent children

▨ 6% comprised couples with non-dependent children. These included:
Married *and* cohabiting couples
Children living with both their own parents *and* in step families: 10% of all families with children were step-families

▨ 10% of households comprised lone parents:
7% had dependent children
3% had only non-dependent children

▨ 29% of households comprised childless couples, married and cohabiting

▨ 29% of households were occupied by people living alone, half of whom were past retirement age.

▨ 1% of households comprised more than one family

▨ 3% of households contained two or more unrelated adults

* The official statistics do not include lesbian and gay couples who would be included in other categories.

Source : ONS, 2006a, Table 2.2 p. 22.

The most telling evidence used to back the claim that there is no normal or typical family is that only a minority of households conform to the standard nuclear family of man, wife and children. Even in 1971, the high point of early marriage and childbearing, only 35 per cent of British households comprised couples with dependent children; by 2005 the proportion had fallen to 22 per cent, a proportion diverse in its composition as a result of rising rates of cohabitation and divorce along with patterns of remarriage and cohabitation after divorce.

These figures can give the impression that family life is in terminal decline, but this is not the whole picture. In the first place, families are not static entities: they change over the life course. Many childless couples will have children in the future or have had children who have grown up and left home; many of those living alone may form couples and families in the future or will have done so in the past. Even if everyone married and there were no divorce or untimely death each one of us would only live in a complete nuclear family household at particular phases of our lives. Moreover, the statistics can tell a different story: looked at from the point of view of people in households (rather than households themselves) and using a more inclusive definition of families, the majority of people in Britain – 83 per cent in 2005 – could be said to live within family-style relationships, in households founded either on heterosexual couples or on parent–child ties or on both. This figure has changed little since 1971, when 85 per cent lived in such households.

---

**FAMILIES RE-DISCOVERED**
**British People in Households in 2005**

▨  25% of the population lived in childless heterosexual couples

▨  46% lived in units of couples with children (including independent and dependent children and step-children)

▨  12% lived in lone-parent households

▨  83%, therefore, lived in heterosexual couples and/or in parent–child relationships

▨  The remaining 17% lived alone (12%) or in 'other households' (5%)

*Source:* ONS, 2006a, derived from Table 2.3 p. 23.

---

The above figures, then, suggest that family life has not ended, but is becoming more complex and varied with the increasing fluidity in adult relationship formation and dissolution. Furthermore, we need to look beyond households to grasp the meanings and practices of family life today.

## Beyond households

In cataloguing variations in domestic living arrangements, it is easy to forget that family ties are not confined within household boundaries: for example, my mother, my sister and I all live in different cities, but we still count each other as family; divorced parents frequently maintain contact with children who live with their ex-spouses (Smart, 1999; Smart and Neale, 1999); some couples in ongoing relationships live apart either through choice or through the constraints of their respective careers (Holmes, 2004a; Levin, 2004); kin, especially grandparents, are among the main providers of child care for working mothers (Lewis, 2001). Family relationships, carrying with them emotional attachments and social obligations, cut across the boundaries of households (Finch and Mason, 1993; Morgan, 1996; Mason, 2004; Smart and Shipman, 2004).

With increased geographical mobility in our globalized world such ties are not only local or even national ones and kin divided by distance may retain a sense of attachment across countries and continents. For example, the importance of kinship documented among families of Pakistani descent in the UK, extends, even after several generations, to kin remaining in Pakistan (Afshar, 1989; Mason, 2004; Smart and Shipman, 2004). More temporary migrants also keep up family connections: for example, a woman from the Philippines might leave children with relatives while working to support them in Saudi Arabia, Japan or Taiwan (Cheng, 2003; Lan, 2003). For more affluent transnational families, ease of international travel and new communications technologies make it possible to maintain meaningful relationships across long distances; a child living in Texas can, through the use of a web-cam, maintain frequent contact with his British grandmother in Yorkshire (Fairbank, 2003).

While it is wise to be cautious about using the concept of '*the* family', we should not lose sight of the continued salience of families in most people's lives. Moreover, too much emphasis on family diversity can conceal important and persistent regularities. Although cohabitation is emerging as an alternative to formal marriage and some countries recognize lesbian and gay partnership, the extent to which heterosexual family relationships remain normative should not be underestimated, nor should the continued gender inequalities associated with institutionalized heterosexuality. In what follows, I will focus on two main issues:

- The extent to which feminist critiques of inequalities between women and men in domestic partnerships (marriage and cohabitation) remain relevant.
- How feminists should make sense of the increasing fluidity and diversity of family life associated in recent debates with the idea of 'postmodern' families.

## Family finances and domestic work

Families are founded on bonds of economic support and cooperation, which also entail economic dependence and unequal divisions of labour. I will explore these issues, and how they shape heterosexual relations, before going on to consider more personal aspects of relationships between women and men in couples and households. Along the way I will also consider the extent to which alternative lifestyles challenge conventional heterosexual arrangements.

With the rise in the number of female-headed households and the increasing participation of women in the labour market, only a minority of households in most of the western world are now wholly dependent on a male breadwinner. From the 1950s to the 1970s, most married men in Britain and the US were their families' sole breadwinners; from the 1980s two earners became the norm (Irwin, 1999; Castells, 2004). In western countries, along with some richer East Asian nations, such as Japan, the gap between men's and women's 'economic activity rates' is closing (see Castells, 2004, tables 4.13 and 4.14 pp. 219–20). It should be noted, though, that there are local variations within the world's regions: fewer women are in paid work in South Korea than in neighbouring Japan (Castells, 2004); in the European Union Sweden and Denmark have the highest rates of women's employment, while Malta has the lowest (ONS, 2006a). There are also variations within countries. In the UK, for example, women with children are more often in paid work if they are living with an employed partner and have educational qualifications (ONS, 2006a); among married or partnered women, white and African Caribbean women are far more likely to take paid work than women of Pakistani or Bangladeshi descent (Dex, 1999).

The general rise in women's employment reflects a growing demand for women's labour and also women's increasing availability for work, as they take less time out of employment for child rearing. Birth rates have been declining in wealthy countries and women now usually return to work after the birth of a child – over two-thirds before their child's first birthday (Dex, 1999); in 2004 the employment rate for married and cohabiting mothers was 71 per cent, only a little lower than the rate for women without dependent children, 73 per cent of whom were employed (ONS, 2006a). The dictates of the 'flexible economy' make income less secure, undermining men's ability to earn a reliable 'family wage' and creating a growing need for two incomes to support a family with children (Stacey, 1996; Irwin, 1999). Most women, however, still earn less than men – a global phenomenon – and are disproportionately employed part-time. Among British couples with dependent children it is usual for women to work shorter hours when their children are under five years old – and a substantial minority still give up work at this stage of their lives (see Lewis, 2001; Irwin, 2005). The typical pattern, then, is not a move from a single male breadwinner to dual breadwinners, but, as Jane Lewis (2001) suggests, to a one and a half breadwinner model of family life. (See also Irving in this volume.)

Where men earn more than their partners they potentially have more control over income, though they can, of course, cede a degree of control to their partners. A number of studies conducted in the 1980s suggested that resources in households were not shared equitably: women contributed a higher proportion of their (smaller) earnings to household expenditure and had less than men to spend on themselves, so that men often enjoyed a higher standard of living than their partners and children (see for example Graham, 1987; Wilson, 1987; Pahl, 1990). As more women gained employment and bank accounts became the norm for all but the poorest households, the complexity and diversity of family financial arrangements increased (Vogler and Pahl, 1993). Jane Lewis's (2001) study indicates that there has been some change in both attitudes and practices. Among the older couples in her sample, the idea of the male breadwinner still prevailed; although most of the women had worked, their earnings were seen as 'pin money'. The younger couples had a much more 'joint' approach to finances, but also placed more importance on both partners having money to call their own. The key issue for these couples was personal spending money and 'where the line was drawn between "own" and "joint" money' (Lewis, 2001:165). While most wanted this to be 'fair', this was not always achieved. For example, taking two couples where women earned far less than their partners, in one precisely equal personal spending was achieved by the man paying much more into the joint account; in the other both paid equally into the joint account so that the woman had far less for herself (Lewis, 2001).

Carolyn Vogler (1998) suggests that women are most able to exert real control over money where they contribute as much as their partners and the couple espouse an egalitarian ideal of equal financial provisioning (Vogler, 1998). Not surprisingly, greater commitment to financial equity has been found in households explicitly committed to anti-sexist living arrangements (VanEvery, 1995) and among lesbian and gay households (Dunne, 1999; Weeks et al., 2001). It is notable, though, that households' financial arrangements 'vary between equality and male power' (VanEvery, 1995:116) – that highly paid women do not turn their earning capacity into power *over* their partners.

Families' financial arrangements continue to be influenced by the assumption that it is women, as wives or partners and mothers, who take primary responsibility for caring for home and children. It is women who tend to give up paid work or take part-time employment after the birth of children; men do so only occasionally, either because of career setbacks (Lewis, 2001) or, in very few cases, because of a commitment to anti-sexist living arrangements (VanEvery, 1995). 'Fathers appear to be fitting family commitments around their working lives...for mothers it is their labour market activity that usually has to be fitted around their family' (Dex, 1999: 37).

Catherine Hakim (1996a, 2000) contends, controversially, that this is a matter of choice. She maintains that only a minority of women, around 20 per cent, are work oriented, another 20 per cent are primarily home-centred, preferring not to work, while the remainder are adaptive, combining work and family in response to changing circumstances (Hakim, 2000:9), and that these preferences are relatively constant across time and social class. Hakim's work has attracted much criticism for ignoring constraints on choices, over-simplifying the ways choices are made and the ways in which choice itself is socially constructed and socially located (Bruegel, 1996; Ginn et al., 1996; Irwin, 2005). Sarah Irwin (2005) argues that those women who most firmly believe that mothers should stay at home with young children are not a random cross-section of women, as Hakim would have it, but are located in a very particular social location: they are white, working class women with few educational qualifications and therefore limited employment opportunities, but they are not the most disadvantaged and are likely to be living with a partner who is in work. Their social location both constrains *and facilitates* their preferences. Jane Lewis (2001) found that working part-time does not necessarily indicate women's lack of orientation to employment. The younger mothers in this situation in her predominately middle-class sample displayed a 'commitment to paid work and an insistence on seeing it as important and often in terms of a career' and in this respect were little different from the mothers in full-time employment (Lewis, 2001:152).

Domestic work, then, still falls largely to women. Men are now more willing to be involved in child care, but have barely increased their participation in routine household chores. A man is likely to do slightly more if his wife is employed full-time, but if she works part-time he will do no more than the husband of a full-time home-maker (Dex, 1999). Earlier qualitative studies documented the long hours and elaborate routines of working mothers and how it was women who were responsible for making the arrangements that enabled both partners to work (Westwood, 1984; Mansfield and Collard, 1988; Hochschild, 1989; Brannen and Moss, 1991). A common feature of such studies was that, while women often said or implied that they felt over-burdened, they rarely questioned their responsibility for housework.

While the actual distribution of domestic labour remains much as it was, it may no longer be so taken for granted. Jane Lewis (2001) found that the older couples in her sample did not question the conventional gendered division of labour, but among the younger couples most women *and* men were willing to admit that, where women were working, it was unfair that they should do all or most of the housework. This did not mean that men did much more housework – only 3 of the 29 couples had negotiated greater flexibility in sharing tasks. In most cases, men's acknowledgement that a problem existed 'was usually enough to mollify their partners, even if no substantial change in their behaviour followed' (Lewis, 2001:154).

Radically different divisions of labour have been found among the small section of the population who are actively pursuing alternative lifestyles. Those in the various anti-sexist living arrangements described by Jo VanEvery (1996) made a conscious effort to disrupt gendered patterns of work and care and most studies of lesbian and gay couples reveal a commitment to egalitarian domestic practices (Dunne, 1997, 1999; Weeks et al., 2001). Among Gill

Dunne's sample of 37 lesbian couples with dependent children, there was near equality in the division of domestic work and child care except for the minority of cases where one partner was employed for much longer hours than the other (Dunne, 1999). This is not, however, a universal finding. Jacqui Gabb found that childcare was not shared equally in lesbian parent families: in most cases 'it remains the "birth mother" who is figuratively and literally left "holding the baby"' (Gabb, 2004:169).

## Conceptualizing domestic labour

The relationship between housework and gender inequality has been central to feminist theories of family relationships. Initially feminists sought to establish that housework *is* work (e.g. Oakley, 1984), but in the 1970s, when Marxism was highly influential, placing it on the theoretical agenda meant establishing its utility for capitalism. Thus housework was conceptualized as (re)producing labour power – servicing the existing labour force and rearing the workers of the future (see Kaluzynska, 1980; Malos, 1980). Marxist feminists, though they acknowledged that men evaded their share of household chores, were reluctant to consider how men might benefit from women's domestic labour (see Barrett, 1988:216–17).

Empirical research, however, revealed how women ordered domestic work to give priority to the desires of others, for example planning meals to fit their husbands' routines and tastes (Charles and Kerr, 1988; DeVault, 1991). Because housework is a personal service, governed by requirements of those for whom it is performed (especially men), it has no boundaries or limits, no job description and no fixed hours. It can be extended to encompass work in a family business, as has been documented in the South Asian and Chinese communities of the UK (Song, 1995; Phizaklea and Ram, 1996), or, for wives of senior managers in large companies, to entertaining his clients and colleagues (Reis, 2002). Conversely, the material rewards a woman receives in return for her labour depend not on the work she does for her partner but on his financial standing and generosity. Every service a woman provides in the home can, of course, be undertaken as waged work and purchased on the market. The peculiarities of domestic labour, therefore, arise not from the specific tasks performed, but from the social relations within which they are performed. French materialist feminists, such as Christine Delphy, have argued – controversially – that these relations are patriarchal and entail men's appropriation of women's labour (see Delphy, 1984; Delphy and Leonard, 1992; Walby, 1986, 1990; Jackson, 1996). From this perspective men do not simply evade their share of domestic work, but have their share done for them. Moreover, as Jo VanEvery (1997) points out, not all the work entailed in running a home is communal: much of it is work done for individuals and could be undertaken by those individuals – there is no reason why a man shouldn't iron his own shirts, just as he cleans his own teeth (see VanEvery, 1997).

The relations within which domestic labour is performed, however, are arguably changing:

- fewer women in wealthier nations are dependent on a male breadwinner;
- paid domestic labour is becoming more prevalent.

With women's increased participation in employment they now spend a smaller proportion of their time working within domestic, or patriarchal, relations (Walby, 1990). Delphy and Leonard (1992), however, have argued that the fact that most married and cohabiting women are now employed – and still doing most of the domestic work – indicates that their exploitation is intensifying. If women are now earning their own keep, they are no longer exchanging domestic labour for maintenance: *they are clearly doing it for nothing*. Materialist feminists have more recently theorized the links between women's work in families and institutionalized heterosexuality, following Monique Wittig's (1992) analysis of the heterosexual contract as both a sexual and work relationship, founded upon the appropriation of women's bodies and labour (see for example Ingraham, 1996, 2001). In their domestic practices heterosexual couples are both 'doing gender' and 'doing heterosexuality' (VanEvery, 1996; Jackson, 1999c), perpetuating a relationship in which women continue to be responsible for the daily maintenance of the social and bodily needs of their male partners and children.

But what if women rear children as lone parents? Insofar as women take responsibility for children, men are exempted from doing the work this entails. When a man pays maintenance for children he has fathered, it is usually intended to cover the financial costs of the children, not the mother's caring work. Retaining custody of children after divorce or separation is generally seen as a gain for women – and one contested by fathers' rights activists. Yet it is worth considering whether asserting mothers' rights over children reinforces women's position as unpaid carers and the assumption that women are 'naturally' suited for this role and serves to claim rights *over* another category of people – children – thus undermining feminism's egalitarian project (see Delphy, 1992, 1994).

Inequality among women is also an issue given that well-paid women in wealthier nations increasingly ease their double burden by buying the services of other, poorer, women in an increasingly international market (Romero, 1992, 1999; Cheng, 2003; Lan, 2003, 2006). Wealthy American women often employ Chicana women (Romero, 1992), while their counterparts in Taiwan and Japan employ maids from the Philippines or South-East Asia (Cheng, 2003; Lan, 2003, 2006). The conditions of this work are often harsh and exploitative, especially for migrant workers. But, as Pei-chia Lan (2003) argues, there are important continuities between paid and unpaid domestic labour. This holds for both employers and employees. Women who do other women's housework are often also responsible for domestic labour in their own homes; if they are migrant workers, they often have to make arrangements for others to care for their children and send money home for this purpose (Romero,

1999; Lan, 2003, 2006). Single migrant domestic workers often marry men from richer countries, exchanging paid for unpaid domestic labour. Some of the Filipina workers in Taiwan interviewed by Lan were well aware of this. One said, 'when you have a husband, you have to provide all the service, cooking, cleaning...for free!' (Lan, 2003:203). Shu-ju Cheng illustrates how women who employ such workers exert a high degree of control over them, but in so doing they do not relinquish their responsibility for running the home; on the contrary, in priding themselves on 'managing' their foreign maids they reconfirm it (Cheng, 2003:183).

For some women, exchanging domestic work for a man's support may still represent the best option for meeting their economic and social needs, but more privileged women can now more easily choose to maintain their independence from men. Thus, while most adult women still live in heterosexual relationships, many now delay or eschew marriage and leave unsatisfactory relationships. The choice of whether or not to marry or cohabit cannot, however, be explained only in terms of rational economic choice. In entering heterosexual partnerships, both women and men expect rewards other than material ones – particularly, in the dominant western culture, love, companionship and security. Here too, some change is discernable.

## Emotional attachments

Western marriage rates have been declining relatively steadily since their high point at the beginning of the 1970s, except in the US where the higher rate is attributed to the frequency of divorce and remarriage (Therborn, 2004), and women are marrying later. In Britain, for example, the average age of first marriage for women in 1971 was 23; by 2003 it had risen to 29 (ONS, 2006a). Cohabitation, a rarity in the early 1970s, has become common-place among young single women and divorced women. Rates vary from one country to another; in Europe they are highest in Denmark and Sweden and lowest in Greece and Portugal (Therborn, 2004). The percentage of non-married women cohabiting continues to rise, in Britain from 13 per cent in 1986 to 25 per cent in 2004 (ONS, 2004), and most couples marrying have previously cohabited. Nonetheless, the majority of women in most western countries marry at least once and at the turn of the century married couples in Britain outnumbered cohabiting couples by more than 6:1 (Lewis, 2001). Marriage is still a common life experience, but it may no longer be for life – divorce rates are also on the increase in the west and in other wealthier countries.

Much of the debate around these trends has been framed in dialogue with Anthony Giddens' (1991) thesis that we are witnessing a 'transformation of intimacy', accompanying the separation of sexuality from reproduction, increasing female autonomy and greater gender equality. The result is the democratized 'pure relationship', where trust is maintained through mutual disclosure and which 'is continued only in so far as it is thought by both parties to deliver enough satisfactions for each individual to stay within it' (1991:58). Giddens maintains that we are moving from romantic love, based on lasting commitment to a 'special person' to a more contingent 'confluent love' in which we seek a 'special relationship' (1991:61–2).

As his feminist critics have noted, Giddens' argument is more conjectural than empirically grounded; in particular, he ignores evidence of continuing inequality in heterosexual relationships (Jamieson, 1999; Langford, 1999; Evans, 2003b): not only material inequalities but also less tangible ones. At the time that Giddens was writing there was already a great deal of research suggesting an emotional divide in marriage, with women seeking a form of intimacy, closeness and togetherness in marriage that men were unable to offer them – and of working hard to sustain relationships in the face of men's preference for a comfortable life unencumbered by women's demands for 'disclosing intimacy' (for example Rubin, 1983; Mansfield and Collard, 1988; Cancian, 1990). More recent studies suggest that this is still the case (Duncombe and Marsden, 1993, 1995; Langford, 1999).

Of course many women do 'vote with their feet' and ultimately end unsatisfactory relationships: most divorces are initiated by women. This does not mean, however, that they saw these relationships as temporary or contingent from the outset. Bernadette Bawin-Legros (2004) claims that her Belgian data support Giddens' thesis in that slightly more than half the men and women in her sample thought it possible to fall in love more than once in a lifetime and most saw lack of love and communication as reasons to end a relationship. Yet over 78 per cent of those living in couple relationships (married or cohabiting) thought that marriage was 'forever', and most thought living together was either forever or long-term. Though this may indicate more willingness to enter into temporary liaisons or end unhappy relationships, it does not indicate the end of the ideal of long-term commitment (see Evans, 2002; Holmes, 2004b).

Women may, as Giddens argues, be leading a move towards more egalitarian partnerships, but the evidence suggests that it is the continuing lack of equality that causes much of the strain and instability in contemporary heterosexual relationships. Many men, it seems, resist democratized relationships and prefer more 'traditional' heterosexual arrangements – but now cannot always find wives willing to comply. One strategy open to them is to turn to the global marriage market, aided by a host of international match-making organizations, leading to an increase in 'global hypergamy' (Constable, 2005) whereby women from poorer countries seek to improve their position by marrying men from richer nations. These men hope to 'fulfil their nostalgia for a prefeminist family romance' by marrying foreign women, in the (often false) expectation that they will be subservient (Lan, 2003:202). European and American men seek wives from Eastern Europe and Asia; men in Japan and Taiwan find brides in poorer, more 'traditional' countries in South-East Asia (Constable, 2005; Suzuki, 2005; Wang, 2005). For instance, in Taiwan, where nearly 1 in 5 weddings now involve foreign brides, match-making companies market South East Asian women as docile, domesticated and virginal (Wang, 2005).

## Towards postmodern, individualized families?

The 'transformation of intimacy' thesis is part of a wider debate on the direction of change in late modern or postmodern families. Two interrelated, but separate kinds of claims are currently made, the first championed by theorists of late modernity, the second more often associated with feminist analysis:

- The individualization thesis: that increasing individuation, reflexivity and choice results in more fluid, fragile and contingent intimate relationships (Giddens, 1991; Beck and Beck Gernsheim, 1995, 2002; Beck-Gernsheim, 2002; Bauman, 2003).
- The de-heterosexualization thesis: that the heterosexual/homosexual binary is becoming less stable and that there is a 'queering' of family relationships (Stacey, 1996; Roseneil, 2000b; Roseneil and Budgeon, 2004).

The individualization thesis emphasizes a breakdown of normative prescription, a disembedding of the individual from the social, freeing us from social constraints. This, as critics have noted, can downplay the extent to which individual conduct and the choices we make continue to be shaped by culture, social context and the immediate social milieu in which our lives are lived (Smart and Shipman, 2004; Irwin, 2005). Such sceptics rarely dismiss the individualization thesis altogether, but they do contest some of its claims.

Even among those whose domestic arrangements are at the vanguard of social change, it is not clear that individualization adequately describes or explains their lives, aspirations and dispositions. Those forming step-families after divorce and separation might be said to exemplify contingent commitments and disembedding from social constraints. Yet their priorities are framed in terms of mutual support and obligations among family members and 'issues of gender, generation and social class still act as powerful mediators of meaning in how people understand and experience their family lives' (Ribbens McCarthy et al., 2003:147). A decision to cohabit rather than marry may indicate a willingness to entertain less permanent relationships, but it may also be an adaptation to particular material circumstances since in the UK the majority of cohabitants with children are young and poor (Lewis, 2001:30.) In Lewis's middle-class sample of married and cohabiting couples, cohabitation did not signal a lack of commitment; for the younger couples, married *and* cohabiting, commitment was balanced with a felt need for autonomy, especially on the part of the women. Couples 'living apart together', a situation often resulting from both partners sustaining a career may, as Mary Holmes (2004a, 2004b) argues, require a great deal of commitment in order to sustain the relationship. It may be, then, that women are aspiring to greater independence within their relationships with men, hoping to combine intimacy with the maintenance of individual autonomy and identity – something that has long been possible for men, but was historically denied to women (see Robinson, 2003).

The individualization thesis is a western idea, formulated from within cultures with a long history of individualism. One aspect of this has been free choice of marriage partners and the idea that marriage should be based on love for another who complements and completes the self – though with changing conceptions of love over time (Evans, 2003b). Most human societies do not share this history. The individualization thesis ignores alternative cultural traditions including those of significant minorities within western societies, for whom marriage may be a matter for the wider family or a means of reaffirming alliances among kin (Afshar, 1989; Smart and Shipman, 2004). 'Arranged marriages', stigmatized as oppressive from the dominant western viewpoint, are not seen by those who contract them as an assault on individual identity, but as a confirmation of an identity embedded in family and kinship. Carol Smart and Becky Shipman suggest that we should not think of alternatives to individualized 'free choice' marriage as 'practices that are yet to catch up in the "individualization race"', but as 'different ways of "doing family"' (2004:496).

Those who argue that we are witnessing a de-heterosexualization or queering of family life also tend to focus on western societies, although with some awareness of ethnic diversity. Writers such as Judith Stacey (1996, 2004) and Sasha Roseneil and Shelly Budgeon (2004) share with the proponents of individualization the idea that we are witnessing radical changes in intimate life towards more fluid relationships and greater individual reflexivity, agency and choice. They distance themselves, however, from the implication that individuals no longer form meaningful social ties or recognize obligations to care for others. Roseneil and Budgeon's study of a sector of the population 'at the cutting edge of social change' (2004:135), those choosing to live outside couple relationships, found that these individuals forged strong networks of care and support provided by friends 'with no biological, legal or social recognized ties to each other' (Roseneil and Budgeon, 2004:152). Judith Stacey (1996) demonstrates the complex ties that form among families linked by divorce and remarriage and more recently, in researching gay men within the 'cruising' culture of Los Angeles, discovered that even a culture based on casual sex can generate 'bonds of kinship and domesticity' (Stacey, 2004:183).

These writers see lesbian, gay and queer lifestyles as in the vanguard of change. Stacey (1996) has suggested that all our families are becoming 'queer' in their diversity and unconventionality as people find new ways of living intimate lives. Roseneil and Budgeon go further, claiming that the 'heterosexual couple, and particularly the married, co-resident heterosexual couple with children, no longer occupies the centre ground of western societies' (2004:140). This over-states the case: there may be a move to less stable and durable heterosexual relationships and a widening of lifestyle choices (at least for the more privileged), but these trends are not universal even in the UK and the US. The majority of adults, as we have seen, continue to live in heterosexual relationships and it seems premature to proclaim the end of the heterosexual couple as a normative style of life. Moreover, and importantly for feminists, the way such couples 'do family' often continues to disadvantage women, although women are exercising agency within such relationships and beginning to effect some change (see Robinson et al., 2004).

The greater visibility and acceptability of lesbian, gay or queer politics and lifestyles does challenge patriarchal and heterosexual norms, but this challenge may have its limits. The normalization of homosexuality could be said to be working towards a re-familialization, rather than de-familialization, of lesbian and gay lives. Roseneil and Budgeon suggest that reconfiguring queer relationships in terms of 'family' may deflect attention away from 'the extra-familial, radically counter-heteronormative nature of many of these relationships' (2004: 137). Whether demands for marriage and parenthood rights are progressive is a matter of debate. Some lesbian feminists suggest that marrying represents a challenge to the patriarchal norms of the heterosexual family (see for example Kitzinger and Wilkinson, 2004). Others are more sceptical about whether such citizenship rights destabilize heteronormativity and are concerned that privileging certain kinds of relationships above others may serve to 'normalize' lesbian and gay lives along heterosexual lines (Donovan, 2004; Jackson and Scott, 2004; Richardson, 2005b). For lesbians, state recognition may have some negative consequences; the introduction of civil partnership in the UK now means than any co-resident lesbian couple, whether in a civil partnership or not, will be treated as each other's dependents for benefit purposes. Not only does this mean that poorer lesbians will lose out financially, but it also imposes on lesbians a heterosexualized norm of economic support and dependence (see also Taylor in this volume). Here as elsewhere, the 'queering' of intimate life has not, so far, dislodged older ideas and practices associated with normative, heterosexual family life.

## Conclusion

In this chapter I have demonstrated that current changes in intimate life are complex, are not unidirectional and do not necessarily undermine family life – although the ways intimate lives are led have become less predictable and more diverse. I have suggested that some caution needs to be exercised in interpreting current trends, so that we take account of change *and* continuity, of diversity *and* regularity in patterns of intimacy and domesticity. This entails awareness of the continuing significance of the idea of 'family' in most women's lives and of the ways in which the social organization of domestic life remains highly gendered, even where the contours of gender relations are shifting. I have also drawn attention to differences among women and to the differential consequences of social change for them. In western societies, more privileged women can now have the opportunity to live outside heteronormative families; the less privileged may live outside them by necessity rather than choice. Only a small minority of western women and men, however, are actively embracing alternative lifestyles and it remains to be seen whether they really are the vanguard of change. When looking beyond the west, even more care needs to be exercised. Superficially similar trends in other parts of the world – later marriage, more divorce, more women working – may not have the same meaning or consequences in countries with different cultural traditions and histories. We may live in a globalized, late modern world, but not everyone's modernity is the same (Rofel, 1999) and it cannot therefore be assumed that modernization will have the same consequences for women's family lives world-wide.

## Further reading

L. Davidoff, M. Doolittle, J. Fink and K. Holden (1999) *The Family Story: Blood, Contract and Intimacy 1830-1960*, London, Longman
This is an eclectic text which engages with historical debates and a useful corrective to the necessarily brief and simplified overview of family history presented in this chapter.

H. Lindeman Nelson (1999) (ed.) *Feminism and Families*, New York, Routledge
Also engaging with recent debates on families, this is an American book , framed from a philosophical perspective, but is interdisciplinary and contains some empirically informed contributions.

E. Silva (1999) (ed.) *The New Family?*, London, Sage
A useful collection of work including recent debates on families, this is British, primarily sociological, and has an empirical focus though informed by theoretical concerns.

G. Therborn (2004) *Between Sex and Power: Family in the World, 1900-2000,* London, Routledge
This offers an encyclopaedic history and sociology of the world's families in the twentieth century, though it does not always address major feminist concerns. It is nonetheless a useful starting point for those wishing to develop a more international perspective on families and the bibliography is invaluable.

# CHAPTER NINE

# Gender and Schooling: Contemporary Issues in Gender Equality and Educational Achievement

JESSICA RINGROSE AND DEBBIE EPSTEIN

## Introduction

In this chapter we will trace the rise of 'educational feminism' and educational debates over gender equality and achievement in schooling, primarily within the UK, as a case study of these issues as they have unfolded in the (over-) developed parts of the Anglophone world. We then map the controversy that erupted when girls were seen to be outperforming and catching up to boys in school in the 1990s. This has led to a 'moral panic' over boys' underachievement that continues into the present and has now spread internationally (Epstein et al., 1998; Ali et al., 2004; Francis and Skelton, 2005).

Broadly speaking the 'failing boys' discourse draws on specific measures of girls' superior educational achievements as compared to boys, to support claims that girls have reached unparalleled levels of success and feminist interventions into schooling have been met, and may have gone 'too far', so that girls' achievements are continuously positioned as won at the expense of boys' (Francis, 2005:9; Arnot et al., 1999).

While many position the failing boys discourses as an anti-feminist backlash, in this chapter we examine how liberal feminist theory has contributed to narrowly conceived, divisive educational debates and policies where boys' disadvantage/success are pitted against girls' disadvantage/success (Jackson, 1998). We examine feminist interventions into educational research and policy, and show how conceptualizing gender in binary terms plays into reversals like the failing boys discourse. The chapter illustrates that gender-only and gender binary conceptions of educational achievement are easily brought into individualizing discourses of educational equality, where narrow measures of exam performance by gender difference are now used by the government to 'prove' gender equality, in ways that obscure how issues of educational equality and achievement in school are related to issues of class, race, ethnicity, religion, citizenship and location, as well as gender (Gillborn and Mirza, 2000; Francis and Skeleton, 2005).

We look at how the gender and achievement debates contribute to a discourse of girl power and a new figure, the successful girl. Through analysis of media reports and public debate, we trace the production of this new 'school girl fiction', this time of unambiguous success where girls' achievement becomes synonymous with an overarching 'feminist victory' – a victory that is at boys' expense (Walkerdine, 1990; Foster, 2000). The failing boys discourse is fuelling a seductive 'postfeminist' discourse of girl power, possibility and choice with massive global reach, where girls' educational performance is increasingly used as evidence that individual success is attainable and educational policies are working in contexts of globalization, marketization and economic insecurity (McRobbie, 2004).

## Historical contexts of girls' inequality in schooling and the development of 'education feminism'

Education has constituted a core issue for women's activism since feminism's 'first wave' where it was viewed as shaping the role women were to play in society (Gamble, 2001). Early proto-feminist texts like Mary Wollstonecraft's *Vindication of the Rights of Women* (1792) dealt extensively with questions of women/girls and education, partly in response to Rousseau's assumption that what girls needed to learn was how to look after men. Much of the political activity during this period and into the nineteenth century, however, took the form of 'a rallying cry to middle-class women', at a time when both British society and educational policy and provision were highly stratified by social class, and women's and girls' were inferior and subordinate in status to men and boys (Sanders, 2001:17). Girls and women were generally not offered many educational opportunities and access to secondary and, especially, higher education for women came as late as the twentieth century in the (over-)developed world (Weiner et al., 1997). At Cambridge, for example, women could not gain degrees until 1921 and were not admitted to full membership of the university until as late as 1948. These questions of access to education persist into the present in developing countries (Aikman and Unterhalter, 2005). For example, girls in Africa receive on average 2.82 years of schooling and only 46 per cent of those enrolling in schools in sub-Saharan Africa are able to complete their primary education (Oxfam, 2005).

Like the first wave, the subsequent 'second wave' women's movement focused on gender equality in education as one of its 'manifesto' goals (Arnot, 2002:5). In the UK context, the 1944 Education Act, which established the principle of free secondary education for all, had paved conditions for greater equality in education (Weiner et al., 1997). Influenced by the women's movement, from the 1970s onward legislative gains concerned with equal opportunities in Britain included the Equal Pay Act (1970), the Sex Discrimination Act (1975) and the Race Relations Act (1976) (Arnot et al., 1999). Arnot et al. (1999:7) note that in the UK in particular, the development of what they call 'educational feminism' was central to the post-war era of social democracy.

Feminists at this time looked at inequalities in schooling, with girls and women excluded and marginalized in the curriculum, content and practices of education (Weiner et al., 1997). Feminist concerns ranged from issues of subject choice by girls and issues of poor performance in mathematics and science (Kelly, 1981, 1985; Northam, 1982; Harding, 1983; Riddell, 1989; Walkerdine, 1989), through the experiences that girls had in schools (for example, Whyte, 1983; Whyte et al., 1988), sexual harassment and lack of space and attention within classrooms (Stanworth, 1981; Spender, 1982), and the question of whether girls and boys should be educated together or separately (Arnot, 1984; Deem, 1984).

With their focus on 'equal opportunities' as a key element of progress for girls and women, liberal feminists placed particular importance on issues of girls' and women's access (to schools, universities), level of achievement and choice of subject. The dominant argument was that girls were doing poorly in school and, later, the workplace because of marginalization and inequality in school culture and gender based subject choice, with more girls in home economics and languages than maths. While research at the time revealed that girls were actually not underperforming in primary school and later in subjects like English, because it was primarily boys who were performing the best in sciences and maths, the dominant feminist trend during this period was a focus on girls' 'underperformance' in these subjects (Walkerdine, 1989).

Arnot (2002) suggests that education feminism of this period, borne out of feminism's second wave, initiated a global social movement which demanded equality of outcome, gender equity in society – in short a 'gender blind approach to education' (quoted from the UNESCO website, http://www.portal. unesco.org/education/, accessed June 2005). Early programmes intended to redress the balance were instituted across the (over-)developed world, virtually always by individual feminist teachers and groups of feminists (such as organisations like GAMMA (Girls/Gender and Mathematics Association)) (Paechter, 1998). In the British context, relative decentralization in education, rather than macro feminist driven policy gains, meant feminist education initiatives for girls were localized with little sustained funding (Weiner er al., 1997). There were also some modest gains (more in some countries than others) in policy terms as liberal feminists, in particular, entered and gained a certain amount of leverage within policy communities. This was particularly noticeable in Australia where a class of what became known as 'femocrats' working with the Commonwealth (i.e. national) government administration grew and assumed influential positions (Eisenstein, 1996).

## Gendered inequalities in education on a global scale

It is worth pausing, at this point, to consider the different imperatives and understandings available in gendering educational equality in those parts of the world not dominated by questions (in policy at least) to do with the problem of 'failing boys'. As pointed out above, there are many parts of the world where it remains difficult for girls even to gain adequate access to primary education. Given the figures (Oxfam, 2005) outlining the massive inequalities in access to education in Africa, it is important to face up to the fact that similar gross inequalities continue to exist in many countries.

Elaine Unterhalter (2007) proposes that we think about gender equality in education in such poverty stricken contexts by drawing on Amartya Sen's capabilities approach. Sen argues that social (including educational) policies must be analyzed in relation to the ways in which they support the development of people's capabilities (Sen, 1992, 1994, 2002). She says:

> The capability approach in education requires us to think about the gendered constraints on functionings and freedoms in educational organisations such as schools or adult literacy classes. It also draws attention to how sometimes, despite relatively high levels of education for girls and women, the legal system, the forms of political participation and economic ownership, or employment and leisure practise limit agency and 'substantive' freedom of girls and women, thus entailing capability deprivation.
>
> (Unterhalter, 2007:103)

In other words, what matters is not just formal access to education, but what this means in the 'outside' world, what powers, capabilities and freedoms women actually have.

In contexts where women and girls are subject to sexual harassment and sexual violence as, for example, in South Africa (Jewkes et al., 2006), where conflict has ravaged all kinds of facilities, including those for education, such as the Sudan or Rwanda (Oxfam, 2005) and where there are few teachers, no running water or electricity and few facilities of any kind, the necessity to approach matters through a social justice and activist lens must take precedence over concerns about whether boys or girls are ahead in the educational 'race'. In such circumstances, Oxfam notes, the education of girls suffers significantly, in part because of the costs incurred in educating them. The work that girls do in, for example, water and fuel collection, care of younger siblings and so on outweigh any potential advantages to the family of sending them to school. This means that not only must education be provided for boys and girls (see the box overleaf for Oxfam's recommendations about the areas needing attention), but interventions to raise women's and girls status in communities, wages and so on, are needed. In other words, the capabilities of women and girls must be substantially improved.

Oxfam (2005: 3) identifies four broad areas that 'need attention and support':

- The provision of education, such as schools, desks, books, and teaching and learning materials

- The ability to determine the different needs of girls and boys, and a political commitment to girls' education

- Administrative capacity, in ministries of education and in the wider civil service

- Pay, conditions, and teacher deployment, as well as school management and regional supervision, data collection and analysis

## The panic over 'failing boys'

The above is all in stark contrast to the situation in developed countries like the UK, where equal opportunities policy was finally formalized in educational practice with the advent of a National Curriculum in England and Wales in 1988, partly in response to feminists' struggles for gender equity (Arnot, 2002). For the first time, girls and boys had to take the same core subjects till the school leaving age. 'League tables' were also introduced to catalogue Geneneral Certificate of Secondary Education (GCSE) results to gauge performance across gender in the wake of this shift to a common curriculum for the sexes. The tables illustrated indisputably that girls were outperforming boys in language subjects and were also rapidly catching up in maths and sciences at a rate not matched by boys' improvements in languages. Figures in 1995 illustrated that seven-year-old girls had gained a head start in mathematics and science (81% of girls reached the expected level of maths compared with 77% of boys, and 86% of girls and 83% of boys reached the expected level in science) (Arnot et al., 1999). By 1996, public debate would be shaped by the new facts of gender equality:

- Girls outperform boys at ages 7, 11 and 14 in National Curriculum assessments in English; achievements in maths and sciences are broadly similar.
- Girls are more successful than boys at every subject in GCSE.
- Girls are succeeding in 'boys' subjects' such as technology, maths and chemistry (adapted from Jackson, 1998: 78).

As Arnot (2002) claims, statistical patterns of female performance were touted as 'one of the most significant transformations in the history of social inequality in the UK' (quoted from the UNESCO website, http://www.portal.unesco.org/education/, accessed June 2005).

Because these findings contradicted earlier assumptions about girls underperformance, particularly in maths and sciences, the results proved shocking vis-à-vis dominant cultural knowledges about boys, girls and schooling, and a 'furore' broke out in British society. From the news that girls were doing better than ever in school, claims of a shocking new 'gender gap' between girls and boys emerged and claims about boys' under-performance were exaggerated and played upon by the media (Epstein et al., 1998). Headlines ranged from 'Girls doing well while boys feel neglected' to 'Is the future female?'; with reports claiming 'the under-achievement of boys has become one of the biggest challenges facing society today' (*Guardian*, 1995, *Panorama*, BBC1, 1995, *Times Educational Supplement*, 1997 in Cohen, 1998).

A 'sex-war' mentality took hold (Jackson, 1998). Girls' apparent new found successes were spelling boys' downfall, and a 'moral panic' over 'failing boys', said to be a consequence of feminist gains in education, was born. What was dubbed a 'crisis' in boys' underachievement in school took on the guise of 'fact' through measures of female vs male achievement in various levels of governmental school testing and subject performance (Reed, 1998).

This concern has carried on unabated ever since (Francis and Skelton, 2005). Indeed, the most recent British research indicates 'the moral panic over boys' perceived underachievement' continues to 'dominate the current gender agenda, and channel debate into a narrow set of perspectives associated with the policy drive to raise "standards" in education' (Ali et al., 2004:1). Moreover, international research indicates the British 'media frenzy over boys' underachievement' has spread to Australian, US and Canadian contexts (at least) influencing an international 'panic... that boys in school are being short-changed' (Davison et al., 2004:50; Francis and Skelton, 2005). Governments in many countries are entrenching a failing boys and successful girls dichotomy through 'shifts in policies which re-focus on the educational needs, body image, mental health and leadership for boys in light of the argument that young women are outperforming young men in school and beyond in almost every aspect of personal development' (Aapola, Gonick and Harris, 2005:8). Australian research has pointed to a discursive shift from a 'deficit framework' that oriented equity policies for helping girls 'measure up to' boys, to a deficit model for boys – 'a current depiction of girls as actively succeeding, and even beating boys in male educational terrain' (Foster, 2000:207). Canadian research is now exploring how a media driven 'perception among some parents/guardians and educators that boys in school are being shortchanged' is being taken up by government organizations responsible for education with as yet unforeseen effects (Davison et al., 2004:50). Francis (2006) notes that, although the US has been slower due to a focus on ethnic inequality rather than gender and performance, recent concern over 'boys' underachievement' has amplified, with such sensationalist titles appearing as *The War against Boys: How Misguided Feminism is Harming our Young Men* (Hoff-Sommers, 2000; Francis, 2006).

Not surprisingly, feminists internationally have responded to this shift with great anxiety and concern calling it variously a 'backlash', a 'reversal' of feminism, and part of an 'anti-feminist' agenda. Jane Kenway (1997) was one of the first to raise concerns about the lines of policy being developed by the Australian government in response to the supposed crisis over boys' education. Epstein et al. (1998), in their edited collection, mapped the field in the UK, describing the moral panic over boys' education as:

> a key opportunity for challenging gender inequalities in schools...but it is one which is fraught with danger. As with all such moments a reactionary recuperation of feminist insights and concerns is also possible.
>
> (Epstein et al., 1998: 14)

More recently Aapolla, Gonick and Harris (2005), working in Finland, the US and Australia respectively, have explored how girls in their different regions of the world are positioned by the consumerist adoption of 'girl power' and the notion's incorporation into right-wing and anti-feminist politics. Rather than view the debate as a clear cut anti-feminist backlash, however, we are concerned next to look at how some forms of feminism and gender analysis are actually complicit in, and productive of, gender binaries. We want to map out how the gender reversal logic still operates, and what can be done to get us out of these binds.

## Testing equality? Educational discourses of achievement and performance

Shifts in debates over educational achievement are linked to massive restructuring of education systems in most western countries over the past few decades in the wake of a rapidly changing global economy and labour markets (Giddens, 1998). Strategies to increase school effectiveness through pupil achievement have continued to gain international importance as a means of making the nation state marketable with increasing pressures on schools to mediate issues of economic insecurity and produce a suitably flexible and adaptable work force (David, 2004).

In this global context, debates on school 'effectiveness' through identifying and measuring standards of teaching and learning performance and excellence are increasingly in line with 'neo-liberal' governmental policy contexts that stress individual attainment, flexibility and adaptation in education and work as the means of succeeding in contexts of social, economic and political transformation and instability (Morley and Rassool, 1999; Francis, 2006; Walkerdine and Ringrose, 2006). In British schools, the drive to 'improve standards' has meant an increased emphasis on exam results. According to Benjamin (2003) a current obsession with testing has international reach, producing a culture of 'curricular fundamentalism' which demands schools and teachers valorise specific, quantifiable versions of 'achievement' and 'performance'. Educational policy discourses which focus on issues of 'performativity' and standards of excellence as part of a wider attention to measurable school improvement have flourished in current economic and governmental contexts (Younger and Warrington, 2003; Youdell, 2004; Francis and Skeleton, 2005).

'Third way' 'New Labour' policies (and similar policies elsewhere) continue to promote assessment as a key way of improving institutional, group and individual standards and effectiveness in schooling (Fairclough, 2000). New Labour policies have emphasized educational achievement as the means of addressing issues of social exclusion and demonstrating governmental 'action' on issues like gender equality (David, 2004). Equity discourses sit alongside demands for 'school improvement' and both issues are to be gauged through specific criteria of 'evidence' about performance like examination results. David notes how in a climate of 'public policy discourses about school improvement and effectiveness ... [equity issues] have been defined in very specific and traditional ways' (David, 2004: 14). One of these 'traditional' ways by which school effectiveness is measured and equity is to be addressed is continued reliance on gendered measurements where girls' and boys' performances on testing are compared. In the UK, the narrow parameters of the gender and achievement debate, oriented toward tracking testing results at the GCSE level (in terms of girls' and boys' performance) continue to produce a dominant educational narrative that gender equity has been attained or even surpassed, because girls' performance at this level exceeds that of boys (Francis, 2005: 9). Students' performance by gender provides an exceptionally easy, though overly simplified, criterion for demonstrating school effectiveness in terms of gender equality.

As noted by Lucey, the concept of 'excellence' promoted by New Labour sets up a difficult binary: 'excellence is produced within dynamic relation to its opposite and therefore depends upon the continued presence rather than eradication of failure' (Lucey, 2001: 182). The dynamic of success and failure plays through a gender binary that continues to reproduce a failing boys discourse, as evident in many recent press reports reminiscent of the mid 1990s like the BBC story: 'Girls keep outstripping boys in exams' (BBC News, 2003). While close attention to the details reveal the article is reporting on how it is at 'the top end [that] the gender gap is widening, with the growth in the number of girls gaining grades A to C being greater than the rate among boys' the message is one of all boys losing out to girls once again (Epstein et al., 1998).

Similarly, an *Observer* headline proclaimed: 'Exam results reveal gender gulf in schools' (Hill, 2005). Drawing on data from the Department for Education and Skills, the article states that surveys of A level results from 1500 schools, both state and independent, showed 'girls are up to 115 percent more likely to achieve an A or B grade than boys' (Hill, 2005: 1). The article declares:

The shocking extent of under-achievement by boys in some of Britain's leading schools has been revealed in a report which for the *first time* shows the huge differences in the performance of girls and boys across the country.

(Hill, 2005: 1, emphasis added)

It is extraordinary that although issues of boys' underachievement have dominated the policy arena and public debates on education for over a decade now, the article represents the findings as groundbreaking in order to underline the grave extent of the problem facing boys.

As Becky Francis has recently argued a 'poor boys' dimension of the failing boys discourse maintains a powerful hegemony (2006). Girls' success is continuously framed through an oppositional dynamic of boys' failure, and the enormous complexity of educational issues involved in struggling for 'equality' greatly muddied. But how and which types of feminisms are implicated in the 'gender seesaw' playing out in educational debates (Collins et al., 2000)?

## Reproducing gender binaries

As we have seen, the debate on gender and achievement is framed through a narrow binary conception of gender so that the unitary category of 'girl' is simplistically pitted against the unitary category 'boy'. This stems from the particular gender perspective in use. Recall that a major goal of education feminists was toward a form of gender neutrality or gender blindness in educational outcome (Arnot et al., 1999). This equality perspective was rooted in the British equal rights feminism of the nineteenth and early twentieth century which aimed to extend to women the same rights and privileges as men through identifying areas of unequal treatment and eliminating them via legal reforms (Pilcher and Whelehan, 2004: 38). Equality became the primary platform of 'liberal feminism', which extends a liberal ethos of equality of rights, and has focused on eradicating gender difference as a way toward gender equality (sameness) (Bryson, 1992). Some feminists argue in contrast that women's inherent difference is to be valued (Irigaray, 1982; Gilligan, 1982), on the grounds that equality strategies which leave the masculine norm intact, against which feminine difference is positioned as something to be transcended towards sameness with men, are inherently patriarchal. But this perspective tends to essentialize feminine difference and miss how gender is differentiated by other forms of difference, which vastly complicates the abstract ideal of gender equality (Young, 1990; Squires, 1999a).

Indeed, more than two decades of poststructural feminism, as well as antiracist, postcolonial, black, and critical race feminist theories have variously illustrated the conceptual problems with gender analysis organized as a binary between man/woman or masculine/feminine that does not account for how gender is always differentiated by other 'intersecting' or 'articulating' axes of experience and identity, and multiple social discourses including those that are productive of social class, race and ethnic based inequalities (Carby, 1982; Mohanty, 1991; Brah, 1996; Bhavnani, 1997; Wing, 2000; see also Reed in this volume). Gender taken as a stand alone variable can be used to prove either the 'facts' of an abstract notion of gender inequality *or* equality, in ways that radically de-contextualize experiences of schooling and achievement from economic and cultural factors:

> Earlier [feminist] work failed to construct a political language – and an activism – around equity beyond competing claims about oppression. We seemed in the 1980s Britain to be unable to 'think through more than one difference at once' – as Kobena Mercer so powerfully phrased it.
>
> (Hey et al., 1998:129)

Liberal feminist equality discourses that focus on gender as a stand alone, undifferentiated, monolithic variable have set the terms for a reactionary debate. The very aims of educational parity by gender sought by educational feminists have created measures of 'equality' that could be used in the reverse.

It is vital for feminists to continue grappling with the ways that measuring for equity through *gender-only* frameworks (manifest as liberal feminist discourses) embeds knowledge into a binary, oppositional framing that actually incites reversal, with very difficult effects for feminist politics or movements, impeding a more complex 'politics of difference' (Brah, 2001). Liberal perspectives work to simplify and individualize the social, to de-contextualize class, cultural and racial issues through which gender manifests as an axis of experience and identity (Collins, 1998). Factors such as social class, ethnicity, race and culture are conveniently obscured despite many suggesting these provide much stronger indicators of performance in school (Gillborn and Mirza, 2000; Lucey, 2001; Reay, 2001). The treatment of gender as an undifferentiated, essentialized and monolithic category of analysis gravely distorts the issues involved with school achievement.

The effects of the gender binary framing and the 'recuperation' of liberal feminism to make claims of equality within the educational terrain of policy, research and schooling have been dire indeed. An overwhelming assumption that girls are 'not a problem' in spaces of school in particular has resulted in a massive neglect of girls' experiences, and a failure to allocate resources to girls' needs in school (Osler and Vincent, 2003; Crudas and Haddock, 2005). There has been a general failure to conceive of gender as a relational category, and a refusal among policy makers to differentiate gender analysis and categories of girl/woman and boy/man so that resources could be allocated to girls and those who fall outside this convenient rhetoric of feminine success and boys' failure (Aapolla, Gonick and Harris, 2005; Archer, 2005; Francis and Skeleton, 2005; Francis, 2006). The educational failing boys' discourse of male disadvantage, which is based almost entirely on gender-differentiated test results, inculcates what Foster (2000) calls in the Australian context, a 'presumptive equality' – the widespread belief that women have achieved equality with men in society. These sets of presumptions orienting educational debates bolster the quintessential *postfeminist* argument 'that girls and women are doing fine, feminism is unnecessary... the movement is over... girls have attained all the power they could ever want' and may actually 'have too much power in the world' (Taft, 2004:72). As Angela McRobbie argues, postfeminist discourses:

> actively draw on and invoke feminism as that which can be taken into account in order to suggest that equality is achieved, in order to install a whole repertoire of meanings which emphasize that it is no longer needed, a spent force.
>
> (McRobbie, 2004:4)

As girl studies scholars are indicating, an increasing consequence of these post-feminist assumptions about girl power, gender equality and feminine success is an overall denial of issues facing girls, which leads to the pathologization of those 'other' 'failing' girls, who fall prey to 'risks' of teen pregnancy, welfare dependency, and criminalization (Harris, 2004b; Ringrose, 2006).

What is also amply evident is that the burgeoning postfeminist discourse of successful girls is not bounded within an educational 'field' or 'domain' (Bourdieu and Wacquant, 1992). The successful girls discourse has a wide scope and powerful reach, spreading in complex ways through the realm of global-ized popular culture, confirming as it does a neo-liberal discourse of personal performance, choice and freedom, and its auxiliary and mutually reinforcing discourse or 'rationale' of individual responsibility for failure in the 'global education race' (Mahoney, 1998; Rose, 1999).

## The proliferating discourse of girls' success

We are witnessing a contemporary 'proliferation' of discourse (Foucault, 1980b) about successful girls. This discursive production incites multiple new meanings and truths about girls' success and a shift in attention to the femi-nine and to girls' educational attainments as evidence that individual success is attainable and educational policies are working. Discourses of girls' successes are being posited as a global phenomenon, where girls everywhere are get-ting ahead in ways that deny both the vast global inequities that structure the gendered outcomes in the various African contexts we've discussed, as well as differential rates of success among girls in (over-)developed countries like the UK, where educational success and 'excellence' is still largely the purview of middle-class girls and boys (via the 'cultural capital' of their parents) (Lucey and Reay, 2002).

These dubious media representations offer insight into the proliferation of postfeminist accounts of the newly successful girl – stories of girl power and girls having it all (Taft, 2004). These representations contribute to a wider shift in the 'gender order' and to a set of discourses where girls are heralded as the new 'global winners' (Connell, 1987; Harris, 2004b; Taft, 2004). The high achievements of some economically privileged girls in western countries are being used to fuel a dangerous story of widespread girl success. What we are arguing, then, is that the educational-based discourse of failing boys and its uptake in the media and popular culture, directly contributes to a much

The portrayal of girls' success as an international phenomenon is evident in three separate 2003 BBC news reports, based on a survey from the Organisation for Economic Co-operation and Development.[1] The first story proclaims a new '*Global* gender gap in education' based on findings that 'girls out-performed boys in reading at the age of 15 in all 43 countries included in the respected study', and women have 'overtaken men at every level of education' (BBC News, 2003, emphasis added).[2] Success at school is directly connected to success at work in the representation of these issues in this article: 'They [girls] are better at school, much more likely to go to university and are expecting to take the better-paid jobs.' A second story based on the survey laments: 'In the space of a generation, boys have gone from expecting to be the best at school, to an assumption that they will be the worst... around the world girls are winning the academic race' (BBC News, 2003).[3] This claim of global equality is made despite the fact that the UN's key Millennium Development Goals for gender and education – that all girls would be able to receive at least primary education were missed by a huge margin in 2005 (Aikman and Unterhalter, 2005). Yet another story 'Girls top of the class worldwide' claims 'the 1990s have seen a remarkable change in women's expectations and achievements' noting 'in the United Kingdom, 63% of girls expect to have white collar, high skilled jobs by the time they are 30, compared to only 51% of boys' (BBC News, 2003).[4] Indeed another 2004 *Guardian* report declares 'across the UK, there has been a *revolution* in educational achievement over the last 30 years, of which girls had been the primary drivers and beneficiaries' (Smithers, 2004, emphasis added). But do these 'great expectations' signal the 'revolution' being claimed, or do they indicate more about the representational dimensions of the issues of gender and achievement where girls are positioned as unambiguous winners, objects of both fear and desire in a brave new postfeminist world?

1. See http://news.bbc.co.uk/1/hi/education/3037844.stm, http://news.bbc.co.uk/1/hi/education/3114208.stm, http://news.bbc.co.uk/1/hi/education/3110594.stm (all accessed July 2005).
2. Quoted from http://news.bbc.co.uk/1/hi/education/3037844.stm (accessed July 2005).
3. Quoted from http://news.bbc.co.uk/1/hi/education/3114208.stm (accessed July 2005).
4. Quoted from http://news.bbc.co.uk/1/hi/education/3110594.stm (accessed July 2005).

wider increasingly international common-sense understanding that *all* girls have come out 'on top' not only in educational spheres but in the world of work, so that 'the complex and rapid socio-economic changes generated by globalization, de-industrialization and the retreat of the welfare state [are seen to] have been more advantageous to young women than young men' (Aapola et. al., 2005:8).

Walkerdine, Lucey and Melody (2001:112) make this argument in the context of the UK in their study, *Growing up Girl*, which analyzes how exam results from high achieving girls at high achieving schools repeatedly obscure how achievement is always a 'class related phenomenon'. They offer longitudinal data on UK girls from both working-class and middle-class backgrounds in order to demonstrate how class cultures continue to shape educational outcomes for girls, and argue that attainment figures based on gender alone, mask how high performance is based in the superior performance of particular girls:

The resounding success by girls that has been spoken of in recent years is primarily about middle class girls and it has set in train a debate about a crisis of masculinity in post-industrial or deindustrialized societies. The effect of this on boys and men has been dramatic. It was formerly relatively easy for boys to obtain employment that did not require high levels of literacy, a particular accent or stylish attractiveness... However, fewer of those kinds of jobs exist in affluent countries and so boys are now being pushed to remake themselves as literate, adaptable and presentable: it is this that has produced a crisis for 'working-class masculinity and it is this that sets girls' educational achievement as a particular problem in the present...It is as though the success of girls has somehow been responsible for the dramatic and distressing changes that have happened over the last twenty or so years.

(Walkerdine et al., 2001:112)

The representational politics around girls' achievement outlined by Walkerdine et al. point to a distinctly postfeminist cultural space, where feminism is blamed for economic change and ensuing masculine 'crisis'. (See also Robinson in this volume.) As this passage indicates, in this gendered terrain girls, women and the feminine can be held accountable for all manner of cultural effects, as the benefactors of a shifting 'gender order' (Connell, 1987). Against the crisis of masculinity, the feminine becomes a site of contestation and anxiety but also desire over what is possible in the brutal conditions of contemporary schooling where success and failure are legitimized through new regimes of testing and achievement.

The shift in focus in debate from the object of the failing boy to the successful girl also, however, marks a shift away from a problem oriented discourse – that there is a problem with the effects of globalizing economic changes for masculinity – onto a success based discourse of femininity. In a context of neo-liberalism and dominant discourses of the self-made, rational, adapting subject, the qualities of adaptation, flexibility, malleability, re-invention, and making over the self ascribed to femininity have a central place in a discourse of economic and familial success (Walkerdine and Ringrose, 2006). The gender shifts we are witnessing require that both men and women increasingly perform what Lisa Adkins (1995) calls an 'aesthetics of femininity' and adaptation. Diane Reay suggests, in contrast, however, that in education (a key site in the production of upward mobility) with its 'growing emphasis on measured outputs, competition and entrepreneurship, it is primarily the assertiveness and authority of masculinity rather than the aesthetics of femininity that is required and rewarded' (Reay, 2001:165). The task for girls then, is to somehow juggle both feminine and masculine attributes in performing academically successful yet also distinctly feminine subjects (Walkerdine et al., 2001; Renold and Allen, 2006). This is the new work of 'doing' what is a specifically 'bourgeois' (middle class) femininity that girls and women must increasingly perform across sites of schooling and work (Walkerdine and Ringrose, 2006).

Femininity is, therefore, marshalled in new ways to sustain an educational area obsessed with academic achievement. We can see also that the discourse of girls' educational success reflects a 'neo-liberal' ethos of individualization, competition and marketization. There is an increasing postfeminist mythology that implies it is possible to win and be successful in the shifting global economy, and girls and feminine subjects, because of their flexibility, adaptability and hard work in spheres of education and work, are held up as the prototypes for this success (McRobbie, 2001).

## Conclusion

As we have suggested, girls' success in school signals massive public 'gender anxieties' and 'gender desires' in rapidly changing institutional and economic contexts (Segal, 1999). Girls' success signifies a brave new 'postfeminist' world, where issues of gender inequality are seen as no longer posing a problem, and where success is held up as there for the taking for 'a kind of young woman celebrated for her "desire, determination and confidence" to take charge of her life, seize chances, and achieve her goals' (Harris, 2004b: 1). Girls' new found 'equality' and success becomes a meritocratic formula, a signifier, a 'metaphor' for the hard work needed to attain educational and career success (McRobbie, 2004).

Educational research is pointing to the devastating effects when girls are positioned as 'not a problem' and resources siphoned away from addressing girls' learning and emotional needs at school (Osler et al., 2002; Crudas and Haddock, 2005). There are also massive contradictions now facing girls and boys within education where masculine levels of assertiveness and performance are rewarded, but it is girls who are viewed primarily to be adapting and succeeding in this context.

What is left for feminists to do? We need to work out the complex effects of the neo-liberal discourse of successful girls in both the 'over developed' and developing global contexts. What are the effects of the mythologies of girls' success in contexts where basic struggles for educational access and human rights remain paramount? Mapping local contexts of educational access and gendered politics of equality are crucial for understanding the complex and uneven effects of globalization (see Aikman and Unterhalter, 2005).

In the UK, pressing questions surround how girls are navigating contradictory demands to live up to ideals of success yet also perform more traditional discourses of femininity in postfeminist, neo-liberal schooling and employment climates. New research is exploring sites of contradiction and 'impossibility' in negotiating these new subject positions of being the 'bright and the beautiful', the 'nurturer and aggressor', and 'hetero-feminine desirable and successful learner', made available through the discourses of successful girls (Archer, 2005; Renold and Allen, 2005; Walkerdine, 2005; Youdell, 2005).

We need a great deal of further research, however, that can map out the effects and implications of the postfeminist, girl power, gender order (in education and beyond) and its meanings in diverse postfeminist global contexts, where the feminine comes to herald success and to signal that gender equality has been met and surpassed (Taft, 2004; Francis, 2005). Particularly important is further attention to the global disparities in educational provision and specific gendered educational outcomes *across* countries, as well as analytical focus on disparities in racialized and classed outcomes *within* national contexts.

In this difficult representational context key issues remain over how feminists can continue to complicate and disrupt these claims to gender equality: How are feminists to continue influencing and shaping debates over education in the current contested 'postfeminist' gender terrain? Most importantly, which feminism(s) do we 'do'?

Gender-only comparisons of boys and girls, used extensively by educational policy makers and news-makers alike, neglect how issues of gender and achievement at school are always cross cut by issues of race and class. When girls are positioned as the new global winners this wilfully ignores the dramatic global inequities and difficulties facing many girls in developing contexts, which we have outlined in this chapter. It is only by staking out the type, scope and complexity of our feminist analysis very carefully that our feminism will not be complicit with simplistic gender analyses, and will not as easily be recuperated into the problematic postfeminist discourse of successful girls.

## Further reading

S. Aikman and E. Unterhalter (2005) *Beyond Access: Transforming Policy and Practice for Gender Equality in Education*, London, Oxfam
This book examines the extent and causes of gender-based inequality in education in developing contexts. The articles analyze government policies and their implications for women's empowerment, and report on original fieldwork in a range of local contexts where gender-equality initiatives have flourished.

M. Arnot (2002) *Reproducing Gender? Critical Essays on Educational Theory and Feminist Politics*, London, Routledge Falmer
This collection introduces key ideas in education feminism. The essays examine the multiple blind spots of masculinist educational theories and the need for feminism in the struggle to democratize education. In particular the ways that gender inequalities continue to be 'reproduced' in educational practices in the UK are explored.

D. Epstein, J. Elwood, V. Hay and J. Maw (1998) *Failing Boys: Issues in Gender and Achievement*, Buckingham, Open University Press
This text presents the issues in the gender and achievement debates, placing the moral panic over failing boys in context. The book challenges the notion that all boys are underachieving in school and provides detailed case studies of educational issues in the UK in relation to the globalizing concerns over the education of boys.

B. Francis and C. Skeleton (2001) *Investigating Gender: Contemporary Perspectives in Education*, Buckingham, Open University Press
This book maps the contemporary and developing theoretical debates in the field of gender and education and recent research and policy. Contributors examine such issues as sexuality, social class, masculinity and femininity in education.

B. Francis and C. Skeleton (2005) *Reassessing Gender and Achievement: Questioning Contemporary Key Debates*, London, Routledge

This volume illustrates that the global debate around boys' underachievement shows no sign of diminishing. It asks why boys are being focused on at this time. How is achievement being conceived? What are the various explanations for the underperformance of boys? The book also highlights the continuing problems experienced by girls in terms of performance and classroom interaction.

# CHAPTER TEN

# Gender and Work

ZOE IRVING

## Introduction

Both as a concept and as a human activity 'work' is profoundly gendered. In the feminist analysis of work we find that much research and theorizing has focused on the ways in which the nature and rewards of men's work are valued more highly than those of women in societies, from the most simple (in the sociological sense) to the most industrially advanced. The idea that, as technological developments occur, men appropriate the most powerful of these as a means to maintain dominance (Cockburn, 1986) fits well with the recent history of industrial employment. Patterns of work established through industrialization certainly reflected the greater strength of men's interests in the workplace, and throughout the twentieth century, women's participation in the public world of paid work has been largely undertaken within the confines of male structures and male norms. The world of work has undoubtedly largely been a 'man's world', and where women have been able to inhabit this world, it has been on men's terms. However, the 21st century presents a slightly different picture; some gender divisions are as deeply embedded as they ever were, but processes of economic development have altered the framework within which the gender relations of work are negotiated and shaped.

While it is impossible to do justice to the entire literature covering gender and work here, this chapter is intended to present an account of the key theoretical questions and practical struggles that feminist writers have engaged with since the emergence of 'second wave' feminism in the 1960s. The structure of the chapter is designed around three enduring themes:

- the meaning(s) of 'work', how these are understood and how they are applied to the daily activities of women and men;
- the gendered experience of work and employment;
- the distribution of work and employment between women and men.

Following discussion and illustration of these themes, the chapter reviews some of the most significant theoretical contributions to the explanation of the enduring gender divisions of labour. Having outlined recent history and current divisions, the final section focuses on economic change and considers the prospects for gender relations presented by a shift from the traditional male breadwinner model of family and working life to, as yet, unestablished models.

## The gendering of work

Sociological enquiry often begins by questioning our common sense understandings of terms and activities and the study of 'work' is no exception. This section thus considers the gendered implications of:

- work as a 'productive' activity;
- work as an 'unproductive' activity;
- the assumed superiority of the productive over the unproductive;
- the skills and attributes associated with 'women's' and 'men's' work.

### *Market and non-market work*

Our understanding of 'work' is inextricably linked to the development of capitalist relations of production. In everyday language, the term work is used synonymously with the term employment reflecting an understanding that 'work' is something we are obliged to do in order to get paid, survive and consume. We contrast 'work' with 'leisure' which is what we do in our unobligated time, mostly utilizing the money we have earned through our 'work'. How we conceive of 'work' then is largely derived from economic theory, both classical and Marxist. To count as 'work' it is widely assumed that an activity has to be productive, a person's labour has to produce something with a market value. This absence of activity with no market value from the conceptualization of work has been at the heart of feminist critiques of reward based accounts of work, and unpaid or 'non-market' work, which has traditionally been undertaken in the domestic domain by women, has only relatively recently been recognized as 'work' at all (UN, 1986). While the term 'housework' has become an accepted description of efforts expended in managing domestic life (buying and preparing food, laundry, general cleaning and so on) the potential to regard this as worthy of economic reward outside the employment relationship has been vigorously debated. (See Jackson in this volume.)

The 'wages for housework' campaign, championed by Selma James and Maria Rosa Dalla Costa in the 1970s (and still active within the 'Global Women's Strike' international movement, http://www.globalwomenstrike.net/) was countered by both arguments based on assumptions of women's natural duties within marriage (see Lewis, 1984) and the non-productive characteristics of domestic labour (Offe and Heinze, 1992), as well as by feminists fearful of the potential for further domestic confinement that such a payment could support (see James and Benn, 2004). Although financial reward for unwaged and 'informal' labour remains elusive, recognition of the significance of women's unpaid labour in the world and national economies has become more apparent in the wealth of time-use survey data, which has become available since the 1990s. Table 10.1 summarizes some of the data on the gendered allocation of time for market and non-market work (UNDP, 2005).

## *Breadwinning and care-giving*

Gershuny's (2000) comprehensive analysis of historical and international time-use data sources suggests a slight trend towards 'gender convergence' in time devoted to paid and unpaid work, but he is also aware that this general trend disguises continuing difference in the detail of work performed. One such ideology is that of a 'male breadwinner' family model which has, to a greater or lesser extent, informed both the development of employment practices and the social policies that support them in industrially advanced economies. There are significant cross-national variations in this model, and as Lewis (2006) points out, the model has for the most part been an ideal rather than a reality. Nevertheless, it remains emblematic of the fundamental separation between the roles of men and women, where 'productive', economically valuable and public activity is assigned to men as 'breadwinners', and 'reproductive', socially necessary but private activity is assigned to women, as 'caregivers'. Keen to counter the essentialist basis of this model, early feminist writing on caring was critical of what was argued to be a flawed conception of care as non-productive and effortless (Finch and Groves, 1983). This work forcefully demonstrated that caring is both a labour-intensive and economically significant activity demanding recognition and reward equal to the status and gains of paid employment outside the home (Finch and Groves, 1983; Showstack Sassoon, 1987; Dalley, 1988), although, as Ungerson (1987) argued, not necessarily in the form of 'wages for caring'. Concerned to prevent the further encroachment of either the market or the state into social relations, feminists such as Himmelweit (1995) have also warned against a struggle to commodify care as 'work'. Contemporary research (for example, the contributions to a special issue of *Critical Social Policy*, 2002 and the CAVA themed section in *Social Policy and Society*, 2004) explores the significance of provision and receipt of care as a central element of fulfilment in intimate social relationships in an age of family fluidity. Calling for an 'ethic of care' as a counterbalance to the dominant work ethic (Sevenhuijsen, 1998; Williams, 2004), this work adds nuance to a critique of 'care as work', and highlights that, as with many false dichotomies, 'care' and 'work' exist along a complex continuum.

**Table 10.1** Gender, work and time allocation in selected countries

| | Year | Female work time (% of male) | Time allocation (%) | | | |
| --- | --- | --- | --- | --- | --- | --- |
| | | | Time spent by women | | Time spent by men | |
| | | | Market activities | Non-market activities | Market activities | Non-market activities |
| **Urban areas** | | | | | | |
| Columbia | 1983 | 112 | 24 | 76 | 77 | 23 |
| Indonesia | 1992 | 109 | 35 | 65 | 86 | 14 |
| Kenya | 1986 | 103 | 41 | 59 | 79 | 21 |
| **Rural areas** | | | | | | |
| Bangladesh | 1990 | 110 | 35 | 65 | 70 | 30 |
| Guatemala | 1977 | 117 | 37 | 63 | 84 | 16 |
| **OECD countries** | | | | | | |
| Australia | 1997 | 104 | 30 | 70 | 62 | 38 |
| Canada | 1998 | 98 | 41 | 59 | 65 | 35 |
| Denmark | 1987 | 98 | 58 | 42 | 79 | 21 |
| Finland | 1987–88 | 105 | 39 | 61 | 64 | 36 |
| France | 1999 | 108 | 33 | 67 | 60 | 40 |
| Germany | 1991–92 | 100 | 30 | 70 | 61 | 39 |
| Italy | 1988–89 | 128 | 22 | 78 | 77 | 23 |
| Japan | 1996 | 108 | 43 | 57 | 93 | 7 |
| Netherlands | 1995 | 98 | 27 | 73 | 69 | 31 |
| New Zealand | 1999 | 101 | 32 | 68 | 60 | 40 |
| Norway | 1990–91 | 108 | 38 | 62 | 64 | 36 |
| UK | 1985 | 100 | 37 | 63 | 68 | 32 |
| USA | 1985 | 106 | 37 | 63 | 63 | 37 |

*Source:* UNDP (2005:315, Table 29)

Because the domain of paid work has evolved around male interests, women's place in employment has largely been determined with reference to the male hegemonic model of industrial labour. This model assumes full-time life-long commitment to employment with minimal responsibilities beyond the economic – a model represented by the archetypal 'breadwinning' Fordist manufacturing worker. The association of 'men's work' with productivity and creativity and 'women's work' with reproduction and the mundane does not simply apply to conceptualizations of the public and the private spheres of activity, but also permeates through to women's involvement in paid work and men's roles as carers. In the post-Second World War period, much of women's increased employment has been located in sectors which represent an extension of the activities traditionally undertaken in the domestic sphere (Elder and Johnson, 2001). The evolution of welfare states rapidly expanded the demand for labour in health, education and welfare services and this has combined with the shift from the masculinized physically demanding jobs (also done by working class women until they were excluded by the nineteenth century Factory Acts) to service, clerical and administrative jobs regarded as more suitable for women. Here, we can identify the gendering of work in the public sphere evolving according to the pre-assigned roles in the private. This is particularly noticeable in the assumptions around the types of skills and attributes required to undertake certain types of paid work. 'Women' as workers have been assumed to represent a qualitatively different kind of workforce, which is submissive in character and limited in skill.

## *Gendered skills*

The construction of women's skills has also been explored in feminist writing which has argued that not only are women's skills generally devalued, but that men are also able to prevent women from acting through exclusionary and discriminatory practices. There are numerous historical and more recent examples of men's denigration of women's skills, often through trades union activity, which sought the protection of men's jobs and the 'family wage' through the restriction of women's access to training and occupational development (Lewis, 1984; Phillips and Taylor 1986; Daune-Richard, 2000). From history, Lewis (1984) reports that 'while oxyacetylene-welding was classed as skilled work prior to 1914, as soon as women entered the trade during the war employers reduced the pay by 50 per cent' (p. 171). While Cockburn's (1983) study of the printing industry demonstrates the extent to which male workers were able to maintain their privileged worker status through their union dominance, and consequent appropriation of new technology, and their ability to exert power over female workers in collective bargaining around wages and promotion. In this way feminized occupations have been devalued since they are constructed as low skilled, and they are designated as low skilled because the skills required are those that women are assumed to possess by nature rather than through recognized processes of acquisition such as apprenticeship. This restricted, masculine account of 'skill' is exposed in scholarship around the concept of 'emotional labour' (Hochschild, 1983; James, 1989), which examines the ways in which 'caring' skills such as empathy and insight, and the ability to manage or regulate emotions, form the basis of the activities required in much paid work in 'new' service industries from airlines to the more established welfare occupations such as nursing and social work (Aldridge, 1994) and to other new and ancient female occupations such as beauty therapy (Sharma and Black, 2001) and erotic dancing (Wood, 2000). While acknowledging the significance of emotional labour in women's experience of paid work, and notwithstanding the explicit and now globalized sex industry (Lee, 1991), from her research in tourist industries, Adkins (1995) points also to the centrality of *sexual* labour as a 'condition of employment' in jobs undertaken by women in the service sector. This is manifested in gendered expectations that the appearance and behaviour of female workers is part of the 'service', and, Adkins argues, is indicative of both gendered economic and power relations.

## The experience of employment

It is established that both common sense and theoretical understandings of work are gendered but what does this imply for practice? In essence the answer to this question lies in the qualitatively different experience of paid and unpaid labour amongst women and men. We can think about this experience in terms of:

- differences in the type and status of jobs that women and men do;
- differences in the financial rewards attached to women's jobs and men's jobs;
- the impact of these occupational divisions on economic and household power relations.

The first point to arise in any consideration of gender differences is that 'women' cannot be analyzed as a homogenous category. Divisions between women according to social class, 'race' and ethnicity, sexuality, disability, age and nationality are fundamental to their experience of paid and unpaid work, and the impact of more recent economic globalization and technological change has particular resonance for the analysis of interactions of class, 'race' and gender. The subsequent discussion is largely focused on gender divisions in advanced economies, but in accounting for these there must also be recognition of both the broader international division of labour and the inequalities that exist between women within national boundaries.

## Gender segregation in paid work

In the British context, a large but temporary influx of women to the labour market occurred during both First and Second World Wars (Lewis, 1984), but the feminization of employment has been facilitated through *post*-war changes in the industrial structure in the advanced economies. Working-class women had been employed in factories throughout the industrial age, and poor women had engaged in market work throughout the preceding centuries. But it was the development of the service economies from the 1960s that opened new doors for the employment of middle-class and married women whose adult lives in previous generations would have revolved around domestic activities rather than paid labour (Scott and Tilly, 1980; Lewis, 1984). A process of deindustrialization was begun as patterns of mass consumption began to be replaced by more individualized consumer demands and the rise of services in, for example, the finance sector (banking, insurance) and in public and welfare services (health, education, civil service), created jobs which have variously been described as 'white collar' in contrast to their 'blue collar' manufacturing equivalents (Crompton and Jones, 1984), 'pink' in terms of their gender association (Gatrell, 2005) and 'secondary' with reference to their place in the economic pecking order (Barron and Norris, 1976).

The feminization and masculinization of particular types of work, is termed *'occupational' or 'horizontal' segregation* (although 'horizontal' is less often used since it tends to refer to a simple manual/non-manual division). Although there is a gradual tendency to a proportionally gender-equal convergence in some occupations (catering and the legal professions for example), in the UK, there remains a clear pattern of occupational segregation where men form the majority of employees in jobs which require 'physical presence', such as security work (88 per cent of security guards are men) and in jobs which require scientific and technical skills such as computer software (86 per cent men) and ICT management (84 per cent men). In contrast, women form the majority of employees in caring (89 per cent of nurses), personal service (89 per cent of hairdressers, 79 per cent of cleaners) and administrative jobs (96 per cent of receptionists and 83 per cent of office assistants) (EOC, 2004a). Therefore, the majority of women do paid work that either mirrors their unpaid work in the home or 'assists' men in their superior position as managers and professionals. These feminized occupations also include the lowest paid occupations and thus, the distribution of women and men across occupations has an important effect on the existence of a gender pay gap, which is compounded by the effects of *vertical segregation* within occupations.

Vertical segregation describes the difference in status (and consequently reward) in the paid work undertaken by women and men, where men are over-represented in positions of seniority within organizations and women are over-represented in junior and less skilled positions. For example, in Britain, more than twice as many men as women are managers, senior officials and professionals (EOC, 2004a) and even in supposedly 'feminized' occupations such as teaching, while 55 per cent of secondary teachers are women they represent only 30.5 per cent of secondary head teachers. If we consider the most extreme everyday examples, despite women's massive over-representation in hairdressing and catering, if asked to name the most prominent UK celebrity chefs and hair stylists in 2007, we would be largely restricted to a shortlist of men. In the global context, Wirth (2001) reports that although women's share of professional and managerial jobs is increasing, 'women's overall share of management jobs rarely exceeds 20 per cent in most countries, yet they represent more than 40 per cent of the world's labour force...in the largest and most powerful organizations, the proportion of top positions held by women is generally 2 to 3 per cent' (p. 243). The stalling of women's careers before they reach senior management and professional status, has been explained through the existence of a 'glass ceiling'. Analysis has suggested that women are excluded from top positions by both discriminatory institutional processes that operate within organizations (sometimes termed 'statistical' discrimination), and also as a result of personal discriminatory attitudes held by their senior male colleagues who operate selection procedures (Snell, 1986; Wirth, 2001). Institutional factors can include job specifications which implicitly disadvantage women through requirements which assume continuous work histories, while personal influences are evidenced in explicit sexism encountered in job interviews, for example. With the enactment of sex discrimination legislation in 1975 in the UK, many sexist practices were outlawed, and since then the advancement of an equal opportunities agenda within the European Union has considerably improved women's working lives (Heide, 2001). However, many sex discrimination cases continue to reach the European Court of Justice, including those based on grounds of sexual harassment (Hodges Aeberhard, 2001), and there is much qualitative evidence to demonstrate the continued operation of discriminatory practices, particularly in relation to working mothers (see for example Heide, 2001; Gatrell, 2005).

## *The gender pay gap*

Given that women are disproportionately found in low paying occupations and in lower status jobs in more highly paid occupations it comes as no surprise that most women earn less than most men. The gender pay gap, that is, the ratio of female to male earnings expressed as a percentage of male earnings, is 16 per cent, on average, in OECD (Organisation for Economic Co-operation and Development) countries (OECD, 2002a). Broadly speaking, OECD refers to countries that are industrialized. In countries such as the UK and US, the gap is at least 20 per cent for full-time employees and higher still if part-time employees are included in the calculations. Evidence regarding gender-differentiated pay is conclusive and the wage gap exists regardless of level of qualification (WWC, 2006). In the UK, pay differences are present despite the existence of the 1970 Equal Pay Act which outlawed differential wage rates offered on grounds of sex, and stated that the lowest paid female employee could not be paid less than the lowest paid male employee in a firm. The law was further amended in 1984 to attend to some of the effects of occupational segregation through the requirement for equal pay for work of 'equal value', but the interpretation of 'equal value' remains rather hazy and again brings us back to the gendered construction of 'skill'. The devaluing of women's skills by both men and the market, however, cannot fully explain the pay and status differences between women and men and to explore these divisions further we have to look at inequalities in paid *and* unpaid work.

## The sharing of work and employment

In Britain, the overall employment rate has not changed significantly since the 1970s, but the gender composition of those employed is very different now to the patterns found in 1976. This section considers some of the following issues, which arise in analyses of gender and work:

- Differences in the patterns of labour force participation between women and men, most noticeably within the part-time/full-time divide and the impact of labour market flexibilization on these gendered divisions.
- The relevance, validity and accuracy of statistical conceptualizations of 'unemployment' and 'economic inactivity' in relation to women's work.
- Differences in the patterns of labour force participation between women depending on their age, family status and ethnic group.
- Gender inequalities in the distribution of unpaid work.

In terms of the 'share' of employment, in 1971 women accounted for just over a third of those employed, not much different to their proportion in 1931 or even in 1951. However, by 1991 the figure had risen to 43.2 per cent and by 1998, 46.4 per cent of those employed were women (Gallie, 2000:293, Table 8.8). It is argued that a gradual 'feminization' of the labour market has occurred as men's rates of employment have declined through redundancy, unemployment and early retirement, while women's rates have increased. Currently, in advanced economies, women's labour force participation rates range from around 50 per cent in countries such as Italy and Greece to over 70 per cent in the Nordic states, the latter almost on a par with men's average rates. In the UK, women's participation rate at 69.6 per cent, is slightly higher than the US (69.2) and considerably higher than the average for women in the 15 pre-accession EU countries (62.8) (OECD, 2005:240, Table B). However, the simple fact that more women are in the labour market cannot be taken to imply that their presence is accepted, valued and rewarded in the same way as that of men, or that their patterns of work are the same. Women's increased entry into the world of paid work has certainly not taken place on an equal basis to men's established position. It was not just the sectoral location of jobs in areas of 'women's work' which drew married women and mothers into the labour market, it was also the manner in which employers chose to organize the offer of employment.

## *The full-time/part-time divide*

In the course of the feminization of employment, the most fundamental difference between women's and men's access to employment is the full-time/ part-time divide. Women undertake more than three-quarters of the part-time employment available in the EU15 and it accounts for 40.4 per cent of women's total employment in the UK (OECD, 2005:253–4, Table E). Part-time employment has been the greatest source of job growth in the OECD countries over recent decades but historically part-time workers have been regarded as a reactionary force in both the process of labour organization and the struggle for gender equality, and the debate continues as to whether women's part-time employment should be considered as a feminist friend or foe (Bonney, 2005). The early development of part-time employment occurred in the face of historical resistance and hostility to women's employment on the part of male dominated trades unions, for whom it represented an employer strategy to undermine wages and the general conditions of employment for male workers (Cockburn, 1983; Charles, 1986). While women generally have been subject to exclusionary practices based on assumptions of their lack of commitment to the aims of organized (male) labour, up until the 1980s, female part-time workers had additionally been regarded as unorganizable. Much has changed since then and although women part-time workers (and other non-standard workers) remain less likely to be unionized (Tam, 1997), most unions in the UK now attempt to incorporate the protection of the interests of part-timers into negotiation and policy (Bradley, 1999). Nevertheless, the absence of unionization amongst the increasing numbers of non-standard workers is likely to contribute to the further erosion of labour as an agent of power, with negative consequences for the pursuit of gender equality.

From a feminist perspective, the offer of part-time employment represents something of a Trojan horse. For many women, particularly those with lower educational attainment, part-time employment represents a 'bridge' (Tam, 1997) to the public world of paid work and opportunities to achieve a measure of financial and personal independence, in other words a step towards greater equality. At the same time, defence of part-timers allows tacit support for a form of paid work which undervalues women's skills and is generally offered under exploitative conditions. In contemporary analyses of part-time employment there is less attention to its structural influence on labour relations, and feminist concern lies in women's restricted access to the full-time labour market and the social and economic consequences of this. Part-time employment is associated with low pay, poor career progression prospects, limited job security and reduced social protection and it is thus constructed as inferior and secondary to the ideal of full-time employment (Blossfeld and Hakim, 1997; O'Reilly and Fagan, 1998; Creighton, 1999). Evidence demonstrates that, although the availability of part-time jobs enables many women to enter paid work, at the same time it compels them to travel on the low road of economic activity (Tam, 1997). In Britain, the gender pay gap between part-time women and full-time men (40 per cent) is much higher than between female and male full-timers. In contrast, it is also the case that in countries where women are politically and/or economically necessary in the labour force, employers have been obliged to offer employment on more attractive terms which allow women to meet the demands of their family responsibilities (Bruegel and Hegewisch, 1994; McRae, 1998) and that part-time employment is not necessarily experienced negatively. In the Nordic countries for example, where parents' option to reduce working hours is an established statutory right, part-time employment is not confined to low-status or low-paid occupations and is regarded as an important element of gender equitable employment policy.

In the UK, an important aspect of difference between women in relation to the part-time/full-time divide is found according to the ethnic group to which they belong. Labour Force Survey data for Great Britain show that in 2000–2002, full-time employment rates were highest amongst Black Caribbean women at 45 per cent and lowest amongst Pakistani and Bangladeshi women at 14 and 9 per cent respectively. These figures compare to a rate of 38 per cent amongst white women and a similar rate of 37 per cent amongst Indian women (Lindley et al., 2004). White women are more likely to work part-time than any other ethnic group with a rate of 28 per cent, while again Bangladeshi women have the lowest rate of part-time employment at 6 per cent. These low rates of both full- and part-time employment for Bangladeshi women reflect low overall rates of economic activity which have been linked to both earlier childbearing and the operation of a more traditional gender regime within this ethnic group, as well as the effects of lower educational attainment and discrimination within the labour market (Walby, 1997; Dale et al., 2002; Lindley et al., 2004). In contrast, explanation of the higher rates of full-time employment amongst black women have focused on the demographic structure of Black families and cultural differences in relation to the construction of women's independence (Duncan and Edwards, 1997) and in critique of cultural explanations: 'quite simply that they [Black households] are poorer and more in need of women's earnings' (Bruegel, 1994: 187). As Bruegel (1994) further demonstrates, Black women's presence in full-time employment should not be taken as evidence of race or gender equality, since it is more likely to be in the kind of low-paid manual jobs associated with white women's part-time employment.

## *Gender and flexibilization*

Employment restructuring since the 1980s has drawn scholarly attention beyond a focus on the part-time/full-time divide to the examination of labour flexibilization (Pollert, 1991; Dex and McCulloch, 1997). Since the early 1990s, there has been polarization between 'work rich' and 'work poor' households (Gregg and Wadsworth, 2003) and an expansion of jobs and conditions of employment variously characterized as 'atypical', 'non-standard' and 'precarious' (Meulders et al., 1994; Allan and Brosnan, 1998; Frade and Darmon, 2005). The latter has been a profoundly gendered process although not uniformly observed in Europe and other advanced economies (Dex and McCulloch, 1997; Fagan and Burchell, 2002). Women's closer relationship to flexible working is not a new phenomenon, the global endurance of homeworking as a female preserve providing a classic example of this historicity (Rowbotham, 1993). Multi-tasking and flexible working were characteristic of women's work in the pre and early industrial periods (Honeyman, 2000), and the assumed temporary nature of women's employment is demonstrated by the existence of the 'marriage bar' which operated to exclude married women from paid employment between the late nineteenth and mid twentieth centuries (Lewis, 1984). Where occupations are feminized, they are more likely to diverge from the male model of employment (Purcell, 1988), and developing the work of Braverman (1974) it has been argued that because women are regarded as a cheap, submissive and secondary workforce, an 'industrial reserve army', that their employment has been subject to greater reorganization than that of men. This characterization of women has been questioned (Bruegel, 1986; Dex, 1988) since historically women have been a permanent feature of the labour market rather than a marginal workforce, but nevertheless, in the low-paid, low-status, feminized occupations (clerical, retailing, and service work such as cleaning) where women comprise over 60 per cent of workers, part-time and other forms of precarious employment are also most prevalent (Fagan and Burchell, 2002).

Two further aspects of flexible employment are significant here: firstly that the various forms of non-standard employment are themselves gendered with men found in greater proportions for example, amongst the self-employed, those working long daily hours, and those with variable work schedules while women are over-represented amongst part-time and homeworkers (Drew and Emerek, 1998; Fagan and Burchell, 2002). Although Fagan and Burchell (2002) report some gender convergence around shift and weekend working, the patterns continue to suggest that, while men are engaged in income maximization strategies in line with the breadwinner model, women attempt to combine paid work with domestic commitments. A second important feature in the gendering of flexibility is that a greater proportion of part-time rather than full-time workers are employed on temporary contracts (Fagan and Burchell, 2002). This has clear implications for women's more acute relationship with flexibilization, and more significant still is the link between precarious employment and unemployment for both women and men.

## Gender, unemployment and inactivity

In addition to the debates around the female 'reserve army of labour', women's unemployment and redundancy has also been explored from a feminist perspective (Coyle, 1984; Rubery, 1988) which challenged the notion that unemployment was, for women, a less significant event. Heterosexist and patriarchal assumptions regarded women's unemployment as merely a return to their primary activity of wifely labour, with limited financial impact on the household since women's earnings were considered secondary. This routine dismissal of the significance of women's unemployment in the 1970s and 1980s remains discernible even in current mainstream writing which implicitly privileges men's assumed greater psychological and financial 'need' for paid work (Van Oorschot, 2002). In most industrialized countries, women's rates of unemployment are higher than those of men (OECD, 2005). This pattern has been linked to the rise in precarious employment which pushes women more readily than men into marginal positions in the labour market where the separation between temporary, part-time employment and unemployment is weak and permeable (Gauvin, 2000; Hegewisch, 2000).

As can be seen from Table 10.2, as well as having one of the lowest rates of female unemployment among the advanced western economies, the UK is one of the few countries where women's unemployment is lower than that of men, a pattern shared with the US and Canada as well as Sweden, Norway and Iceland. In the UK, one explanation of the under-representation of women rests on the basis of the measurement of unemployment which is linked to the operation of a male-biased social security benefit system. Consequently, in the UK many women are 'discouraged workers', that is people who would like to gain employment but who have little expectation of rejoining the labour market. In other European countries, long-term unemployment figures for women reflect this phenomenon and have shown a substantial increase in the

**Table 10.2** Unemployment rates for women and men in selected OECD countries, 2004 (%)

|           | Women | Men  |
|-----------|-------|------|
| Australia | 5.6   | 5.4  |
| Denmark   | 5.5   | 5.1  |
| France    | 10.7  | 8.7  |
| Germany   | 9.4   | 10.3 |
| Greece    | 16.0  | 6.5  |
| Italy     | 10.6  | 6.4  |
| Spain     | 15.1  | 8.2  |
| UK        | 4.3   | 5.0  |
| US        | 5.5   | 5.7  |
| EU15      | 9.1   | 7.5  |

*Source:* OECD (2005: 239–40, Table B).

decade 1994–2004, with an average of 43.3 per cent of unemployed women in the EU15 having been unemployed for twelve months or more (OECD, 2005:260, Table G). Women in this group are often in disguised unemployment and show up in statistics as 'economically inactive' having described themselves as being full-time mothers or carers, housewives or students. In the UK, this misrepresentation of women's activity and aspiration has been particularly noticeable in relation to lone mothers. Thus, women are over-represented on the 'fringes' of unemployment as well as amongst the officially defined unemployed (Gauvin, 2000).

Unemployment is also a highly racialized condition in the UK for both women and men. With reference to data from the 2001 Census, the Equal Opportunities Commission (EOC, 2004b) suggests that rates of unemployment 'were influenced more by ethnic group than gender' (p. 7) with rates above 12 per cent for Pakistani, Bangladeshi and Black African women and men and Black Caribbean men compared to rates of 3.8 per cent and 5.6 per cent for white women and men. At just under 8 per cent, the unemployment rate for Black Caribbean women was much lower than for Black Caribbean men. Educational achievement and length of settlement are factors which may impact on the likelihood of unemployment. However, in his critique of Modood et al.'s (1997) explanations for the 'closing' of the employment gap between minority ethnic groups and the white population in the UK, Virdee (2006) emphasizes the gains made through political struggle. This anti-racist activism he argues, was particularly successful in the efforts of public sector unions and has facilitated the employment of ethnic minority women within junior non-manual occupations. Age is also a significant factor in differences in women's unemployment rates by ethnic group and an indication of this can be found in Table 10.3. Ethnic minority groups in the UK have much younger population structures than the white population (EOC, 2004b) and recent research suggests that differences in unemployment by ethnicity between women are greatest amongst the oldest and youngest age groups (Lindley et al., 2004). In a British study of Bangladeshi and Pakistani women, these more general statistical trends are supported by qualitative data which draw attention to both gender ideology within these communities, which places less emphasis on women's economic activity, and the impact of employer discrimination based on cultural and religious stereotyping of Muslim women (Dale et al., 2002).

## Employment patterns over the life course

Women's tendency to be found in economically inactive categories and their more complex relationship with employment leads us to consider women's work over the life course. The most significant factor in the difference between women and men's lifetime work patterns is the presence of children. The presence of dependent children decreases women's employment rates while it has the opposite effect on those of men (EOC, 2004a). What this suggests is that while women reduce their participation in paid work in order to care for children, men increase their participation (often through the use of overtime) in order to meet the additional household costs of a child and often to compensate for the mother's lost earnings. While the employment rates of men and women without dependent children are broadly similar at around 75 per cent, for women and men with dependent children aged 0–15 years the rates are 62 per cent and 82 per cent respectively (DTI, 2004).

Nevertheless, as Figure 10.1 shows, more recently the 'M' shaped curve of women's lifetime employment rates has flattened out indicating that fewer women are withdrawing from the labour market upon the birth of children. Research also demonstrates that not only are women returning to work after having children, but they are also returning much more quickly than in the past (Smeaton, 2006). In the UK, the existence of statutory maternity provisions enacted in 1978 and 1993 are of course influential in facilitating the continuity of women's employment and, following further improvements in 2003 and 2006, women are currently entitled to 39 weeks paid leave with a further 13 weeks unpaid leave with job protection. However, women returning to work following childbirth are much more likely to be part-time with

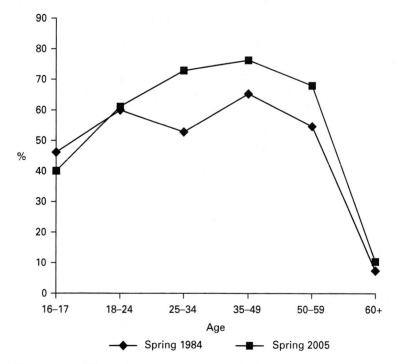

**Figure 10.1** Women's employment rates by age, Great Britain, 1984 and 2005

*Source:* Adapted from ONS Labour Force Survey (2006b), not seasonally adjusted.

71 per cent of women with children under 2 years working part-time, compared to 28 per cent of women without dependent children (DTI, 2004) and the employment rates of 'unskilled' women with preschool children are half those of professional women. In addition to divisions between women according to social class and age, again women from black and other minority ethnic groups present different lifetime employment profiles to those of white women, reflecting both demographic differences and the operation of a racialized labour market (Walby, 1990). As can be seen from Table 10.3, Pakistani and Bangladeshi mothers for example, are much more likely to remain out of the labour market when they have dependent children whereas Black Caribbean mothers are more likely to remain in full-time employment even when they are lone parents. A general trend for all women however, is the greater likelihood of economic inactivity in the presence of children, particularly when they are under school age.

## *The gendered distribution of unpaid work*

While women's work histories are characterized by weak lifetime links to the labour market due to intermittent and partial participation, until recently men's work histories were characterized by strong, continuous and full-time participation and this is still true for a significant proportion of men. The converse of the unequal distribution of paid work of course is the equally unequal distribution of unpaid work within the home. Following a substantial literature review in her book *The Workings of the Household*, Morris (1990) concluded that, despite changes in women's participation in paid work, men's contribution to domestic work did not compensate for their work outside the home. Delamont (2001) reaches the same conclusion just over a decade later. The essence of the 'male breadwinner' model is the primacy of men's full-time paid employment, the onus therefore has always remained on women to accommodate the desire, demand or necessity to undertake paid work within their caregiver role. Dual breadwinning usually means dual burden for women and the unequal distribution of domestic work within dual earning households persists into the twenty-first century, as is demonstrated both in comparative quantitative time use surveys (OECD, 2001; European Foundation, 2002; Kodz et al., 2003) and qualitative case studies (Windebank, 2001). Responsibility for care and domestic work is not shared equally between women and men regardless of women's employment status, and on average in the advanced economies women spend more than double the amount of time spent by men on non-market activities (see Table 10.1, and also Jackson in this volume). The Scandinavian countries are often quoted as demonstrating greater gender egalitarianism at the household level (Plantenga and Hansen, 2001). However, Björnberg's (1998) qualitative study of Swedish fathers injects a measure of caution into the conflation of men's desire to be involved in the care of their children with a desire to share equally in the less fulfilling domestic chores.

**Table 10.3** Proportions of women* in selected ethnic groups by economic activity status and life stage, Great Britain, 2000–2002 (%)

| | No partner, no dependent children and aged under 35 | Partner, no dependent children and aged under 35 | No partner, with children | Partner, youngest child aged 0–4 | Partner, youngest child aged 5–15 | No partner, no dependent children and aged 35 and over | Partner, no dependent children and aged 35 and over |
|---|---|---|---|---|---|---|---|
| **White** | | | | | | | |
| Economically inactive | 8 | 4 | 47 | 35 | 19 | 24 | 28 |
| Unemployed | 5 | 2 | 6 | 3 | 2 | 1 | 4 |
| Full-time employment | 70 | 84 | 16 | 20 | 27 | 40 | 49 |
| Part-time employment | 18 | 10 | 30 | 42 | 52 | 35 | 19 |
| All | 100 | 100 | 100 | 100 | 100 | 100 | 100 |
| **Black Caribbean** | | | | | | | |
| Economically inactive | 13 | 2 | 36 | 26 | 10 | 19 | 26 |
| Unemployed | 12 | 2 | 10 | 8 | 10 | 3 | 8 |
| Full-time employment | 56 | 84 | 33 | 39 | 43 | 58 | 57 |
| Part-time employment | 19 | 12 | 21 | 28 | 38 | 20 | 10 |
| All | 100 | 100 | 100 | 100 | 100 | 100 | 100 |
| **Black African** | | | | | | | |
| Economically inactive | 14 | 9 | 58 | 36 | 15 | 25 | 28 |

|  |  |  |  |  |  |  |  |
|---|---|---|---|---|---|---|---|
| Unemployed | 16 | 13 | 10 | 7 | 7 | 8 | 9 |
| Full-time employment | 41 | 56 | 21 | 36 | 55 | 56 | 51 |
| Part-time employment | 29 | 22 | 11 | 20 | 23 | 11 | 12 |
| All | 100 | 100 | 100 | 100 | 100 | 100 | 100 |
| **Indian** |  |  |  |  |  |  |  |
| Economically inactive | 7 | 18 | 49 | 43 | 29 | 34 | 44 |
| Unemployed | 7 | 3 | 11 | 4 | 3 | 3 | 7 |
| Full-time employment | 63 | 71 | 19 | 26 | 37 | 44 | 37 |
| Part-time employment | 22 | 8 | 21 | 27 | 31 | 19 | 13 |
| All | 100 | 100 | 100 | 100 | 100 | 100 | 100 |
| **Pakistani/Bangladeshi** |  |  |  |  |  |  |  |
| Economically inactive | 19 | 42 | 76 | 82 | 79 | 81 | 85 |
| Unemployed | 15 | 9 | 6 | 2 | 2 | 2 | 3 |
| Full-time employment | 38 | 41 | 6 | 6 | 8 | 12 | 8 |
| Part-time employment | 28 | 8 | 12 | 11 | 10 | 4 | 5 |
| All | 100 | 100 | 100 | 100 | 100 | 100 | 100 |

*Women aged 19–59. Excludes economically inactive full-time students.
*Source:* Labour Force Survey unweighted data, CCSR, in Lindley et al. (2004: 162, Table 9).

## Explaining gendered patterns of work

Explanation of the existence of feminized occupations and gender segregation in the labour market broadly follows two separate paths. These diverge on the relative strength which authors accord to:

- individual agency, that is the extent to which women and men choose to be different (and unequal); and
- structural processes, that is the set of power relationships between groups (including women and men), which restrict the opportunities of weaker groups to achieve equality.

Early theorizing of gendered patterns of work tended to rest on either:

- the effects of patriarchy on the structures of capitalism, emphasizing the benefits of women's inferior labour market status which accrue to capital, and the benefits to men gained by restricting women's access to economic resources (Hartmann, 1979; Molyneux, 1979); or
- theories that emphasize women's choice of investment in their employability, and commitment or 'orientation' to paid work outside the home (Mincer and Polachek, 1980; Becker, 1991; Hakim, 1991).

Both of these sets of explanations have been subject to critique and elaboration, and clearly the restrictive impact of the sexual division of domestic labour on the formation of women's roles, terms of engagement and reward in paid employment is central to the explanation of gendered work. (See also Jackson in this volume.) However, as noted earlier in relation to 'skill', the recognition of the significance of other aspects of male domination of industrial development is also essential in broadening our understanding of gender relations (Beechey, 1986; Cockburn, 1986; Dex, 1988; Bergmann, 1995; Honeyman, 2000). In her study of economic development in late medieval Europe, Howell (1986) observed that, as the site and relations of production moved away from the family unit, women's power was lost because, unlike men, women remained tied to the domestic sphere and were thus unable to re-establish power in the public domain. In her conclusion, Howell also raises the possibility that women gave up control, rather than having it wrenched from them. Howell's analysis also documents the ways in which men actively pursued women's removal from economic life, however, and the question of the extent to which women exercise agency in the determination of their work, employment and life choices rather than being at the mercy of men and the market remains central in the debates on gender inequalities, their origins and remedies.

### *Agency and structure, choice and constraint*

Voluntarism, or the exercise of agency is central to Catherine Hakim's important, though controversial (Bruegel, 1996; Ginn et al., 1996; Crompton and

Harris, 1998; Marks and Houston, 2002) contribution to research on women and work. Hakim's 'preference' theory (2000) develops the theme of female heterogeneity (Hakim, 1996), which places women's lack of collective interests (and consequent differences in choice to be a 'worker', 'homemaker' or both) at the centre of any explanation of their social and economic disadvantage to men. Hakim argues that men have less choice of social and economic roles and, thus, an obvious collective interest to compete and succeed in public life at women's expense. As Walby (1997:7) reminds us, echoing Marx, 'women act, but not always in circumstances of their choosing'.

Human capital theory derives from classical economic approaches that assume that markets are neutral and people are rational. In contrast to these approaches there is a wealth of literature concerned with the ways in which markets are political and rationality is not primarily economic (for example, Duncan and Edwards, 1997; Duncan, 2003). Particularly influential has been Walby's (1990) development of Hartmann's (1979) 'dual systems' analysis, which Walby presents in the operation of six structures of patriarchy: paid work; household production; culture; sexuality; violence and the state, and in a historical account of a shift from 'private' to 'public' forms of patriarchy. Private patriarchy, Walby argues, is found in systems of household production and operates through the exclusion of women *from* the public realms of male power. In contrast, systems of public patriarchy operate through the segregation and subordination of women *within* the public sphere of politics and culture (Walby, 1990: 173–9). What is important in Walby's analysis is the emphasis given to women as political actors, particularly in the period of 'first wave feminism' from the mid nineteenth century to the 1930s, in place of a simplistic reduction of changes in gender relations to the forces of capitalism. Walby (1997) is also interested in differences between women, but in contrast to Hakim (1996, 2000), who frames this in terms of a homemaker–worker 'choice' continuum, Walby's concern is that economic, political and cultural changes are creating new and wider divisions between women than have existed in the past, particularly between younger and older women. Walby's attention to the social and economic disparities between different groups of women beyond the full-time/part-time divide gives us a clearer picture of the ways in which gender relations are re-negotiated over time and place and according to the interplay with other aspects of social division. In the contemporary context, explanations of gender inequalities in employment stretch outside the capitalism/patriarchy 'dual systems' approach in an attempt to address the non-economic dimensions of gender relations that cannot be separated from economic behaviour.

The significance of international comparative analysis is crucial in further developing our understanding of why and how women and men establish particular patterns of employment and how these fit into the other facets of everyday life in the current era of de-industrialization and the rise of global, political and economic forces. Daly and Rake, for example, clearly account for women's heterogeneity, but also demonstrate the power of welfare states in 'opening up' or 'closing down' choices and opportunities across the life course (Daly and Rake, 2003:159). The opportunities available to women and thus the choices they make: whether and when to have children, form partnerships, get married, pursue study and qualifications and so on, largely determine their immediate and subsequent social and economic wellbeing, but also the choices available in the future (Walby, 1997; Daly and Rake, 2003). The extent to which welfare systems treat women as mothers, workers, independent citizens, or combinations of all three varies widely across welfare states and the influence of these institutional factors combined with socio-cultural practices within gender regimes, cannot be underestimated in the explanation of the cross-national variation in gendered patterns of paid and unpaid work (Sainsbury, 1994; Crompton, 1999).

## Work: is the future female?

From the preceding discussion, it might appear that the story of work relations between women and men was one of historical inequality endlessly repeating itself with little hope of a happy ending. Reference to the past, however, shows that times of acute economic restructuring are also points at which existing social orders can be challenged and resettled (Howell, 1986; Honeyman, 2000). For the advanced economies at least, we may well have reached such a crossroads and it is important to consider some of the areas in which indicators of this resettlement can be found:

- The shift towards a more universalized 'female' model of partial and intermittent employment;
- The rise of 'work–life balance' strategies and their political significance.

The recent history of women's employment has been characterized by their shadowing of and aspiration to the hegemonic male model. Some writers have applauded and championed women's direct competition with men, arguing that women following the male model are challenging the gender order while those following the female model are promoting it (Hakim, 1996). There is research evidence to suggest that the presence of women in senior positions is beneficial to the transformation of work culture (Belloni et al., 2000), but women in positions of power cannot be assumed to promote the interest of women more generally. Women who 'choose' to follow the male model, adopt masculine values and goals and inhabit men's employment structures may have little to gain and much to lose from a gender transformation.

### *The rise of the female model of employment and the rebalancing of work and life*

Regardless of what women and men desire either collectively or as individuals, industrial restructuring has encouraged a gradual seepage of employment relationships previously considered 'female' into many industries which are not characterized by a preponderance of women, and this could be expected to have an impact on domestic gender relations. What have not been borne out in practice, as Bradley (1999) notes, are the predictions of a gender homogenization of employment resulting from processes of economic globalization. The late 1990s did not witness busloads of pink-collared men seeking work in the caring professions, and we remain a long way from the 'universal caregiver' social model (Fraser, 1997b). Nonetheless, rather than the jobs done, it is the terms under which jobs are offered and undertaken which are drifting towards a female model. Male part-time employment is increasing in many advanced economies; the Netherlands is argued to be 'the first part-time economy in the world' (Visser, 2002) and France recently experimented with a reduction in working time for all. Thus, despite the assumed attachment of men to the reality or aspiration of full-time work, the trends suggest that the conditions of post-industrial employment favour an imposition of the female model.

There is certainly a discernible policy trend in the direction of the renegotiation of the distribution of paid and unpaid work. Developed from debates around family–work reconciliation begun in the EU policy context, the concept of 'work–life balance' has emerged. Political interest in the achievement of balance between the demands of paid work and caring responsibilities has emerged in the context of global economic competitiveness, changes in the demographic structure of advanced economies and debates around the affordability of welfare states, or more specifically the costs of non-participation in the labour market (OECD, 2002b). Despite the use of gender-neutral language in official accounts of strategies to assist in the combination of paid and unpaid work, terms like 'families' and 'parents', as has been well established by feminist studies of care, in practice means 'women' and 'mothers' (Finch and Groves, 1980). In fact it is somewhat disingenuous to present the 'business case' for work–life balance strategies in non-gendered terms since the core of this case is the labour market mobilization and retention of (skilled) female employees (Dex and Smith, 2002; OECD, 2001, 2002b). The key elements of work–life balance policies are located in flexible working arrangements, entitlements to paid or unpaid leave and assistance with the care of children whether this is paid or in kind. In practice it is clear that work–life balance strategies are directed towards female employees (and potential employees). British evidence suggests that family-friendly policies are more common in organizations with greater numbers of female employees (Dex and Smith, 2002; OECD, 2002b) and that it is predominantly women who request the now statutory gender-neutral opportunities for flexible working (CIPD, 2003).

Work–life balance policy may be employer-led but it has evolved partly from women's political agency and has great symbolic significance. Given the progress of such measures, it seems that the transformation of men remains as the biggest obstacle in the course of gender equality in work. Emerging debates concern the place of men in caring roles, particularly as fathers (Popay et al., 1998; Pease and Pringle, 2001; Hatten et al., 2002; Hobson, 2002; EOC,

2003). There is dissent around the level of choice enjoyed by women and men in relation to their roles and responsibilities in 'work' and 'life'. Clarke and Popay (1998) argue that 'motherhood is mandated and fatherhood discretionary' (p. 226) but, as with women's 'choices', the structural constraints on men's desires to share domestic responsibilities are largely overlooked, and assumptions of male homogeneity and men's rejection of the private are deeply embedded. Despite the incontrovertible historical record of men's absence from domestic work, there is also evidence to suggest that in the last decade men's employment/family priorities have begun to change (Dex, 2003), often in response to their female partner's employment decisions and career status (Reeves, 2002; Baldock and Hadlow, 2005). There is also evidence that the domestic division of labour is sensitive to changes in men's own un/employment experience (Wheelock, 1990). Nevertheless, no matter how strong the aspiration to greater equity within households, men's working time, work practices and workplace culture offer powerful resistance to this becoming a reality (Fagan, 1996; OECD, 2002b). It is for this reason though that identified changes in at least the former two aspects of men's working lives are so important. If men are not to share in the domestic work that increasingly employed women do not have time to complete, then a further polarization between women will occur, as the more highly skilled buy in the services of the less skilled, with little or no impact on the gender distribution. These forms of class difference in the experience and distribution of employment have already been alluded to in previous sections, what is more significant here is the way in which longstanding patterns of racialization of women's work (Bhavnani, 1997) are being re-established through the operation of a global care industry (Yeates, 2005). While benefiting better-off employed women in rich countries, these processes situate migrant women from the global South (and Central and Eastern Europe) as insecure and exploited domestic labourers, and serve as a clear reminder that within the relationship between work and gender, women's interests and experience are far from universal.

## Conclusion

Like an aerial photograph, this chapter has presented a snapshot overview, which necessarily comprises aspects of breadth, rather than depth. In the picture of the study of gender and work presented here, however, some of the most prominent landmarks have been identified. The gendering of work is an evolutionary process and the contemporary picture continues to reflect many of the sexual divisions established in both pre-industrial and industrial eras. These divisions are shaped and experienced by women in ways that reflect female heterogeneity in social position and identity. What the picture also tells us, however, is that these landmarks are not fixed over time, the buildings and monuments of gender inequality and difference have been, and can be, demolished and rebuilt. Audre Lorde (1994) has argued that 'the master's tools

will never dismantle the master's house', and certainly it is unlikely that a few 'fully-involved dads' (Hatten et al., 2002), limited occupational desegregation (Witz, 1997) and the extension of flexible employment practices (Dex, 2003) will successfully transform gender relations. Nevertheless, the current economic and political context does offer some potential for change in the social relations of gender, workplace culture and the relationship between work and life.

## Further reading

R. Crompton (2006) *Employment and the family: The Reconfiguration of Work and Family Life in Contemporary Societies,* Cambridge, Cambridge University Press
The most recent cross-national work by an important contributor to the study of gender and employment. With a focus on economic and political change, Crompton presents an analysis of developments in gender relations in a wide range of work and family contexts. Chapters address issues such as caring, organizations and careers, work and life, the role of the state and the household in determining patterns of work; and the significance of class in framing women's choices around paid and unpaid work.

*Feminist Review* (eds) (1986) *Waged Work: A Reader,* London, Virago
This is a classic collection of articles originally published in the journal *Feminist Review* from the mid 1970s to mid 1980s. The book represents a wide range of scholarly contributions to debates in the key areas of feminist analysis of work and employment in that period. Despite changes in economy, family and politics the perspectives and ideas offered in this book continue to inform our understanding of gender inequality.

J. Jenson, J. Laufer and M. Marunani (eds) (2000) *The Gendering of Inequalities: Women, Men and Work,* Aldershot, Ashgate
This edited collection draws together a range of European and North American contributors who are all well-established in the field of gender and work. It provides a fascinating map of contemporary theoretical and applied study, and includes sections on historical and recent developments in gender relations, education and training, the impact of labour market restructuring and the evolution of social and employment policy.

D. Perrons, C. Fagan, L. McDowell, K. Ray and K. Ward (2006) *Gender Divisions and Working Time in the New Economy,* Cheltenham, Edward Elgar
This comparative study of four European countries and the US explores national and household level responses to recent changes in the labour market and daily life. It addresses policy development and family adaptation in relation to work–life balance and the distribution of work and employment. The conclusions suggest that while there is scope for difference in the extent to which gender roles are reinforced or challenged, ultimately the breadwinner model is retained at the household level whatever the policy environment.

# SECTION FOUR
## CULTURES AND CONTEXTS

This section is concerned with culture, in different contexts, to illustrate how gender is both reflected in, and constructed through, images, the media, discourse and technology. In the first chapter in this section, **Media and Popular Culture**, the media and popular culture are utilized to examine past and contemporary feminist theorizing in feminist and gender studies on a range of issues. Whether women are situated in these contexts as 'cultural dopes', that is unthinking subjects manipulated by both capitalism and patriarchy, or afforded agency through the individual and collective pleasures to be had from reading women's magazines or watching soaps or reality TV programmes, is a debate which has concerned feminists from the 1980s to the present. Through an examination of advertising and shopping, this central concern is re-visited through the current interest with theories of consumption. Then, the focus shifts to an exploration of 'texts' such as women's and men's magazines, films, romantic fiction and television. In this way, the chapter looks at both how femininity and masculinity are constructed, in different ways, within a variety of media. In addition, the case study of the 'film noir' genre allows us to see how 'looking' at images of women on screen has been debated by feminists in terms of the pleasures allowed to female (and male) spectators. Are such pleasures a reflection of male fantasies, or do such films afford women more positive readings? The chapter also considers the issue of sexuality in relation to the significance of TV programmes for a lesbian and gay audience, as well as whether soaps, nationally and more globally, can be read for progressive, even feminist messages. This chapter, therefore, gives a general context for the reading of the following chapter. Chapter 12, **Cyberspace, Feminism and Technology: Of Cyborgs and Women**, is centrally concerned with technology, its implications for women, and its connection to the body, to which you have been introduced in Section Two (Bodies–Identities). The chapter argues that through both shifts in technology and theorizing by feminists on the body, debates within cyberfeminism have been concerned, especially in Haraway's work, with feminism's interest in theorizing new connections between humans and machines. Thus, the chapter ends by a consideration of the possibilities of a re-imagined body through technology, but also asks if the new gender identities which may emerge in online spaces are informed by class and race.

# CHAPTER ELEVEN

# Media and Popular Culture

RUTH HOLLIDAY

This chapter outlines some of the landmark feminist and gender studies of popular culture and explores the ways in which contemporary debates have moved on since these early positions were developed. The material presented is necessarily selective, since popular culture is such a vast and diverse subject. I focus primarily on media content, showing how some adverts, movies, TV shows, magazines and popular literature address and represent gender. There is a central tension running through feminist work on popular culture between writers who emphasize the ways in which women are frequently represented in highly negative ways, and those that foreground the pleasure that women gain from consuming media texts. The chapter begins by outlining early debates about gender and representation in advertising – one of feminism's first engagements with popular culture. It then explores gender and consumption more generally, particularly more recent debates examining the pleasure of the consumer. Next the chapter focuses on the production and consumption of texts such as film, television, romantic fiction and magazines. I end by examining the recent growth in 'lifestyle TV' as a media form that links entertainment, advertising and consumption in very direct ways.

## Gender and consumption

Marxist writers argue that capitalist organizations own both the means of producing products and the media industries that advertise them – capitalism therefore both produces our desires and fulfils them. To think outside of this artificially created set of needs is impossible according to many writers such as Adorno (1991) or Baudrillard (1993) – except in their own cases, of course. In addition, since capitalism's aim is to generate ever-expanding profits it must sell cheap, mass produced products in a way that fools us into thinking they are designed for us as individuals (Althusser, 1971). This also applies to media products that compete for viewing figures in order to secure advertising revenue and which also carry ideological messages about the world to ensure our compliance with the capitalist system as workers and consumers.

Many feminist writers (for example Williamson, 1978) have a lot of sympathy with this position, but they claim a Marxist analysis is incomplete (for example Hartmann, 1997). Women, they argue, are doubly disadvantaged since big businesses are not just run by capitalists but by capitalist *men*. Women are therefore at the mercy of both capitalist and patriarchal ideologies. Media and advertising images continuously display idealized versions of women – as good, beautiful, glamorous and feminine women caring for their husbands and children, or bad seducers and manipulators of men and uncaring 'career bitches'. Marxism has not been able to address the specific problems of women, and in many ways has added to their negative representation. If women are seen primarily as consumers then it is women who are most duped by, and most supportive of, capitalism. This allows for Marxist models that celebrate the collective heroism of the masculine worker/producer whilst condemning the individualistic selfishness of the feminine consumer. But where did this perception originate? And what is the actual relationship of gender and consumption? I will firstly take a closer look at the ideological messages that feminist writers have identified, and then take a brief look at the history of consumer culture and shopping practices in particular, to demonstrate how consumption has come to be seen as a gendered practice.

## Advertising – selling (to) women

Marketing is the broad term given to the scoping, design, development, advertising and sale of commodities, but many writers on gender have turned their attention to advertising as a particularly important cultural force. Erving Goffman (1976) was one of the first people to write about this. Goffman examined the ways in which men and women were differently placed in advertising images in the 1970s. He argued that certain poses represent power and others subordination, some represent activity and others passivity. For instance, men were frequently positioned standing over seated women or smaller children. Men therefore seemed to be surveying or protecting whilst women and children were protected or surveyed. Women were often pictured cradling or caressing a commodity, whilst men grasped or manipulated objects, demonstrating their active role in relation to the world. In general women were depicted in passive and subordinate poses – a female nurse looking on as a male doctor performed an operation, for example, or a man adjusts a sail whilst a woman stands on a boat in her bikini – being looked at, rather than participating in the activities.

Judith Williamson (1978) drew on the work of Roland Barthes (1957) to show how commodities are woven into a network of meanings in advertising. Barthes talks about 'mythologies' or ideologies and a system of 'signs' through which certain images come to stand in for certain other things. This system of linking things and meanings, and the process of uncovering those meaning is called semiotics. One of Barthes' best known examples is of red roses. He explains that we cannot give someone a bunch of roses without the associated meaning of love – or passion. We use roses to express love or passion. However, there is nothing about the rose itself that is connected to love.

Love could just as easily be connected to an onion or a cauliflower. However, over time using roses to express love has become congealed into a taken-for-granted idea. We can no longer think about roses without thinking about love, a connection that has become naturalized. Importantly, in order to express our love we have to purchase roses – a commodity.

Williamson drew on semiotics and applied a feminist analysis to demonstrate how advertisers attempt to create naturalized associations between the commodities they are commissioned to sell and positive characteristics that we might aspire to. Products are frequently linked to idealized families where a mother provides healthy meals (breakfast cereals) or clean fresh laundry (washing powders) for her family. Advertisements for alcoholic drinks, for instance, frequently position men and women in groups of friends, laughing, joking and flirting with each other. In this way advertisers try to fix their products to the positive connotations of friendship, romance and sexual attraction/attractiveness. In particular, women's bodies are central to adverts for both women's and men's products. Groomed, slender, attractive, made-up (mostly white) women's bodies are semiotically linked to products from the bar snacks you can buy in your local pub (removing each packet of peanuts from a card background uncovers more of a scantily clad woman's body) to top of the range cars (a woman in a bikini is draped over the bonnet). This advertising links, for example, fast cars with sexual prowess with the message that if you buy this car you can attract this woman because it displays your wealth and women desire wealthy men. These kinds of adverts are so ubiquitous they mostly pass without comment. However, they have been a catalyst for feminist activism and direct actions have focused on defacing posters. A billboard near to my home for a L'Oreal product, for instance, whose tag line was 'Because you're worth it' was altered to say 'Because you're anorexic' instead. However, it was a campaign for Lee Jeans in the 1990s that featured a woman's stiletto heeled foot poised behind a naked male ass with the tag line 'Put the Boot In' that attracted so many complaints from the public it had to be withdrawn. The furore prompted claims from male ad agents that gender equality has 'gone too far'.

Advertising cannot simply reproduce the same old images over and over because contemporariness and fashion are also highly valued. Thus, more recently the 'cereal packet' (or idealized) families, formerly a staple of ad campaigns, have evolved to represent more realistic and up-to-date family forms, see below.

---

One washing powder advert shows a son washing his mother's cardigan before she goes out on her date. Far from the idealized family, then, this is a single-parent household where the son takes his share of the domestic responsibilities. This might be construed as a positive step for the representation of women in advertising, were it not for the reason the son washes his mother's cardigan – to cover up her cleavage exposed by her revealing dress. In other words the son is trying to control his mother's sexuality by covering her up with a cardigan!

---

Advertising must constantly evolve in order to address its markets. Globalization has led many companies to target wealthy elites in an ever expanding number of countries – China, Japan, Korea, and India, for instance – who represent eager consumers for high end products. Expanding global markets for fashion, for example, have significantly increased the number of black, Asian and East Asian fashion models represented, breaking with the tradition of using only light-skinned, blonde models to connote success. In addition, older models are now being used to appeal to women in their 40s and 50s who represent an independently successful and highly lucrative target market. Because of the pressure on the advertising industry to capture the zeitgeist, it has also had to deal with feminism. As a significant cultural force that has been highly critical of the representation of women, feminism couldn't be ignored by advertisers, so instead it has been largely incorporated into advertising and used to sell commodities. Goldman (1992) calls this 'commodity feminism' (a play on commodity fetishism discussed by Karl Marx). Goldman argues that advertisers have appropriated feminism to such an extent that one can now be a feminist by consuming certain kinds of products. An advert for Jean-Paul Gaultier perfume clearly illustrates this point:

The ad depicts a watery landscape. In the foreground the top of the Arc de Triomphe is visible upon which sits a beautiful mermaid singing through a loudhailer. Floating past her, not meeting her gaze but joining in her song, are two sailors kept afloat by red and white striped lifebelts. They are dressed in trademark Gaultier Breton jerseys. In the background the Eiffel Tower lists dramatically to one side and in the foremost corner Gaultier perfume, styled in a bottle shaped like a woman's corseted torso, floats innocently past. Using a semiotic analysis we can 'decode' this advert to explore the use of feminism to sell the perfume. Most perfume adverts use mythology to link their products with (hetero)sexual desirability – women using this perfume will be more attractive to men. The Gaultier ad forecloses this interpretation in a number of ways. Firstly, the woman is not a woman, she is a mermaid (and thus because she cannot be penetrated, she cannot be heterosexual). Second, the men in the picture are clearly coded as gay, using the twin connotations of the Gaultier jersey (Gaultier is gay and something of a gay icon) and of the sailor – another classic gay icon. Even the best perfume would not result in their attraction to her. In addition to this, the traditional symbols of masculinity within the picture are subverted, the phallic Eiffel Tower is leaning (drooping) and the Arc de Triomphe – a celebratory symbol of war – barely breaks the surface of the water. The primary message of the ad, then, is that the old male-dominated world is gone, and in the new flooded one the woman/ mermaid has evolved to flourish. Heterosexual men are drowned, we assume, since they are absent, perished in the shipwreck precipitated by the woman/mermaid/siren who sings together with the gay men – the only male survivors. The perfume bottle, designed like a corseted woman, also draws on naturalized signifiers. The corset – the very symbol of women's oppression, that quite literally controlled her body – was reclaimed by the notorious pop star Madonna. Her corset, designed by Gaultier, more closely resembled armour than underwear, and signified women's sexuality as strength. This new world, the advert tells us, is a woman's world. Thus, feminism (and cosmopolitanism) are firmly linked to the Gaultier perfume. A woman can signify her feminism by purchasing and wearing this exclusive (highly expensive) product – a far cry from feminism's roots in socialism.

However, we have to be careful about the assumptions we make about how adverts are actually understood by consumers. Signs, as Barthes says, are 'polysemic'. This means that any image or text can have multiple meanings depending on the frame of reference of the viewer/reader. The Gaultier ad is clearly designed to appeal to women 'in the know' (influenced by feminism) who can recognize the signs (and afford the perfume). Increasingly such codes are being used to create middle-class (feminist) identities based on being in the know about gender, sexuality and 'race', such as the 'cosmopolitan' or the 'metrosexual' (see Hollows and Moseley, 2005). To decode the Gaultier advert effectively the reader must understand and be aware of feminist critiques of phallic architecture, the difference between restraining corsets and the subverted version modelled by Madonna, the connections between Gaultier, sailors and gayness, and many others. In fact the advert congratulates those who can effectively decipher all of these signs, and in validating the reader's detailed knowledge it signals to them that this is certainly the perfume for them simultaneously producing them as a lifestyle category. However, women as the target of adverts rather than the objects of them have a long history and that is because historically women have been most strongly associated with consumption.

## Gender and consumption – a brief history

Shopping as we understand it today is a relatively new experience. Better transport networks developed in the nineteenth century west eased the flow of materials, products and people into and out of cities and facilitated the birth of department stores which carried a huge range of products, on a number of floors. These stores used advertising to bring customers in and displays to provide a spectacle, inviting customers to walk around and to browse, not only to purchase the product they went in for. However, consumption took place within a particular set of gender relations. Whilst working-class women in the nineteenth century were working long hours in sometimes gruelling conditions, bourgeois women, were pushed into a life of enforced inactivity (McClintock, 1995). Only aristocrats could really refrain from working, but by emulating the aristocracy the bourgeois classes could accrue status by association. To be 'respectable', then, meant to stay within the home and this caused a number of problems for retailers. Department stores compensated for the problem of respectability by turning themselves into a largely female-only space – an 'Adamless Eden' as Gail Reekie (1992) puts it in her Melbourne-based study. Although the products they sold were often relatively cheap, they cultivated an aristocratic aura of luxury through extravagant décor and personalized service. By deliberately employing middle-class women as shop assistants they simultaneously created a respectable feminine occupation – and a new set of customers. Stores also hosted fashion shows (10,000 women over 4 days attended a fashion show in Melbourne's McWhirters store in 1931) and even made free meeting rooms available for women's organizations (Reekie, 1992). As a public space where women could go unchaperoned, away from the possibility of bumping into family friends and neighbours, the city centre department store offered middle-class women the exciting possibility of reinventing themselves. Women could be free of masculine surveillance and could themselves gaze upon city life from the safety of the store.

In terms of extravagance, department stores were surpassed only by shopping malls that originated in the US in the 1980s. Such spaces constitute shopping as something far from necessity, as a day out, and a leisure activity in and of itself. However, whilst the Marxists continue to condemn such spaces as 'temples of consumption' designed for the 'worship of commodities', malls afford many benefits for women. Car parking is conveniently close to the shops and for a mother with young children this is an important factor. Multiple lifts accommodate pushchairs and prams but if she does not want to take them around the shops with her a mother can leave her children securely in the crèche. Security guards and bright lighting mean that women shoppers feel safer than they might do outside on the streets, especially during winter evenings. Shopping malls are public buildings that have quite simply been designed (unusually) with women in mind (Miller et al., 1998).

Unlike Marxists, John Fiske (1989) celebrates the shopping mall as a 'feminine' space. Reading a bumper sticker that states 'When the going gets tough, the tough go shopping', he demonstrates how this ironic subversion of the more usual phrase 'When the going gets tough, the tough get going' undoes a central tenet of masculinity through its association with the feminine. Fiske explains that whilst toughness and masculinity are linked to production, femininity is linked to consumption. In this sticker, shopping as a tough activity (toil and labour) disrupts its association with leisure and femininity. At the same time the idea that men work and women spend also undermines the heroism attached to labour and being a breadwinner – providing for one's family. Providing is at the heart of masculinity, but when women celebrate shopping they trivialize this – he works so she can frivolously spend. Heroic labour and provision are undone via a few credit cards. However, what Fiske misses is that men accompanied by young, beautiful, fashionable women also demonstrate their wealth and power, not just in being able to attract such a woman (signifying sexual prowess) but also in being able to maintain her (looking young, beautiful and fashionable takes considerable labour and is usually incompatible with full-time employment). Shopping may undo one kind of masculinity, but it also perpetuates others.

What all of the theorists cited above fail to discuss, however, is that most shopping, far from being leisurely and glamorous, is actually food shopping, or 'provisioning' as Danny Miller (1998) calls it. In fact, then, most shopping is simply another domestic chore primarily undertaken by women. But this does not mean it is an activity without meaning. Miller demonstrates that many women use food shopping to express love and care for their families. Buying low-fat yogurts or sugar-free drinks expresses the women's concern for the health and well-being of their families. Miller says that, despite the fact that all of the women in his study were well aware of the discourse of the selfish consumer, none of them actually behaved according to this model. Instead he conceptualized shopping as a sacrifice made on the part of the woman for her household.

We should not be seduced into thinking, however, that men do not consume. Many recent writers have talked about the increasing importance of men's consumption in areas like health, fashion and skincare. However, similar claims were being made as far back as the 1950s and 1960s when the bachelor was a prominent feature of the popular imagination (Osgerby, 2001). Bachelors lived in 'pads' decorated with the latest modernist furniture, they entertained, they skied, they holidayed abroad and were resoundingly condemned as irresponsible sufferers of 'arrested development'. Unlike the breadwinner, the bachelor's limited responsibilities and excessive consumption failed to make him a 'proper man'. Yet even the breadwinner of the 1950s had his own room within the family home – the music room – where he listened to his often extensive music collection. Men have always consumed small things like music, films and gadgets and large things such as cars, sports equipment and yachts, and unlike women's consumption, men's is much less likely to have a purpose beyond leisure. However, much of men's consumption remains invisible in the Marxist 'discourse of shopping' since shopping is always already constituted as a feminized activity. This poses particular problems for producers and marketers of products which are also designed to fit a gendered script.

Cynthia Cockburn and Susan Ormrod (1993) present us with an excellent example of what happens when marketers fail to address their targeted customers when they discuss the marketing of the microwave in the 1980s. The microwave was initially designed for use on submarines and constituted a high-tech development of space-age proportions. Marketers presumed that because of its technical nature women would be unable to understand its operation and would reject the product. Microwaves were therefore developed as 'brown goods', adorned with complicated dials and switches and accompanied by a substantial manual. They were placed amongst the other brown goods – hi-fis, video players and televisions (men's leisure products) and marketed as gifts for wives. This strategy proved totally unsuccessful as men were reluctant to buy ovens even on behalf of their partners. The microwaves were simplified and repackaged as 'white goods'. Placed among the fridges, washing machines, and dryers (women's labour products), they were sold with a cookbook instead of a manual. This proved the more successful strategy and the microwave is now an essential appliance in most western kitchens.

## Men producing culture

Many writers now argue that we live in a media saturated society, and that our consumption of media content structures and perpetuates our ideas about gender (for example see Van Zoonen, 1994; Gauntlett, 2002). Furthermore, since media organizations are mostly owned and run by powerful white men, this inevitably has an impact on the kinds of products they produce, and in particular, on the ways in which women and men are represented. This was made particularly stark in an early study by Angela McRobbie (1978) of girls' comics. Focusing on *Jackie* magazine, aimed at pre-teen girls, she showed how the company that produced it was run almost exclusively by men. McRobbie looked at the impact this had on the actual content of the magazine and found that there were a number of specific codes that structured the magazine's features. The first code was the code of heterosexual romance which advised girls, in both the stories and the problem pages, that their ideal destiny was marriage. Ideal girls were represented as passive – for example, in stories where a girl's boyfriend goes off with her best friend, the ideal outcome is that the girl waits patiently for the boy to come back to her. The stories were always about love and romance and never about sex. 'Feelings' for other girls expressed on the letters pages were always dealt with as a problem the reader will soon grow out of. Ideal girls were always blonde, other girls were brunette bitches, only represented as competitors for the affections of a boy. Black or Asian girls were almost never seen on the pages of *Jackie*. Much of the magazine was given over to beauty tips, and in particular, what beauty products to consume. In contrast boys' comics focused on action and adventure, or sports and hobbies.

McRobbie claimed that capitalism and patriarchy combine in the girls' magazines to create particularly powerful ideologies, and that these are particularly hard to resist since girls read the comics alone in their bedrooms during their leisure time. This prevents any kind of collective action they might engage in to resist the comic's messages. McRobbie received some criticism for her work, mostly because she never tried to find out what messages girls actually took from the comics. By focusing only on the comic's production and content, she missed the practice of consumption – reading – that the girls engaged in (Frazer, 1987). Subsequent writers suggested that girls may be more able to resist the restricted versions of femininity presented in them than McRobbie gave them credit for. More recently McRobbie (2000) has revisited this theme in her analyses of *Just Seventeen* and *More* magazine. She found some changes to more contemporary magazines – such as a focus on sex and careers rather than love and marriage, and a broader range of girls and young women represented in terms of 'race' or sexuality. This, she claimed, was largely because of changes in the production process as more women were actively involved in putting the magazine together. A major shift was in the tone of the problem page – now an advice column – which previously addressed girls in rather moralistic and authoritarian ways. The new columns adopted the style of 'big-sisterly' advice. However, the focus on consumption, body maintenance and beauty was still a major element, suggesting that sex and careers are simply added on to existing definitions of femininity prevalent in earlier magazines. These characteristics still pervade many women's magazines such as *Cosmopolitan* and *Elle*.

Another significant development since McRobbie's study has been the massive growth in men's and 'lifestyle' magazines. Style magazines, a new and self-consciously ungendered format, such as *Face* and *i-D* in the UK, grew from humble beginnings to define the look and content of a new breed of magazines. Combining fashion spreads, music and film reviews, interviews and commentary, and employing some of the best known lifestyle journalists and columnists of the era, the style press knowingly played with magazine stereotypes as well as the pretensions of their readership, imagined as a metrocentric, taste-making elite (Nixon, 1996). These magazines showed that there was a market for new formats, and crucially that men were an important target market – opening enough space for the creation of a new type of men's magazines, which shared the style press's interest in fashion and grooming, but which now began to target an idealized 'new man' reader – a man sufficiently at ease with his own masculinity to be able to look at male fashion models, and to consider shopping, grooming and lifestyle as suitable topics for a man to read about. However, subtle shifts in the form and content of men's magazines across the 1990s in the UK suggested that a limit to the ease of this reader had been reached, and the men's magazines shifted in emphasis and tone. Where early issues of magazines such as *GQ* (Gentlemen's Quarterly) had centrally focused on men, for example always featuring a male celebrity on the cover, across the decade images of women came to dominate, and the overall content of the magazines refocused, crucially around heterosexual sex. The pictures of male fashion models and skin and haircare products had to be counterbalanced with soft-core images of women in order for men to escape the suggestion of homosexuality that would otherwise hang uneasily over the act of looking at another man. This trend reached its acme with the arrival of the so-called lads' mags, epitomized in the UK by *Loaded*, a magazine which, with alleged postmodern irony, championed 'politically incorrect' male interests and pursuits (Jackson et al., 2001). The 'laddification' of men's magazines arguably infected the entire genre, and even the ungendered *Face* fell victim, closing down in May 2004. The lads' mags proliferated and diversified, segmenting the market further until it was extended beyond saturation, and a number of titles folded (such as *Loaded*'s food-based stablemate *Eat Soup*). Weekly lads' mags such as *Zoo* and *Nuts* represent a more recent addition, aimed at capturing a more time-sensitive market than the more common monthlies. However, after impressive initial sales figures, magazines like these have struggled in the marketplace, their predicament attributed by industry pundits to either the end of the 'new lad' movement, or the availability of laddish content, especially pornography, more widely across other media such as cable television and the internet.

## Negative representations?

So both women's and men's magazines have traditionally represented women in fairly restrictive ways. Feminist investigations of film have painted a depressingly similar picture (Creed, 1993; Stacey, 1993; Tasker, 1998). In cinema then, women in the past have frequently been restricted to a limited range of roles and were most highly valued for their looks (sometimes accessed via the notorious 'casting couch'). In addition, representations of women seemed to be divided into two kinds – good women and bad women, known as the 'Madonna/whore' dichotomy. Good women in the west (just like in the *Jackie* comics) were most often blonde and backlighting was used to effect a kind of 'halo' at key moments in the film. These good women were passive, seeking love and marriage, and care for the male hero. On the other hand, bad women usually had dark hair and were sexually predatory and seductive. The most extreme of these caricatures is the femme fatale, most frequently found in 'film noir' of the 1940s and 1950s (see Kaplan, 1980, for a classic study). The femme fatale was profoundly dangerous and usually served to distract the hero from his real business. She was a destructive force, someone who seduced the hero, not because she loved him, but to confuse and distract him for some ulterior motive. At the end of the film the femme fatale was almost always punished by plot devices such as being killed, going blind or losing everything she had worked so hard to gain. This narrative is still evident in many countries' film productions, especially perhaps postcolonial and nationalist ones. Postcolonial national cultures often look to pre-colonial times to reclaim their 'authentic' values. Because women more than men often symbolize nationhood they carry the burden of representing moral values from history. Issues of women's morality are central to the Nigerian 'home video' genre (produced cheaply and circulated via copied video tape or dvd), for example. The women at the centre of these films are frequently implicitly represented in opposition to 'immoral' western women: African women's sexuality is represented by contrast as loyal, subservient and desexualized, and any deviation from this model is severely punished.

Film noirs included movies such a *Double Indemnity* (1944), *The Postman Always Rings Twice* (1946) and *Kiss Me Deadly* (1955). However, the genre made a resurgence from the 1980s – now known as 'new noir' or 'neo-noir' – with films such as *The Grifters* (1990), *Red Rock West* (1992) and *Pulp Fiction* (1994). Mary Ann Doane (1992) theorized that film noirs appear at times when women make political and economic gains – when women took over men's jobs during the Second World War, for instance – and that they reflect a kind of paranoia on the part of the misogynist film industry about women taking power. However, new noirs such as the Cohen Brothers' *Fargo* (1996) which stars Frances McDormand as a pregnant and extremely tenacious police chief investigating a kidnap and murder, or the Wachowski brothers' *Bound* (1996) in which Corky, a tough female ex con, and her gangster's moll lover Violet, concoct a scheme to steal millions of dollars of mob money, for instance, offer more progressive roles for women. In addition films made by female directors, such as Kathryn Bigelow's *Blue Steel* (1990) have been credited with transforming the noir genre and offering more positive and interesting roles (and role models) for women. However, there has also been some debate by feminists about what constitutes a 'positive' film noir since the powerful figure of the femme fatale is both the phallic woman of men's paranoid fantasies and a key source of viewing pleasure for female audiences. An argument over the John Dahl film *The Last Seduction* (1994) exemplifies this:

> *The Last Seduction* features a woman, Bridget, who pushes her doctor husband, Clay to get involved in a $700,000 drug deal. Clay thinks the money is to secure his and Bridget's future, but she has other plans -- why split the money when she can keep it all for herself? She grabs the money and runs off to a small town, Beston, where she can hide out until she can divorce Clay or have him killed. Whilst in Beston, Bridgit meets the homely country boy Mike Swale who thinks the town is too small for him and longs for adventure. To her, he's a means to an end, another pawn in her manipulative games. To him, she's the love of his life, offering the excitement and adventure of big city life. Bridgit discovers that Mike's last foray into the big city resulted in him getting unwittingly married to a transsexual woman. She uses the possibility of disclosing this information in conservative small-town Beston to involve Mike in an insurance scam, killing adulterous husbands and splitting the life insurance money with their widows. She uses the small town's sexism and racism to her advantage, claiming protection from its inhabitants to hide from an 'abusive' husband and to avoid prosecution for the murder of a black detective her husband sent to find her. In the final scene, Bridgit manipulates Mike into killing Clay and then frames Mike for her rape, walking away free with the $700,000. Unlike earlier film noirs, Bridgit is not punished in the plot.

Films like *The Last Seduction* split feminist opinion. Some writers claim that Bridgit is the worst kind of male paranoid fantasy, the ultimate negative representation of womanhood. However, there is no denying that many women find femme fatale characters such as Bridgit extremely pleasurable to watch. Identifying with the 'good' woman positions the female viewer as virtuous, but ultimately passive and rather boring. Identifying with the femme fatale, on the other hand, positions her as active, controlling and exciting. Many women enjoy watching a woman hold all the cards, giving the hopeless and inept male hero the run around. The femme fatale is always an emasculating force and enables the fantasy of power and control over men that women frequently lack in their 'real' lives. However, the femme fatale gains her power through a highly sexualized form of ruthlessness, reinforcing the myth that women control men via their sexuality. In reality, however, men more usually control women's sexuality. Men's perception of women's infidelity, whether real or not, is a major cause of domestic violence or even the murder of women by their partners or ex-partners all over the world, and is even used in court as mitigation, seeming to justify the man's actions, in many countries.

We also need to question the heterosexual male viewer's pleasure in watching film noir. Despite the 'weak' hero, there are still many benefits for male viewers according to many feminists. One central feminist writer on men's viewing pleasure is Laura Mulvey (1975). Mulvey argues in her famous article 'Visual Pleasure and Narrative Cinema' that men and women in films have profoundly different roles. Men *act* and women *appear*. Men move the plot forward, they solve mysteries, beat enemies, rescue women in trouble and so on, and women are their reward for all this activity. Women, on the other hand, simply look good and embody 'to-be-looked-at-ness'. They 'sell' the movie by adding beauty and glamour. Furthermore, since films are produced, directed, filmed and edited (mostly) by men, this also structures how an audience can see the activities and characters in a film. Routine camera techniques have a point of view so that when an audience watches a film they also take that view – as if behind the camera. The audience therefore watches the film through men's eyes, or through the 'male gaze' as Mulvey calls it. Drawing on Freud, she says that men obtain 'scopophilic' pleasure from looking. Scopophilia in Freud is the pleasure that (male) infants obtain from gazing upon their mothers' bodies and fantasizing about controlling them. This is particularly evident in 'romantic' scenes when we are encouraged to experience the man's pleasure. For instance, many sex scenes are filmed from 'on top', looking down on the woman. In the classic 'missionary position' this replicated the man's view of the woman, thus the woman's sexual point of view is ignored. More generally, women are frequently shown in a fragmented way, when the camera pans up and down her body, lingering on her buttocks and breasts (or in 'erotic' or pornographic film on her penetrated vagina, mouth or anus). In this sense women's bodies are constructed as objects for male consumption. We might think then, that women who go to the cinema are educated in lesbianism. However, Mulvey forecloses this possibility by saying that woman watch cinema in a 'transsexual' way. Women cannot watch as women, only as men, since the very act of looking is intrinsically masculine, she argues. This, of course, poses a number of problems for lesbian filmmakers, or visual artists who stand accused of appropriating masculinity if they present erotically charged images of women – no matter how those images are styled and constructed. However, a key dilemma for feminists, as Margaret Marshment (1993, 1997) observes is whether to try, using the conventions of Hollywood, to reach a mass audience with a watered-down feminist politics, or whether to stick to a clear feminist agenda and address a smaller audience, probably already informed of the key issues concerned. However, 'positive' or realistic representations of women are not always positively received.

The debate about 'positive images' has also focused on 'race' and sexuality (see Young, 1995). Mark Simpson (1996), for example, examined the fate of a popular lesbian and gay TV magazine show called *Out*, which was broadcast by the UK's Channel 4 in the 1980s. One of *Out*'s primary aims was to combat homophobia and sexism in the media by representing extraordinary lesbians and gay men; in other words, creating positive representations. The show was broadcast just before a re-run of the popular US TV serial *The Golden Girls*. *The Golden Girls* were four single middle-aged women who shared a house together. Each woman had a very different personality and in many ways this series can be seen as a forerunner to *Sex in the City*. The fact that the women all lived together, in a shared house, pursuing individual lives but also supporting each other, appealed to lesbians and gay men who frequently lived in similar arrangements. The UK's Conservative government of the 1980s pejoratively labelled non-heterosexual families as 'pretended families'. In many ways *The Golden Girls* could be read by a queer audience as constituting a 'pretended family'. This was especially important in the 1980s as there were no shows like *Will and Grace, Queer as Folk, The L Word* or *Six Feet Under* that routinely represent the lives of gay men, and sometimes lesbians. Instead queer audiences had to undertake 'queer readings' of straight TV programmes.

Because all representations are polysemic (subject to multiple interpretations) there is always space available for texts to be read against their intended meanings. Thus, we can use highly conventional products and 'subvert' their meanings by manipulating signs. In the case of *The Golden Girls* the programme's makers became aware of its queer following and camped the show up a little bit more – but never introduced overtly lesbian characters. Eventually, *The Golden Girls* was pulled, and viewing figures for *Out* dropped from 4 million to under 1 million. Mark Simpson speculates that this is because reading against the intended meanings of texts is more fun and offers more creative possibilities for viewers than watching positive representations. In fact, he argues, positive representations may actually make us feel bad – guilty – for not living up to the high and principled standards of the heroic people depicted in programmes such as *Out*. This might explain why books and films like *Bridget Jones,* for instance are so popular amongst women, because they represent our faults and insecurities and make us laugh when we recognize them (although they offer men as the only solution to these problems).

## Feminine forms

So, if idealized representations of women or lesbians don't really bring us pleasure, what does? Several feminists have looked at the problem of 'mass culture' aimed at women – in other words, from a Marxist perspective, culture produced according to clear formulae that are repeated over and over again and marketed to a mass audience. If this mass culture is so bad, then why do women like it so much? This has been a key question (and frustration) for feminists since the 1970s. Perhaps the answers to this question could not be found in the books, films or TV shows themselves; feminists had to ask women themselves what they liked about them. One landmark investigation was carried out by Janice Radway in 1987 (see box overleaf).

Since the early romantic novels, a more 'raunchy' genre of romantic fiction began to develop. Known as 'bodice-rippers' these novels incorporated highly explicit sex scenes, to the extent that they have been called 'pornography for women' by Lewallen (1988). Despite the failure of pornographic magazines aimed at heterosexual women in the 1990 (largely due to the illegality of showing an erect penis, perhaps), this genre has grown and developed such that Mills and Boon in the UK have launched a new brand of erotic fiction aimed at women and informed by feminism known as Red Dress books.

Radway studied the reading habits of a group of women in a small American town known as Smithton. They all read a brand of romantic fiction, known as Harlequin Romances (equivalent to Mills and Boon in the UK). Janice Radway was highly sceptical about the benefits of romantic fiction when she began her study. She felt that reading romance detracted from the women's potential to become feminists – both ideologically in terms of presenting men and marriage as the solution to their problems, and in terms of taking up their free time. Radway concludes that romances provide a set of key functions. Firstly, they provided a sense of escape from the boring drudgery of domestic chores. Secondly, they compensated for the lack of emotional care that men give women and allowed women to interpret their husbands' indifference towards them as 'inadequate expression', rather than inadequate feeling. Finally, the act of reading the novels allowed women a break from domestic chores and time for themselves away from the demands of their families.

Another similar publisher, Black Lace, is discussed by Hardy (2001) as part of a growing market for 'chick lit' – popular fiction (exemplified by *Bridget Jones' Diary*) aimed at cosmopolitan 20–30 somethings that addresses the themes of work, sex and relationships.

## The pleasure of the text

Debates about viewing pleasure have also focused on another key cultural form – soap opera. Soap operas tend to address domestic lives and relationships between people (Geraghty, 1990) and therefore have a particular resonance with women's concerns that other media forms don't (excepting perhaps the melodrama, see Gledhill, 1988). However, soaps receive enormous criticism from male TV viewers which sometimes makes it difficult for women to explain why they like them. Ien Ang (1985) analyzed viewers of the American soap opera *Dallas*. She split her respondents into Dallas 'haters', 'lovers' and ironic viewers. The 'haters' deployed what Ang called the 'ideology of mass culture'. This began as an academic criticism of popular TV but has now become part of common knowledge. 'Lovers' on the other hand found it very difficult to explain why they liked the show and tended to make excuses. Ironic viewers said they enjoyed the show because, or despite the fact that, it was 'bad'. But some of these ironic viewers displayed a detailed knowledge of the show and performed what Ang called 'surface irony' (they were really lovers). She concluded that 'feminine' popular forms, such as soaps, are so denigrated by the (masculinist) 'ideology of mass culture' that it is impossible for women to justify their viewing habits without claiming ironic distance. However, the pleasure that soaps offer women comes from their 'emotional realism' that other kinds of media forms fail to address.

This focus on domestic and emotional life may also explain why soaps have become a particularly 'translatable' form of popular culture, and have often been successful at reversing global flows of culture from west to east and north to south. For example, the popular Colombian telenovela (soap opera) *Betty la fea* was initially broadcast on the Columbian network RCN and then Telemundo – the US's second largest Spanish language TV network – to a massive Latin American audience. The show was so popular, perhaps because it centred on the life of an (ordinary) 'ugly' woman working in the glamorous fashion industry, that it was subsequently adapted and/or shown in a huge number of countries around the world, for instance as *Jassi Jaissi Koi Nahin (There's No One Like Jassi)* in India, *Esti Ha'mechoeret (Ugly Esti)* in Israel, *Ne Rodis' Krasivoy (Don't Be Born Beautiful)* in Russia, and *Yo soy Bea (I am Bea)* in Spain, to name just a few. In the US the show was remade as *Ugly Betty* and achieved huge viewing figures both in the US and UK. The show is billed as a 'dramedy' or comedy-drama, a style of television in which there is an equal balance of humour and serious content. Thus soap opera has in some cases moved to *incorporate* the very irony which women initially used to *justify* their viewing pleasure.

In recent years, British soaps have also tried to tackle serious issues like rape or domestic violence in realistic and responsible ways, making visible issues that are frequently silenced in women's real lives. For example, 'Little Mo', a character who became the victim of domestic violence in *EastEnders*, first worked with scriptwriters and feminists from Women's Refuges to ensure the accuracy of the representation and subsequently became the 'face' of a campaign designed to assist women leaving violent relationships. So soap operas sometimes present feminist issues in responsible ways and work with feminist groups to do so.

A similar link between 'real-life' and TV has been made by critics in relation to the hit teen TV show *Buffy the Vampire Slayer*. *Buffy* has been largely well received by feminists and there is an entire journal devoted to 'Buffy Studies' (see *Slayage: The Online Journal of Buffy Studies*). Buffy is a regular small-town American teenager who discovers she has a special calling – to defeat and destroy vampires and demons intent on taking over the earth for the forces of evil. College student (of popular culture) by day, slayer by night, Buffy is assisted by a circle of friends, in particular, one of the few positive lesbian characters on TV, Willow, a nerdish but powerful witch. *Buffy* mixes genres. The series focuses on both personal relationships – the problems of falling for a vampire, or a demon, for instance – with lots and lots of action, featuring at its centre a slim, blonde, teenage girl who 'kicks ass'. *Buffy* builds on a new genre of 'action heroine' movies such as *Alien, The Terminator, The Long Kiss Goodnight* as well as martial arts (Wǔxiá) films featuring 'warrior women' such as the Chinese *Crouching Tiger, Hidden Dragon* and *Hero*. These in turn have inspired US films like *Kill Bill* and arguably connect to 'girl power', a concept popularized by the British band The Spice Girls (Tasker, 2004). It would seem that Buffy has done much to inspire a generation of young women. For instance, a TV documentary broadcast in 2003 interviewed young women who had been attacked by men. The women explained how they had fought off their assailants after thinking 'what would Buffy do in a situation like this'.

However, before we prematurely celebrate the dawn of a new era of gender-neutral TV, we also need to address a new genre of 'lifestyle' TV. In many ways lifestyle TV takes us back to the beginning of this chapter. Shows like *The Swan, Extreme Makeover* and *America's Next Top Model* in the US and *Ten Years Younger* and *What Not to Wear* in the UK are essentially programmes aimed at women which instruct us how to improve our bodies through consumption. Each of these shows takes 'ordinary' members of the public and remodels them through aesthetic surgery, cosmetic dentistry, hair restyling, fashion and make-up instruction and dieting and exercise regimes. Women are instructed that in order to 'feel good' they need to look good, and consuming commodities is the way to achieve this. The global market for aesthetic surgery is booming. Women have obviously made significant gains since the 1970s in terms of careers, education and legal rights, but perhaps this new-found independence comes on the condition that women look good. Women may have more of their own money than ever before, but they are increasingly spending it on maintaining their appearances (Black, 2004), and the media is clearly promoting this.

And there is some evidence that representations of women are perpetuating, maybe even intensifying, women's concern with their bodies. A rise in labia trimming, and anal bleaching, for instance, has been attributed to the growing influence of pornography, where female actors' bodies are cropped, clipped and airbrushed in the production process such that they cease to resemble 'real' women's bodies at all (Blum, 2003). In addition, there has been an apparent rise in young women aspiring to become strippers and glamour models. Many feminists have criticized young women (sometimes called ladettes) who go out on the town, drinking excessively and dressing scantily whilst claiming the status of 'liberated women'. Ariel Levy, in her book on 'women and the rise of raunch culture' (2005), argues that this 'new liberation' looks just like the 'old objectification' and that women are simply being duped by popular culture into becoming 'female chauvinist pigs', making themselves into male fantasies on behalf of men. However, there are serious questions to be debated here. Many young women clearly feel empowered in this guise. Beverley Skeggs (1997) talks at length about respectability and how young women needed to be respectable (desexualized, but ironically also heterosexual) in order to accrue status in society. In addition the bodies of 'other' (working-class, colonized or enslaved) women have traditionally been represented as overtly sexual, (busty barmaids, for instance, or black women with large bottoms) and therefore unrespectable. This is why, arguably, when generations of middle-class white women have anxiously wondered 'does my bum look big in this?' they have worried less about their figure than about maintaining their status as different from 'other' women. When white middle-class feminists criticize 'ordinary' women for watching make-over shows or for having cosmetic surgery and for demonstrating overt sexuality, they also need to be wary of how their class and ethnic privilege (not just their feminism) informs this position

(Holliday and Sanchez Taylor, 2006). Of course, it is one thing if young women feel pressurized to conform to a set of masculinist and unobtainable norms but quite another if they experience getting ready and going out in a group as pleasurable and collective 'dressing up' to mark the end of a boring working week.

## Conclusion

To conclude, then, this chapter has explored the problems of negative representations of women in the media and popular culture but it has also been careful to point out that 'mass culture' also offers women many pleasures. In addition positive representations have been identified as presenting problems for viewers by sometimes setting unachievable standards or reducing audience engagement by reducing their role as 'active readers'. The chapter has also highlighted the impact of feminism on media and popular culture and the uneven and sometimes contradictory ways in which it gets taken up. It should be obvious from the examples presented here that feminism's relationship with popular culture is a difficult one, and that there is much disagreement within feminism about how to deal with it. But perhaps there is one fundamental reason for this. We can find as many positions within feminism as there are types of representation in the media. For every make-over show there is always another looking at the negative experiences of women undergoing cosmetic surgery. What does it mean when attractive young women are also saving the world by fighting demons, or when Germaine Greer becomes a contestant on *Celebrity Big Brother*, for instance? You decide!

## Further reading

J. Hollows (2000) *Feminism, Femininity and Popular Culture*, Manchester, Manchester University Press
This introductory guide to feminism and popular culture identifies key feminist approaches to popular culture from the 1960s to the present and demonstrates how the relationship between feminism, femininity and popular culture has often been a troubled one. The book introduces the central ideas of both second wave feminism and feminist cultural studies and demonstrates how they inform feminist debates about a range of popular forms and practices through a series of case studies including the woman's film, romantic fiction, soap opera, consumption and material culture.

P. Jackson, N. Stevenson and K. Brooks (2001) *Making Sense of Men's Magazines,* Cambridge, Polity
The last decade witnessed the phenomenal growth of the men's magazine market, raising important questions about the significance of the rise of men's lifestyle magazines for gender politics. The book questions whether or not we are witnessing a backlash against feminism or instead are men's magazines simply harmless fun? It examines how the 'new man' gave way to the 'new lad' and the political issues this raises within the context of the information society.

A. McRobbie (2000) *Feminism and Youth Culture*, Basingstoke, Palgrave Macmillan
This volume collects together eight separate essays written by Angela McRobbie over a period of almost 13 years about youth culture focusing on young women and girls. Topics include the changing place of romance in girls' comics and magazines, the everyday culture of working-class girls, the appeal of dance narratives for pre-teenage readers and viewers, teenage mothers and feminist critiques of subcultural theory. The book illustrates how McRobbie in particular, and feminists more generally have shifted in their analyses of popular and youth culture from early approaches arising out of Marxist analysis to later, more nuanced accounts.

J. Stacey and S. Street (eds) (2007) *Queer Screen*, London, Routledge
This is a collection of articles published in *Screen* between 1990 and 2004, spanning the period during which queer studies and the 'New Queer Cinema' flourished. It includes ground-breaking articles by Teresa De Lauretis, Chris Straayer and Andy Medhurst, and addresses issues of bodies and technologies.

# CHAPTER TWELVE

# Cyberspace, Feminism and Technology: Of Cyborgs and Women

STACY GILLIS

## Introduction

The ability to create and use technology is commonly understood as one of the key markers of what it means to be human. Certainly some other animals – notably apes and monkeys – use technology to assist particular activities. It is only us humans, however, who use technology regularly. We arguably could no longer survive if all forms of technology – from the car to the needle – were removed from our grasp as we are now defined – and, to some extent, controlled – by the technological forms which we use daily. Partly as a result of our reliance on technology, since the late eighteenth century, western culture has been particularly keen to define its progress and knowledge through technological developments (Kaplan, 2004). Whether thinking about the steam engines that enabled the economic expansion of the Industrial Revolution or Henry Ford's Model-T Ford assembly line, technological development is often accompanied by a rhetoric which endorses its progress, forward expansion and improvement. This notion of technological progress has accelerated in the second half of the twentieth century as *cybernetics* has come to dominate our understanding of both technology and of the body in the west and increasingly in developing nations. Developments in military technologies during the Second World War, the Cold War and the war on terrorism have gone hand-in-hand with the popular account of technology as possessing an unlimited potential for development.

The rapid rise in cybernetic technology since the 1950s has also resulted in a widespread theorizing of the new interfaces between human and machine, between the organic and the technological. These shifts in technological histories, combined with the rise in feminist and body theories since the 1970s, have opened up new debates about human relationships with machines. This chapter will discuss the ways in which current feminist and gender studies have both responded to and informed these technological histories. Much of this discussion will necessarily be taken up with a discussion of the *cyborg* as this figure has been an important one, both for feminists and for those working more broadly in cybertheory and in science and technology studies. The term cyborg – or cybernetic organism – was coined by Manfred E. Clynes and Nathan S. Kline in 1960. For Clynes and Kline, this term referred to a human being who had been enhanced so as to survive in extraterrestrial environments.

Since the publication of Donna Haraway's 'A Manifesto for Cyborgs' (1985) – the revised version, 'A Cyborg Manifesto' was published in 1991 – the meat/ metal hybrid of the cyborg has dominated much of the feminist debate concerning the relationship between gender and technology. Haraway's metaphor of the cyborg has been claimed by some as a way out of the Enlightenment body, the model of the body (i.e. white, able-bodied, male, rational) that has been dominant since the early eighteenth century. However, for others, it has merely consolidated Enlightenment ideas about the body. This chapter will trace these debates, paying particular attention to those proposed by those working in the field of cyberfeminism. After moving on to a discussion of theoretical alternatives to Haraway's metaphor of the cyborg, notably the idea of the posthuman (Hayles, 1999) and the 'soft' cyborg (Zylinksa, 2005), the chapter will conclude by considering the cultural distinctions between the human and the machine.

## The Enlightenment body

The Enlightenment refers to a specific point in European philosophical thought which is associated with broader cultural shifts that took place in the eighteenth century. We now understand the Enlightenment as a complex cultural period (Porter, 2001; Outram, 2005), one which can be loosely summarized as a European intellectual movement which endorsed reason, progress and rational thought. In other words, it was during the eighteenth century that reason was widely advocated as the way in which to establish a coherent and rational system of intellectual argument, ethics, politics and aesthetics – a system of thinking which has formed the basis for much scientific and intellectual work through to the present day. Rationality and reason were – and are – believed to enable humans to obtain objective truths about the world in which they lived. The beliefs sustaining Enlightenment thought are largely to do with forward-thinking progress: for example, the insistence on the notion of absolute and definite truth which can be pursued through science. The eighteenth century is also the period of history in the west when systematic and scientific thinking gained widespread approval and application.

Why is the Enlightenment vital in thinking about the relationship between the body and technology? Precisely because it was during this period that current models and conceptions of the body were developed and endorsed. This body was ultimately *knowable*: a body which was and continues to be understood through metaphors of science, progress and improvement. The

Enlightenment – as both a historical period as well as an intellectual movement – is concurrent with modernity, or the move away from Mediaeval and Renaissance thought and perceptions into a 'modern' world. Refigurations of the body were understood as key to this change. Think, for example, of how the body was understood differently from the Classical Roman period to the body in late Mediaeval Europe to the body today. Culturally, the body held different and varying levels of signification in each of the points in history: that is, the way in which we understand and represent the body is the result of cultural and social forces.

One way to think through this refiguration of the body in the Enlightenment is to consider the ideas of René Descartes. Descartes' *Meditations on First Philosophy* (1641/1996) identified the mind with consciousness and with self-awareness. He differentiated between the mind and the brain – the latter, for him, was the seat of intelligence. The definition of a body within this equation is as something solid and, in some ways, *separable*. The physical here is distinct from the mental (or spiritual). Descartes was one of the first to propose this mind/body binary – what we now refer to as *Cartesian dualism* (see also Woodward in this volume). This understanding of the body as something separate from the mind – the latter being the seat of rationality and thought – is crucial in understanding why the figure of the cyborg has been regarded as a transgressive figure.

Fantasies and fictions of cyborgic possibilities have been circulating in Western literature and thought for centuries, and particularly since the Industrial Revolution. As the machine become paramount in the popular consciousness as a site of economic and scientific progress, so too did the possibilities of a human *augmented* by machinery. The monster in Mary Shelley's *Frankenstein* (1818/1994) can be understood as an example of thinking about the possibilities of constructing humans like machines. In this novel, Victor Frankenstein 'builds' a human form through body parts from others. Much of the novel is concerned with questions of Cartesian dualism – what is the mind that animates the matter of this mechanically-constructed and monstrous human form? As the Industrial Revolution spread across Europe, concerns about the mechanizing of human activity became more prevalent. These concerns were addressed most overtly in science fiction although questions about the impact of widespread mechanization were a common site of discussion. The notions of the human/machine hybrid, or the machine which behaved as a human, were common in science fiction throughout the earlier half of the twentieth century, for example, L. Frank Baum's *The Marvelous Land of Oz* (1904), Jean de La Hire's *L'Homme qui peut vivre dans l'eau* (1908), Fritz Lang's *Metropolis* (1927) or Edmund Hamilton's *The Comet Doom* (1928). It was, however, the cybernetic developments linked to the demands of military technology in the Second World War which foregrounded the possibilities of the cyborgic body. As knowledge of computers became more widespread, so too did the general awareness of a body enhanced by cybernetic technology. While this 'new' cyborg should be understood as emerging from the American–USSR space race, it is also clear that the second half of the twentieth century has been marked by a desire to investigate the possibilities of an intimate relationship between machine and human.

The use of the cyborg to question notions of the Enlightenment body is most commonly identified with Donna Haraway's work (1985, 1991), referred to earlier. Her argument is primarily concerned with the ways in which feminism might move beyond binary ways of thinking. For Haraway, this can occur through considering how the cyborg *disrupts* our expectations of what it means to be in that Enlightenment body. The human/machine interface of the cyborg is what Haraway proposes can reconfigure our understandings of the body and of Cartesian dualism. Providing a number of examples of the possibilities of the cyborgic, her argument collapses the distinction between metaphor and reality. She argues that the cyborg – part organic and part artificial – can be found throughout western culture: from 'human babies with baboon hearts' (Haraway, 1991:164) to the replicants in Ridley Scott's *Blade Runner* (1982). A key feature of Haraway's cyborg metaphor is hybridity. She uses the idea of the figure of the cyborg to explore hybrid bodies, subjectivities and identities and to disrupt binary dualisms.

This hybridity allows the notion of the cyborg to break down the binary dualism of culture and nature. This breaking down results in other dualisms being brought into question: such as male/female, mind/body and subject/object. Indeed, Haraway's metaphor of the cyborg destabilizes the strict boundaries between subject categories.

What is important here is the emphasis that Haraway places on the pleasure wrought by the confusion which the cyborg engenders. As a hybrid, the cyborg disrupts such traditionally accepted accounts of the world as the Enlightenment body. That is, the hierarchical domination of the white, able-bodied male body which has for so long represented *all* bodies – and that has been the accepted norm for bodies – is disrupted by the confusion offered by the machine/human dyad that is the cyborg. Boundary breakdowns are thus a component of a cyborg world. Haraway's metaphor has been so seductive for feminist theory, postmodern theory and for cybertheory precisely because it provides a useful way of critiquing Enlightenment ideas, and offers an opportunity to think about the body without the boundaries of gender.

While Haraway's manifesto was influenced by work in cybernetics, it must also be located within the Cold War culture of the 1980s. The Cold War resulted in a technological determinism, a determinism which promised multiple possibilities for bodily alteration and interaction with machines. Pointing up the breakdown of boundaries, Haraway indicated how this technological determinism – despite its promises of transgression and progress – was merely reproducing traditional models of dominance (Schneider, 2005). By (re)appropriating technology, her metaphor of the cyborg seems to use science's own weapons against itself: the cyborg offers resistance from within the dominant models. However, some criticism of her work has noted that this cyborg relies too heavily upon a model of linear progression. An example of this is the

'Informatics of Domination' which dominates her essay. This list of discursive shifts is based upon a series of discernable breaks from a knowable past. What some see as problematic about such a list is that it would not be possible for the current categories to exist without an engagement with their previous incarnations – that is, the current category exists only *because* of the category which it replaces. Notions of progress are thus contained within her argument. Indeed, it could be argued that Haraway's metaphor of the cyborg does not provide an alternative to Cartesian dualism but rather reinforces its strengths.

Some have critiqued the seductiveness of the cyborg metaphor (Balsamo, 1996; Kember, 2002). For example, Judith Squires argues that we have been too quick in rejecting the entirety of the Enlightenment body: 'we may want to use the cyborg as a positive icon in our political imagination, but we cannot allow ourselves to take an apolitical stance with regard to the form and operation of developing technologies' (Squires, 2000:361). Squires is concerned that the political considerations surrounding the cyborg may have been ignored. For her, the cyborg fails to critique convincingly the gendered body. The mind/body split locates female identity as being 'more embodied' or bound by the body than masculine identity and, for Squires, this is not adequately dealt with by the cyborg. Arguing that the 'appropriation of the cyborg for the mapping of possible feminist futures has the potential to be a subversive act', she also warns us to 'not imagine that persuasive rhetoric alone is sufficient to shift the distribution of power' (Squires, 2000:370). This is of particular relevance when one considers how the cyborg has been used as a site of liberation by some feminist theorists like Rosi Braidotti (1996), Susan Hawthorne (1999), Renate Klein (1999) and Sadie Plant (2000). For Squires, one of the reasons that the cyborg is dangerous is because of the implicit ways in which masculinity and maleness are always present within the technocultural narratives which enable its existence. One only has to think of popular representations of the cyborg – the hard, masculine body of the male Terminator in *The Terminator* (1984) versus the sexualized and sometimes hysterical body of female Seven of Nine in the *Star Trek: Voyager* series (1995–2001) – to see how traditional gender politics are played out in the supposedly gender-less body of the cyborg.

Haraway's work has been crucially instrumental in retheorizing the relationship between gender and technology through its articulation of cyborg feminism. However, bearing in mind the points which Squires makes, feminist theorists need to think through the implications of the cyborgic to make us more aware of the political ramifications of new forms of technology. That is, we must consider the body as cyborgic, rather than the human as cyborg. This would allow for a more complex understanding of how the body is technologically mediated, assembled and re-assembled. In turn, this reconfiguration of the body would mean that we are able – whether in reality or in potential – to move beyond the confines of the Enlightenment body. It is to the ways in which the figure of the cyborg has been appropriated by feminist theory and practice that this chapter will now turn.

---

**Characteristics of the Contemporary Cyborg**

**Fusion** – The cyborg is always a combination of meat and metal. It does not have to take human form although this is how it is commonly represented. This is in contrast with the android which looks like a human but has no organic components.

**Hybrid** – Containing both organic and inorganic materials, the cyborg is at its core always a hybrid entity. As such, it should be understood as an intersection of different kinds of bodies and subjectivities.

**Liminal** – Existing at the boundaries of the organic and the technological, the cyborg does not and cannot occupy traditional subject positions. Its hybridity means that it always remains as liminal – neither wholly human nor wholly technological.

**Transgressive** – The cyborg has been claimed as transgressive precisely because of its fusion of meat and metal and its subsequent hybridity and liminality. Because it does not occupy traditional subject positions, it challenges these positions and provides possibilities for rethinking bodies and identities.

---

## Cyberfeminism

The potential in the transgressive qualities of the figure of the cyborg led to the claims for a new kind of feminism in the 1990s: *cyberfeminism*. The term 'cyberfeminism' appeared at roughly the same time in the work of Sadie Plant in the UK and in the artwork of VNS Matrix in Australia. From the outset, cyberfeminism was particularly concerned with online gender politics and the possibilities for women in the new spaces of the World Wide Web. The 'future cunt' claimed by VNS Matrix in their 'Cyberfeminist Manifesto' (1991) has been picked up by numerous digital artists, including the work at the First Cyberfeminist International event which took place in Germany in September 1997. It is thus little surprise that it is in digital artwork that cyberfeminism has been the most prevalent. An example of this is Karen Keifer-Boyd's online installation *Cyberfeminist House: Challenging Inscriptions of Normalcy from Our Embodied Experiences* (2002). The installation seeks to 'explore perception, production, and dissemination of visual cultural practices in terms of inclusion and exclusion from power and privilege' (par. 1). subRosa is another example of cyberfeminist activity on the Web, proclaiming itself as a 'reproducible cyberfeminist cell of cultural researchers committed to combining art, activism, and politics to explore and critique the effects of the intersections of the new information and biotechnologies on women's bodies, lives, and work' (par. 2). Unlike Keifer-Boyd's work, however, subRosa's artwork, while engaged with digital technologies, results in IRL (in real life) installations. These art-as-activism installations often draw upon feminist and queer theory, and particularly current theories of the body, to interrogate gendered and sexed identities and behaviours.

Much of the work grouped under the title of cyberfeminism has been art-related. These installations could certainly be described as feminist and many of them employ postmodern techniques of pastiche. Alison Booth and Mary Flanagan have noted that the form of the Internet lends itself and these art forms: 'The style of many cyberfeminist works and Web sites, like the style of the Internet or digital culture itself, is not linear, but is a collage, an assembly, of stories, facts, theories, drawings, quotes, and parenthetical comments' (Booth and Flanagan, 2002:11–12). As I have asked in more detail elsewhere, however, what precisely ensures that these installations should be labelled cyberfeminist (Gillis, 2007)? If this is just feminist activity, why the need to distinguish a clear category of separate feminist activity online? Other feminist work online, such as the activist website Feminist.com, does not label itself as cyberfeminist and this raises the question of whether or not the category of cyberfeminism is, indeed, a useful category for feminism. Thinking about the relationship between gender and technology can certainly focus attention on the ways in which women are using the Internet as a tool to organize as it makes it possible for information to be shared rapidly between groups. Activism has been one activity which cyberfeminist groups have been keen to claim as particularly 'feminist': for example, subRosa describes itself as combining art and activism. Nina Wakeford has noted the 'new types of feminist activism and possibilities of resistance to male power available through these new technologies' (Wakeford, 1999:185). Similarly, Krista Hunt is clear that 'the Internet is used by groups working on global feminist issues to gain publicity, to solicit donations, to serve as an education resource, to create organizational networks' (Hunt, 2001:155–6). The combination of feminism and globalization has certainly demonstrated the ways in which the Internet can bring together disparate groups. Yet we must not lose sight of the fact that the Internet is merely a faster form of communication technology and that, while it may allow groups to communicate more quickly and efficiently, it does not solely enable this communication.

Cyberfeminism has often been conflated with new forms or 'brands' of feminism, notably third wave feminism and postfeminism. Cyberfeminists tend, as do many third wave feminists, to depict previous versions of feminism – second wave or otherwise – as monolithic and anti-technology: 'Removed from any kind of location, 1970s and 1980s feminisms are frequently condemned as a unified block of misguided political and theoretical essentialisms' (Stacey, 1997:68). These designations and fixed definitions of certain kinds of feminism certainly subscribe to an account of politics which is embedded within Enlightenment models of progress: the notion that things can only get better and that current incarnations of a movement are always better than previous ones. Jackie Stacey has identified the disturbing 'way in which the developments [in feminist histories] are characterised as a radical break between past and present. In these kinds of Enlightenment narratives the conservative past is replaced by the radical present' (Stacey, 1997:63). This model of a feminist history which is always getting better works nicely for cyberfeminism's notion of the futurist utopia which supposedly is to be found in cyberspace. There is a problem here, however, in that the futurist utopias of cyberspace which were advanced in the 1990s were not grounded in a full understanding of feminist politics and history.

Alison Adam reminds us that cyberculture or, more broadly, the representations and articulations of cyberspace are fundamentally conservative and that they endorse a technological determinism 'which is uncritical of technological advances, which accepts as inevitable that technology will be used in a particular way and which also relies on developments in technology which may or may not even happen; e.g. intelligent computers or completely realistic virtual reality environments' (Adam, 1997:20). Adam goes on to point out that for cyberculture to be overly critical of science and technology would be to bite the hand that feeds it. Similar to the cyberutopian writing in the 1980s and 1990s, which vaunted the infinite (and often genderless) possibilities of cyberspace, cyberfeminism often disregards the material conditions of the Internet and embraces the notion of cyberspace as a futurist utopia. Squires (1996:360) dismisses this sort of writing as 'a sea of tehnophoric cyberdrool', and it is true that much of the cyberfeminist rhetoric endorses a transformative image of cyberspace. The belief in the transformative quality of cyberspace, to bring about new bodies and identities, is based upon a belief in the community-building and communication of cyberspace, activities and qualities which are traditionally linked with feminism. For example, Dale Spender argues that, because cyberspace 'has the capacity to create community; to provide untold opportunities for communication, exchange, and keeping in touch', it is a medium 'more attuned to women's way of working in the world than to men's' (Spender, 1995:229). Similarly, Scarlet Pollock and Jo Sutton find that 'the Internet offers the possibility of working in ways feminists have often aspired to', such as 'interaction, diversity, and transparency in an open process which can lead to action and change' (Pollock and Sutton, 1999:33). The belief that the new technologies associated with cyberspace provide radical shifts in how we think about the body and identity, thereby allowing for powerful opportunities for women's politics, is a commonly held one in cyberfeminism.

It should be noted, however, that to use the category of 'cyberfeminism' is to imply a coherent and self-aware movement. While some cyberfeminists – like Sadie Plant – attempt to provide a theoretical model for cyberfeminism, they do not however provide a convincing account of its politics and it is troubling that a movement devoid of politics should be termed feminist. While some of those claiming to be cyberfeminists do have a political aspect to their work, this work often does not reference the long history of politics and theory in feminist history or the relationship between women and technology. The notion of the politically-savvy web-grrrls effecting change in and through the Internet has never been anything more than an idea which the media, at one point, referenced in popular discussions of the 'new' kinds of activities taking place online. In other words, the activities which Spender, Pollock and Sutton above claim as cyberfeminist should be recognized as such: as feminist activity in cyberspace.

While Haraway has been associated, to some degree, with cyberfeminism, she should be identified with a cyborg feminism, one which resists models of unity and thus eschews the essentialist positions which mark much cyberfeminist exchange. It is through the work of writers such as Plant, as well as in the digital artists, that cyberfeminism has found its strongest proponents. For Plant cyberfeminism is 'an insurrection on the part of the goods and material of the patriarchal world, a dispersed, distributed emergence composed of links between women, women and computers, computers and communication links, connections and connectionist nets' (Plant, 1996:82). So while Haraway is concerned with how the metaphor of the cyborg could be used to understand the position of women, and to provide a way of thinking about how we can move beyond the Enlightenment body, Plant is more concerned with how women can use the new information and communication technologies (ICTs), particularly the Internet. Plant argues that women are using cybernetic technologies to subvert patriarchy as they find connections through cyberspace. Celebrating women's supposed connection with machines, Plant argues that virtual reality 'undermines both the world view and the material reality of two thousand years of patriarchal control' (Plant, 1996:170). In other words, she claims that the digital matrix is a new sexual revolution: 'The Internet promises women a network of lines on which to chatter, natter, work and play; virtuality brings a fluidity to identities which once had to be fixed; and multi-media provides a tactile environment in which women artists can find their space' (Plant, 1996:265). However, as Adam points out, Plant's 'image of women subverting the internet for their own ambitions is a cyberfeminism that, following cyberculture itself, tries to set itself above and beyond politics' (Adam, 1997:19). Adam goes on to point out that empirical studies have not supported Plant's argument. Haraway's metaphor of the cyborg allows us to articulate how women have historically experienced fragmented subjectivities; Plant's version of cyberfeminism is one without politics and one which does not meaningfully address the fraught relationship between women and technology.

The question of *who* has access to the Internet, while paramount, is often omitted in discussions of feminism and cyberspace. While Radhika Gajjala argues that cyberfeminists too often assume 'that silence on-line implies a general lack of off-line voice and power, thus conflating "power" with having a visible presence on-line and being adept at using digital technologies' (Gajjala, 2001:115), there is the question of access to information and communication technologies – bringing to the forefront race and class. The futurist utopias of cyberfeminism often endorse what might be considered a conservative feminist approach in their account of woman as implicitly white, middle-class and literate. So much of cyberfeminism has been predicated upon utopian imaginings of cyberspace. Cyberfeminism has thus been ostensibly concerned with gender politics and the possibilities for women in the new spaces of the World Wide Web. In short, it assumes that the development in information and communication technologies offers women a space in which to create new definitions of being-woman and femininity: this, in turn, will result in a repositioning of woman within the patriarchy. However, the liberatory claims of cyberfeminism for the new environs of cyberspace should take note of the ways in which technology often reproduces long-familiar power dynamics in terms of sex, race and class inequalities. As Renate Klein asks: 'who has access to these technologies?; who holds power and is in control?; in whose interest is cyberlife developed?; how does the fragmentation of cyberculture fit within the framework of knowledges of indigenous and other marginalised people?' (Klein, 1999: 187). It is these questions which should be at the heart of feminist debate about technology and gender, whether or not these debates are termed cyberfeminist.

## Bodies of thought

Armed with the language of cybernetics, Haraway, Plant and others have launched what could be termed projects of a radical critique of technoscientific narratives and of the technologized body. It is Haraway's cyborg which has, however, remained the most seductive and best-known of these critiques. Her cyborg has been deployed in contemporary thought as a way of thinking through the relationship between humans and technology as well as opening up discussion among feminists. Central to these discussions is the question of embodiment. The question of embodiment – just what kind of body is being enacted and/or understood when we talk about the cyborg – is crucial to these technology debates. (See also Woodward in this volume.)

Hayles (1999) has suggested ways in which to move beyond the model of the cyborg in offering ways of thinking about embodiment and the body in cyberspace, and her model of the posthuman is a useful contribution to the debate. In its consideration of the union of the human and the intelligent machine, her notion of the posthuman, like the cyborg, encompasses a number of technologically-mediated reconfigurations of human identity and subjectivity. Hayles argues that the cyborg emerged as '*a technological and cultural icon*' (Hayles, 1999: 2; emphasis in original) in the years after the Second World War and that we are currently experiencing 'how a historically specific construction called *the human is giving way to a different construction called the posthuman*' (Hayles, 1999: 2; emphasis in original). What is vital here is her identification of a 'historically specific construction'– this returns us, once again, to that Enlightenment body and Cartesian dualism. For Hayles, the late twentieth and early twenty-first centuries are witness to a shift from the human to the posthuman which leaves behind Cartesian dualism. Using ideas of embodiment as articulated by such feminist theorists as Elizabeth Grosz (1994, 1995) and Moira Gatens (1996), Hayles allows us to think about identity without relying on Cartesian dualism.

The mind/body dualism which positions the body as an entity to be mastered by the rational self that *possesses* it becomes highly unstable if we do not locate consciousness as *the* defining characteristic, then models of understanding based on Cartesian dualism are no longer tenable. Hayles is aware, however, of the dangers of Enlightenment mind/body dualism being mapped onto the posthuman and argues that '[i]n the posthuman, there are no essential differences or absolute demarcations between bodily existence and computer simulation, cybernetic mechanism and biological organism, robot teleology and human goals' (Hayles, 1999: 3). This posthuman subjectivity is one which incorporates both the possibilities and limits of the organic and the technological:

> [My] dream is a version of the posthuman that embraces the possibilities of information technologies without being seduced by fantasies of unlimited power and disembodied immortality, that recognizes and celebrates finitude as a condition of human being, and that understands human life is embedded in a material world of great complexity, one on which we depend for our continued survival.
>
> (Hayles, 1999: 5)

This idea of posthuman, while drawing upon Haraway's metaphor of the cyborg, provides the possibility of an identity which is not bound by traditional understandings of the body and is thus removed from the confines of Cartesian dualism. While Hayles is concerned more with the machine/human interface and tracing the post-Second World War evolution of what it means to be human, rather than with understandings of the body in feminist histories, her work has obvious relevance for feminist theory.

Another way of building upon the potential of the cyborg as proffered by Haraway is offered by Joanna Zylinska. She explicitly references feminist histories, arguing that cyberfeminism still has potential. This is one way of moving beyond the hyper-gendered representation of the cyborg in popular culture which, as Anne Balsamo has persuasively argued, 'reinserts us into dominant ideology by reaffirming bourgeois notions of human, machine and femininity' (Balsamo, 1996: 156). For Zylinska, the meat/metal model of the 1990s cyborg has undergone a radical shift in the last fifteen years. In other words, the potent, hard materialism of the Terminator, with its hyper-masculinized body and its foregrounding of the meat/metal interface, has given way to more subtle insertions of the cyborgic into the cultural landscape. Zylinska points to 'OncoMouseTM, Dolly the sheep, and inhabitants of the SimLife computer game designed as a "genetic playground"', as examples of 'soft' cyborgs (Zylinska, 2005: 140). She is thus seeking to reposition the cyborg metaphor. As opposed to the noisy cyborgs of Haraway's vision, Zylinska's soft cyborgs do not reveal themselves. Rather, they exist only in the implication of monstrosity and the potential for radical otherness.

Zylinska is adamant that these 'soft' cyborgs must be assessed in terms of their qualification as ethically respectable. She goes on to outline what she terms 'a (modest) proposal for a feminist cyberbioethics' (Zylinska, 2005: 140). This interrogates the prevalent discourse on bioethics, which she regards as implicated in a project to strategically close down the consideration of certain forms of difference and 'set a limit to the subjectivity of ethical judgements' (Zylinska, 2005:141). Zylinska's notion of the soft cyborg is used to open up, once again, alternative possibilities of thinking of the body beyond the confines of the Enlightenment body. Moreover, in bringing in the question of ethics, Zylinska seeks to re-introduce politics to the cyberfeminist debates and, more broadly, to both feminist and technology debates. So, for example, for Zylinksa, the focus on soft cyborgs, such as OncoMouseTM, a patented mouse engineered to be born with certain genetic characteristics associated with a form of cancer in order that it can be used for medical research, creates 'fundamental problems for the traditional moral principles that would be derived from human rationality and rooted in the idea of the human common good' (Zylinska, 2005:144).

Cyberbioethics is a responsibility for accounting for our encounters with these new formations such as the cyborg. It is this which Zylinska sees as forming the basis of a feminist political project. She has begun the mapping of how a 'cyberbioethics' can sidestep the danger of universalizing narratives such as the Enlightenment body. This latter engagement will allow for a further interrogation of categorical boundaries such as, once again, the Enlightenment body. This does not necessarily imply the construction of new boundaries, merely a reconfiguration. Indeed, for Zylinska, the performance of cyberbioethics is actually a responsibility in accounting for our encounters with the unknowable 'other'. She argues that this can form the basis of a political project for 'hospitality' to the other, as unsettling as this may turn out to be, which can re-invigorate feminist debate. Like the hybridity of Haraway's cyborg and the power of Hayles' posthuman, embracing the monstrosity of the soft cyborg can enable us to move beyond the expectations and confines of the body as traditionally represented and enacted.

These differing accounts can provide a launching point for arguments about the body and technology, which are at the heart of gender and women's studies. For feminist scholarship, at the heart of all these debates must be the question of whether or not cyberspace merely reproduces and magnifies traditional renditions of sex and gender. Judith Halberstam suggests one way around this question, drawing upon the feminist work on the artificiality of gender: 'The mistake lies in thinking that there is some "natural" or "organic" essence of woman that is either corrupted or contained by any association with the artificial. However, femininity is always mechanical and artificial – as is masculinity' (Halberstam, 1991:454). Yet the transgressive promise of the cyborg and the posthuman has not always been evident – particularly when considering the popular representations of these figures. Indeed, a hyper-sexualization of the female cyborg too often marks the representation of the meat/metal hybrid, raising the question of whether it is possible to leave the (female) body behind in cyberspace. Austin Booth and Mary Flanagan remind us that 'the cyborg as metaphor is fraught with difficulties precisely because it is already such a ubiquitous image in popular culture, an image that, unfortunately, replicates traditional ways of thinking about gender' (Booth and Flanagan, 2002:15). We need, therefore, to carefully negotiate the debates about precisely *how* the relationship between the body and technology has resulted in a reconfiguration of human subjectivity, in particular gendered and sexual identities.

# Conclusion

## *Of cyborgs and women*

As technology has enabled us to do more, our perceptions of technology have shifted. An increasing lack of distinction between the human body and newer forms of technology, combined with an increased use of digital and communication technologies, has resulted in the acknowledgement that many daily activities are now technologically mediated. Technology is used to reify the human, while we are increasingly using technology to define the human. With technology both altering our bodies as well as altering our understandings of our bodies, it has become necessary to think through the political and historical ramifications of these distinctions. The possibility of the body being reconfigured and re-imagined through technology is enticing. This is a body, however, which all too often retains its gendered embodiment and one which often ignores other politics of the body. For example, Wakeford (1999) points out that technology has traditionally – in terms of class – been associated with masculinity. While some argue that the cyborg can offer a way of moving beyond the binaries associated with inequalities, gendered or otherwise, it remains based upon the Enlightenment body. Removing the body from the equation in a way that the metaphor of the cyborg cannot, the posthuman may offer us the opportunity of moving beyond the Enlightenment body into a post-gendered space. This will require us, however, to more carefully examine the ways in which feminist theories are based upon all forms of technology.

While the feminist and science debates have begun to interrogate the implications of this, too often the cybercultural debates remain stuck in apolitical and ahistorical accounts of the relationship between women and technology. As we understand ourselves as technologically mediated, we must account for the political and historical ramifications of the body/technology hybrid, whether this is cyborgic or posthuman: and this ranges, for feminism, from the work of Karen Throsby (2004) on IVF and of Deborah Wheeler (2001) on women's use of the Internet in Kuwait. Contemporary feminism – rather than cyberfeminism – must and often does endorse and embrace hybridity and fluidity. This is not, however, a feminism which sits comfortably within the claims of the futurist utopias of cyberspace. Websites written by and for women and online feminist networks are undoubtedly a positive thing, but the fact remains that it is in pornography that women are most prevalent on the Internet. Bearing this in mind, we need to ask whether it is possible to subvert and control the Internet, as cyberfeminists often propose, or whether we should think of new forms of engagement with technology and the technology/body interface. Are the new gender identities proposed for online spaces really that new? Do they ignore the politics of race and class? Do they disrupt in a tangible way the politics of the Enlightenment body? What are the political implications of labelling theory and/or activism as 'cyberfeminist'? Should the Internet provide a space for global feminisms to rethink identity politics and political activism? Contemporary gender and women's studies needs to think through critically the implications of the body, cyberspace and technology in order to address their political, as well as theoretical, ramifications for feminism.

## Further reading

A. Adam (2005) *Gender, Ethics and Technology*, Basingstoke, Palgrave Macmillan
Although she is a firm critic of the apolitical nature of cyberfeminism, Adam's work has overall largely been concerned with the relationship between gender and technology. This book addresses hacking, software crime, e-harrassment, privacy and online communities from a feminist perspective. It is particularly concerned with feminist ethics. Interdisciplinary in approach, it draws upon science and technology studies, communication and media studies, feminist theory, and information systems theory.

A. Booth and M. Flanagan (2002) (eds) *Reload: Rethinking Women + Cyberculture*, Cambridge, MA, MIT Press
This collection seeks to move beyond cyberfeminism and to investigate women and cyberspace. It provocatively mixes critical theory essays with examples of fiction. This mixed approach is thought-provoking, but the links between the texts and the criticism can sometimes be tenuous.

E. Graham (2002) *Representations of the Post/Human: Monsters, Aliens and Others in Popular Culture*, Manchester, Manchester University Press
This book draws upon a wide range of cultural texts – from *Frankenstein* to *Galaxy Quest*, and from the Human Genome Project to *Star Trek: The Next Generation* – to theorize the impact of contemporary technologies on popular culture. The book examines current debates on the posthuman and explores the various representations of artificial humans, with particular attention paid to the attitudes towards science and religion which these representations enact.

L. Nakamura (2002) *Cybertypes: Race, Ethnicity, and Identity on the Internet*, London, Routledge
One of the first works to examine the category of race in cyberspace, this book demonstrates the power with which such embodied identities are performed online – despite the claims for the Web as a race-less (and gender-less) utopia. This book engages both with the politics of the Web itself but also with advertisements for software companies and cyberpunk films and novels. Grounded in current cybertheory, this book is crucial reading for those interested in race and digital cultures.

J. Wolmark (1999) (ed.) *Cybersexualities: A Reader on Feminist Theory, Cyborgs and Cyberspace*, Edinburgh, Edinburgh University Press
The essays in this collection explore how cyberspace, the cyborg and cyberpunk have given feminist scholars new ways in which to theorize embodiment and identity in relation to technology. Its sections on embodiment, cyberpunk, and cyborgs mean that it covers all the key debates and reprints the key contributions to this field. It includes an excellent and extensive introduction which surveys the ways in which cyborg and cyberspace metaphors have been used in relation to current theory.

# SECTION FIVE

## METHODOLOGIES

---

Chapter 13, the only chapter in this section, argues that methodology is about much more than knowing about which methods to use when conducting feminist research. For feminists, methodology has been seen to matter because it is connected to the production of (feminist) knowledge and, crucially allows us to be concerned with issues such as knowledge and power, the ethics of the relationship between the researcher and the researched, how feminist knowledge connects to other disciplines within the academy and whether or not the knowledge produced within gender and women's studies is accountable knowledge, for example, to those outside the academy. Chapter 13, **Feminist Methodology Matters!**, is concerned with many of these issues, which have been at the heart of debates about feminist methodology for over three decades. Furthermore, it chooses to examine these and other issues in a different and innovative way, one which invites you to engage with debates around methodology by using the original texts of some classic and well known studies by feminists. These texts are research (and theoretical) studies on a wide range of issues, which have captured the imagination of gender and women's studies scholars. The chapter first gives you some reference points to allow you to go off and learn about key feminist debates around methodology over the last 30 years or so, but it does more than that. It is fundamentally concerned with looking at 'real world' research by different feminist researchers who use different types of methodology. By grounding debates about feminist methodology in this way, the authors of this chapter encourage you to see that there is no single or 'right' way to do feminist research. The chapter allows you to compare and contrast a number of these key feminist research studies, by using a 'reading frame', which is explained to you in the chapter. What is more, the selection of 'exemplars' (examples of feminist research using interviews or documentary evidence, for instance, and here the selection is a global one, with research considered from Europe, New Zealand and Kenya amongst other countries), will allow you to consider the chapters in this volume in a new light. The chapter will enable you to reflect on why we are often convinced by the last thing we have read, even if it conflicts with something just read previously, or to think why often we reject something new we have read if it does not fit in with our own views and beliefs. The 'reading frame' you will develop from this chapter will allow you to 'ethically' read different and sometimes opposing texts and ideas, and do so in a way which gives you more confidence that you are doing justice to the many feminist (and other) ideas you will encounter in this book.

CHAPTER THIRTEEN

# Feminist Methodology Matters!

LIZ STANLEY AND SUE WISE

## Introduction: why feminist methodology matters

What is a chapter on feminist methodology doing in an introduction to women's and gender studies? Surely this is much less important than feminist theory, women's history and politics, family and work...? Anyway, doesn't feminist research mean just learning some simple methods, like how to interview people or produce an ethnography? Methodology is, in fact, the basis of making good convincing theoretical arguments and of advancing good convincing facts about the social world, so feminist methodology is an absolutely essential and crucial part of women's and gender studies.

'Methodology' is a shorthand term for a theoretical or practical idea to be explored together with a set of tools which specify how it is to be investigated – including what is appropriate and also sufficient evidence for doing so and how this should be produced, what counts as good arguments about this evidence, and what conclusions can be justifiably drawn from this. Considerations of feminist methodology have been an important part of women's and gender studies and engaged the energies of successive generations of feminist scholars. Methodology encourages us to ask interesting and important questions about, for example, what makes an idea feminist or not, what is the best way to investigate the things that women's and gender studies is concerned with, and which theory or research can we trust – and which should we be sceptical of or even reject. Feminist methodology matters because it enables us to ask and also begin to answer such questions.

Debates about feminist methodology have been central to women's studies since the late 1970s. Sara Delamont (2003:60–1) notes that: 'None of the attempts by feminists to reinstate founding mothers, or enthrone contemporary women thinkers have captured the attention... in the way methodological debates have', pointing out that: 'Over-arching these debates are very serious methodological and epistemological disputes about the very nature of research'. We agree: while questions of methodology are often presented in a purely technical way in mainstream textbooks, at root methodology is concerned with the fundamentally important matter of the 'getting of knowledge'. As women's and gender studies has long recognized, feminist methodology matters because it is the key to understanding the relationship between knowledge/power and so it has epistemological reverberations. It also provides important tools for helping to produce a better and more just society, and so it has political and ethical reverberations too.

So, what do the key terms we have used so far mean? 'Research' involves investigating something in depth, in theoretical and abstract as well as substantive and grounded ways. A 'method' is a procedure for collecting information relevant to a topic being investigated. 'Methodology' involves harmonizing theoretical ideas, choices of methodology and procedures for doing research. And 'epistemology' is a theory of knowledge in which what is seen as knowledge, who are thought to be accredited 'knowers', the definition of facts, and ways of evaluating competing knowledge-claims are specified. Feminist methodology is at the heart of the feminist project of changing the world because it is the focal point for bringing together theory, practical research methods, and the production of new knowledge. Feminist methodology matters!

Some useful overviews of the key ideas of, and debates about, feminist methodology have been published (Reinharz, 1992; Ramazanoglu with Holland, 2002; Letherby, 2003; Hesse-Bieber and Yaiser, 2004). However, one of the problems with even the best textbook discussions is that they focus on debates about feminist methodology that occurred some years ago now, and/or they discuss methodology in an abstract way. What they rarely do is look in any depth at 'real world research' carried out by feminist researchers using, in their own particular ways, a feminist methodology (as argued by Wise and Stanley, 2003). This is what our chapter does, explore real world feminist research and 'feminist methodology' in action.

The chapter's aims are to show that carrying out feminist research is a complicated business, to emphasize that there is no single 'right way' to do feminist research, to point out that the core ideas of feminist methodology can be put into practice very differently but in ways that are still feminist, and to convey how wide-ranging and truly global are the concerns of feminist research. It starts by explaining the importance of close, in-depth analytical reading as the basic tool of all feminist methodology, and explores how to devise a 'reading frame' to ensure consistency and enable valid comparisons across a range of comparator writings. It then shows in detail how this works, by using our own reading frame to 'compare and contrast' a number of exemplars of feminist research writing. 'Exemplars' does not mean that these are exemplary or near-perfect examples, but that they are useful examples of 'research of their kind'. We have chosen exemplars across all of the main methods of researching a topic – ethnography, interviewing, documentary research, surveys, auto/biographical research, and theoretical work. Some of these research texts are historical while others are contemporary; the authors come from Australia, Germany, Kenya, New Zealand, the UK and the US, and their topics involve a wide range of countries and ethnic and gender configurations.

## Reading real-world feminist research

Academic publications, including feminist ones, are produced from a wide range of often disagreeing viewpoints. Evaluating these in terms of whether the reader agrees or disagrees with their contents can mean that work is criticized or even rejected just because it expresses a perspective different from the reader's. Consequently a more defensible and more feminist way of reading needs to be found; our preferred way of doing this is to use a 'reading frame', a structured set of points, to think systematically about examples of actual research. Doing this makes evaluations of research transparent and provides a coherent basis for comparing a number of examples. Our reading frame is concerned with how and to what extent the examples of feminist research we go on to discuss use key ideas associated with feminist methodology:

- *Social location:* knowledge is necessarily constructed from where the researcher/theoretician is situated, and so feminist knowledge should proceed from the location of the feminist academic and work outwards from this.
- *Groundedness and specificity:* all knowledge is developed from a point of view, and all research contexts are grounded and specific, and therefore the knowledge-claims which feminist researchers make should be modest and recognize their particularity and specificity.
- *Reflexivity:* producing accountable feminist knowledge requires analytical means of looking reflexively at the processes of knowledge production, rather than bracketing or dismissing such things as unimportant.

There are different ways that a reading frame could be devised for evaluating the methodological aspects of feminist research. For instance, readers could comb through books and articles (or even just one, if this is thought very good) which discuss feminist methodology, listing the most important points made. These could then be put in a logical order and used to evaluate research by considering the extent to which it follows these criteria or not. Something similar could be produced by 'brain-storming' to compile a list of topics which readers think should characterize good feminist methodology. A reading frame could also be developed by reading books and articles which discuss feminist methodology, but this time by listing the things which readers *disagree* with and then re-writing these negatives into positive statements – often the ideas we disagree with can help us think better and more productively than those we agree with. The reading frame used in this chapter is a simple one which:

- provides a summary of the content and methodology of each research text and points the reader to key sections concerned with methodology matters;
- discusses the overall approach to methodology in each example;
- examines the relationship between its questions, analysis, conclusions and discussions of the processes of feminist enquiry;

- considers how feminism is deployed within the text and whether it matters if some of the ideas associated with feminist methodology are absent;
- discusses the light thrown on important methodological issues by considering some comparator examples of feminist research;
- indicates how readers might develop the ideas discussed and questions asked.

## Reading the research exemplars

The exemplars of feminist research we discuss raise interesting questions about the methodological aspects of 'feminists researching'. In addition, the Bibliography provides short overviews of three more examples of research which used a similar methodological approach to each of the five exemplars – these have been chosen because they 'do it differently' from the exemplar, because it is important to recognize that 'good feminist research' can be done in sometimes very different ways. We will look at these exemplars in the following order: ethnography, interviewing, documentary research, surveys, autobiography and, finally, theory.

---

**ETHNOGRAPHY EXAMPLE**

**Marjorie Shostak (1981) *Nisa: The Life and Words of a !Kung Woman***

*Nisa* investigates women's lives among the gatherer-hunter !Kung people who live on the northern edge of the Kalahari desert. This is explored in particular through the ideas and viewpoints of fifty-year-old Nisa, in interviews covering Nisa's childhood, family life, sex, marriage, childbirth, lovers, ritual and healing, loss and growing older.

*Methodology*

- Twenty months of ethnographic fieldwork carried out in the late 1970s, plus interviews with eight women in addition to Nisa herself
- Its particular interest is in cultural differences and also 'the universals, if any', of human emotional life
- Consists of fifteen thematically edited interviews, around thirty hours of taped conversations, between Nisa and Shostak carried out over a two week period
- Nisa is described as having articulated highly organized and rich stories with a clear beginning, middle and end
- Focuses on Nisa's words and stories and omits Shostak's part in the interviews in asking and responding to questions
- Shostak has edited the interviews, so the chronological sequence of the thematic narratives does not necessarily reflect the order in which stories were told in the interviews

*Methodology reading*

'Introduction', 1–43
'Epilogue', 345–71

---

Marjorie Shostak's (1981) *Nisa: The Life and Words of a !Kung Woman* provides an interesting and informative account of the lives and experiences of !Kung women through the lens of her interviews with the woman, Nisa. This is an engaging read, in which Shostak discusses her fieldwork generally and in particular her meetings with Nisa, and readers come to share Shostak's fascination with Nisa's character and the extent to which the stories she told in her interviews are representative or not of !Kung women generally. In addition, there is a full discussion of confidentiality and consent and the strategies used to analyze the identity of the group and Nisa as an individual, as well as concerning the location where these !Kung people lived. The overall impression is of *Nisa* as a very open text with methodology matters dealt with fully. However, the important matters of Shostak's involvement in the interviews, and the role that possible bystanders played, plus details of how the interviews were translated and edited under the thematic headings used in *Nisa*, are dealt with fairly cursorily. These important methodological omissions have enormous implications for how readers understand the interpretation of Nisa's stories. Two further criticisms have been made of *Nisa* as well.

The first concerns Shostak's comment that she is interested in cultural differences and 'the universals, if any' of human emotional life. This led to the charge, incorrectly, that Shostak was suggesting that biology determines social behaviour across cultural difference and proposing an essentialist argument. The second criticism is that Nisa could have had little if any idea about what giving consent to publication in a book actually meant. However, it is difficult to reconcile this criticism, based on the assumption of Nisa's naïveté or lack of knowledge, with interviews in the book in which she comes across as very savvy, and also with the details subsequently provided by Shostak (2000) in *Return to Nisa*.

An interesting methodological and ethical question is raised here: are uneducated, 'third-world' or otherwise disempowered research subjects 'by definition' unable to give knowing consent? In thinking about this, readers should look at the overviews of the comparators for *Nisa* and also read the sections referenced on methodology matters. These three comparators are all ethnographies, but deal with the relationship between researcher and researched in different ways.

Diane Bell's (1983) study of Australian aboriginal women's and men's roles *Daughters of the Dreaming* has also been criticized regarding the 'knowing consent' issue, although Bell fully discusses this matter. Because Aboriginal women's and men's knowledges are kept separate and secret from each other, the assumption has been the women in her research did not fully realize what they were consenting to. Was Bell perhaps naïve about consent? There are, however, other possible explanations: perhaps the women concerned gave their consent while other community members objected, perhaps it was men who objected rather than women, perhaps the women were constrained after the event to rescind consent, and so on. Such ethical matters are a burning issue for Judith Stacey's (1991) study of the 'modern family' in the US, *Brave*

*New Families*, where the ethical complications that arise in her ethnography are treated as discrediting the method, rather than being something that 'just happens' in any long-term research, or perhaps produced by the relationships established by a particular researcher. *Brave New Families* is actually a sociological departure from 'typical' ethnography, and Stacey participating in people's lives as a kind of acquaintance or friend is likely to have increased the possibility that these issues would arise. Sallie Westwood's (1984) *All Day Every Day* is also by a sociologist, but is a 'shopfloor' ethnography by someone who worked in the factory she writes about. Her relationship with her co-workers is different again, involving her and them in common activities and common cause vis-à-vis management.

Are some research methods 'in themselves' more exploitative than others? This is the implication of *Brave New Families* and Stacey's associated writings about ethnography. After going through the ethnography readings suggested in the Bibliography, readers might want to list the different factors to take into account, concerning the researcher/researched relationship, whether what people say and do is fully recorded or only summarized, how matters of consent and confidentiality are handled, who decides on the final form that publications take, and then compare the different research examples. It is important both to be clear about how 'exploitation' and 'ethics' are defined, and to think about whether it is the method, or whether it is the particular practice of it, that has such characteristics.

Catherine Kohler Riessman's (1990) *Divorce Talk: Women and Men Make Sense of Personal Relationships* provides an accessible and engaging account of this research and the ideas underpinning the analysis, including an explanation of the change that occurred in its methodological and analytical direction. Why narrative analysis was adopted is discussed, as are the specific ways it was used, through providing detailed examples using sections of original data. Its research questions, the analysis and the arguments drawn from these, and also the processes of research and its evolving methodological framework, are all fully accounted for. *Divorce Talk* situates itself in relation to feminist scholarship on marriage and the family and structural gender inequalities, and it also comments on the impact of the women's movement regarding marriage and what is seen as acceptable or not within it. Interestingly, however, its approach as feminist methodology remains implicit in the choice of topic, questions asked, analysis carried out and arguments developed, rather than being explicitly stated. Does *Divorce Talk* use a feminist methodology or not?

This raises the interesting methodological (and political) question of what to call research that employs some or all of the characteristics of feminist methodology but does not use 'the F word' as an explicit characterization of its approach. In thinking about this, readers should look at the overviews of the comparators for *Divorce Talk* and read the sections referenced on methodology matters. These comparators all use an interview method, but structure their interviews and analyze their data in very different ways and also make different kinds of knowledge-claims.

---

**INTERVIEWING EXAMPLE**

**Catherine Kohler Riessman (1990)** *Divorce Talk: Women and Men Make Sense of Personal Relationships*

*Divorce Talk* focuses on how women and men talk about making sense of divorce, what led to it, and their lives afterwards. It discusses their recognition that, although divorce is difficult, it is not all bad and that 'interpretive work' helps. It also deals with the processes which people go through in reconstituting the history of their marriages and the end of these. Regarding selves, men and women make different sense of their divorces, remember their marriages differently, and interact with the researcher differently too.

*Methodology*

▓ Began as a survey of divorce adaptation patterns in a joint research project with a psychiatrist colleague

▓ Taped interviews were carried out with fifty-two women and fifty-two men, all divorced or not living with their spouses, chosen to be representative of the wider population of people going through marital dissolution

▓ 'Hearing' what people did in the interviews, in which they multiply departed from structured questions and interactions, led Riessman to her intensive narrative study of how people made sense of their experiences in these interviews

▓ Focuses on four narrative genres (story, habitual, hypothetical and episodic), so as to provide detailed interpretive readings of the interview materials

▓ These are transcribed in a detailed (but not conversation analytic) way

▓ Long segments of shared talk are provided, including Riessman's part in this, marked up to show the narrative structures perceived in them

*Methodology reading*

'Preface', ix–xiv
'The Teller's Problem: Four Narrative Accounts of Divorce', 74–119
'A Narrative About Methods', 221–30

---

Sarah Mirza and Margaret Strobel's (1989) *Three Swahili Women: Life Histories From Mombasa, Kenya* has an even more tacit relationship to feminist methodology. Its key concern is with making visible the lives of Swahili women in Mombasa, in a context where there was almost no published literature: a 'breaking silence' motivation that has underpinned much feminist research. Together with Mirza and Strobel's emphasis on publishing for a Swahili-speaking as well as US readership, the authors' equal partnership in producing the published book, and Strobel's institutional location in women's studies as well as history, this strongly implies that their research was consonant with aspects of feminist methodology – however, this is nowhere explicitly stated. Jayne Ifekwunigwe's (1998) *Scattered Belongings: Cultural Paradoxes of 'Race', Nation and Gender* is similarly concerned with 'giving voice', in this case to 'mixed race' women whose lives were previously little researched. It assumes a feminist or at least pro-women readership and was certainly marketed by its publisher in this way. However, while it describes itself as a feminist auto-ethnography, feminism is not discussed, suggesting some ambivalence. It might be supposed that Ann Oakley's (1974) *The Sociology of Housework* would help resolve where the boundaries between an explicit and implicit feminist methodology are, but in fact it confirms how complex these boundaries can be. The background is the women's movement, gender inequalities, the recognition of sexism in sociology and other social sciences, and Oakley's concern with domestic labour as *work* and the gender dynamics governing it. However, *The Sociology of Housework* describes itself as carrying out a sociological analysis rather than a feminist one; it characterizes feminism simply as a perspective which keeps women in the mind's forefront; while its research design, concern with a representative sample, and its analysis of the interview data and utilization of significance testing on small numbers, are strongly 'scientific'.

While certainly feminist research, *The Sociology of Housework* does not employ a feminist methodology, while the statuses of *Divorce Talk* and *Three Swahili Women* are harder to pin down. Readers here should think about whether they agree with our assessment or not, because of course this 'all depends' on how feminist methodology is being defined.

Janet Finch's (1983) *Married to the Job* is a clearly written and engaging discussion of a topic – wives' incorporation into men's work – which is important for the feminist analysis of marriage and women's labour market participation. It involves documentary research – its data are pre-existing documents rather than interviews or participant observation and so on – and in particular these are secondary sources, mainly academic research concerned with the same topic and questions that Finch herself is. It provides an exemplary account of its methods, spelling out its research questions and what it sets out to do, then discussing the details of this and what the sources tell, and also overviewing what conclusions can be drawn from the data sources used.

*Married to the Job* asks feminist questions, its analysis of its sources has these questions clearly in mind and its conclusions about the mechanisms of incorporation are similarly, incontrovertibly, feminist ones. At the same time, it contains few methodological details on the research process engaged in, the issues in working with secondary sources and any methodological or political deficiencies these might have. Also, Finch is interested in a specific group of women, those who are incorporated into men's work, and the many women who do not have 'incorporated' marriages lie outside the investigation. Relatedly, the group who were 'incorporated' will have included women who resisted or rebelled against this, but there is no discussion of this because the analytical concern is not with 'women's lives' or 'the complexities of marriage and work', but rather the mechanisms by which incorporation is lived out, so that complexities and fractures also lie outside the focus of investigation. This again raises the question of whether it matters if some features of feminist methodology criteria are not present when others, equally important, are. *Married to the Job* is a good piece of feminist research and the clarity with which it explains its research methods is highly commendable. At the same time, some

---

**DOCUMENTARY RESEARCH EXAMPLE**

**Janet Finch (1983)** *Married to the Job*

*Married to the Job* explores what happens when women marry into their husband's occupations. It suggests this typically involves a two-way process – men's
work imposes structures on wives, and wives directly contribute to the work men
do. The extent and character of this varies by occupation, in a pattern termed
'incorporation'.

*Methodology*

- A documentary and secondary analysis of relevant pre-existing research
- Specifies the conceptual starting point to enable other researchers to evaluate
  the analysis pursued, because different starting points and different questions
  could have been validly chosen
- Uses four main sources for a secondary analysis of published research: research which directly addresses wives' relationship to men's work in particular occupations, studies of occupations from which wives' incorporation can
  be gleaned, studies of family and marriage with enough on men's work to
  draw some conclusions of wives' relation to it, and self-reported material generated by organizations representing particular occupations
- Explores the different forms of incorporation and accounts for the underlying
  processes
- Uses 'special cases' rather than common experiences to show what forms of
  incorporation are possible, not just those which are typical
- Provides overviews of its approach and analysis in the three parts of the book,
  on how men's work structures wives' lives, on wives' contributions to men's
  work, and the theoretical framework for analyzing wives' incorporation

*Methodology reading*

'Introduction', 1–19
'Introduction to Part One', 21–3
'Introduction to Part Two', 75–7
'Introduction to Part Three', 121–3

---

of the current hallmarks of feminist methodology are absent from its pages
and also from its research process, and it is interesting to think about why this
might be so. The reasons are likely to include personal preference, the fact that
in the early 1980s there was no normative expectation of what feminist methodology 'ought' to consist of, and that feminist research with policy concerns
even now tends to be more 'mainstream' in its approach and presentation. We
also think the use of secondary analysis of documentary materials is important, because both the context and depth of an investigation can be lost when
published research reports become the analytic focus. Is this inevitable when
doing documentary research, or is it perhaps a feature of secondary analysis?
Reading our comparator examples we think will suggest the latter.

At this point, readers should look at the three comparators for Finch's research and read the recommended sections on methodology. The comparators

all use documentary materials (one uses interview material as well) and some secondary sources, while none of them focuses exclusively on these in the way *Married to the Job* does.

Leonore Davidoff and Catherine Hall's (1987) *Family Fortunes* is a highly influential 'mainstream' piece of UK historical research which also has clear feminist analytical questions and aims. It uses some secondary materials (the historical Census), alongside personal and family papers in building an in-depth account of some families and their female and male members in three different places, to explore similarities and differences. Hilary Lapsley's (1999) *Margaret Mead and Ruth Benedict: The Kinship of Women*, a biography of the relationship of Mead and Benedict and their friendship network, is similarly 'mainstream' in its approach and writing style. It utilizes some secondary sources (published biographies and autobiographies), but its primary sources are newly-available collections of letters and these provide considerable depth to this reading of women's lives and relationships. Dorothy Smith's (1999) *Writing the Social* is concerned with organizational documents of different kinds. Smith does not use their contents as a proxy for people's actual behaviours, but as an indication to the concerns and ways of recording of the organizations involved, while her clearly articulated 'method of inquiry' locates it within a feminist methodology of considerable sophistication which situates the researcher as a knowing subject at its centre.

Finch's choice of secondary analysis, rather than working with documents as such, importantly impacted on the focus of her investigation, what is discussed and what is not, and the rather distanced stance adopted regarding matters of feminist methodology. Readers should look for some more examples of feminist research that carries out a secondary analysis of existing data, to see whether these are similar to or different from *Married to the Job* concerning the discussion or absence of feminist methodology matters. It would also be interesting to do this with other feminist research published in the early 1980s, to explore how important the conventions of the time might have been in influencing the authorial 'voice' Finch writes in.

Shere Hite's (1981) *The Hite Report On Male Sexuality* is one of a series of books published from 1977 on investigating links between women's unequal position in US society and sexual behaviours and feelings (usefully overviewed in Hite, 2006). Hite's research utilizes survey research and large-scale datasets, but radically departs from conventional 'scientific' ideas about how to achieve a representative sample, the structure and organization of a questionnaire, how research should be carried out, and the kind of analysis which ought to result. The research for *On Male Sexuality* started in 1974, at a time when it took considerable courage to carry out feminist research concerned with men (the orthodoxy was that, to be feminist, research must focus on women). It clearly demonstrates that a survey can be feminist in its process and methodology, not just regarding its questions and conclusions, and also that it need not conform to mainstream positivist methodological thinking (that is 'scientific' and 'objective' thinking) to have social impact. *On Male Sexuality* is

## SURVEY EXAMPLE

### Shere Hite (1981) *The Hite Report On Male Sexuality*

*The Hite Report On Male Sexuality* sees male sexuality as a microcosm of US society: male sexuality is central to the definition of masculinity and masculinity is central to the 'world-view' of US culture. The investigation uses a specially designed kind of survey approach. It aims to provide a new cultural interpretation of male sexuality, by radically reworking how a questionnaire is designed and redefining how 'sex' and 'male sexuality' are understood.

*Methodology*

- Over 7200 questionnaires from US men aged 13–79 were collected and analysed, relating their sexual behaviours and feelings to their wider view of themselves, women and society
- Uses a written 'essay-type' questionnaire very different from the usual design of questionnaires, and encourages the participating men to reflect on and depart from its questions and to write about these in detail if they wish
- Rejects conventional definitions of 'representative' samples, but also emphasizes that there is a close fit between its sample and the US male population aged 18+
- Points out that patterns in men's responses occur across socio-economic groupings, and interprets these patterns as a matter of 'character', rather than the product of class or race
- Readers are provided with unfolding sequences of lengthy quotations from a number of particular men, adding depth and complexity to discussion of the range of responses to questions
- At points the report combines responses to different questions for particular men, showing how behaviours, ideas and feelings were linked for them

*Methodology reading*

'Preface,' xiii–xix
'Questionnaire IV', xxi–xxxiii
'Who answered the questionnaire: population statistics and methodology', 1055–7
'Towards a new methodology in the social sciences', 1057–60

interested not only in general patterns, but also in variations in responses from sample members, while mainstream survey research tends to treat such variations as insignificant 'ends' and discuss only majority responses. It is also concerned with exploring linked responses from some men across the questions, as part of interpreting and making sense of their written responses.

At this point, readers will find it helpful to look at the overviews of the three comparators for Hite's book, all of which use 'numbers', although in different ways, with relevant sections on methodology referenced in the Bibliography. The methodological question we are interested in here concerns whether a feminist survey and use of large-scale datasets can be feminist in its *process*, not just its questions and conclusions, or whether surveys are by definition positivist. For many people, surveys and other large-scale datasets are seen as inherently in conflict with the ideas of feminist methodology. We do not agree: any research can be foundationalist, for this depends on how a method is put into practice and the claims made about the information it provides, and not the method itself. *On Male Sexuality* shows that the feminist use of a survey approach can radically re-work what this is and put a feminist methodology fully into practice within it. It is also important here to realize that the now dominant understanding of 'a survey' is actually fairly recent: until post-Second World War, the term meant providing a general overview of a field of inquiry and did not necessarily include numbers, let alone those produced through a questionnaire asked of a random representative sample.

Clementina Black's (1915/1983) *Married Women's Work* is an early feminist example of survey research to provide an overview, in this case of women's labour market and household work, with the same approach used in other Women's Industrial Council's investigations. The reports in *Married Women's Work* contain different kinds of data, some numerical and generalized to whole groups, some more focused and originating from particular women and groups. Diana Gittins' (1982) *Fair Sex* uses the UK's 1921 and 1931 Censuses to show the considerable downturn in family size that occurred. However, this kind of data cannot explain *why* many people changed their behaviour, only that the change is a demonstrable fact, although Gittins' interview and case study data do enable her to explain why it happened: these women were able to change their husbands' behaviours, as well as their own, because better employment provided them with greater equality. Census data and the large-scale datasets resulting from random sample surveys convincingly show broad trajectories of behaviours; but while having breadth about matters of 'what', they do not provide the depth necessary for explaining the 'why' questions Gittins is interested in. However, are there circumstances in which 'what' should override 'why', in the name of feminist politics? Diane Russell's (1982/1990) *Rape in Marriage* investigates an important feminist topic, the rape of women by their husbands or partners, asks feminist questions about this, and its analysis has firmly in mind the need to change the prevailing view that such things do not happen or are not particularly important. It is also insistent that a mainstream random sample survey is essential for making valid generalizations that will influence policy-makers.

Since the early 1980s, it has become a truism in 'sensitive' and policy-related areas of feminist research that such research has to be rigorously mainstream in everything or it will not be seen as scientifically valid and so will not have the desired impact. This begs interesting questions about why policy changes come about and whether it is academic research findings, or more complex sets of factors, including the media and well-placed political sponsorship, that produce change. In thinking about the issues here, readers should think about their own response to survey research, and consider why the split exists between 'born-again' feminist survey research in policy areas and the more generally negative response in women's and gender studies about numerical analysis. Also, might there be a middle ground, with Hite's approach providing a way forward consonant with feminist methodology? And if this is so, then why don't other feminist survey researchers try harder to include feminist methodology?

---

### AUTO/BIOGRAPHICAL EXAMPLE

**Frigga Haug and Others (1983)** *Female Sexualization: A Collective Work of Memory*

*Female Sexualization* combines the investigation/analysis/theorization of the self-construction of normative expectations concerning 'female sexualization' and women's body experiences, carried out by members of a socialist feminist network in late 1970s/early 1980s Germany. It involves the collective engagement by network members with the idea and practice of 'memory-work', including exploring memory practices and then speaking together analytically about these.

*Methodology*

- Refuses the 'theory/research' binary as well as the 'subjectivity/objectivity' and 'researcher/subjects' binaries
- Insists that the object of feminist research has to be the researcher as the vehicle for interpretation, analysis, theorizing
- Produces a collective analysis of women's socialization as sexualized beings through memory-work as a means of disrupting the taken-for-granted, so as to better interpret memory practices
- Focuses on themes connected with the body, using written memories of past events which are not treated as 'objective fact' but as examples of socialization as an active process involving the self
- Argues that the collective process is fundamental to memory-work and has to be made visible in writing – writing is not separate from analysis or theory
- Re-works theory as a usable language which meshes with everyday narratives

*Methodology reading*

'Translator's Foreword', 11–19
'Preface to English Edition', 21–32
'Introduction', 29–32
'Memory work', 33–72

---

Frigga Haug et al.'s (1983) *Female Sexualization: A Collective Work of Memory* departs from many of the conventions for doing and writing about feminist research. Within *Female Sexualization*, the researcher is both subject and object of analytical attention, and this 'researcher' is actually a collective group, engaged in a collective co-process of talking, thinking, analyzing and also writing about all this. Moreover, theory is not seen as separate from these grounded research activities and is treated as part of narrativizing the processes of female sexualization and then analyzing and writing about this – in effect, theory is 'methodologized' by the group. And as these comments will indicate, writing is seen as fully a part of research; indeed, the close relationships insisted upon by the collective could be expressed as 'writing-as-research/as-theory'. The basis of this extremely interesting research and writing project is the conviction that the lives and experiences of the co-researchers, but, more precisely and importantly, their *collective* interrogation, analysis and interpretation of these, should be as central to emancipatory research as they are to emancipatory politics.

Does feminist methodology require treating the researcher in this way? That is, must the feminist researcher always be the combined subject/object in any reflexive engagement with the specific topic or focus of a piece of research, as Haug et al. imply? While *Female Sexualization* is fascinating and extremely insightful, we do not think that all versions of feminist research reflexivity need to take this specific form. And at this point, readers should look at the overviews of the three comparators for *Female Sexualization*, all of which use auto/biography (Stanley, 1992) and/or memory work as an important tool of feminist methodology. The methodological question we shall explore in relation to them concerns how they use ideas about reflexivity.

Carolyn Steedman's (1986) *Landscape For a Good Woman* deals with the 'disruptive narratives' told by her mother, concerning the lives of herself and her two daughters. This is the focus both for its own sake and because it provides an analytical route into the untold stories of working-class women and girls more generally. The result is what *Landscape For a Good Woman* refers to as a 'non-celebratory case study' regarding class and gender, an in-depth focus on specific lives in order to tell a different kind of story, an analytically and politically informed story about working-class women. *Landscape For a Good Woman*, then, is reflexively engaged and traverses the researcher/researched line, but in a very different way from *Female Sexualization*. Ruth Linden's (1993) *Making Stories, Making Selves* too is very reflexively aware and engaged, but also fully aware that 'the point' of her research concerns the people who lived through the Shoah and how to respond to its aftermaths. Reflexivity in *Making Stories, Making Selves* is concerned with important matters of ethics, emotion and interpretation in researching a topic so sensitive on all levels as interviews with people who survived the Nazi concentration camps, and it demonstrates that reflexivity is at the heart of interpretation and is neither an optional extra nor an indulgence. Rebecca Campbell's (2002) *Emotionally Involved: The Impact of Researching Rape* is centrally concerned with the emotional impact on people who work with rape survivors and the importance of them 'doing things' to ameliorate the potentially damaging effects in order to better help others. It provides a thoughtful and insightful investigation of the relationship between intellectual thought and human emotion within feminist research which treats emotion as capable of rational inquiry, and something that can be shaped and used rather than being outside of people's control. The origins of *Emotionally Involved* lie in Campbell's long-term experiences in rape crisis work and is a reflexive project engaged in by someone who is both researcher and worker. While more 'mainstream' in its presentation than the other auto/biographical texts discussed here, Campbell and the rape crisis workers interviewed are effectively co-researchers within the project. The research also has direct implications for how people can best learn to 'handle' powerful emotional reactions to such upsetting things as rape, and so it has some of the attributes of action research as well.

Is it always important to write about the emotional component of research – or might there be circumstances when this would detract from the importance of the research topic? It is also useful to remember the range of meanings that the term 'reflexivity' has – in some feminist research, it has been reduced to locating the researcher as a person, while the examples we have provided here all treat reflexivity much more analytically. Readers might also find it useful to pick one or two examples of mainstream/malestream research and think about whether researcher reflexivity and/or the role of emotion in research are discussed in these, if so in what ways, and how this compares with how the examples of feminist research discussed here do so.

---

**THEORY EXAMPLE**

**Judith Butler ([1990] 1999 with new Preface)** *Gender Trouble*

*Gender Trouble* contends that a pervasive assumption about heterosexuality in 1990s (implicitly, US) feminist theory restricted the meaning of gender to then-current ideas about masculinity and femininity. It explores how non-normative sexual practices can question the stability of gender as a category of analysis. It also outlines a theory of performativity, that gender is 'manufactured' through sustained sets of social acts organized through the gendered stylization of the body. However, it rejects applying this to the psyche, seeing some aspects of internality as 'given' and lying beyond (or beneath) the social.

*Methodology*

- A theoretical exposition, written mainly in an 'it is so' and apparently removed and detached authorial voice
- Its argument is structured in a mainly critical mode, by interrogating the ideas advanced in other people's theoretical writings, particularly ones which have been important in a US academic context
- It proposes that feminist theoretical discussion relates to feminist politics through parody and subversion and the deconstruction of the terms in which identity is articulated
- 'I' is used mainly in the 1999 Preface and Conclusion to disavow notions of fixed self or identity, with 'author identity' similarly questioned.

*Methodology reading*

'Preface' (1999), vii–xxvi
'Preface' (1990) xxvii–xxiv

Readers may be surprised to find theory included among discussions of feminist methodology, because theory and research are often treated as binaries, as alternative ways of working. However, substantive research or investigation which is 'ideas free' is, quite simply, bad research; and any theoretical investigation that does not have a coherent basis to its use of argument, evidence, interpretation and conclusion (that is, a good methodology) is deficient theory. Theorizing has a methodological frame which links evidence, arguments and conclusions by, typically, using other people's ideas or writings as the source or data, but usually without explaining why they have been selected for commentary and others not (see Thompson, 1996).

Judith Butler's *Gender Trouble* is a much cited influential theorization of the socially constructed and performative nature of gender, a topic absolutely central to the feminist analysis of gender relations and how to achieve social change in a move 'from parody to politics', as Butler puts it. How can ideas about feminist methodology be used to think about feminist theory? And wherein does the feminism of *Gender Trouble* lie and is this similar to or different from other important works of feminist theory?

The underlying assumptions about the gender order and the 'speculative questions' that *Gender Trouble* addresses, also its topic and its conclusions emphasizing the implications for feminist politics, all mark this as a feminist text. At the same time, it is written in a very opaque way, utilizes an 'it is so' authorial voice that inhibits readers from answering back, and uses the work of other feminists in a mainly critical way. What results is a fairly closed text, in the sense that it provides few means for readers to engage with or dispute its arguments – it has a strong 'take it or leave it' quality. For many people, this is what high-class social theory 'is' by definition, and clearly many feminist readers have responded positively to its combination of content and authorial 'voice'. However, there is little which indicates its engagement with any of the ideas of feminist methodology. Relatedly, it positions the reader very much outside of the text, as a recipient of it, rather than someone who should or could directly engage with it. It is important to ask, then, whether feminist theory necessarily positions the reader in this way – is this the textual politics of all theory and so an inevitable aspect of the feminist variant, or can – perhaps even should – feminist theory be different?

At this point, readers should look at the overviews of the three comparators for Butler's text and read the sections on methodology referenced in the Bibliography. They are extremely influential examples of feminist theory, having a major impact when published and, in the case of Woolf's *Three Guineas*, for many decades after as well. All three have different approaches from *Gender Trouble*, regarding the open or closed character of the text, how it positions readers, and related matters of feminist methodology. Readers at this point might want to contemplate what they think that 'theory' consists of. Does theory need to be difficult to read, can it be fiction or fictionalized, must it be abstract and without detailed content? Also, crucially important, should feminist theory be different and embody at least some of the principles of feminist methodology?

bell hooks' (1984) *Feminist Theory* shares some important characteristics with *Gender Trouble*: it proceeds from critiquing other people's ideas, and its authorial 'voice' is a declaratory one stating a position rather than persuading an active reader. Its message is a moral as well as political one about white feminists and it is difficult to find a way of arguing back that does not seem like rejecting the importance of racism. However, other writing by the author, in 'real life' Gloria Watkins, comments that the pseudonym 'bell hooks' was adopted specifically for her to engage in passionate polemics. Therefore, the reader who is aware of this knows that texts by bell hooks are writings of a polemical kind, with the relationship of readers to these that of an appreciative (or unappreciative) audience, rather than having any detailed engagement with them. R.W. Connell's (2005) *Masculinities*, by contrast, is written in a processual way that takes readers through the process of enquiry that the author engaged in. It also provides many examples from around the world to put across its points, and discusses work by other people in a positive way, by deploying their arguments within the developing framework of this theorization of masculinities. (See Robinson in this volume for further discussion of Connell's work.) The result is that readers are continually encouraged to engage with the ideas being worked out and discussed. Readers are even more directly addressed in Virginia Woolf's (1938) *Three Guineas*, because the reader is a proxy for a man Woolf writes three fictionalized letters to. The addressee becomes the reader, who is not only engaged with, but their possible responses to her comments are anticipated by Woolf and she responds to these in a thoughtful and respectful and also very witty way. Woolf's reader is not only engaged with, but is also treated as someone important to be persuaded and entertained.

A good next step here is for readers to think about these matters concerning their favourite (and/or most disliked) works of feminist theory. Here whether their writing styles are open and processual or closed and declaratory, if readers are encouraged to be responsive and engage with the ideas and arguments presented, and also whether the authors explicitly engage with any important components of feminist methodology, are all useful things to consider.

## Conclusion

### *Reading research writing methodologically*

The aims of this chapter have been to show that carrying out feminist research is a complicated business, to emphasize that there is no single 'right way' to do feminist research, to point out that feminist methodology can be put into practice very differently but in ways that are still feminist, and to convey the wide-ranging concerns of feminist research. In doing these things, we have used a reading frame for looking in detail at the methodological aspects of five exemplars of feminist research and fifteen more comparators to these, a reading frame which not only provides a transparent set of themes for evaluating this work but also encourages research writing to be read and compared in a systematic way.

Readers may want to use some of our ideas but not others within an alternative reading frame, or to supplement these with additional or alternative methodological ideas, or indeed to devise a reading frame composed by entirely different things. What is important we think is not the specific components of a reading frame, but instead that the criteria used to read and evaluate feminist research work should be made explicit and transparent, so that other people can engage, and if necessary disagree, with these.

Many people find themselves completely convinced by the last thing they have read, even when this directly conflicts with the previous thing they read and were convinced by; or else they criticize or reject work just because it departs from their pre-existing ideas and beliefs. Developing and using a reading frame, as we have done in this chapter, will provide the means of engaging in a detailed and thoughtful way with wide-ranging examples of feminist research. It will also help readers to feel more 'in charge' of their reading and more secure that the evaluations they make of it will do justice to what the authors have written. Bon voyage!

## Bibliography

### A. SHOSTAK COMPARATORS

These comparators all use ethnographic or participant observation methods.

#### Diane Bell (1983) *Daughters of the Dreaming,* London, Allen & Unwin

*Topic:* Explores Australian aboriginal women's importance in religious and ritual aspects of their society.

*Methodology:* A feminist anthropological ethnography of the late 1970s, when Bell lived in Warrabri in Australia for over two years, with her presence treated as part of the fieldwork dynamics. Women's and men's roles in ritual are kept secret from each other, so the problems of researching this are discussed, while the acknowledged importance of women's ritual activities is stressed.

*Methodology reading:* Methodology discussions are interwoven into substantive discussions in all chapters, but see in particular 'Into the Field', 7–40; 'The Problem of Women', 229–54.

#### Judith Stacey (1991) *Brave New Families,* New York, Basic Books

*Topic:* Investigates the demise of the 'modern family' in the US due to the combined impacts of post-industrialization, postmodernity and postfeminism. Sees the 'postmodern family' (where there is no normative or dominant family form) as a transitional form.

*Methodology:* Calls its methodology an ethnography, but in practice combines formal interviews with participating in people's lives as a kind of acquaintance or friend. Focuses on two white women and their family/kinship networks in California's 'Silicon Valley'. Concludes ethnography is 'far less benign or feminist than anticipated'.

*Methodology reading:* 'The Making and Unmaking of Modern Families', 3–19; 'Land of Dreams and Disasters', 20–38; 'Epilogue', 272–8.

**Sallie Westwood (1984)** *All Day Every Day,* **London, Pluto Press**

*Topic:* Investigates 'factory and family in women's lives', particularly the inherent contradictions of women's lives under patriarchal capitalism. Explores how these are played out through a shopfloor culture oppositional to management which forges bonds of solidarity and sisterhood.

*Methodology:* A shopfloor ethnography carried out over fourteen months in the early 1980s in 'StitchCo', a UK hosiery factory making jerseyknit material in which over a third of the female workforce were Asian. The methodological aspects are only briefly discussed.

*Methodology reading:* 'Introduction', 1–12.

## B. RIESSMAN COMPARATORS

These comparators all produce and analyse interview data.

**Jayne Ifekwunigwe (1998)** *Scattered Belongings: Cultural Paradoxes of 'Race', Nation and Gender,* **London, Routledge**

*Topic:* Explores cultural paradoxes of 'race', nation and gender, in which 'mixed race' hybridities disrupt assumptions of binary, black or white, racializations. Extracts from personal testimonies are placed in a 'critical dialogue' with extracts from cultural theories, together with brief discussion of how to theorize such identities in a global context.

*Methodology:* Focuses on six testimonies as 'narratives of belongings for future generations of metis(se) children and adults in England', from two sets of sisters and two women raised by mother surrogates. Short extracts are provided, together with 'culled extracts' from cultural theorists, and extracts from an ethnography Ifekwunigwe did in a Bristol, UK, community.

*Methodology reading:* 'Prologue', xii–xiv; 'Returning(s): the critical feminist auto-ethnographer', 29–49; 'Setting the stage', 50–61; 'Let blackness and whiteness wash through', 170–93.

**Ann Oakley (1974)** *The Sociology of Housework,* **London, Martin Robertson**

*Topic:* Part of Oakley's larger study of housewives in early 1970s London. Treats housework as 'a job' which can be researched like paid employment, carried out in the context of the then 'invisibility' of women within sociological research of the early 1970s.

*Methodology:* Forty interviews carried out (with black and Indian women removed to make the sample 'more homogeneous') with a sample drawn from middle- and working-class women with at least one child under 5. Utilizes similar measurement techniques to those for researching occupational groups, proxy measures to produce dis/satisfaction scales, and a 'ten statement test' to assess women's 'domestic role identity' and questions about 'who am I?'.

*Methodology reading:* 'Description of Housework Study', 29–40; 'Conclusions', 181–97; 'Appendix I, Sample Selection and Measurement Techniques', 198–207, 'Appendix II, Interview Schedule', 208–19.

**Sarah Mirza and Margaret Strobel (eds and trans., 1989)** *Three Swahili Women: Life Histories From Mombasa,* **Kenya, Bloomington, IN, Indiana University Press**

*Topic:* Provides three 'narrative texts' by Swahili-speaking women from Mombasa, Kenya. At the time this and a parallel Swahili text were published, there was little published in Swahili about women. Therefore these narratives, by women of different ages and different social groups, are seen as promoting understanding of this society and change within it.

*Methodology:* Life history interviews were carried out in Swahili by Strobel in 1972–3 and 1975, while transcription and editing involved both researchers, resulting in what are called 'narrative texts'. The details of editing are not discussed, the involvement of the researcher and any bystanders is omitted, and the texts are smoothly edited and chronologically ordered. There is also little interpretation or comparison of content.

*Methodology reading:* 'Preface', ix–xi; 'Introduction', 1–14; 'Appendix', 117–21.

## C. FINCH COMPARATORS

These comparators are all examples of feminist documentary analysis.

### Leonore Davidoff and Catherine Hall (1987) *Family Fortunes*, London, Routledge

*Topic:* Focuses on family and gender differences in the English middle class 1780 to 1850, a period of rapid change. Moves beyond 'separate spheres' ideas, to show the public prominence of men is embedded in networks of familial and female support, and therefore it focuses on sexual divisions of labour in the family and beyond.

*Methodology:* Uses an archive-based methodology, only briefly discussed. Compares three locations so the analysis covers a wide spectrum of English life. In each location, research on named individuals, families and their interrelationships is supplemented by studying a sample of wills and the dispensation of property, how the particular local communities were organized, and a sample of middle-class households are investigated using 1851 Census data.

*Methodology reading:* 'Prologue', 13–35; 'Epilogue', 450–4.

### Hilary Lapsley (1999) *Margaret Mead and Ruth Benedict: The Kinship of Women*, Amherst, MA, University of Massachusetts Press

*Topic:* A biographical study of the life-long friendship between US anthropologists Margaret Mead and Ruth Benedict, encompassing sexuality, love and close intellectual bonds. Carried out around present-day interest in new forms of family and kinship relationships, it explores the anthropological work of each woman in the context of the central relationship with each other and their wider friendship networks.

*Methodology:* Only briefly discusses its archive-based methodology. Uses newly-available correspondences as well as earlier biographies and the women's own autobiographical writings. Written in a 'standard biography' form, but as a narrative of two interconnected lives, it also has a revisionist intention, influenced by feminist and lesbian studies, to emphasize the women's friendship networks.

*Methodology reading:* 'Introduction', 1–8.

### Dorothy Smith (1999) *Writing the Social: Critique, Theory, and Investigations*, Toronto, University of Toronto Press

*Topic:* Interconnected chapters explore the intertextuality of Smith's position *as a reader*, focusing on fissures in the relations of ruling, with Smith conceiving organizational texts as material means of bringing together ruling ideas, and local settings and what people do in these. For Smith, all relations of ruling are textually-mediated and so the analysis of organizational texts is crucially import for feminist politics.

*Methodology:* Combines theory and methodology. Smith analytically joins up *writing* the social and *reading* the social through a six-point 'method of inquiry'. This encompasses the situated knower; the ongoing coordinated activities of the social; the 'how' of this coordination; organizational practices and the social relations they engender; avoiding a theory/practice split; recognition that texts join up local activities and the organizational relations of ruling; and that the politics of this method are foundational. Positions Smith as both subject and agent.

*Methodology reading:* 'Introduction', 3–12; 'Sociological Theory: Methods of Writing Patriarchy into Feminist Texts', 45–69; '"Politically Correct": An Organiser of Public Discourse', 172–94; 'Conclusion', 225–8.

## D. HITE COMPARATORS

These comparators all use numbers and/or a survey approach.

### Clementina Black (1915/1983) *Married Women's Work* (ed. Ellen Mappen), London, Virago Press

*Topic:* Presents the results of a survey of married women's lives, including household as well as industrial work, carried out in many areas of Britain by members of the Women's Industrial Council (WIC). The WIC investigated the social conditions and employment circumstances of women's lives and acted as a pressure group arguing for political changes using research findings from this and other investigations.

*Methodology:* The methodology is a survey in the sense, then current, of overviewing married women's work. The reports were written by the various investigators using a combination of individual responses, case studies and numerical data about the people interviewed in a particular area.

*Methodology reading:* 'New Introduction' (Ellen Mappen), i–xxi; 'Preface' (Clementina Black), xxiii-xxiv; 'Introduction' (Clementina Black), 1–15; 'Appendices', 254–83.

### Diana Gittins (1982) *Fair Sex: Family Size and Structure, 1900–39*, London, Hutchinson

*Topic:* Investigates why English working-class family size fell sharply between 1900 and 1939. Concludes this was not due to the diffusion of middle-class attitudes, as had been assumed, but because of the impact of socio-economic factors, particularly those which enabled women to earn reasonable wages from employment and, as a consequence, helped them establish more egalitarian marriages.

*Methodology:* Uses three kinds of data to throw light on each other: the analysis of 1921 and 1931 Census demographics; documentary analysis of the records of an early birth control clinic; and material from thirty in-depth interviews with women of the appropriate age group.

*Methodology reading:* 'Preface', 9–10; 'Introduction', 11–32; 'Conclusion', 181–7; 'Appendix: The interviews', 197–200.

### Diane Russell ([1982] 1990 expanded edition) *Rape in Marriage*, New York, Stein & Day

*Topic:* A 'breaking the silence' study of marital rape, carried out in the early 1980s context of marital rape exemption laws in many US states, and the denial of its incidence and impact. The key finding is that around 14% of ever-married women had been raped by ex/husbands. Explores a continuum of sex and violence, and also analyzes factors that can help stop marital rape.

*Methodology:* Set up to generalize from the study to the US population, it insists a random representative sample was essential because non-random sampling can only raise hypotheses and present exploratory thinking, but cannot test hypotheses or make valid generalizations to the whole population.

*Methodology reading:* 'Introduction to the New Edition', ix–xxx; 'Preface', xxxi–xxxiii; 'Acknowledgements', xxxiv–xxxviii; 'The Rape Study', 27–41; 'Why Men Rape Their Wives', 132–66.

## E. HAUG ET AL. COMPARATORS

These comparators all use aspects of the researcher's auto/biographies as part of the research process and also its product.

### Rebecca Campbell (2002) *Emotionally Involved: The Impact of Researching Rape*, New York, Routledge

*Topic:* Emotions are part of all social research, especially when the topic concerns painful things: regarding *Emotionally Involved*, this involves long-term work with rape survivors. Discusses emotions, coping and knowing, with the focus on 'how to think straight' when working with pain, to gain insights into violence against women generally, and to achieve a balance between intellectual thought and human emotion within research.

*Methodology:* Builds on a large interview project with rape survivors and experience in a Violence Against Women Project. Its 'collective case study' involves a three-stage analysis: 'data reduction' into sections of coded text; 'data display', looking across cases for similarities and differences; and 'data interpretation', checking its credibility and meaningfulness with interviewees. Issues of feelings as well as confidentiality arose, making writing about the research difficult.

*Methodology reading:* 'Preface', 1–13; 'Creating Balance – Thinking and Feeling', 123–50; 'Appendix A: The Development, Process, and Methodology of the Researching-the-Researcher Study', 151–68; 'Appendix B: The Researching-the-Researcher Interview Protocol', 169–72.

### R. Ruth Linden (1993) *Making Stories, Making Selves*, Columbus, OH, Ohio State University Press

*Topic:* Provides feminist analytical explorations of the interconnections between remembering, story-telling and self-fashioning around the Holocaust. Discusses autobiographical and ethnographic materials and Linden's many interviews with survivors, to explore how selves and times are fashioned through the times, places and audiences of story-telling.

*Methodology:* A montage bringing together Linden's 200-plus interviews with death camp survivors and ethnographic examinations of her lived experience and interpretations of survivors' stories. Rejects treating people's memory in terms of failed referentiality and instead emphasizes its synchronic truth. Also insists that writing is central to methodology, including to interpretation, and this needs to be fully recognized.

*Methodology reading:* The whole book disrupts any theory/methodology separation, but in particular see: 'Preface', ix–x; 'Prologue', 1–11; 'Bearing Witness', 61–70; 'Reflections on "Bearing Witness"', 70–83; 'Reflections on "The Phenomenology of Surviving"', 103–12.

### Carolyn Steedman (1986) *Landscape For a Good Woman*, London, Virago

*Topic:* Analytically interrogating the disruptive narratives of her own childhood, including those told in her mother's stories. These 'secret stories' of lives lived on the class and gender borderlands of dominant culture are re-interpreted in a way that eschews notions of a 'real biographical past' while also insisting on people's real lives and experiences.

*Methodology:* A case study at the boundaries of biography and autobiography with history. Because these 'real lives' and the theories that explain them are disjunctural, a narrative methodology is used to disrupt canonical facts by confronting them with the stories of working-class women and girls.

*Methodology reading:* The entire book is both methodology and theory, but see: 'Stories', 5–24; 'Childhood for a Good Woman', 140–4.

## F. BUTLER COMPARATORS

These comparators are all examples of pro/feminist theorizing.

### R.W. Connell (2005) *Masculinities*, Cambridge, Polity

*Topic:* Argues that different masculinities are associated with different configurations of power and different social locations and social practices. Discusses historical changes in theorizing masculinities and uses the life histories of different groups of men to underpin its theorizations. Also examines whether 'hegemonic masculinity' needs reconsidering in relation to non-hegemonic forms.

*Methodology:* A theoretical argument stemming from the empirical research it extensively draws on. Emphasizes that good argument cannot remain abstract and proposes a 'situational' approach which ties theory to specific practice/context. Uses a first person and processual authorial 'voice' in an inclusive way that takes the reader through the processes of finding out, and uses world-wide examples to illustrate the key arguments made.

*Methodology reading:* 'Introduction to the Second Edition', xi–xxv; 'The Science of Masculinity', 3–44; 'Introduction to Part II', 89–92.

### bell hooks (1984) *Feminist Theory: From Margin to Center*, Boston, MA, South End Press

*Topic:* Uses the margin/centre metaphor to characterize early 1980s (implicitly, US) feminist theory regarding the location of black (and other non-privileged) women. Insists a much wider set of experiences and analyses must be included within feminist theory and that feminism must be a mass movement to achieve social transformation.

*Methodology:* A theoretical approach based on assertion and proceeding from what it calls a 'sometimes harsh and unrelenting' critique. Generalizes to white women always dominating 'the center' of feminism. Sees new theory as produced by those who experience both margins and centre, a form of theoretical vanguardism. Written mainly in a first person emphatic authorial 'voice' and uses 'they', 'we' and 'our' in a largely exclusive way to mark out divisions and separations. Few examples, all US ones, are discussed.

*Methodology reading:* 'Preface', ix–x; 'Black Women: Shaping Feminist Theory', 1–15.

### Virgina Woolf (1938) *Three Guineas*, Harmondsworth, Penguin

*Topic:* Three closely interlinked essays exploring and theorizing links between the position of women, militarism and fascism. Published around the rise of fascism in Europe, the Spanish Civil War, and the widespread certainty in the UK that a wider war was going to occur. Written as letters replying in a feminist voice to a man who had requested Woolf to donate money to a peace organization.

*Methodology:* Complexly mixes factual and fictional elements in a theoretical argument presented in detail to the reader (who 'stands in for' the man requesting the donation),for evaluation. Written in a first person inclusive authorial 'voice', with the fictional male appeal-writer directly addressed in an inquiring, sceptical but even-handed way. Argues feminism as an analytical position should not be ignored in discussions of politics and war because patriarchy is closely related to militarism and fascism.

*Methodology reading:* No separate discussion of methodology matters, but the first essay dazzlingly explains why they were written and how Woolf will respond to the appeal made to her; see 'One', 5–46.

# Bibliography

Aapola, S., Gonick, M. and Harris, M. (2005) *Young Femininity: Girlhood, Power and Social Change*, Basingstoke: Palgrave Macmillan.

Abdel-Shehid, G. (2005) *Who Da Man?; Black Masculinities and Sporting Cultures*, Toronto: Canadian Scholars' Press.

Acker, J. (1990) 'Hierarchies, Jobs, Bodies: A Theory of Gendered Organisations', *Gender and Society*, 4: 139-58.

Adam, A. (1997) 'What Should We Do with Cyberfeminism?', *Women in Computing* R. Lander and A. Adam (eds) Exeter: Intellect Books.

Adkins, L. (1995) *Gendered Work: Sexuality, Family and the Labour Market*, Buckingham: Open University Press.

Adkins, L. and Skeggs, B. (2004) *Feminism After Bourdieu* London: Routledge.

Adorno, T. W. (1991) *The Culture Industry: Selected Essays on Mass Culture*, Routledge: London.

Adu-Poku, S. (2001) 'Envisioning (Black) Male Feminism: A Cross Cultural Perspective' *Journal of Gender Studies*, 10 (2): 157–67.

Afshar, H. (1989) 'Gender Roles and the "Moral Economy of Kin" Among Pakistani Women in West Yorkshire', *New Community*, 13 (2) 211–25.

Afshar, H. and Maynard, M. (2000) 'Gender and Ethnicity at the Millennium: From Margin to Centre', *Ethnic and Racial Studies*, 23 (5): 805–819.

Ahmed, S. (1996) 'Beyond Humanism and Postmodernism', *Hypatia*, 11 (2): 71–93.

Aikman, S. and Unterhalter, E. (2005) *Beyond Access: Transforming Policy and Practice for Gender Equality in Education*, London: OXFAM.

Akrich, M. and Pasveer, B. (2004) 'Embodiment Ads Disembodiment in Childbirth Narratives', *Body and Society*, 10 (2–3): 63–84.

Albertyn, C. (2003) 'Towards Substantive Representation: Women and Politics in South Africa', in A. Dobrowolsky and V. Hart (eds), *Women Making Constitutions: New Politics and Comparative Perspectives*, Basingstoke: Palgrave Macmillan.

Aldridge, M. (1994) 'Unlimited Liability? Emotional Labour in Nursing and Social Work', *Journal of Advanced Nursing*, 20 (4): 722–8.

Alexander, C. (1996) *The Art of Being Black*, Oxford: Clarendon Press.

Alexander, C. (2000) *The Asian Gang: Ethnicity, Identity and Masculinity*, Oxford: Berg.

Alexander, C. and Alleyne, B. (2002) 'Introduction: Framing Difference: Racial and Ethnic Studies in Twenty-First-Century Britain', *Ethnic and Racial Studies*, 25 (4): 541–51.

Alexander, W. (2000) 'Women and the Scottish Parliament', in A. Coote (ed.) *New Gender Agenda*, London: Institute for Public Policy Research.

Ali, S. (2003) *Mixed-Race, Post-Race: Gender, New Ethnicities and Cultural Practices*, Oxford: Berg.

Ali, S., Benjamin, S. and Muthner, M. (2004) *The Politics of Gender and Education: Critical Perspectives*, Basingstoke: Palgrave Macmillan.

Alibhai-Brown, Y. and Montague, A. (1992) *The Colour of Love: Mixed Race Relationships*, London: Virago.

Allan, C. and Brosnan, P. (1998) 'Non-Standard Working-Time Arrangements in Australia and New Zealand', *International Journal of Manpower*, 19 (4): 234–49.

Allen, S. and Barker, D.L. (eds) (1976) *Dependence and Exploitation in Work and Marriage*, London: Longman.

Alsop, R., Fitzsimons, A. and Lennon, K. (eds) (2002) *theorizing gender*, Oxford: Polity.

Althusser, L. (1971) 'Ideology and Ideological State Apparatuses', in L. Althusser (ed.) *Lenin and Philosophy and Other Essays*, London: New Left Books.

Amos, V. and Parmar, P. (1984) 'Challenging Imperial Feminism', *Feminist Review Special Issue, 'Many Voices One Chant'*, 17 (July): 3–19.

Anderson, M. (1980) *Approaches to the History of the Western Family 1500–1914*, London: Macmillan.

Ang, I. (1985) *Watching Dallas*, London: Methuen.

Anzaldua, G. (1999) *Borderlands = La Frontera*, San Francisco: Aunt Lute Books.

Archer, L. (2005) 'The Impossibility of Girls' Educational "Success": Entanglements of Gender, "Race", Class and Sexuality in the Production and Problematisation of Educational Femininities', paper presented at ESRC seminar series: Girls and Education 3–16, Cardiff University, November.

Arnot, M. (1984) 'How Shall We Educate Our Sons?', in R. Deem (ed.), *Co-Education Reconsidered*, Milton Keynes: Open University Press.

Arnot, M. (2002) *Reproducing Gender? Critical Essays on Educational Theory and Feminist Politics*, London: RoutledgeFalmer.

Arnot, M., David, M. and Weiner, G. (1999) *Closing the Gender Gap: Post-War Education and Social Change*, Cambridge: Polity Press.

Arnot, M. and Dillabough, J. (eds) (2000) *Challenging Democracy? International Perspectives on Gender, Education and Citizenship*, London: RoutledgeFalmer.

Bahovic, E. (2000) 'A Short Note on the use of "Sex" and "Gender" in Slavic Languages', in R. Braidotti and E. Vonk (eds), *The Making of European Women's Studies*, Utrecht: Drukkerij Zuidam and Uithof.

Baldock, J. and Hadlow, J. (2005) 'Managing the Family: Productivity, Scheduling and the Male Veto', in T. Kröger and J. Sipilä (eds), *Overstretched, European Families up against the Demands of Work and Care*, Oxford: Blackwell.

Balsamo, A. (1996) *Technologies of the Gendered Body: Reading Cyborg Women*, Durham, NC: Duke University Press.

Banton, M. (2001) 'Progress in Ethnic and Racial Studies', *Ethnic and Racial Studies*, 24 (2): 173–94.

Barrett, M. (1988) *Women's Oppression Today*, 2nd edn, London: Verso.

Barrett, M. (1992) *The Politics of Truth: From Marx to Foucault*, Cambridge: Polity.

Barrett, M. and McIntosh, M. (1982) *The Anti-Social Family*, London: Verso.

Barron, R. and Norris, E. (1976) 'Sexual Divisions and the Dual Labour Market' in D. Barker and S. Allen (eds), *Dependence and Exploitation in Work and in Marriage*, London: Longman.

Bartky, S. (1998) 'Foreword', in T. Digby (ed.), *Men Doing Feminism*, London: Routledge.

Barthes, R. (1957) *Mythologies*, trans. Annette Lavers, New York: Hill & Wang.

Battersby, C. (1998) *The Phenomenal Woman*, Cambridge: Polity Press.

Baudrillard, J. (1993) *Symbolic Exchange and Death*, London: Sage.

Bauman, Z. (2003) *Liquid Love*, Cambridge: Polity.

Bawin-Legros, B. (2004) 'Intimacy and the New Sentimental Order', *Current Sociology*, 52 (2): 241–50.

Beal, B. (1995) 'Disqualifying the Official: An Exploration of Social Resistance Through the Subculture of Skateboarding', *Sociology of Sport Journal*, 12 (3): 252–67.

Beal, B. (1999) 'Skateboarding: an Alternative to Mainstream Sports', in J. Coakly and P. Donnelly (eds) *Inside Sports*, London: Routledge.

Beasley, C. (2005) *Gender and Sexuality: Critical Theories, Critical Thinkers*, London: Sage.

Beck, U. and Beck-Gernsheim, E. (1995) *The Normal Chaos of Love*, Cambridge, MA: Blackwell.

Beck, U. and Beck-Gernsheim, E. (2002) *Individualization*, London: Sage.

Beck-Gernsheim, E. (2002) *Reinventing the Family*, Cambridge: Polity.

Becker, G. (1991) *A Treatise on the Family*, enlarged edn, Cambridge, MA: Harvard University Press.

Beechey, V. (1986) 'Studies of Women's Employment', in *Feminist Review* (ed.), *Waged Work: A Reader*, London: Virago.

Bell, D. (1983) *Daughters of the Dreaming*, London: Allen & Unwin.

Bell, D. and Binnie, J. (2000) *The Sexual Citizen: Queer Politics and Beyond*, Cambridge: Polity.

Bell, D. and Valentine, G. (1995) 'The Sexed Self: Strategies of Performance, Sites of Resistance', in S. Pile and N. Thrift (eds), *Mapping the Subject: Geographies of Cultural Transformation*, London: Routledge.

Bell, S.E. and Reverby, S.M. (2005) 'Vagina Politics: Tensions and Possibilities in The Vagina Monologues' *Women's Studies International Forum*, 28: 430–44.

Belloni, M.-C., Boulin, J.-Y. and Junter-Loiseau, A. (2000) 'Rethinking Time: There is More to Life than Working Time', in J. Jenson, J. Laufer and M. Maruani (eds), *The Gendering of Inequalities: Women, Men and Work*, Aldershot: Ashgate.

Benhabib, S. (1994) 'Feminism and the Question of Postmodernism', in *The Polity Reader in Gender Studies*, Cambridge: Polity.

Benjamin, S. (2003) 'What Counts as 'Success'? Hierarchical Discourses in a Girls' Comprehensive School', *Discourse*, 24 (1): 105–18.

Bergmann, B. (1995) 'Becker's Theory of the Family: Preposterous Conclusions', *Feminist Economics*, 1 (1): 141–50.

Bernardes, J. (1997) *Family Studies: An Introduction*, London: Routledge.

Bernard, J. (1972) *The Future of Marriage*, New Haven, CT: Yale University Press.

Bernard, J. (1982) *The Future of Marriage*, 2nd edn, New Haven, CT: Yale University Press.

Bernard, J. (1989) 'The Dissemination of Feminist Thought 1960–1988', in R.A. Wallace (ed.), *Feminism and Sociological Theory*, London: Sage.

Berger, M.T. (2004) *Workable Sisterhood: The Political Journey of Stigmatized Womanhood with HIV/AIDS*, Princeton, NJ: Princeton University Press.

Bhabha, H. (1994) *The Location of Culture*, London: Routledge.

Bhattacharrya, G. (1999) 'Teaching Race in Cultural Studies: A Ten Step Programme of Personal Development', in M. Bulmer and J. Solomos (eds) *Ethnic and Racial Studies Today*, London: Routledge.

Bhavnani, K. (1997) 'Women's Studies and its Interconnections with "Race", Ethnicity and Sexuality', in V. Robinson and D. Richardson (eds), *Introducing Women's Studies*, 2nd edn, Basingstoke: Macmillan.

Bhavnani, K. and Coulson, M. (1986) 'Transforming Socialist Feminism: The Challenge of Racism', *Feminist Review*, 23: 81–92.

Bhopal, K. (1997) *Gender, Race and Patriarchy: Study of South Asian Women* (Interdisciplinary Research Series in Ethnic, Gender & Class Relations), Aldershot: Ashgate.

Bindel, J. *The Telegraph* (2003), *The Guardian* (2004).

Binnie, J. (2000) 'Cosmopolitanism and the Sexed City', in D. Bell and A. Haddour (eds), *City Visions*, Harlow: Prentice Hall.

Binnie, J. (2004) *The Globalization of Sexuality*, London: Sage.

Birke, L. (1986) *Women, Feminism and Biology: The Feminist Challenge*, New York: Methuen.

Bishop, K. (2004) 'Working Time Patterns in the UK, France, Denmark and Sweden', *Labour Market Trends*, March: 113–22.

Björnberg, U. (1998) 'Family Orientation Among Men', in E. Drew, R. Emerek and E. Mahon (eds), *Women, Work and the Family in Europe*, London: Routledge.

Björnberg, U. (2002) 'Ideology and Choice between Work and Care: Swedish Family Policy for Working Parents', *Critical Social Policy*, 22 (1): 33–52.

Black, C. (1915/1983) *Married Women's Work* (ed. E. Mappen), London: Virago.
Black, P. (2004) *The Beauty Industry: Gender, Culture, Pleasure*, London: Routledge.
Blossfeld, H-P. and Hakim, C. (eds) (1997) *Between Equalization and Marginalization, Women Working Part-time in Europe and the United States of America*, Oxford: Oxford University Press.
Blum, Virginia L. (2003) *Flesh Wounds: The Culture of Cosmetic Surgery*, Berkeley: University of California Press.
Blunt, A. (2005) *Domicile and Diaspora: Anglo-Indian Women and the Politics of Home*, Oxford: Blackwell Publishing.
Bogues, A (2001) 'Review of The Racial Contract', in *Constellations*, 8 (2): 267–85.
Bolle, P. (2001) 'Parental Leave', in M. Loutfi (ed.), *Women, Gender and Work*, Geneva: International Labour Office.
Bonney, N. (2005) 'Overworked Britons? Part-time Work and Work-life Balance', *Work, Employment and Society*, 19 (2): 391–401.
Booth, A. and Flanagan, M. (2002) 'Introduction', in M. Flanagan and A. Booth (eds) *Reload: Rethinking Women + Cyberculture*, Cambridge, MA: MIT Press.
Borden, I. (2001) *Skateboarding, Space and the City: Architecture and the Body*, Oxford: Berg.
Bornstein, K. (1994) *Gender Outlaw: Men, Women and the Rest of Us*, New York: Routledge.
Bourdieu, P. (1984) *The Logic of Practice*, Oxford: Blackwell.
Bourdieu, P. (1986) *Distinction: A Social Critique of the Judgement of Taste*, trans. R. Nice, London: Routledge.
Bourdieu, P. and Wacquant, L.J.D. (1992) *An Invitation to Reflexive Sociology*, Chicago: Chicago University Press.
Bourque, S. and Grossholtz, J. (1998) (first published 1974) 'Politics an Unnatural Practice: Political Science Looks at Female Participation', in A.Phillips (ed.), *Feminism and Politics*, Oxford: Oxford University Press.
Bradley, H. (1996) *Fractured Identities: Changing Patterns of Inequality*, Oxford: Blackwell.
Bradley, H. (1999) *Gender and Power in the Workplace: Analysing the Impact of Economic Change*, Basingstoke: Macmillan.
Brah, A. (2001) 'Difference, Diversity, Differentiation', in K.K. Bhavnani (ed.), *Feminism and Race*, London: Oxford University Press.
Braidotti, R. (1994) *Nomadic Subjects: Embodiment and Sexual Difference in Contemporary Feminist Thought*, New York: Columbia University Press.
Braidotti, R. (1996) 'Cyberfeminism with a Difference', accessed 1 March 2007. Available online: http://www.let.uu.nl/womens_studies/rosi/cyberfem.htm.
Braidotti, R. (2000) 'Key Terms and Issues in the Making of European Women's Studies', in R. Braidotti and E. Vonk (eds), *The Making of European Women's Studies*, Utrecht: Drukkerij Zuidam and Uithof.
Braidotti, R. (2002) *Metamorphoses: Towards a Materialist Theory of Being*, Cambridge: Polity.
Brannen, J. and Moss, P. (1991) *Managing Mothers: Dual Earner Households after Maternity Leave*, London: Unwin Hyman.
Braun, V. and Wilkinson, S. (2005) 'Vaginal Equals Woman? On Genitals and Gendered Identity', *Women's Studies International Forum*, 28: 509–22.
Braverman, H. (1974) *Labor and Monopoly Capital: The Degradation of Work in the Twentieth Century*, New York: Monthly Review Press.
Brickell, C. (2001) 'Whose 'Special Treatment'? Heterosexism and the Problems with Liberalism', *Sexualities*, 4(2): 211–35.
Brittan, A. (1989) *Masculinity and Power*, New York: Blackwell.
Brod, H. (1987) *The Making of Masculinities: The New Men's Studies*, Boston: Allen & Unwin.

Brooks, A. (1997) *Postfeminisms: Feminism, Cultural Theory and Cultural Forms*, New York: Routledge.

Browne, K. (2004) 'Genderism and the Bathroom Problem: (Re)materialising Sexed Sites, (Re)creating Sexed Bodies', *Gender, Place and Culture*, 11(3): 331–46.

Bruegel, I. (1986) 'The Reserve Army of Labour 1974–79', *Feminist Review* (ed.), *Waged Work: A Reader*, London: Virago.

Bruegel, I. (1994) 'Sex and Race in the Labour Market', in M. Evans (ed.), *The Woman Question*, 2nd edn, London: Sage.

Bruegel, I. (1996) 'Whose Myths are they Anyway?', *British Journal of Sociology*, 47 (1): 175–7.

Bruegel, I. and Hegewisch, A. (1994) 'Flexibilisation and Part-time Work in Europe', in P. Brown and R. Compton, *A New Europe? Economic Restructuring and Social Exclusion*, London: UCL Press.

Bryson, V. (1992) *Feminist Political Theory*, London: Macmillan.

Bulmer, M. and Solomos, J. (eds) (1999) *Ethnic and Racial Studies Today*, London: Routledge.

Bunch, C. (1975) 'Not for Lesbians Only', *Quest, A Feminist Quarterly* (Fall), republished in C. Ingraham and R. Hennessey (eds) (1999), *Materialist Feminism*, New York: Routledge.

Burrell, B.C. (1994) *A woman's Place is in the House*, Ann Arbor, MI: University of Michigan Press.

Burrows, R. and Ellison, N. (2004) 'Sorting Places Out? Towards a Politics of Neighbourhood Informalization', *Information, Communication and Society*, 7: 321–6.

Butler, J. (1990) *Gender Trouble: Feminism and the Subversion of Identity*, New York: Routledge.

Butler, J. (1993) *Bodies That Matter: On the Discursive Limits of 'Sex'*, London: Routledge.

Butler, J. (1994) 'Against Proper Objects', *differences*, 6 (2/3): 1–26.

Butler, J. (1997) 'Critically Queer', in S.Phelan (ed.), *Playing with Fire: Queer Politics, Queer Theories*, London: Routledge.

Butler, J. and Scott, J.W. (eds) (1992) *Feminists Theorize the Political*, New York: Routledge.

Byne, W. (1995) 'Science and Belief: Psychobiological Research on Sexual Orientation', *Journal of Homosexuality*, 28 (3/4): 303–44.

Byrne, B. (2006) *White Lives: The Interplay of 'Race', Class and Gender in Everyday Lives*, London: Routledge.

Campbell, R. (2002) *Emotionally Involved: The Impact of Researching Rape*, New York: Routledge.

Canaan, J.E. and Griffin, C. (1990) 'The New Men's Studies: Part of the Problem or Part of the Solution', in J. Hearn and D. Morgan (eds), *Men, Masculinities and Social Theory*, London: Unwin Hyman.

Cancian, F. (1990) *Love in America*, Cambridge: Cambridge University Press.

Carabine, J. (ed.) (2004) *Sexuality: Personal Lives and Social Policy*, Buckingham: Open University Press.

Carby, H. (1982) 'White Women Listen! Black Feminism and the Boundaries of Sisterhood', in Centre for Contemporary Cultural Studies, *The Empire Strikes Back: Race and Racism in 70s Britain*, London: Hutchinson.

Carby, H. (2000) 'White Woman Listen!', in L. Back and J. Solomos (eds), *Theories of Race and Racism: A Reader*, London: Routledge.

Carrigan, T., Connell, B. and Lee, J. (1985) 'Towards a New Sociology of Masculinity', *Theory and Society*, 14 (5): 551–604.

Casey, M. (2004) 'De-dyking Queer Space(s): Heterosexual Female Visibility in Gay and Lesbian Spaces', *Sexualities*, 7 (4): 446–61.

Castells, M. (2000) *The Rise of Network Society*, Oxford: Blackwell.

Castells, M. (2004) *The Power of Identity*, 2nd edn, Oxford: Blackwell.

Chaney, P., Mackay, F. and McAllister, L. (forthcoming, 2007) *Women, Politics and Constitutional Change: The First Years of the National Assembly for Wales*, Cardiff: University of Wales Press.

Chanter, T. (2006) *Gender: Key Concepts in Philosophy*, London: Continuum.

Charles, M. (2005) 'National Skill Regimes, Postindustrialism and Sex Segregation', *Social Politics*, Summer: 289–316.

Charles, N. (1983) 'Women and Trade Unions in the Workplace', *Feminist Review*, 15: 3–22.

Charles, N. (1986) 'Women and Trade Unions', in *Feminist Review* (ed.), *Waged Work: A Reader*, London: Virago.

Charles, N. (1996) 'Feminist Practices: Identity, Difference, Power', in N. Charles and F. Hughes-Freeland (eds), *Practising Feminism: Identity, Difference, Power*, London: Routledge.

Charles, N. (2000) *Feminism, the State and Social Policy*, Basingstoke: Macmillan.

Charles, N. (2002) *Gender in Modern Britain*, Oxford: Oxford University Press.

Charles, N. and Hintjens, H. (1998) 'Gender, Ethnicity and Cultural Identity: Women's "Places"', in N. Charles and H. Hintjens (eds), *Gender, Ethnicity and Political Ideologies*, London: Routledge.

Charles, N. and Kerr, M. (1988) *Women, Food and Families*, Manchester: University of Manchester Press.

Chasin, A. (2000) *Selling Out.:The Gay And Lesbian Movement Goes To Market*, New York: St. Martin's Press.

Cheng, S.A. (2003) 'Rethinking the Globalization of Domestic Service; Foreign Domestics, State Control and the Politics of Identity in Taiwan', *Gender and Society*, 17 (2): 166–86.

Chesler, P. (1978) *About Men*, London: The Women's Press.

Childs, S. (2004) *New Labour's Women MPs: Women Representing Women*, London and New York: Routledge.

Christian, H. (1994) *The Making of Anti-Sexist Men*, London: Routledge.

CIPD (2003) 'A Parent's Right to Ask, a Review of Flexible Working Arrangements, Survey Report', October, London: Lovells/Chartered Institute of Personnel and Development.

Clarke, S. and Popay, J. (1998) 'I'm Just a Bloke Who's had Kids: Men and Women on Parenthood', in J. Popay, J. Hearn and J. Edwards (eds), *Men, Gender Divisions and Welfare*, London: Routledge.

Clatterbaugh, K. (1990) *Contemporary Perspectives on Masculinity*, Oxford: Westview Press.

Clavering, E. (2004) *Singled Out? An Ethnographic Study of Lone Parents Consumption Strategies in East End Newcastle*, unpublished PhD thesis, University of Newcastle.

Cockburn, C. (1983) *Brothers: Male Dominance and Technological Change*, London: Pluto Press.

Cockburn, C. (1986) 'The Material of Male Power', *Feminist Review* (ed.), *Waged Work: A Reader*, London: Virago.

Cockburn, C. and Ormrod, S. (1993) *Gender and Technology in the Making*, London: Sage.

Cohen, M. (1998) '"A Habit of Healthy Idleness": Boys' Underachievement in Historical Perspective', in D. Epstein, J. Elwood, V. Hey and J. Maw (eds), *Failing Boys? Issues in Gender and Achievement*, Buckingham: Open University Press.

Cohen, P. (1997) 'Labouring under Whiteness', in R. Frankenberg (ed.), *Displacing Whiteness*, Durham, NC: Duke University Press.

Colebrook, C. (2004) *Gender*, Basingstoke: Palgrave Macmillan.

Collins, C., Kenway, J. and McLeod, J. (2000) 'Gender Debates We Still Have to Have', *Australian Educational Researcher*, 27 (3): 37–48.

Collins, P.H. (1996) 'Black Women and the Sex/Gender Hierarchy', in S. Jackson and S. Scott (eds), *Feminism and Sexuality: A Reader*, Edinburgh: Edinburgh University Press.

Collins, P.H. (1998) *Fighting Words: Black Women and the Search for Justice*, Minneapolis: University of Minnesota Press.

Collinson, P. (1999) 'Valentine's Vows: No Sentiment in Financial Affairs', *The Guardian*, quoted in M. Tyler (2004) 'Managing Between the Sheets: Lifestyle Magazines and the Management of Sexuality in Everyday Life', *Sexualities*, 7(1): 81–106.

Comer, L. (1974) *Wedlocked Women*, Leeds: Feminist Press.

Connell, B. (1995) *Masculinities: Knowledge, Power and Social Change*, Berkeley: University of California Press.

Connell, R.W. (1987) *Gender and Power*, Cambridge: Polity Press.

Connell, R.W. (1995) *Masculinities*, Cambridge: Polity Press.

Connell, R.W. (2000) *The Men and the Boys*, Cambridge: Polity Press.

Connell, R.W. (2002) *Gender*, Oxford: Polity.

Connell, R.W. (2005) *Masculinities*, 2nd edn, Cambridge: Polity Press.

Constable, N. (2005) 'Cross-border Marriages, Gendered Mobility and Global Hypergamy', in N. Constable (ed.), *Cross-Border Marriages: Gender and Mobility in Transnational Asia*, Philadelphia: University of Pennsylvania Press.

Cornwall, A. and Lindisfarne, N. (eds) (1994) *Dislocating Masculinity: Comparative Ethnographies*, London: Routledge.

Coyle, A. (1984) *Redundant Women*, London: The Women's Press.

Creed, B. (1993) *The Monstrous-feminine: Film, Feminism, Psychoanalysis*, London: Routledge.

Creedon, P. J. (ed.) (1994) *Women, Media and Sport: Challenging Gender Values*, London: Sage.

Creighton, C. (1999) 'The Rise and Decline of the "Male Breadwinner Family" in Britain', *Cambridge Journal of Economics*, 23: 519–41.

Crompton, R. (ed.) (1999) *Restructuring Gender Relations and Employment: The Decline of the Male Breadwinner*, Oxford: Oxford University Press.

Crompton, R. and Harris, F. (1998) 'Explaining Women's Employment Patterns "Orientations to Work" Revisited', *British Journal of Sociology*, 49 (1):118–37.

Crompton, R. and Jones, G. (1984) *White Collar Proletariat*, London: Macmillan.

Crompton, R., Devine, F., Savage, M. and Scott, J. (eds) (2000) *Renewing Class Analysis*, Oxford: Blackwell.

Crossley, N. (2001) *The Social Body: Habit, Identity and Desire*, London: Sage.

Crudas, L. and Haddock, L. (2005) 'Engaging Girls Voices: Learning as Social Practice', in G. Lloyd, *Problem Girls: Understanding and Supporting Troubled and Troublesome Girls and Young Women*, London: RoutledgeFalmer.

Dahlerup, D. (1988) 'From a Small to a Large Minority: Women in Scandinavian Politics', *Scandinavian Political Studies*, 11: 275–98.

Dahlerup, D. (2006) 'The Story of the Theory of Critical Mass', *Politics and Gender*, 2 (4).

Dale, A., Fieldhouse, E., Shaheen, N. and Kalra, V. (2002) 'The Labour Market Prospects for Pakistani and Bangladeshi Women', *Work Employment and Society*, 16 (1): 5–25.

Dalley, G. (1988) *Ideologies of Caring, Rethinking Community and Collectivism*, London: Macmillan.

Daly, M. and Rake, K. (2003) *Gender and the Welfare State*, Cambridge: Polity.

Daune-Richard, A.-M. (2000) 'The Social Construction of Skill', in J. Jenson et al. (eds), *The Gendering of Inequalities: Women, Men and Work*, Aldershot: Ashgate.

David, M. (2004) 'A Feminist Critique of Public Policy Discourses about Educational Effectiveness', in. S. Ali, S. Benjamin, and M.L Muthner (eds), *The Politics of Gender and Education: Critical Perspectives*, Basingstoke: Palgrave Macmillan.

Davidoff, L. and Hall, C. (1987) *Family Fortunes: Men and Women of the English Middle Class 1780–1850*, London: Routledge.

Davidoff, L., Doolittle, M., Fink, J. and Holden, K. (1999) *The Family Story: Blood, Contract and Intimacy 1830–1960*, London: Longman.

Davis, K., Evans, M. and Lorber, L. (eds) (2006) *Handbook of Gender and Women's Studies*, London: Sage.

Davison, K.G., Lovell, T.A., Frank, B.W. and Vibert, A.B. (2004) 'Boys and Underachievement in the Canadian context: No Proof for Panic', in A.S. Benjamin, and M.L. Mauthner (eds), *The Politics of Gender and Education: Critical Perspectives*, Basingstoke: Palgrave Macmillan.

de Beauvoir, S. (1953) *The Second Sex*, first pub. 1949, reprinted Vintage Books 1997.

Deem, R. (1984) 'Coeducation, equal education', in R. Deem (ed.), *Coeducation Reconsidered*, Buckingham: Open University Press.

Delamont, S. (2001) *Changing Women, Unchanged Men?*, Buckingham: Open University Press.

Delamont, S. (2003) *Feminist Sociology*, London: Sage.

Delphy, C. (1984) *Close to Home: A Materialist Analysis of Women's Oppression*, London: Hutchinson.

Delphy, C. (1992) 'Mothers' Union?', *Trouble & Strife*, 24: 12–19.

Delphy, C. (1993) 'Rethinking Sex and Gender', *Women's Studies International Forum*, 16 (1): 1–9.

Delphy, C. (1994) 'Changing Women in a Changing Europe: Is Difference the Future for Feminism?', *Women's Studies International Forum*, 27 (2): 187–201.

Delphy, C. and Leonard, D. (1992) *Familiar Exploitation: A New Analysis of Marriage in Western Societies*, Cambridge: Polity.

Delsen, L. (1997) 'A New Concept of Full Employment', *Economic and Industrial Democracy*, 18: 119–35.

Descartes, R. (1641/1996) *Meditations on First Philosophy: With Selections from the Objections and Replies*, J. Cottingham (ed.) 2nd rev. edn, Cambridge: Cambridge University Press.

DeVault, M. (1991) *Feeding the Family*. Chicago: University of Chicago Press.

Dex, S. (1988) 'Gender and the Labour Market', in D. Gallie (ed.) *Employment in Britain*, Oxford: Blackwell.

Dex, S. (1999) *Families and the Labour Market: Trends, Pressures and Policies*, London: Family Policy Studies Centre/Joseph Rowntree Foundation.

Dex, S. (2003) *Families and Work in the Twenty-First Century*, York: Joseph Rowntree Foundation/The Policy Press.

Dex, S. and McCulloch, A. (1997) *Flexible Employment, the Future of Britain's Jobs*, Basingstoke: Macmillan.

Dex, D. and Smith, C. (2002) *The Nature and Pattern of Family-Friendly Employment Policies in Britain*, Bristol: The Policy Press.

Dickens, P., Gregg, P. and Wadsworth, J. (eds) (2003) *The Labour Market Under New Labour, the State of Working Britain*, Basingstoke: Palgrave Macmillan.

Doane, M.A. (1992) *Femmes Fatales: Feminism, Film Studies and Psychoanalysis*, New York: Routledge.

Dobash, R. and Dobash, R. (1980) *Violence against Wives*, London: Open Books.

Donovan, C. (2004) 'Why Reach for the Moon? Because the Stars aren't Enough', *Feminism and Psychology*, 14 (1): 24–9.

Doyle, J.A. (1994) Editorial, *The Journal of Men's Studies*, 3 (2).

Dreger, A.D. (2000) *Hermaphrodites and the Medical Invention of Sex*, Cambridge, MA: Harvard University Press.

Drew, E. and Emerek, R. (1998) 'Employment, Flexibility and Gender', in E. Drew, R. Emerek and E. Mahon (eds) *Women, Work and the Family in Europe*, London: Routledge.

DTI (Department for Trade and Industry) (2004) 'Gender Briefing 2004', London: Women and Equality Unit, Department for Trade and Industry.

Duncan, S. (2003) 'Mothers, Care and Employment: Values and Theories', CAVA Working Paper No. 1, Leeds, CAVA Research Group.

Duncan, S. and Edwards, R. (1997) 'Lone Mothers and Paid Work – Rational Economic Man or Gendered Moral Rationalities?', *Feminist Economics*, 3 (2): 29–61.

Duncombe, J. and Marsden, D. (1993) 'Love and Intimacy: The Gender Division of Emotion and "Emotion Work"', *Sociology*, 27 (2): 221–41.

Dunne, G.A. (1997) *Lesbian Lifestyles. Women's Work and the Politics of Sexuality*, London: Macmillan.

Dunne, G. (1999) 'A Passion for Sameness? Sexuality and Gender Accountability', in E. Silva (ed.) *The New Family?*, London: Sage.

Dunning, E. (1999) *Sport Matters: Sociological Studies of Sport, Violence and Civilization*, London: Routledge.

Dworkin, A. (1981) *Pornography: Men Possessing Women*, London: The Women's Press.

Dyer, R. (1997) *White*, London: Routledge.

Edholm, F. (1982) 'The Unnatural Family', in E. Whitelegg, M Arnot, E. Bartels, V. Beechey and L. Birke (eds), *The Changing Experience of Women*, Oxford: Martin Robertson.

Edwards, T. (1994) *Erotics and Politics: Gay Male Sexuality, Masculinity and Feminism*, London: Routledge.

Edwards, T. (2006) *Cultural Masculinities*, London: Routledge.

Eisentein, H. (1996) *Inside Agitators: Australian Femocrats and the State (Women in the Political Economy)*, Philadelphia: Temple University Press.

Elder, S. and Johnson, L.J. (2001) 'Sex-Specific Labour Market Indicators: What They Show', in M. Loutfi (ed.), *Women, Gender and Work*, Geneva: International Labour Office.

EOC (Equal Opportunities Commission) (2003) *Fathers: Balancing Work and Family*, Research Findings, Manchester: Equal Opportunities Commission.

EOC (2004a) *Facts about Women and Men in Great Britain*, Manchester: Equal Opportunities Commission.

EOC (2004b) *Ethnic Minority Women and Men*, Manchester: Equal Opportunities Commission.

Epstein, D., Elwood, J., Hey, V. and Maw, J. (1998) *Failing Boys? Issues in Gender and Achievement*, Buckingham: Open University Press.

Essen, P., Goldberg, D.T. and Kobayashi, A. (2004) *A Companion to Gender Studies*, Oxford: Blackwell.

European Foundation for the Improvement of Living and Working Conditions (2002) 'Quality of Women's Work and Employment, Tools for Change', Foundation Paper No. 3, Luxembourg, OOPEC

Eurostat (2006) 'Gender Pay Gap in Unadjusted Form' (online statistics at http://epp.eurostat.cec.eu.int/portal/page?_pageid=1996,45323734&_dad=portal&_schema=PORTAL&screen=welcomeref&open=/&product=EU_population_social_conditions&depth=2, extracted on 16 February 2006).

Evans, D. (1993) *Sexual Citizenship. The Material Construction of Sexualities*, London: Routledge.

Evans, M. (1997) *Introducing Contemporary Feminist Thought*, London: Polity.

Evans, M. (2003a) *Gender and Social Theory*, Milton Keynes: Open University Press.

Evans, M. (2003b) *Love: An Unromantic Discussion*, Cambridge: Polity.

Eves, A. (2004) 'Queer Theory, Butch/Femme Identities and Lesbian Space', *Sexualities* 7 (4): 480–96.

Eyerman, R. and Jamison, A. (1991) *Social Movements: A Cognitive Approach*, Cambridge: Polity.

Fagan, C. (1996) 'Gendered Time Schedules: Paid Work in Great Britain', *Social Politics*, Spring: 72–106.

Fagan, C. and Burchell, B. (2002) 'Gender, Jobs and Working Conditions in the European Union, Dublin', European Foundation for the Improvement of Living and Working Conditions.

Fagan, C. and Rubery, J. (1996) 'The Salience of the Part-time Divide in the European Union', *European Sociological Review*, 12 (3): 227–50.

Fairbank, A. (2003) 'Grandmotherhood: Theory, Experience and Practice', unpublished PhD Thesis, University of York.

Fairclough, N. (2000). *New Labour, New Language?*, London: Routledge.

Faludi, S. (1999) *Stiffed: The Betrayal of The American Man*, New York: William Morrow.

Fausto-Sterling, A. (1992) *Myths of Gender; Biological Theories about Women and Men*, 2nd edn, New York: Basic Books.

Fausto-Sterling, A. (2000) *Sexing the Body: Gender Politics in the Constructions of Sexuality*, New York: Basic Books.

Fausto-Sterling, A. (2005) 'The Bare Bones of Sex', *Signs: Journal of Women in Culture and Society*, 30 (21): 1491–527.

Featherstone, M. (1991) *Consumer Culture and Postmodernism*, London: Sage.

Feinburg, L. (1993) *Stone Butch Blues*, Ithaca, NY: Firebrand.

Feld, V. (2000) 'A New Start in Wales: How Devolution is Making a Difference', in A. Coote (ed.), *New Gender Agenda*, London: Institute for Public Policy Research.

*Feminist Review* (ed.) (1986) *Waged Work: A Reader*, London: Virago.

Finch, J. (1983) *Married to the Job* London: Allan & Unwin.

Finch, J. and Groves, D. (1980) 'Community Care and the Family: A Case for Equal Opportunities', *Journal of Social Policy*, 9 (4): 487–511.

Finch, J. and Groves, D. (eds) (1983) *A Labour of Love, Women, Work and Caring*, London: Routledge & Kegan Paul.

Finch, J. and Mason, J. (1993) *Negotiating Family Responsibilities*, London: Routledge.

Firestone, S. (1970) *The Dialectic of Sex: The Case for Feminist Revolution*, London: Jonathan Cape.

Fiske, J. (1989) *Reading the Popular*, London: Routledge.

Flax, J. (1997) 'Postmodernism & Gender Relations in Feminist Theory', in S. Kemp and J. Squire (eds), *Feminisms*, Oxford: Oxford University Press.

Foster, V. (2000) 'Is Female Educational "Success" Destabilizing the Male Learner Citizen?', in M. Arnot, and J.A. Dillabough (eds), *Challenging Democracy, International Perpectives on Gender, Education and Citizenship*, London: RoutledgeFalmer.

Foucault, M. (1972) *The Archaeology of Knowledge and the Discourse of Language*, London: Pantheon.

Foucault, M. (1979) *The History of Sexuality, Volume One*, London: Allen Lane.

Foucault, M. (1980a) *Herculine Barbin*, Place: Colophon.

Foucault, M. (1980b) *Power/Knowledge: Selected Interviews and Other Writings, 1972–77* (trans. C. Gordon, L. Marshall, J. Mepham, J. and K. Soper, ed by C. Gordon, New York: Pantheon Books.

Frade, C. and Darmon, I. (2005) 'New Modes of Business Organization and Precarious Employment: Towards the Recommodification of Labour', *Journal of European Social Policy*, 15 (2): 107–21.

Francis, B. (2005). 'Not Know/ing Their Place: Girls' Classroom Behaviour', in G. Lloyd, *Problem Girls: Understanding and Supporting Troubled and Troublesome Girls and Young Women*, London: RoutledgeFalmer.

Francis, B. (2006) 'Heroes or Zeroes? The Discursive Positioning of "Underachieving Boys" in English Neo-liberal Educational Policy', *Journal of Education Policy*, 21 (2): 187–200.

Francis, B. and Skelton, C. (2005) *Reassessing Gender and Achievement: Questioning Contemporary Key Debates,* London: Routledge.

Frankenberg, R. (1993) *White Women, Race Matters: The Social Construction of Whiteness*, Minneapolis: University of Minnesota Press.

Fraser, M. (1999) 'Classing Queer: Politics in Competition', *Theory, Culture and Society*, 16(2): 107–31.

Fraser, M. and Greco, M. (eds) (2005) *The Body. A Reader*, London, Routledge.

Fraser, N. (1997a) 'Heterosexism, Misrecognition and Capitalism: A Response to Judith Butler', *Social Text*, 52/53 (15): 3–4.

Fraser, N. (1997b) *Justice Interruptus, Critical Reflections on the 'Postsocialist' Condition*, London: Routledge.

Fraser, N. (2003) 'Social Justice in the Age of Identity Politics: Redistribution, Recognition, and Participation', in N. Fraser and A. Honneth, *Redistribution or Recognition?*, London and New York: Verso.

Frazer, E. (1987) 'Teenage Girls Reading Jackie', *Media, Culture and Society*, 9 (4): 407–25.

Friedan, B. (1965) *The Feminine Mystique*, Harmondsworth: Penguin.

Gabb, J. (2004) 'Critical Differentials: Querying the Incongruities within Research on Lesbian Parent Families', *Sexualities*, 7 (2): 167–82.

Gabb, J. (2005) 'Locating Lesbian Parent Families: Everyday Negotiations of Lesbian Motherhood in Britain', *Gender, Place and Culture* 12(4): 419–32.

Gajjala, R. (2001) 'Studying Feminist E-spaces: Introducing Transnational/Post-Colonial Concerns', in S. Munt (ed.), *Technospaces: Inside the New Media*, London: Continuum.

Gallie, D. (ed.) (1988) *Employment in Britain*, Oxford: Blackwell.

Gallie, D. (2000) 'The Labour Force', in A.H. Halsey and J. Webb (eds), *Twentieth Century British Social Trends*, Basingstoke: Macmillan.

Gamble, S. (2001) *The Routledge Companion to Feminism and Postfeminism*, New York: Routledge.

Gardiner, M.E. (2000) *Critiques of Everyday Life*, London, Routledge.

Gatens, M. (1991) *Feminism and Philosophy: Perspectives on Difference and Equality*, Cambridge: Polity.

Gatens, M. (1996) *Imaginary Bodies: Ethics, Power and Corporeality*, London: Routledge.

Gatrell, C. (2005) *Hard Labour, the Sociology of Parenthood*, Maidenhead: Open University Press.

Gauntlett, D. (2002) *Media, Gender and Identity: An Introduction*, London: Routledge.

Gauvin, A. (2000) 'Female Unemployment in France and the Rest of Europe', in J. Jenson et al. (eds), *The Gendering of Inequalities: Women, Men and Work*, Aldershot: Ashgate.

Gavron, H. (1966) *The Captive Wife*. Harmondsworth: Penguin.

Geraghty, C. (1990) *Women and Soap Opera*, Cambridge: Polity.

Gershuny, J. (2000) *Changing Times, Work and Leisure in Postindustrial Society*, Oxford: Oxford University Press.

Giddens, A. (1991) *Modernity and Self-Identity*, Cambridge: Polity.

Giddens, A. (1992) *The Transformation of Intimacy: Sexuality, Love and Eroticism in Modern Societies*, Cambridge: Polity Press.

Giddens, A. (1998) *The Third Way: The Renewal of Social Democracy*, Cambridge: Polity.

Giffney, N. (2004) 'Denormatizing Queer Theory: More Than (Simply) Lesbian and Gay Studies', *Feminist Theory*, 5(1): 73–8.

Gillborn, D. and Mirza, H. (2000) *Educational Inequality: Mapping Race, Class and Gender*, London: HMI.

Gilligan, C. (1982) *In a Different Voice: Psychological Theory and Women's Development*, Cambridge, MA: Harvard University Press.

Gillis, S., Howie, G. and Munford, R. (2007) *Third Wave Feminism: A Critical Exploration*, 2nd edn, Basingstoke: Palgrave Macmillan.

Gillis, S. (2007) 'Neither Cyborg nor Goddess: The (Im)Possibilities of Cyberfeminism', in S. Gillis, G. Howie and R. Munford. (eds), *Third Wave Feminism: A Critical Exploration*, 2nd edn, Basingstoke: Palgrave Macmillan.

Gilroy, G. (1993) *The Black Atlantic: Double Consciousness and Modernity*, Cambridge, MA: Harvard University Press.

Ginn, J., Arber, S., Brannen, J., Dale, A., Dex, S. and Elias, P. (1996) 'Feminist Fallacies: A Reply to Hakim on Women's Employment', *British Journal of Sociology*, 47 (1): 167–72.

Gittins, D. (1982) *Fair Sex: Family Size and Structure, 1900–39*, London: Hutchinson.

Glass, R. (assisted by Harold Pollins) (1960) *Newcomers: the West Indians in London*, London: Centre for Urban Studies and Allen & Unwin.

Gledhill, C. (1988) *Home Is Where the Heart Is: Studies in Melodrama and the Woman's Film*, London: BFI.

Goffman, E. (1976) 'Gender Advertisements', *Studies in the Anthropology of Visual Communication*, 3 (2): 69–154.
Goffman, E. (1979) *Gender Advertisements*, New York: Harper & Row.
Goldman, R. (1992) *Reading Ads Socially*, London: Routledge.
Goot, M. and Reid, E. (1975) *Women and Voting Studies: Mindless Matrons or Sexist Scientism?*, Contemporary political sociology series, 1 (6), London: Sage professional paper.
Gorz, A. (1999) *Reclaiming Work, Beyond the Wage Based Society*, Cambridge: Polity.
Graham, H. (1983) 'Caring: a Labour of Love', in J. Finch and D. Groves (eds), *A Labour of Love, Women, Work and Caring*, London: Routledge & Kegan Paul.
Graham, H. (1987) 'Women's Poverty and Caring', in C. Glendinning and J. Millar (eds), *Women and Poverty in Britain*. Brighton: Wheatsheaf.
Gregg, P. and Wadsworth, J. (2003) 'Workless Households and the Recovery', in P. Dickens, P. Gregg and J. Wadsworth (eds), *The Labour Market Under New Labour, the State of Working Britain*, Basingstoke: Palgrave Macmillan.
Grewal, I. and Kaplan, C. (eds) (1994) *Scattered Hegemonies: Postmodernity and Transnational Feminist Practice*, Minneapolis: University of Minnesota Press.
Grewal, I. and Kaplan, C. (2000) 'Postcolonial Studies and Transnational Feminist Practices', in *Jouvert: A Journal of Postcolonial Studies*, 5 (1), http://social.chass.ncsu.edu/jouvert/v5i1/grewal.htm (accessed April 2007).
Grewal, I. and Kaplan, C. (2001) *An Introduction to Women's Studies: Gender in a Transnational World*, New York: McGraw-Hill.
Griffin, G. (ed.) (2005) *Doing Women's Studies. Employment Opportunities, Personal Impacts and Social Consequences*, London: Zed Books.
Grimshaw, D. and Rubery, J. (1997) 'Workforce Heterogeneity and Unemployment Benefits: The Need for Policy Reassessment in the European Union', *Journal of European Social Policy*, 7 (4): 291–318.
Grosz, E. (1994) *Volatile Bodies: Towards a Corporeal Feminism*, Bloomington: Indiana University Press.
Grosz, E. (1995) *Space, Time and Perversion: Essays on the Politics of Bodies*, New York: Routledge.
Guerrina, R. (2002) 'Mothering in Europe, Feminist Critique of European Policies on Motherhood and Employment', *European Journal of Women's Studies*, 9 (1): 49–68.
Haaken, J. (1998) *Pillar of Salt: Gender, Memory, and the Perils of Looking Back*, New Brunswick, NJ: Rutgers University Press, quoted in S.E. Bell and S.M. Reverby (2005) 'Vagina Politics: Tensions and Possibilities in The Vagina Monologues', *Women's Studies International Forum*, 28: 430–44.
Hakim, C. (1991) 'Grateful Slaves and Self-made Women: Fact and Fantasy in Women's Work Orientations', *European Sociological Review*, 7 (2): 101–21.
Hakim, C. (1995) 'Five Feminist Myths about Women's Employment', *British Journal of Sociology*, 46: 429–55.
Hakim, C. (1996) *Key Issues in Women's Work: Female Heterogeneity and the Polarization of Women's Employment*, London: Athlone.
Hakim, C. (2000) *Work-Lifestyle Choices in the 21st Century*, Oxford: Oxford University Press.
Halberstam, J. (1991) 'Automating Gender: Postmodernism Feminism in the Age of the Intelligent Machine', *Feminist Studies*, 17 (3): 439–60.
Halberstam, J. (1994) 'F2M: The Making of Female Masculinity', in L. Doan (ed.), *The Lesbian Postmodern*, New York: Columbia University Press.
Halberstam, J. (1998) *Female Masculinity*, Durham, NC: Duke University Press.
Halberstam, J. (2005) *In a Queer Time and Space: Transgender Bodies, Subcultural Lives*, New York: New York University Press.
Hall, C. (1992) *White, Male and Middle Class: Explorations in Feminism and History*, Cambridge: Polity.

Halperin, D. (1995) *Saint Foucault: Towards a Gay Hagiography*, New York: Oxford University Press.

Halsey, A.H. and Webb, J. (eds) (2000) *Twentieth Century British Social Trends*, Basingstoke: Macmillan.

Hanmer, J. (1978) 'Violence and the Social Control of Women', in G. Littlejohn (ed.), *Power and the State*, London: Croom Helm.

Hanmer, J. (1990) 'Men, Power and the Exploitation of Women', in J. Hearn and D. Morgan (eds), *Men, Masculinities and Social Theory*, London: Unwin Hyman.

Hanmer, J. (1997) 'Women and Reproduction', in V. Robinson and D. Richardson (eds), *Introducing Women's Studies: Feminist Theory and Practice*, Basingstoke: Palgrave.

Haraway, D. (1985) 'A Manifesto for Cyborgs: Science Technology and Socialist Feminism in the 1980s', *Socialist Review*, 80: 65–107.

Haraway, D. (1989) 'The Biopolitics of Postmodern Bodies: Determinations of Self in Immune System Discourse', *differences: A Journal of Feminist Cultural Studies*, 1: 34–43.

Haraway, D. (1991) *Simians, Cyborgs, and Women: The Reinvention of Nature*, New York: Routledge.

Haraway, D. (2000) *How Like a Leaf: An Interview with Thyrza Nichols Goodeve*, London: Routledge.

Harding, J. (1983) *Switched Off: the Science Education of Girls*, New York: Longman.

Harding, S. (1995). *The Science Question in Feminism*, Ithaca: Cornell University Press.

Hardy, S. (2001) 'More Black Lace: Women, Eroticism and Subjecthood', *Sexualities*, 4 (4): 435–53.

Hargreaves, J. (1994) *Sporting Females*, London: Routledge.

Harper, P.B. (1999) *Are We Not Men?: Masculine Anxiety and the Problem of African-American Identity*, Oxford: Oxford University Press.

Harris, A. (ed.) (2004a) *All About the Girl: Culture, Power and Identity*, New York: Routledge.

Harris, A. (2004b) *Future Girl: Young Women in the Twenty First Century*, New York: Routledge.

Hartmann, H. (1976) 'Capitalism, Patriarchy and Job Segregation by Sex', *Signs*, 1 (1): 137–68.

Hartmann, H. (1979) 'Capitalism, Patriarchy and Job Segregation by Sex', in Z. Eisenstein (ed.), *Capitalist Patriarchy and the Case for Socialist Feminism*, New York: Monthly Review Press.

Hartmann, H. (1997) 'The Unhappy Marriage of Marxism and Feminism', in L.J. Nicholson (ed.), *The Second Wave Feminism Reader: Feminist Theoretical Writings*, London: Routledge.

Hatten, W., Vintner, L. and Williams, R. (2002) 'Dads on Dads, Needs and Expectations at Home and at Work', *Research Discussion Series*, Manchester: Equal Opportunities Commission.

Haug, F. et al. (1983) *Female Sexualization: A Collective Work of Memory*, London: Verso.

Hausman, B. (1995) *Changing Sex: Transsexualism, Technology, and the Idea of Gender*, Durham, NC: Duke University Press.

Hawthorne, S. and Klein, R. (eds) (1999) *Cyberfeminism: Connectivity, Critque and Creativity*, Melbourne: Spinifex Press.

Hayles, N.K. (1999) *How We Became Posthuman: Virtual Bodies in Cybernetics, Literature, and Informatics*, Chicago: Chicago University Press.

Haywood, C. and Mac an Ghaill, M. (2003) *Men and Masculinities*, Buckingham: Open University Press.

Head, E. (2005) 'The Captive Mother? :The Place of Home in the Lives of Lone Mother"', *Sociological Research Online*, 10 (3) <http://socresonline.org.uk/10/3/head.html>

Hearn, J. (1998a) *The Violences of Men*, London: Sage.

Hearn, J. (1998b) 'Theorizing Men and Men's Theorizing: Varieties of Discursive Practices in Men's Theorizing of Men', *Theory and Society*, 27: 781–816.

Hearn, J. (2004) 'From Hegemonic Masculinity to the Hegemony of Men', *Feminist Theory*, 5 (1): 49–72.

Hearn, J. and Morgan, D. (eds) (1990) *Men, Masculinities and Social Theory*, London: Unwin Hyman.

Heath, S. and Cleaver, E. (2003) *Young, Free and Single? Twenty-Somethings and Household Change*, Basingstoke: Palgrave Macmillan.

Heckman, S.J. (2000) 'Beyond Identity: Feminism, Identity and Identity Politics', *Feminist Theory*, 1 (3): 289–308.

Hedges, W. (1997) 'Queer Theory Explained', SOU English Department, http://www.sou.edu

Hegewisch, A. (2000) 'Moving Towards the American model? Women and Unemployment in Great Britain', in J. Jenson et al. (eds), *The Gendering of Inequalities: Women, Men and Work*, Aldershot: Ashgate.

Heide, I. (2001) 'Supranational Action against Sex Discrimination: Equal Pay and Equal Treatment in the European Union', in M. Loutfi (ed.), *Women, Gender and Work*, Geneva: International Labour Office.

Helie-Lucas, M.-A. (1994) 'The Preferential Symbol for Islamic Identity: Women in Muslim Personal Laws', in V.M. Moghadam (ed.) *Identity Politics and Women: Cultural Reassertions and Feminisms in International Perspective*, Boulder, CO: Westview.

Hennessy, R. (1995) 'Queer Visibility in Commodity Culture', in L. Nicholson and S. Seidman (eds), *Social Postmodernism: Beyond Identity Politics*, Cambridge: Cambridge University Press.

Hennessy, R. (2000) *Profit and Pleasure: Sexual Identities in Late Capitalism*, London: Taylor & Francis.

Hennessy, R. (2006) 'The Value of a Second Skin', in D. Richardson, J. McLaughlin and M.E. Casey (eds), *Intersections in Feminist and Queer Theory*, Basingstoke: Palgrave Macmillan.

Hesse-Bieber, S. and Yaiser, M. (eds) (2004) *Feminist Perspectives on Social Research*, New York: Oxford University Press.

Hey, V. (2003) 'Joining the Club? Academia and Working-class Femininities', *Gender and Education*, 5(3): 319–35.

Hey, V., Leanord, D., Daniels, H. and Smith, M. (1998) 'Boys' Underachievement, Special Needs Practices and Questions of Equity', in D. Epstein, J. Elwood, V. Hey and J. Maw (eds), *Failing Boys? Issues in Gender and Achievement*, Buckingham: Open University Press.

Heyes, C.J. (2000) 'Reading Transgender, Rethinking Women's Studies, *NWSA*, 12 (2): 170–80.

Hill, A. (2005) 'Exam Results Reveal Gender Gulf in Schools', *The Observer*, 15 May.

Hill-Collins, P. (1998) *Fighting Words: Black Women and the Search for Justice*, Minneapolis: University of Minnesota.

Hills, J. (1981) 'Britain', in J. Lovenduski and J. Hills (eds), *The Politics of the Second Electorate*, London: Routledge & Kegan Paul.

Himmelweit, S. (1995) 'The Discovery of Unpaid Work: The Social Consequences of the Expansion of Work', *Feminist Economics*, 1 (2): 1–19.

Hines, S. (2006) 'What's the Difference?: Bringing Particularity to Queer Studies of Transgender', *Journal of Gender Studies*, 15(1): 49–67.

Hines, S. (2007) *TransForming Gender: Transgender Practices of Identity, Intimacy and Care*, Abingdon: Policy Press.

Hird, M. (2000) 'Gender's Nature: Intersexuality, Transsexualism and the "Sex/Gender" Binary', *Feminist Theory*, 1 (3): 347–64.

Hird, M.J. (2002) 'For a Sociology of Transsexualism', *Sociology*, 36 (3): 577–95.

Hite, S. (1981) *The Hite Report On Male Sexuality*, London: Macdonald.

Hite, S. (2006) *The Shere Hite Reader: New and Selected Writings on Sex, Globalization, and Private Life*, London: Seven Stories Press.

Ho, P.S.Y. and Tsang, A.K.T. (2005) 'Beyond the Vagina-Clitoris Debate – From Naming the Genitals to Reclaiming the Woman's Body', *Women's Studies International Forum*, 28: 523–34.

Hobson, B. (2002) *Making Men into Fathers, Men, Masculinities and the Social Politics of Fatherhood*, Cambridge: Cambridge University Press.

Hochschild, A.R. (1983) *The Managed Heart: Commercialisation of Human Feeling*, Berkeley: University of California Press.

Hochschild, A. (1989) *The Second Shift: Working Parents and the Revolution in the Home*, London: Piatkus.

Hockey, J., Meah, A. and Robinson, V. (2007) *Mundane Heterosexualities: From Theory to Practices*, Basingstoke: Palgrave Macmillan.

Hodges Aeberhard, J. (2001) 'Sexual Harassment in Employment: Recent Judicial and Arbitral Trends', in M. Loutfi (ed.), *Women, Gender and Work*, Geneva: International Labour Office.

Hoff-Somers, C. (2000) *The War against Boys (How Misguided Feminism is Harming our Young Men)*, New York: Simon & Schuster.

Holland, J., Ramazanoglu, C., Sharpe, S. and Thomson, R. (1998) *The Male in the Head: Young People, Heterosexuality and Power*, London: Tufnell Press.

Holliday, R. and Sanchez Taylor, J. (2006) 'Aesthetic Surgery as False Beauty', *Feminist Theory*, 7 (2) 179–95.

Hollows, J. and Moseley, R. (eds) (2005) *Feminism In Popular Culture*, Oxford: Berg.

Holmes, M. (2004a) 'An Equal Distance? Individualisation, Gender and Intimacy in Distance Relationships' *Sociological Review*, 52 (2): 180–200.

Holmes, M. (2004b) 'The Precariousness of Choice in the New Sentimental Order: A Reply to Bawin-Legros', *Current Sociology*, 52 (2): 251–7.

Honeyman, K. (2000) *Women, Gender and Industrialisation in England, 1700–1870*, Basingstoke: Macmillan

Hood-Williams, J. (1996) 'Goodbye to Sex and Gender', *Sociological Review*, 44 (4): 1–16.

hooks, b. (1981) *Ain't I a Woman?: Black Women and Feminism*, Boston, MA: South End Press.

hooks, b. (1984) *Feminist Theory: From Margin to Center*, Boston, MA: South End Press.

hooks, b. (1990) 'Postmodern Blackness', *Postmodern Culture*, 1 (1); http://jefferson.village.virginia.edu/pmc/text-only/issue.990/hooks.990 (accessed 15 September 2005).

hooks, b. (1996) 'Continued Devaluation of Black Womanhood', in S. Jackson and S. Scott (eds), *Feminism and Sexuality: A Reader*, Edinburgh: Edinburgh University Press.

hooks, b. (2000) 'Racism and Feminism', in L. Back and J. Solomos (eds), *Theories of Race and Racism: A Reader*, London: Routledge.

Howarth, C. (2002) '"So you're from Brixton?" The Struggle for Recognition and Esteem in a Stigmatized Community', *Ethnicities*, 2 (2): 237–60.

Howell, M. (1986) *Women, Production and Patriarchy in Late Medieval Cities*, Chicago: University of Chicago Press.

Howson, A. (2005) *Embodying Gender*, London: Sage.

Humm, M. (ed.) (1992) *Feminisms: A Reader*, Hemel Hempstead: Harvester Wheatsheaf.

Hunt, K. (2001) 'On the Edge of Connection: Global Feminism and the Politics of the Internet', in K. Hunt and C.Saulnier (eds), *Feminism(s) on the Edge of the Millennium: Rethinking Foundations and Future Debates*, Toronto: Inanna Publications and Education.

Hussain, Y. (2005) *Writing Diaspora: South Asian Women, Culture and Ethnicity*, Aldershot: Ashgate.

Ifekwunigwe, J. (1997) 'Diaspora's Daughters, Africas Orphans? On Lineage, Authenticity and Mixed Race Identity', in H. Mirza (ed.), *Black British Feminism*, London: Routledge.

Ifekwunigwe, J. (1998) *Scattered Belongings: Cultural Paradoxes of 'Race', Nation and Gender*, London: Routledge.

Inglehart, R. and Norris, P. (2003) *Rising Tide: Gender Equality and Cultural Change Around the World,* Cambridge: Cambridge University Press.

Ingraham, C. (1996) 'The Heterosexual Imaginary', in S. Seidman (ed.), *Queer Theory/ Sociology,* Oxford: Blackwell.

Ingraham, C. (2001) *White Weddings: Romancing Heterosexuality in Popular Culture,* New York: Routledge.

Ingraham, C. (ed.) (2005) *Thinking Straight: The Power, the Promise, and the Paradox of Heterosexuality,* New York: Routledge.

Irigaray, L. (1982) 'Sexual Difference', in M Whitford (ed,) (1990), *The Irigaray Reader,* trans. D. Macey, London: Blackwell.

Irigaray, L. (1985a) *Speculum of the Other Woman,* trans. G.C. Gill, Ithaca, NY: Cornell University Press.

Irigaray, L. (1985b) *This Sex Which is Not One,* trans. C. Porter, Ithaca, NY: Cornell University Press.

Irwin, S. (1999) 'Resourcing the Family: Gendered Claims and Obligations', in E. Silva (ed.), *The New Family?* London: Sage.

Irwin, S. (2005) *Reshaping Social Life,* London: Routledge.

Jackson, D. (1998) 'Breaking out of the Binary Trap: Boys' Underachievement, Schooling and Gender Relations', in D. Epstein, J. Elwood, V. Hey and J. Maw (eds), *Failing Boys? Issues in Gender and Achievement,* Buckingham: Open University Press.

Jackson, P., Stevenson, N. and Brooks, K. (2001) *Making Sense of Men's Magazines,* Cambridge: Polity.

Jackson, S. (1982) *Childhood and Sexuality,* Oxford: Blackwell.

Jackson, S. (1996) 'Heterosexuality and Feminist Theory', in D. Richardson (ed.), *Theorising Heterosexuality,* Buckingham: Open University Press.

Jackson, S. (1999a) 'Theorising Gender and Sexuality', in S. Jackson and J. Jones (eds), *Contemporary Feminist Theories,* Edinburgh: Edinburgh University Press.

Jackson, S. (1999b) 'Feminist Sociology and Sociological Feminisms: Recovering the Social in Feminist Thought', *Sociological Research Online,* 4 (3): 1–20 (http://www.socresonline.org.uk/socresonline/4/3/jackson.html).

Jackson, S. (1999c) *Heterosexuality in Question,* London: Sage.

Jackson, S. (2001) 'Why a Materialist Feminism is (Still) Possible – and Necessary', *Women's Studies International Forum,* 24 (3/4): 283–93.

Jackson, S. (2005) 'Sexuality, Heterosexuality and Gender Hierarchy: Getting Our Priorities Straight', in C. Ingraham (ed.), *Thinking Straight: The Power, the Promise, and the Paradox of Heterosexuality,* New York: Routledge.

Jackson, S. (2006) 'Heterosexuality, Sexuality and Gender: Re-thinking the Intersections', in D. Richardson, J. McLaughlin and M.E. Casey (eds), *Intersections Between Feminist and Queer Theory,* Basingstoke: Palgrave Macmillan.

Jackson, S. and Scott, S. (1996) *Feminism and Sexuality. A Reader,* Edinburgh: Edinburgh University Press.

Jackson, S. and Scott, S. (1997) 'Gut Reactions to Matters of the Heart: Reflections on Rationality, Irrationality and Sexuality', *The Sociological Review,* 45(4): 551–75.

Jackson, S. and Scott, S. (2004) 'Sexual Antinomies in Late Modernity', *Sexualities,* 7 (2): 241–56.

Jagose, A. (1996) *Queer Theory: An Introduction,* New York: New York University Press.

James, N. (1989) 'Emotional Labour: Skill and Work in the Social Regulation of Feelings', *Sociological Review,* 37: 15–42.

James, S. and Benn, M. (2004) 'Home Truths for Feminists', *The Guardian,* 21 February (http://www.guardian.co.uk/comment/story/0,,1152715,00.html, last accessed 29 June 2006).

Jamieson, L. (1998) *Intimacy: Personal Relationships in Modern Societies,* Cambridge: Polity.

Jamieson, L. (1999) 'Intimacy Transformed?', *Sociology,* 33 (3): 477–94.

Jaumotte, F. (2003) 'Female Labour Force Participation: Past Trends and Main Determinants in OECD Countries', Economics Department Working Papers No. 376, Paris: OECD.

Jeffreys, S. (1997a) 'Transgender Activism: A Feminist Perspective', *Journal of Lesbian Studies*, 1 (3/4): 55–74.

Jeffreys, S. (1997b) 'The Queer Disappearance of Lesbians', in B. Mintz and E. Rothblum (eds), *Lesbians in Academia: Degrees of Freedom*, New York: Routledge.

Jeffreys, S. (2003) *Unpacking Queer Politics: A Lesbian Feminist Perspective* Oxford: Polity.

Jeffreys, S. (2006) 'Judicial Child Abuse: The Family Court of Australia, Gender Identity Disorder, and the "Alex" Case', *Women's Studies International Forum*, 29: 1–12.

Jewkes, A.N., Laubscher, R. and Hoffman, M. (2006) 'Intimate Partner Violence: Prevalence and Risk Factors for Men in Cape Town, South Africa', *Violence and Victims*, 21 (2): 247–64.

Jenson, J., Laufer, J. and Maruani, M. (eds) (2000) The *Gendering of Inequalities: Women, Men and Work*, Aldershot: Ashgate.

Johnson, P. (2004) 'Haunting Heterosexuality: The Homo/Het Binary and Intimate Love', *Sexualities*, 7(2): 183–200.

Johnson, P. and Lawler, S. (2005) 'Coming Home to Love and Class', *Sociological Research Online*, 10(3): 1–25 (http://www.socresonline.org.uk/10/3/johnson.html).

Kaluzynska, E. (1980) 'Wiping the Floor with Theory', *Feminism Review*, 6: 27–54.

Kaplan, D. (ed.) (2004) *Readings in the Philosophy of Technology*, Lanham: Rowman & Littlefield.

Kaplan, E.A. (ed.) (1980) *Women in Film Noir*, London: British Film Institute.

Kegan Gardiner, J. (ed.) (2002) *Masculinity Studies and Feminist Theory*, New York: Columbia University Press.

Keifer-Boyd, K. (2002) *The Cyberfeminist House* (http://sva74.sva.psu.edu/~cyberfem/, accessed 1 March 2007).

Kelly, A. (ed.) (1981) *The Missing Half: Girls and Science Education*, Manchester: Manchester University Press.

Kelly, A. (1985) 'The Construction of Masculine Science', *British Journal of Sociology of Education*, 6(2): 133–54.

Kember, S. (2002) *Cyberfeminism and Artificial Life*, London: Routledge.

Kenway, J. (1997) *Will Boys be Boys? Boys' Education in the Context of Gender Reform*, Deakin West, ACT: Australian Curriculum Studies Association.

Kershen, A. (ed.) (1998) *A Question of Identity*, Aldershot: Ashgate

Kessler, S. (1998) *Lessons from the Intersexed*, Rutgers: Rutgers University Press.

Kessler, S.J. and McKenna, W. (1978) *Gender: An Ethnomethodological Approach*, New York: Wiley.

Kessler, S.J. and McKenna, W. (2000) 'Gender Construction in Everyday Life: Transsexualism (Abridged)', *Feminism and Psychology*, 10: 11–29.

Kidger, J. (2005) 'Stories of Redemption? Teenage Mothers as the New Sex Educators', *Sexualities*, 8(4): 481–96

Kimmell, M. (1990) 'After Fifteen Years: The Impact of the Sociology of Masculinity on the Masculinity of Sociology', in J. Hearn and D. Morgan (eds), *Men, Masculinities and Social Theory*, London: Unwin Hyman.

Kitzinger, C. and Wilkinson, S. (2004) 'The Re-Branding of Marriage: Why We Got Married Instead of Registering a Civil Partnership', *Feminism & Psychology*, 14 (1): 127–50.

Klugman, B. (2000) 'Sexual Rights in Southern Africa: A Beijing Discourse or a Strategic Necessity?', *Health and Human Rights*, 4(2): 155–73.

Knowles, K. (2003) *Race and Social Analysis*, London: Sage.

Kodz, J. et al. (2003) 'Working Long Hours: A Review of the Evidence: Volume 1 Main Report, Employee Relations Research Series 16', London: Institute of Employment Studies.

Komarovsky, M. (1962) *Blue Collar Marriage*, New Haven, CT: Yale University Press.
Koyama, E. (2003) 'Transfeminist Manifesto', in R. Dicker and A. Piepmeier (eds), *Catching a Wave: Reclaiming Feminism for the 21st Century*, Boston, MA: Northeastern University Press.
Kröger, T. and Sipilä, J. (eds) (2005) *Overstretched, European Families up Against the Demands of Work and Care*, Oxford: Blackwell.
Laclau, E., Butler, J. and Zizek, S. (2000) *Contingency, Hegemony and Universality: Contemporary Dialogues on the Left*, London: Verso.
Lan, P. (2003) 'Maid or Madam? Filipina Migrant Workers and the Continuity of Domestic Labour', *Gender and Society*, 17 (2): 187–208.
Lan, P. (2006) *Global Cinderellas*, Durham, NC: Duke University Press.
Langford, W. (1999) *Revolutions of the Heart*, London: Routledge.
Lapsley, H. (1999) *Margaret Mead and Ruth Benedict: The Kinship of Women*, Amherst, MA: University of Massachusetts Press.
Laqueur, T.W. (1990) *Making Sex: Body and Gender from the Greeks to Freud*, Cambridge, MA: Harvard University Press.
Lawler, S. (2000) *Mothering the Self. Mothers, Daughters, Subjects*, London: Routledge.
Lawler, S. (2002) 'Mobs and Monsters. Independent Man meets Paulsgrove Woman', *Feminist Theory*, 3 (1): 103–13.
Lawler, S. (2005) 'Disgusted Subjects: The Making of Middle-Class Identities', *Sociological Review*, 53 (3): 429–46.
Lea, R. (2003) 'The "Work-Life Balance" revisited', UK Institute of Directors Employment Comment, London: IoD.
Lee, W. (1991) 'Prostitution and Tourism in South-East Asia', in N. Redclift and M.T. Sinclair (eds), *Working Women, International Perspectives on Labour and Gender Ideology*, London: Routledge.
Lempiainen, K. (2000) 'A Short Introduction to the Use of "Sex" and "Gender" in the Scandanavian Languages', in R. Braidotti and E. Vonk (eds), *The Making of European Women's Studies*, Utrecht: Drukkerij Zuidam and Uithof.
Letherby, G. (2003) *Feminist Research in Theory and Practice*, Buckingham: Open University Press.
Levin, I. (2004) 'Living Apart Together: A New Family Form', *Current Sociology*, 52(2): 223–40.
Lewallen, A. (1988) 'Lace: Pornography for Women?', in L. Gamman and M. Marshment (eds), *The Female Gaze*, London: The Women's Press.
Lewis, J. (1984) *Women in England 1870–1950, Sexual Divisions and Social Change*, Brighton: Wheatsheaf.
Lewis, J. (1992) 'Gender and the Development of Welfare Regimes', *Journal of European Social Policy*, 2 (3): 159–73.
Lewis, J. (2001) *The End of Marriage? Individualism and Intimate Relations*, London: Edward Elgar.
Lewis, J. (2003) 'Economic Citizenship: A Comment', *Social Politics*, 10 (2): 176–85.
Lewis, J. (2006) 'The Adult Worker Model Family, Care and the Problem of Gender Equality', *Benefits*, 14 (1): 33–8.
Levy, A. (2005) *Female Chauvinist Pigs. Women and the Rise of Raunch Culture*, New York: Free Press.
Liddle, J. and Michielsens, L. (2000) 'Gender, Class and Political Power in Britain', in S.M. Rai (ed.), *International Perspectives on Gender and Democratisation*, Basingstoke: Macmillan.
Liddle, J. and Michielsens, L. (2007) '"NQOC": Social Identity and Representation in British Politics', *British Journal of Politics and International Relations*, 7.
Linden, R. (1993) *Making Stories, Making Selves* , Columbus, OH: Ohio State University Press.

Lindley, J., Dale, A. and Dex, S. (2004) 'Ethnic Differences in Women's Demographic, Family Characteristics and Economic Activity Profiles, 1992 to 2002', *Labour Market Trends*, April: 153–65.

Lobel, K. (ed.) (1986) *Naming The Violence: Speaking Out About Lesbian Battering*, Seattle: Seal.

Lorde, A. (1994) 'The Master's Tools will Never Dismantle the Master's House'. in M. Evans (ed.), *The Woman Question*, 2nd edn, London: Sage.

Loutfi, M. (ed.) (2001) *Women, Gender and Work*, Geneva: International Labour Office.

Lovenduski, J. (1996) 'Sex, Gender and British Politics', in J. Lovenduski and P. Norris (eds), *Women in Politics*, Oxford: Oxford University Press.

Lovenduski, J. (1999) 'Sexing Political Behaviour in Britain', in S. Walby (ed.), *New Agendas for Women*, Basingstoke: Macmillan.

Lovenduski, J. (2005a) *Feminizing Politics*, Cambridge: Polity.

Lovenduski, J. (ed.) (2005b) *State Feminism and Political Representation*, Cambridge: Cambridge University Press.

Lovenduski, J. and Randall, V. (1993) *Contemporary Feminist Politics: Women and Power in Britain*, Oxford: Oxford University Press.

Lucey, H. (2001) 'Social Class, Gender and Schooling', in B. Francis and C. Skelton (eds), *Investigating Gender: Contemporary Perspectives in Education*, Buckingham: Open University Press.

Lucey, H. and Reay, D. (2002) 'Carrying the Beacon of Excellence: Social Class Differentiation and Anxiety at a Time of Transition', *Journal of Education Policy*, 17 (3): 321–36.

Mac an Ghaill, M. (1994) *The Making of Men: Masculinities, Sexualities and Schooling*, Buckingham: Open University Press.

Mac an Ghaill, M. (1996) (ed.) *Understanding Masculinities*, Buckingham: Open University Press.

MacClancy, J. (1996) *Sport, Identity and Ethnicity*, Oxford: Berg.

MacDonald, E. (1998) 'Critical Identities: Rethinking Feminism through Transgender Politics', *Atlantis*, 23 (1): 3–12.

MacEwen Scott, A. (1994) *Gender Segregation and Social Change*, Oxford: Oxford University Press.

Mackay, F. (2004) 'Gender and Political Representation in the UK: The State of the 'Discipline', *British Journal of Politics and International Relations*, 6: 99–120.

MacKinnon, C.A. (1982) 'Feminism, Marxism, Method and the State: An Agenda for Theory', *Signs: Journal of Women in Culture and Society*, 7(3): 515–44.

MacKinnon, C. (1987) *Feminism Unmodified: Discourses on Life and Law*, Cambridge, MA: Havard University Press.

Mahoney, P. (1998) 'Girls will be Girls and Boys will be First', in D. Epstein, J. Elwood, V. Hey and J. Maw (eds), *Failing Boys? Issues in Gender and Achievement*, Buckingham: Open University Press.

Malos, E. (1980) *The Politics of Housework*, London: Allison & Busby.

Mani, L. (1989) 'Multiple Mediations: Feminist Scholarship in the Age of Multinational Reception', *Inscriptions*. 5 (http://humwww.ucsc.edu/CultStudies/PUBS/Inscriptions/vol_5/v5_top.html, accessed April 2007).

Mansfield, P. and Collard, J. (1988) *The Beginning of the Rest of Your Life: A Portrait of Newlywed Marriage*, London: Macmillan.

Marchbank, J. and Letherby, G. (eds) (2007) *Introduction to Gender. Social Science Perspectives*, Harlow: Pearson Longman.

Marks, G. and Houston, D. (2002) 'Attitudes Towards Work and Motherhood Held by Working and Non-working Mothers', *Work, Employment and Society*, 16 (3): 523–36.

Marshment, M. (eds) (1998) *The Female Gaze*, London: Women's Press.

Martin, B. (1998a) 'Sexualities without Genders and Other Queer Utopias', in M. Merck, N. Segal and E. Wright (eds), *Coming Out of Feminism?*, Oxford: Blackwell.

Martin, B. (1998b) 'Feminism, Criticism and Foucault', in I. Diamond and L. Quinby (eds), *Feminism and Foucault: Reflections on Resistance,* Boston, MA: Northeastern University Press.

Mason, D. (1999) 'The Continuing Significance of Race? Teaching Ethnic and Racial Studies in Sociology', in J. Solomos and M. Bulmer (eds), *Ethnic and Racial Studies Today,* London: Routledge.

Mason, D. (ed.) (2003) *Explaining Ethnic Differences,* Bristol: The Policy Press.

Mason, J. (2004) 'Managing Kinship Over Long Distances: The Significance of the Visit', *Social Policy and Society,* 3 (4): 421–9.

Maushart, S. (2001) *Wifework: What Marriage Really Means for Women,* Melbourne: Text Publishing.

McClintock, A. (1995) *Imperial Leather: Race, Gender and Sexuality in the Colonial Context,* London: Routledge.

McKay, J., Messner, M.A. and Sabo, D. (eds) (2000) *Masculinities, Gender Relations and Sport,* London: Sage.

McKenna, W. and Kessler, S.J. (2000) 'Retrospective Response', *Feminism and Psychology,* 10: 235–50.

McLaughlin, J. (2003) *Feminist Social and Political Theory: Contemporary Debates and Dialogues,* Basingstoke: Palgrave Macmillan.

McLaughlin, J. (2006) 'The Return of the Material: Cycles of Theoretical Fashion in Lesbian, Gay and Queer Studies', in D. Richardson, J. McLaughlin and M.E. Casey (eds), *Intersections in Feminist and Queer Theory,* Basingstoke: Palgrave Macmillan.

McLaughlin, J., Casey, M.E. and Richardson, D. (2006) 'At the Intersections of Feminist and Queer Debates', in D. Richardson, J. McLaughlin and M.E. Casey (eds), *Intersections Between Feminist and Queer Theory,* Basingstoke: Palgrave Macmillan.

McRae, S. (1998) 'Part-time Employment in a European Perspective', in E. Drew, R. Emerek and E. Mahon (eds), *Women, Work and the Family in Europe,* London: Routledge.

McRobbie, A. (1978) *Jackie: An Ideology of Adolescent Femininity,* CCCS Stencilled Papers.

McRobbie, A. (1996) 'More! New Sexualities in Girls' and Women's Magazines', in J. Curran et al. (eds), *Cultural Studies and Communications,* London: Arnold.

McRobbie, A. (2000) *Feminism and Youth Culture,* London: Routledge.

McRobbie, A. (2001) 'Sweet Smell of Success? New Ways of Being Young Women', unpublished keynote address at A New Girl Order? Young Women and the Future of Feminist Inquiry Conference, London, 12–14 November.

McRobbie, A. (2004) 'Notes on Postfeminism and Popular Culture: Bridget Jones and the New Gender Regime', in A. Harris (ed.), *All About the Girl: Culture, Power and Identity,* New York: Routledge.

Mead, M. (1963) *Sex and Temperament in Three Primitive Societies,* New York: William Morrow. First published 1935.

Melkas, H. and Anker, R. (2001) 'Occupational Segregation by Sex in Nordic Countries: An Empirical Investigation', in M. Loutfi (ed.), *Women, Gender and Work,* Geneva: International Labour Office.

Merck, M., Segal, N. and Wright, E. (eds) (1998) *Coming Out of Feminism?,* Oxford: Blackwell.

Merleau-Ponty, M. (1962) *Phenomenology of Perception,* trans. C. Smith, London: Routledge.

Messner, M.A. (1992) *Power at Play: Sports and the Problem of Masculinity.* Boston: Beacon Press.

Messner, M. and Sabo, D. (eds) (1994) *Sex, Violence and Power in Sports: Rethinking Masculinity* , Freedom, CA: Crossing.

Meulders, D., Plasman, O. and Plasman, R. (1994) *A Typical Employment in the European Community,* Aldershot: Dartmouth Publishing Company.

Miller, D. (1998) *A Theory of Shopping*, Cambridge: Polity.

Miller, D., Jackson, P., Thrift, N., Holbrook, B. and Rowlands, M. (1998) *Shopping, Place and Identity*, London: Routledge.

Mincer, J. and Polachek, S. (1980) 'Family Investments in Human Capital: Earnings of Women', in A. Amsden (ed.), *The Economics of Women and Work*, Harmondsworth: Penguin.

Minh-Ha, T.T. (1988) 'Not You/Like You: Post-colonial Women and the Interlocking Questions of Identity and Difference', 3/4 (http://humwww.ucsc.edu/CultStudies/PUBS/Inscriptions/vol_3-4/v3-4top.html, accessed April 2007).

Mirza, H. (1997) 'Introduction: Mapping a Genealogy of Black British Feminism', in H. Mirza (ed.), *Black British Feminism*, London: Routledge.

Mirza, S. and Strobel, M. (eds and trans, 1989) *Three Swahili Women: Life Histories From Mombasa, Kenya*, Bloomington: Indiana University Press.

Modood, T. et al. (eds) (1997) *Ethnic Minorities in Britain*, London: Policy Studies Institute.

Mohanty, C.T. (1988) 'Under Western Eyes: Feminist Scholarship and Colonial Discourses', *Feminist Review*, 30: 65–88.

Mohanty, C.T. (1991) 'Under Western Eyes: Feminist Scholarship and Colonial Discourses', in C.T. Mohanty, A. Russo and L. Torres (eds), *Third World Women and the Politics of Feminism*, Bloomington: Indiana University Press.

Mohanty, C.T. (2003) '"Under Western Eyes" Revisited: Feminist Solidarity through Anti-capitalist Struggles', *Signs: Journal of Women in Culture and Society*, 28: 499–535.

Moi, T. (1999) *What is a Woman?: And Other Essays*, Oxford: Oxford University Press.

Molyneux, M. (1979) 'Beyond the Domestic Labour Debate', *New Left Review*, 116: 3–28

Money, J. and Erhardt, A. (1972) *Man and Woman, Boy and Girl*, Baltimore: Johns Hopkins.

Moore, H. (1988) *Feminism and Anthropology*, Cambridge: Polity.

Moraga, C. and Anzaldúa, G. (1983) *This Bridge Called Me Back: Writings by Radical Women of Color*, New York: Kitchen Table, Women of Color Press.

Morgan, D. (1992) *Discovering Men*, London: Routledge.

Morgan, D. (1996) *Family Connections*, Cambridge: Polity.

Morley, L. and Rasool, N. (1999) *School Effectiveness: Fracturing the Discourse*, Brighton: Falmer Press.

Morris, L. (1990) *The Workings of the Household: A US–UK Comparison*, Cambridge: Polity.

Mulvey, L. (1975) 'Visual Pleasure and Narrative Cinema', *Screen* 16(3): 6–18.

Munt, S. (2001) 'The Butch Body', in R. Holliday and J. Hassard (eds), *Contested Bodies*, London: Routledge.

Murray, C. (1997) *The Racial Contract*, Ithaca, NY: Cornell University Press.

Myrdal, A. and Klein, V. (1956) *Women's Two Roles*, London: Routledge & Kegan Paul.

Namaste, K. (1996) 'Genderbashing: Perceived Transgressions of Normative Sex-Gender Relations in Public Spaces', *Environment and Planning D – Society and Space*, 14(2): 221–40.

Nicholson, L. (1994) 'Interpreting Gender', *Signs: Journal of Women in Culture and Society*, 20(1): 79–105.

Nicholson, L. (1999) 'The Myth of the Traditional Family', in H. Lindeman Nelson (ed.), *Feminism and Families*, New York: Routledge.

Nixon, S. (1996) *Hard Looks: Masculinities, Spectatorship and Contemporary Consumption*, New York: Palgrave.

Nnaemeka, O. (ed.) (2005) *Female Circumcision and the Politics of Knowledge: African Women in Imperialist Discourses*, Westport, CT: Praeger.

Norris, P. (1996) 'Women Politicians: Transforming Westminster?', in J. Lovenduski and P. Norris (eds), *Women in Politics*, Oxford: Oxford University Press.

Norris, P. (1999) 'Gender: a Gender-Generation Gap?', in G. Evans and P. Norris (eds), *Critical Elections: British Parties and Voters in Long-term Perspective*, London: Sage.

Norris, P. and Lovenduski, J. (1995) *Political Recruitment: Gender, Race and Class in the British Parliament*, Cambridge: Cambridge University Press.

Northam, J. (1982) 'Girls and Boys in Primary Maths Books', *Education*, 10 (1), Spring: 11–14.

Novas, C. and Rose, N. (2000) 'Genetic Risk and the Birth of the Somatic Individual', *Economy and Society*, 29: 485–513.

Nussbaum, M.C. (1999) 'The Professor of Parody', *New Republic*, 22 February: 37–45.

Oakley, A. (1972) *Sex, Gender and Society*, London: Maurice Temple Smith.

Oakley, A. (1974) *The Sociology of Housework* London: Martin Robertson.

Oakley, A. (1984) *The Sociology of Housework*, 2nd edn, London: Blackwell.

OECD (Organisation for Economic Co-operation and Development) (2001) *Employment Outlook 2001*, Paris: OECD.

OECD (2002a) *Employment Outlook 2002*, Paris: OECD.

OECD (2002b) *Babies and Bosses, Reconciling Work and Family Life*, Paris: OECD.

OECD (2005) *Employment Outlook 2005*, Paris: OECD.

Offe, C. and Heinze, R. (1992) *Beyond Employment*, Cambridge: Polity.

Ohms, C. (ed.) (2002) *Against Violence. Guidelines for Counselling Services on Dealing with Violence in Lesbian Partnerships*, Anti-Violence Project of the Lesbian Information and Counselling Service Frankfurt.

Okin, S.M. (1998) 'Gender, the Public, and the Private', in A. Phillips (ed.), *Feminism and Politics*, Oxford: Oxford University Press.

ONS (Office of National Statistics) (2006a) *Social Trends 2006*.

ONS (2006b) *Labour Force Survey Historical Quarterly Supplement, Table 2, Employment by Age*. Statistics online at http://www.statistics.gov.uk/StatBase/ssdataset.asp?vlnk=7902 &Pos=1&ColRank=1&Rank=272, extracted 13 July 2006.

Orbach, S. (2006) *Fat is a Feminist Issue*, Arrow Omnibus Edition, London: Arrow.

O'Reilly, J. and Fagan, C. (eds) (1998) *Part-time Prospects, an International Comparison of Part-Time Work in Europe, North America and the Pacific Rim*, London: Routledge.

Oriel, J. (2005) 'Sexual Pleasure as a Human right: Harmful or Helpful to Women in the Context of HIV/AIDS?', *Women's Studies International Forum*, 28: 392–404.

Osgerby, B. (2001) *Playboys in Paradise: Masculinity, Youth and Leisure-style in Modern America*, Oxford: Berg.

Osler, A. and Vincent, K. (2003) *Girls and Exclusion: Rethinking the Agenda*, London: RoutledgeFalmer.

Osler, A., Street, C., Lall, M. and Vincent, C. (2002) *Not a Problem? Girls and Exclusion from School*, York: Joseph Rowntree Foundation.

Ortner, S. (1974) 'Is Female to Male as Nature to Culture?', in M.Z. Rosaldo and L. Lamphere (eds), *Women, Culture and Society*, Stanford, CA: Stanford University Press.

Outram, D. (2005) *The Enlightenment*, 2nd edn, Cambridge: Cambridge University Press.

Oxfam (2005) Programme Insights. Education and Gender Equality Series 8: Girls' Education in Africa, Oxford: Oxfam (http://www.oxfam.org.uk/what_we_do/issues/education/downloads/edPaper8.pdf, accessed 18 April 2007).

Paechter, C.F. (1998) *Educating the Other: Gender, Power and Schooling*, London: RoutledgeFalmer.

Pahl, J. (1989) *Money and Marriage*, London: Macmillan.

Pahl, J. (1990) 'Household Spending, Personal Spending and the Control of Money in Marriage', *Sociology*, 24 (1): 119–38.

Parker, D. (1995) *Through Different Eyes: The Cultural Identities of Young Chinese People in Britain*, Aldershot: Ashgate.

Parker, D. and Song, M. (2001) (eds) *Rethinking Mixed Race*, London: Pluto Press.

Parmar, P. (1988) 'Gender, Race and Class: The Challenge to Youth Work Practice', in P. Cohen. and H.S. Baines (eds), *Multi-Racist Britain*, London: Macmillan.

Parsons, T. (1951) *The Social System*, London, Routledge & Kegan Paul.

Pateman, C. (1988) *The Sexual Contract*, Cambridge, Polity.

Pateman, C. (1989) *The Disorder of Women*, Cambridge: Polity.

Patterson, S. (1963) *Dark Strangers*, Harmondsworth: Penguin.

Pease, B. and Pringle, K. (eds) (2001) *A Man's World? Changing Men's Practices in a Globalized World*, London: Zed Books.

Perrigo, S. (1996) 'Women and Change in the Labour Party 1979–1995', in J. Lovenduski and P. Norris (eds), *Women in Politics*, Oxford: Oxford University Press.

Petchesky, R.P. (2000) 'Sexual Rights: Inventing a Concept, Mapping an International Practice', in R. Parker, R.M. Barbarosa and P. Aggleton (eds), *Framing the Sexual Subject: The Politics of Gender, Sexuality and Power*, Berkeley: University of California Press.

Phillips, A. (1991) *Engendering Democracy*, Cambridge: Polity.

Phillips, A. (1998a) 'Democracy and Representation: or, Why Should it Matter Who Our Representatives Are?', in A. Phillips (ed.), *Feminism and Politics*, Oxford: Oxford University Press.

Phillips, A. (ed.) (1998b) *Feminism and Politics*, Oxford: Oxford University Press.

Phillips, A. and Taylor, B. (1986) 'Sex and Skill', in *Feminist Review* (ed.), *Waged Work: A Reader*, London: Virago.

Phizacklea, A. and Ram, M. (1996) 'Being Your Own Boss: Ethnic Minority Entrepreneurs in Comparative Perspective', *Work, Employment and Society*, 10 (2), 319–39.

Pilcher, J. and Whelehan, I. (2004) *50 Key Concepts in Gender Studie*s, Thousand Oaks, CA: Sage.

Plant, S. (1996) 'On the Matrix: Cyberfeminist Simulations', in F. Hovenden et al. (eds), *The Gendered Cyborg: A Reader*, London: Routledge.

Plantenga, J. and Hansen, J. (2001) 'Assessing Equal Opportunities in the European Union', in M. Loutfi (ed.), *Women, Gender and Work*, Geneva: International Labour Office.

Plummer, K. (1995) *Telling Sexual Stories. Power, Change and Social Worlds*, London: Routledge.

Pollert, A. (ed.) (1991) *Farewell to Flexibility?*, Oxford: Basil Blackwell.

Pollock, S. and Sutton, J. (1999) 'Women Click: Feminism and the Internet', in S. Hawthorne and R. Klein (eds), *CyberFeminism: Connectivity, Critique and Creativity*, Melbourne: Spinifex Press.

Popay, J., Hearn, J. and Edwards, J. (eds) (1998) *Men, Gender Divisions and Welfare*, London: Routledge.

Porter, R. (2001) *The Enlightenment*, 2nd edn, Basingstoke: Palgrave.

Price, J. and Shildrick, M. (1999) *Feminist Theory and the Body. A Reader*, Edinburgh: Edinburgh University Press.

Prosser, J. (1998), *Second Skins: The Body Narratives of Transsexuality*, New York: Columbia University Press.

Purcell, K. (1988) 'Gender and the Experience of Employment', in D. Gallie (ed.), *Employment in Britain*, Oxford: Blackwell.

Puwar, N. (2004) 'Thinking about Making a Difference', *British Journal of Politics and International Relations*, 6: 65–80.

Rahman, M. (2000) *Sexuality and Democracy: Identities and Strategies in Lesbian and Gay Politics*, Edinburgh: Edinburgh University Press.

Rahman, M. (2004) 'The Shape of Equality: Discursive Deployments During the Section 28 Repeal in Scotland', *Sexualities*, 7(2): 150–66.

Ramazanoglu, C. with J. Holland (2002) *Feminist Methodology: Challenges and Choices* London: Sage.

Randall, V. (2002) 'Feminism', in D. Marsh and G. Stoker (eds), *Theory and Methods in Political Science*, Basingstoke: Palgrave.

Raymond, J. (1980*) The Transsexual Empire*, London: Women's Press.

Reay, D. (2001) 'The Paradox of Contemporary Femininities in Education: Combining Fluidity with Fixity', in B. Francis and C. Skelton (eds), *Investigating Gender: Contemporary Perspectives in Education*, Buckingham: Open University Press.

Reay, D. (2004) '"Mostly Roughs and Toughs": Social Class, Race and Representation in Inner City Schooling', *Sociology*, 38(5): 1005–23.

Redclift, N. and Sinclair, M.T. (eds) (1991) *Working Women, International Perspectives on Labour and Gender Ideology*, London: Routledge.

Reed, K. (2000) 'Dealing with Difference: Researching Health Beliefs and Behaviours of British Asian Mothers' *Sociological Research Online*, 4 (4) (http://www.socresonline.org.uk/4/4/reed.html).

Reed, K. (2003) *Worlds of Health*, Westport, CT: Praeger.

Reed, K. (2006) *New Directions in Social Theory: Race, Gender and the Canon*, London: Sage.

Reed, L.R. (1998) '"Zero Tolerance": Gender Performance and School Failure', in D. Epstein, J. Elwood, V. Hey and J. Maw (eds), *Failing Boys? Issues in Gender and Achievement*, Buckingham: Open University Press.

Reekie, G. (1992) 'Changes in the Adamless Eden: the Spatial and Sexual Transformation of a Brisbane Department Store, 1930–1990', in R. Shields (ed.), *Shopping for Subjectivity: the Subject of Consumption*, London: Routledge.

Reeves, R. (2002) *Dad's Army: The Case for Father-Friendly Workplaces*, London: The Work Foundation.

Reinharz, S. (1992) *Feminist Methods in Social Research*, New York: Oxford University Press.

Reis, C. (2002) 'The Private and Public Lives of Men Managers in a European Multinational Company', unpublished PhD thesis, Institute of Education, University of London.

Renold, E. and Allan, A. (2006) 'Bright and Beautiful: High-achieving Girls, Ambivalent Femininities and the Feminisation of Success', *Discourse: Studies in the Cultural Politics of Education*, 27 (4): 457–73.

Rex, J. (1967) 'Race, Community and Conflict: A Study of Sparkbrook' (by John Rex and Robert Moore with the assistance of Alan Shuttleworth, Jennifer Williams), published for the Institute of Race Relations, Oxford: Oxford University Press.

Ribbens, M., Edwards, J.R. and Gillies, V. (2003) *Making Families: Moral Tales of Parenting and Step-Parenting*, York: Sociology Press.

Rich, A. (1980) 'Compulsory Heterosexuality and Lesbian Existence', *Signs*, 5 (4): 631–60.

Rich, E. (2005) 'Young Women, Feminist Identities and Neo-Liberalism' *Women's Studies International Forum*, 28: 495–508.

Richardson, D. (ed.) (1996a) *Theorising Heterosexuality*, Buckingham: Open University Press.

Richardson, D. (1996b) 'Heterosexuality and Social Theory', in D. Richardson (ed.), *Theorising Heterosexuality*, Buckingham: Open University Press.

Richardson, D. (1997) 'Sexuality and Feminism', in V. Robinson and D. Richardson (eds), *Introducing Women's Studies: Feminist Theory and Practice*, 2nd edn, Basingstoke: Macmillan.

Richardson, D. (1998) 'Sexuality and Citizenship', *Sociology*, 32 (1): 83–100.

Richardson, D. (2000) *Rethinking Sexuality*, London: Sage.

Richardson, D. (2004) 'Locating Sexualities: From Here to Normality' *Sexualities* 7(4): 391–411.

Richardson, D. (2005a) 'Desiring Sameness? The Rise of a Neoliberal Politics of Normalisation', *Antipode*, 37 (3): 514–34.

Richardson, D. (2005b) 'Claiming Citizenship? Sexuality, Citizenship and Lesbian Feminist Theory', in C. Ingraham (ed.), *Thinking Straight*, New York: Routledge.

Richardson, D. (2006) 'Bordering Theory', in D. Richardson, J. McLaughlin and M.E. Casey (eds), *Intersections Between Feminist and Queer Theory*, Basingstoke: Palgrave Macmillan.

Richardson, D. (2007) 'Patterned Fluidities: (Re)Imagining the Relationship Between Gender and Sexuality', *Sociology*, 41 (3): 457–74.

Richardson, R. and Robinson, V. (eds) (1993) *Introducing Women's Studies: Feminist Theory and Practice*, London: Macmillan and New York: New York University Press.

Richardson, D. and Robinson, V. (1994) 'Theorizing Women's Studies, Gender Studies and Masculinity: The Politics of Naming', *European Journal of Women's Studies*, 1 (1): 11–27.

Richardson, D., McLaughlin, J. and M.E. Casey (eds) (2006) *Intersections Between Feminist and Queer Theory*, Basingstoke: Palgrave Macmillan.

Riddell, C. (1996) 'Divided Sisterhood: A Critical Review of Janice Raymond's *The Transsexual Empire*', in R. Ekins and D. King, *Blending Genders: Social Aspects of Cross-Dressing*, London: Routledge.

Riddell, S. (1989, reprinted 2005) 'Pupils, Resistance and Gender Codes: A Study of Classroom Encounters', in C. Skelton and B. Francis (eds), *A Feminist Critique of Education*, London: RoutledgeFalmer.

Riessman, C.K. (1990) *Divorce Talk*, New Brunswick: Rutgers University Press.

Ringrose, J. (2006) 'A New Universal Mean Girl: Examining the Discursive Construction and Social Regulation of a New Feminine Pathology', *Feminism and Psychology*, 16 (4): 405–24.

Robinson, V. (1997) 'Introducing Women's Studies', in V. Robinson and D. Richardson (eds), *Introducing Women's Studies: Feminist Theory and Practice*, 2nd edn, Basingstoke: Macmillan.

Robinson, V. (2001) 'Men's Studies', in C. Kramarae and D. Spender (eds), *The Routledge International Encyclopedia of Women's Studies*, London: Routledge.

Robinson, V. (2003) 'Radical Re-visionings?: The Theorising of Masculinities and (Radical) Feminist Theory', *Women's Studies International Forum*. 26 (2): 129–37.

Robinson, V. (2004) 'Taking Risks: Identity, Masculinities and Rockclimbing', in B. Wheaton (ed.), *Understanding Lifestyle Sports: Consumption, Identity and Difference*, London: Routledge.

Robinson, V. (2006) 'Internal and External Shifts and Constraints on Women's Studies and Gender Studies: Implications For the "Canon"', in M. Bidwell-Steiner and K.S. Wozonig (eds), *A Canon of Our Own? Kanonkritik und Kanonbildung in den Gender Studies*, Wien, Innsbruck: Studienverlag.

Robinson, V. (2007) 'Heterosexuality', in M. Flood, J.K. Gardiner, B. Pease and K. Pringle (eds), *The International Encyclopedia of Men and Masculinities*, London: Routledge.

Robinson, V. (2008) *Everyday Masculinities and Extreme Sport: Male Identity and Rock Climbing*, Oxford: Berg.

Robinson, V. and Richardson, D. (1994) 'Publishing Feminism: Redefining the Women's Studies Discourse', *Journal of Gender Studies*, 3 (1): 87–94.

Robinson, V. and Richardson, D. (eds) (1997) *Introducing Women's Studies*, 2nd edn, Basingstoke: Macmillan.

Robinson, V., Hockey, J. and Meah, A. (2004) '"What I Used to Do ... On My Mother's Settee": Spatial and Emotional Aspects of Heterosexuality in England', *Gender, Place and Culture*, 11(3): 417–35.

Robinson, V., Hockey, J. and Hall, A. (forthcoming, 2008) 'Occupational Cultures and the Embodiment of Masculinity: Hairdressing, Estate Agency and Firefighting', *Journal of Gender, Work and Organisation*.

Rofel, L. (1999) *Other Modernities: Gendered Yearnings in China after Socialism*. Berkeley: University of California Press.

Romero, M. (1992) *Maid in the USA*, New York: Routledge.

Romero, M. (1999) 'Who Takes Care of the Maid's Children? Exploring the Costs of Domestic Service', in H. Lindeman Nelson (ed.), *Feminism and Families*, New York: Routledge.

Rose, N. (1996) *Inventing Our Selves*, Cambridge: Cambridge University Press.

Rose, N. (1999) *Powers of Freedom: Reframing Political Thought*, Cambridge: Cambridge University Press.

Rose, S. (1998) *Lifelines: Biology, Freedom, Determinism*, Harmondsworth: Penguin.

Roseneil, S. (1995) *Disarming Patriarchy: Feminism and Political Action at Greenham* Buckingham: Open University Press.

Roseneil, S. (2000a) *Common Women Uncommon Practices: The Queer Feminisms of Greenham*, London and New York: Cassel.

Roseneil, S. (2000b) 'Queer Frameworks and Queer Tendencies: Towards an Understanding of Postmodern Transformations of Sexuality', *Sociological Research Online*, 5(3): 1–22 (http://www.socresonline.org.uk/5/3/rosenel.html).

Roseneil, S. (2002) 'The Heterosexual/Homosexual Binary: Past, Present and Future', in D. Richardson and S. Seidman (eds), *Handbook of Lesbian and Gay Studies*, London: Sage.

Roseneil, S. and Budgeon, S. (2004) 'Cultures of Intimacy and Care Beyond "The Family": Personal Life and Social Change in the Early 21st Century', *Current Sociology*, 52 (2): 135–59.

Rowbotham, S. (1993) *Homeworkers Worldwide*, London: Merlin Press.

Rubery, J. (ed.) (1988) *Women and Recession*, London: Routledge & Kegan Paul.

Rubin, G. (1975) 'The Traffic in Women: Notes on the "Political Economy" of Sex', in R. Reiter, *Toward an Anthropology of Women*, New York: Monthly Review Press.

Rubin, G. (1984) 'Thinking Sex: Notes for a Radical Theory of the Politics of Sexuality', in C.S. Vance (ed.), *Pleasure and Danger: Exploring Female Sexuality*, London: Routledge.

Rubin, G. with J. Butler (1998) 'Sexual Traffic', in M. Merck, N. Segal, and E. Wright (eds), *Coming Out of Feminism?*, Oxford: Blackwell.

Rubin, H. (1996) 'Do You Believe in Gender?', *Sojourner*, 21: 6.

Rubin, L. (1983) *Intimate Strangers: Men and Women Together*, New York: Harper & Row.

Russell, D. ([1982] 1990 expanded edition) *Rape in Marriage*, New York: Stein & Day.

Sainsbury, D. (ed.) (1994) *Gendering Welfare States*, London, Sage.

Sanders, V. (2001) 'First Wave Feminism', in S. Gamble (ed.), *The Routledge Companion to Feminism and Postfeminism*, New York: Routledge.

Sapiro, V. (1998) 'Feminist Studies and Political Science – and Vice Versa', in A. Phillips (ed.), *Feminism and Politics*, Oxford: Oxford University Press.

Schiebinger, L. (1993) *Gender in the Making of Modern Science*, Boston: Beacon Books.

Schneider, J. (2005) *Donna Haraway: Live Theory*, London: Continuum.

Scott, J. and Tilly, L. (1980) 'Women's Work and the Family in Nineteenth Century Europe', in A. Amsden (ed.), *The Economics of Women and Work*, Harmondsworth: Penguin.

Sedgwick, E.K. (1990) *Epistemology of the Closet*, Berkeley: University of California Press.

Segal, L. (1990) *Slow Motion: Changing Masculinities, Changing Men*, London: Virago.

Segal, L. (1994) *Straight Sex*, London: Virago.

Segal, L. (1999) *Why Feminism?: Gender, Psychology, Politics*, London: Polity Press.

Segal, L. (2007) *Slow Motion: Changing Masculinities, Changing Men*, 3rd edn, Basingstoke: Palgrave Macmillan.

Seidler, V. (1994) *Unreasonable Men: Masculinity and Social Theory*, London: Routledge.

Seidler, V. (2006) *Transforming Masculinities*, London, Routledge.

Seidman, S. (1993) 'Identity and Politics in a "Postmodern" Gay Culture: Some Historical and Conceptual Notes', in M. Warner (ed.), *Fear of a Queer Planet: Queer Politics and Social Theory*, Minneapolis: University of Minnesota Press.

Seidman, S. (1995) 'Deconstructing Queer Theory or the Under-Theorization of the Social and Ethical', in L. Nicholson and S. Seidman (eds), *Social Postmodernism: Beyond Identity Politics*, Cambridge: Cambridge University Press.

Seidman, S. (ed.) (1996) *Queer Theory/Sociology*, Oxford: Blackwell.

Seidman, S. (1997) *Difference Troubles. Queering Social Theory and Sexual Politics*, Cambridge: Cambridge University Press.

Sen, A. (1992) *Inequality Re-examined*, Oxford: Oxford University Press.

Sen, A. (1994) 'Freedom and Needs', *New Republic*, January 10–17: 31–8.

Sen, A. (2002) *Rationality and Freedom*, Cambridge, MA: Harvard University Press.

Sevenhuijsen, S. (1998) *Citizenship and the Ethics of Care*, London: Routledge.

Sharma, U. and Black, P. (2001) 'Look Good, Feel Better, Beauty Therapy as Emotional Labour', *Sociology*, 35 (4): 913–31.

Shelley, M. (1994) *Frankenstein: Or, 'The Modern Prometheus'.*, first published 1818, ed. M. Butler, Oxford: Oxford University Press.

Shilling, C. and Mellor, P. (2001) *The Sociological Ambition: The Elementary Forms of Social Life*, London: Sage.

Shostak, M. (1981) *Nisa: The Life and Words of a !Kung Woman*, London: Allan Lane.

Shostak, M. (2000) *Return to Nisa*, Cambridge, MA: Harvard University Press.

Showstack Sassoon, A. (ed.) (1987) *Women and the State*, London: Routledge.

Siltanen, J. and Stanworth, M. (1984) 'The Politics of Private Woman and Public Man', in J. Siltanen and M. Stanworth (eds), *Women and the Public Sphere: A Critique of Sociology and Politics*, London: Hutchinson.

Simpson, M. (1996) *It's a Queer World*, London: Vintage.

Skeggs, B. (1997) *Formations of Class and Gender*, London: Sage.

Skeggs, B. (1999) 'Matter out of Place: Visibility and Sexualities in Leisure Spaces', *Leisure Studies*, 18(3): 213–32.

Skeggs, B. (2001) 'The Toilet Paper: Femininity, Class and Mis-recognition', *Women's Studies International Forum*, 24(3/4): 295–307.

Skeggs, B. (2004) *Class, Self and Culture*, London: Routledge.

Smart, C. (1999) 'The "New" Parenthood: Fathers and Mothers after Divorce', in E. Silva (ed.), *The New Family?*, London: Sage.

Smart, C. and Neale, B. (1999) *Family Fragments?* Cambridge: Polity.

Smart, C. and Shipman, B. (2004) 'Visions in Monochrome: Families, Marriage and the Individualization Thesis', *British Journal of Sociology*, 55 (4): 491–509.

Smeaton, D. (2006) 'Work Return Rates after Childbirth in the UK: Trends, Determinants and Implications: A Comparison of Cohorts Born in 1958 and 1970', *Work, Employment and Society*, 20 (1): 5–25.

Smith, A.-M. (1994) 'The Imaginary Inclusion of the Assimilable "Good Homosexual": The British New Right's Representations of Sexuality and Race', *Diacritics*, 24 (2–3): 58–70.

Smith, A.-M. (1997) 'The Good Homosexual and the Dangerous Queer: Resisting the "New Homophobia"', in L Segal (ed.), *New Sexual Agendas*, London: Macmillan.

Smith, D. (1990) *Texts, Facts and Femininity*, London: Routledge.

Smith, D. (1999) *Writing the Social: Critique, Theory, and Investigations*, Toronto: University of Toronto Press.

Smith, S. (1993) 'Residential Segregation and the Politics of Racialisation', in M. Cross and M. Keith (eds), *Racism, the City and the State*, London: Routledge.

Smithers, R. (2004) 'Minister Backs Split-Sex Lessons in Some Subjects', *The Guardian*, 17 November.

Snell, M. (1986) 'Equal Pay and Sex Discrimination', in *Feminist Review* (ed.), *Waged Work: A Reader*, London: Virago.

Sobchack, V. (2004) *Carnal Thoughts. Embodiment and Moving Image Culture*, Berkeley: University of California Press.

Solomos, J. (1993) *Race and Racism in Britain*, London: Macmillan.

Solomos, J. and Back, L. (1996) *Racism and Society*, Basingstoke: Macmillan.

Somerville, J. (2000) *Feminism and the Family: Politics and Society in the UK and USA*, Basingstoke: Macmillan.

Song, M. (1995) 'Between "the Front" and "the Back" – Chinese Women's Work in Family Business', *Women's Studies International Forum*, 18(3): 285–98.

Spence, J. and Stephenson, C. (2007) 'Female Involvement in the Miners' Strike 1984–5: Trajectories of Activism', *Sociological Research Online*, 12 (1) (http://www.socresonline.org.uk/12/1/spence.html, accessed 16 February 2007).

Spender, D. (1982) *Invisible Women: The Schooling Scandal*, London: Writers and Readers Publishing Cooperative.

Spender, D. (1995) *Nattering on the Net: Women, Power and Cyberspace*, Melbourne: Spinifex Press.

Spivak, C.G. (1990) *The Post-Colonial Critique*, London: Routledge.

Squires, J. (1996) 'Fabulous Feminist Futures and the Lure of Cyberculture', in J. Dovy (ed.), Fractal Dreams: New Media in Social Context, London:Lawrence & Wishart.

Squires, J. (1999a) *Gender in Political Theory*, Cambridge: Polity.

Squires, J. (1999b) 'Rethinking the Boundaries of Political Representation', in S. Walby (ed.), *New Agendas for Women*, Basingstoke, Macmillan.

Squires, J. (2000) 'Fabulous Feminist Futures and the Lure of Cyberculture', in. D. Bell and B. Kennedy (eds), *The Cybercultures Reader*, London: Routledge.

Stacey, Jackie (1993) *Star Gazing: Hollywood Cinema and Female Spectatorship*, London: Routledge.

Stacey, Jackie (1997) 'Feminist Theory: Capital F, Capital T', in V. Robinson and D. Richardson (eds), *Introducing Women's Studies: Feminist Theory and Practice*, Basingstoke: Macmillan.

Stacey, Judith (1991) *Brave New Families*, New York: Basic Books.

Stacey, Judith (1996) *In the Name of the Family: Rethinking Family Values in the Postmodern Age*, Boston: Beacon Press.

Stacey, Judith (2004) 'Cruising to Familyland: Gay Hypergamy and Rainbow Kinship', *Critical Sociology*, 52 (2): 181–97.

Stanley, L. (1984) 'Should "Sex" Really be "Gender" or "Gender" Really be "Sex"?', in R. Anderson and W. Sharrock (eds), *Applied Sociology*, London: Allen & Unwin.

Stanley, L. (ed.) (1990) *Feminist Praxis: Research, Theory and Epistemology in Feminist Sociology*, London: Routledge.

Stanley, L. (1992) *The Auto/biographical: Theory and Practice of Feminist Auto/biography*, Manchester: Manchester University Press.

Stanley, L. (2004) 'A Methodological Toolkit for Feminist Research: Analytical Reflexivity, Accountable Knowledge, Moral Epistemology and being "A Child of Our Time"', in H. Piper and I. Stronach (eds), *Educational Research: Difference and Diversity*, Aldershot: Gower.

Stanley, L. and Wise, S. (2006a) 'Having it All: A Future for Feminist Research', in K. Davies et al. (eds), *Sage Handbook on Gender & Women's Studies*, London: Sage.

Stanley, L. and Wise, S. (2006b) 'Putting it into Practice: Using Feminist Fractured Foundationalism in Researching Children in the Concentration Camps of the South African War', *Sociological Research Online* 11 (1) (http://www.socresonline.org.uk/11/1/stanley.html).

Stanley, L. and Wise, S. (2006c) 'Commentary: Using Feminist Fractured Foundationalism in Researching Children in the Concentration Camps of the South African War', in S. Hesse-Biber (ed.), *Handbook on Feminist Research*, New York: Sage.

Stanworth, M. (1981) *Gender and Schooling: A Study of Sexual Divisions in the Classroom*, London: Hutchinson.

Stead, J. (1987) *Never the Same Again: Women and the Miners Strike*, London: The Women's Press

Steedman, C. (1986) *Landscape For a Good Woman*, London: Virago.

Stefano, D.C. (1990) 'Dilemmas of Difference: Feminism, Modernity, and Postmodernism', in L. Nicholson (ed.), *Feminism/Postmodernism*, New York and London: Routledge.

Steinberg, D.L. (1997) *Bodies in Glass*, Manchester: Manchester University Press.

Stephenson, M. (1998) *The Glass Trapdoor: Women , Politics and the Media during the 1997 General Election*, London: Fawcett.

Stokes, W. (2005) *Women in Contemporary Politics*, Cambridge: Polity.

Stoller, R. (1968) *Sex and Gender, Vol 1: On the Development of Masculinity and Femininity*, London: Hogarth Press.

Stone, S. (1991) 'The Empire Strikes Back: A Posttranssexual Manifesto', in J. Epstein and K. Straub (eds), *Body Guards: The Cultural Politics of Sexual Ambiguity*, London: Routledge.

subRosa. *subRosa*. N. pub. 24 March 2006. <http://www.cyberfeminist.net>.

Suleri, S. (1992) 'Women Skin Deep: Feminism and the Postcolonial Condition', *Critical Inquiry*, 18 (4): 756–69.

Sullivan, B. (2003) 'Trafficking in Women', *International Feminist Journal of Politics*, 5 (1): 67–91.

Sullivan, N. (2003) *A Critical Introduction to Queer Theory*, Edinburgh: Edinburgh University Press and Melbourne: Circa Books.

Suzuki, N. (2005) 'Filipina-Japanese Marriages and Fantasies of Transnational Traversal', in N. Constable (ed.), *Cross-Border Marriages: Gender and Mobility in Transnational Asia*, Philadelphia: University of Pennsylvania Press.

Taft, J. (2004) 'Girl Power Politics: Pop-Culture Barriers and Organizational Resistance', in A. Harris (ed.), *All About the Girl: Culture, Power and Identity*, New York: Routledge.

Tam, M. (1997) *Part-time Employment: A Bridge or a Trap*, Aldershot: Ashgate.

Tasker, Y. (1998) *Working Girls: Gender and Sexuality in Popular Cinema*, London: Routledge.

Tasker, Y. (2004) *Action and Adventure Cinema*, London and New York: Routledge.

Taylor, Y. (2004) 'Negotiation and Navigation: An Exploration of the Spaces/Places of Working-Class Lesbians', *Sociological Research Online*, 9 (1): 1–24 (http://www.socresonline.org.uk/9/1/taylor.html).

Taylor, Y. (2005a) 'The Gap and How to Mind It: Intersections of Class and Sexuality', *Sociological Research Online*, 10(3): 1–17.

Taylor, Y. (2005b) 'Inclusion, Exclusion, Exclusive? Sexual Citizenship and the Repeal of Section 28/2a', *Sexualities*, 8(3): 375–80.

Taylor, Y. (2005c) 'Real Politik or Real Politics? Working-Class Lesbians' Political "Awareness" and Activism', *Women's Studies International Forum*, 28(6): 484–94.

Taylor, Y. (2007a) *Classed Outsiders: Working-Class Lesbian Life Experiences*, Basingstoke: Palgrave Macmillan.

Taylor, Y. (2007b) '"If your Face Doesn't Fit…": The Misrecognition of Working-Class Lesbians in Scene Space', *Leisure Studies*, 26 (2): 161–78.

Temkina, A. and Zdravomyslova, E. (2006) 'Gender and Women's Studies in Contemporary Russia', in M. Bidwell-Steiner and K.S. Wozonig (eds), *A Canon of Our Own? Kanonkritik und Kanonbildung in den Gender Studies*, Wien and Innsbruck: Studienverlag.

Terry, J. (1999) *An American Obsession. Science, Medicine and Homosexuality in Modern Society*, Chicago: University of Chicago Press.

Therborn, G. (2004) *Between Sex and Power: Family in the World, 1900–2000*, London: Routledge.

Thompson, A. (1996) *Critical Reasoning*, London: Routledge.

Thorne, B. (1982) 'Feminist Rethinking of the Family: An Overview', in B. Thorne and M. Yalom (eds), *Rethinking the Family: Some Feminist Questions*, New York: Longman.

Throsby, K. (2004) *When IVF Fails: Feminism, Infertility and the Negotiation of Normality*, Basingstoke: Palgrave Macmillan.

Turner, B. (1992) *Regulating Bodies: Essays in Medical Sociology*, London: Routledge.

Tyler, M. (2004) 'Managing Between the Sheets: Lifestyle Magazines and the Management of Sexuality in Everyday Life', *Sexualities*, 7(1): 81–106.

UN (United Nations) (1986) 'Forward Looking Strategies for the Advancement of Women', Report of the World Conference to Review and Appraise the Achievements of the United Nations Decade for Women: Equality, Development and Peace, Nairobi, 1985, New York: UN (http://www.un.org/esa/gopher-data/conf/fwcw/nfls/nfls.en, last accessed 29 June 2006).

UNDP (United Nations Development Programme) (2005) *Human Development Report, 2005*, New York: United Nations Development Programme.

Ungerson, C. (1983) 'Why do Women Care?', in J. Finch and D. Groves (eds), *A Labour of Love, Women, Work and Caring*, London: Routledge & Kegan Paul.

Ungerson, C. (1987) *Policy is Personal, Sex, Gender and Informal Care*, London: Tavistock.

Unterhalter, E. (2007) 'Gender Equality, Education and the Capability Approach', in M. Walker and E. Unterhalter (eds), *Sen's Capability Approach and Social Justice in Education*, Basingstoke: Palgrave Macmillan.

Urry, J. (2002) 'Mobility and Proximity', *Sociology*, 36 (2): 255–74.

Valentine, G. (1993) 'Hetero-Sexing Space: Lesbian Perceptions and Experiences of Everyday Spaces', *Environment and Planning D – Society and Space*, 9 (3): 395–413.

Valentine, G. (1999) 'A Corporeal Geography of Consumption', *Environment and Planning D – Society and Space*, 17: 329–51.

VanEvery, J. (1995) *Heterosexual Women Changing the Family: Refusing to be a 'Wife'*, London: Taylor & Francis.

VanEvery, J. (1996) 'Heterosexuality and Domestic Life', in D. Richardson (ed.), *Theorizing Heterosexuality: Telling it Straight*, Buckingham: Open University Press.

VanEvery, J. (1997) 'Understanding Gendered Inequality: Reconceptualizing Housework', *Women's Studies International Forum*, 20 (2): 411–20.

Van Oorschot, W. (2002) 'Miracle or Nightmare? A Critical Review of Dutch Activation Policies and their Outcomes', *Journal of Social Policy*, 31 (3): 399–420.

Van Zoonen, L. (1994) *Feminist Media Studies*, London: Sage.

Virdee, S. (2006) 'Race, Employment and Social Change: A Critique of Current Orthodoxies', *Ethnic and Racial Studies*, 29 (4): 605–28.

Visser, J. (2002) 'The First Part-time Economy in the World: A Model to be Followed?', *Journal of European Social Policy*, 12 (1): 23–42.

Vogler, C. (1998) 'Money in the Household: Some Underlying Issues of Power', *Sociological Review*, 46 (4): 687–714.

Vogler, C. and Pahl, J. (1993) 'Social and Economic Change in the Organisation of Money within Marriage', *Work, Employment and Society*, 7 (1): 723–34.

Waddington, D, Wykes, M. and Critcher, C. (1991) *Split at the Seams?*, Milton Keynes: Open University Press.

Wakeford, N. (1999) 'Gender and the Landscapes of Computing in an Internet Café', in M. Crang, P. Crang and J. May (eds), *Virtual Geographies: Bodies, Spaces and Relations*, London: Routledge.

Walby, S. (1986) *Patriarchy at Work*, Cambridge: Polity.

Walby, S. (1988) *Gender Segregation at Work*, Milton Keynes: Open University Press.

Walby, S. (1989) 'Theorising Patriarchy', *Sociology*, 23 (2): 213–34.

Walby, S. (1990) *Theorizing Patriarchy*, Oxford: Blackwell.

Walby, S. (1997) *Gender Transformations*, Routledge: London.

Walby, S. (2004) 'The European Union and Gender Equality: Emergent Varieties of Gender Regime', *Social Politics*, 11 (1): 4–29.

Walkerdine, V. (1989) *Counting Girls Out*, London: Virago.

Walkerdine, V. (1991) *Schoolgirl Fictions*, London: Verso.

Walkerdine, V. (2003) 'Reclassifying Upward Mobility: Femininity and the Neo-Liberal Subject', *Gender and Education*, 15(3): 238–49.

Walkerdine, V. (2005) 'Remember Not to Die – Young Girls and Video Games', paper presented at ESRC seminar series: Girls and Education 3–16 November, Cardiff University.

Walkerdine, V., Lucey, H. and Melody, J. (2001) *Growing up Girl: Psychosocial Explorations of Gender and Class*, Basingstoke: Palgrave.

Walkerdine, V. and Ringrose, J. (2006) 'Femininities: Reclassifying Upward Mobility and the Neo-liberal Subject', in B. Francis and C. Skelton (eds), *Gender and Education Handbook*, Thousand Oaks, CA: Sage.

Walters, S.D. (2005) 'From Here to Queer: Radical Feminism, Postmodernism, and the Lesbian Menance', in I. Morland and A. Willox (eds), *Queer Theory*, Basingstoke: Palgrave Macmillan.

Wang, Y. (2005) 'Invisible Violence: Objectifying "Foreign Brides" and Cross-National Marriage Agents in Taiwan', paper presented at the 18th Conference of the Feminist and Women's Studies Association (UK and Ireland), University of Aberdeen, September.

Ware, V. (1992) *Beyond the Pale: White Women, Racism and History*, London: Verso.

Warner, M. (ed.) (1993) *Fear of a Queer Planet: Queer Politics and Social Theory*, Minneapolis: University of Minnesota Press.

WASS (2007) 'Gender Transformations in Higher Education' in *Sociological Research Online*, 12 (1) (http://socresonline.org.uk/12/1/lambert.html.

Watson, J.L. (1977) *Between Two Cultures*, Oxford: Basil Blackwell.

Weeks, J. (2003) *Sexuality*, London: Routledge.

Weeks, J., Heaphy, B. and Donovan, C. (2001) *Same Sex Intimacies: Families of Choice and Other Life Experiments*, London: Routledge.

Weiner, G., Arnot, M. and David, M. (1997) 'Is the Future Female? Female Success, Male Disadvantage and Changing Gender Patterns in Education', in A. Halsey, P. Brown, H. Lauder and A. Stuart-Wells (eds), *Education, Culture, Economy and Society*, Oxford: Oxford University Press.

Weston, K. (1991) *Families We Choose: Gays, Lesbians, Kinship*, New York: Columbia University Press.

Weston, K. (1995) 'Get Thee to a Big City: Sexual Imaginary and the Great Gay Migration' *GLQ*, 2: 253–77.

Westwood, S. (1984) *All Day, Every Day: Factory and Family in Women's Lives*, London: Pluto.

Wetherell, M. and Griffin, C. (1991) 'Feminist Psychology and the Study of Men and Masculinity: Part 1: Assumptions and Perspectives', *Feminism and Psychology*. 1 (3): 133–68.

Wheaton, B. (2000) '"New Lads"? Masculinities and the "New Sport" Participant', *Men and Masculinities*, 2 (4): 434–56.

Wheaton, B. (ed.) (2004) *Understanding Lifestyle Sports: Consumption, Identity and Difference*, London: Routledge.

Wheeler, D. (2001) 'New Technologies, Old Culture: A Look at Women, Gender, and the Internet in Kuwait.' in C. Ess (ed.), *Culture, Technology, Communication: Towards an Intercultural Global Village*, New York: State University of New York Press.

Wheelock, J. (1990) *Husbands at Home. The Domestic Economy in a Post-Industrial Society*, London: Routledge.

Whelehan, I. (1995) *Modern Feminist Thought from the Second Wave to 'Post Feminism'*, Edinburgh: Edinburgh University Press (US edn *Feminist Thought: From the Second Wave to 'Postfeminism'*, New York: New York University Press).

Whelehan, I. (2004) *Having It All?*, Paper presented to the ESRC New Femininities Seminar Series, London School of Economics, 19 November.

Whitehead, S. (2000) 'Masculinities, Race and Nationhood – Critical Connections', *Gender and History*, 12 (2): 472–6.

Whitehead, S. (2002) *Men and Masculinities: Key Themes and New Directions*, Cambridge: Polity.

Whitford, M. (1991) *Luce Irigaray: Philosophy of the Feminine*, London: Routledge.

WHO (World Health Organization) (2003) *Integrating Gender into HIV/AIDS Programmes*, Geneva: WHO.

Whyte, J. (1983) *Beyond the Wendy House: Sex Role Stereotyping in Primary Schools*, York: Longman

Whyte, J., Deem, R., Kant, L. and Cruickshank, M. (eds) (1985) *Girl Friendly Schooling*, London: Methuen.

Whyte, J., Deem, R. and Cruickshank, M. (1988) *Girl Friendly Schooling*, New York: Routledge.

Williams, F. (2004) *Rethinking Families*, London: Calouste Gulbenkian Foundation.

Williamson, J. (1978) *Decoding Advertisements*, London: Marion Boyars.

Wilson, A. (1978) *Finding a Voice: Asian Women in Britain Today*, London: Virago.

Wilson, G. (1987) 'Patterns of Responsibility and Irresponsibility in Marriage', in J. Brannen and G. Wilson (eds), *Give and Take in Families*, London: Allen & Unwin.

Wilson, M. (2002) '"I am the Prince of Pain, For I am a Princess in the Brain": Liminal Transgender Identities, Narrative and the Elimination of Ambiguities', *Sexualities*, 5 (4): 425–48.

Wilton, T. (1996) 'Which One's the Man? The Heterosexualisation of Lesbian Sex', in D. Richardson (ed.), *Theorising Heterosexuality*, Buckingham: Open University Press.

Wilton, T. (2000) 'Out/performing Our Selves: Sex, Gender and Cartesian Dualism', *Sexualities*, 3 (2): 237–54.

Windebank, J. (2001) 'Dual Earner Couples in Britain and France: Gender Divisions of Domestic Labour and Parenting Work in Different Welfare States', *Work, Employment and Society*, 15 (2): 269–90.

Wing, A.K. (2000) *Global Critical Race Feminism: An International Reader*, New York: New York University Press.

Wirth, L. (2001) 'Women in Management: Closer to Breaking through the Glass Ceiling?', in M. Loutfi (ed.), *Women, Gender and Work*, Geneva: International Labour Office.

Wischermann, U. (2000) 'The Sex/Gender Debate in Germany', in R. Braidotti and E. Vonk (eds), *The Making of European Women's Studies*, Utrecht: Drukkerij Zuidam and Uithof.

Wise, S. and Stanley, L. (2003) 'Looking Back, Looking Forward: Recent Feminist Sociology Reviewed" *Sociological Research Online*, 8 (3) (http://www.socresonline.org.uk/8/3/wise.html).

Wittig, M. (1981) 'One is not Born a Woman', *Feminist Issues*, 1 (2): 47–54. Reprinted in M. Wittig (1992) *The Straight Mind and Other Essays*, Hemel Hempstead: Harvester.

Wittig, M. (1992) *The Straight Mind and Other Essays*. Hemel Hempstead: Harvester Wheatsheaf.

Witz, A. (1997) 'Women and Work', in V. Robinson and D. Richardson (eds), *Introducing Women's Studies: Feminist Theory and Practice*, 2nd edn, Basingstoke: Palgrave.

Witz, A. (2000) 'Whose Body Matters? Feminist Sociology and the Corporeal Turn in Sociology and Feminism', *Body and Society*, 6: 1–24.

Wollstonecraft, M. (1792/1975) *The Vindication of the Rights of Women*, ed. M. Kramnick, Harmondsworth: Penguin.

Wood, E. (2000) 'Working in the Fantasy Factory: The Attention Hypothesis and the Enacting of Masculine Power in Strip Clubs', *Journal of Contemporary Ethnography*, 29 (1): 5–31.

Woodward, K. (1997) 'Motherhood: Myths and Meanings', in K. Woodward (ed.), *Identity and Difference*, London: Sage.

Woodward, K. (2002) *Understanding Identity*, London: Arnold.

Woodward, K. (2005) 'On and Off the Pitch: Diversity Policies and Transforming Identities', CRESC Working Paper 8, www.cresc.ac.uk.

Woodward, K. (2006) *Boxing, Masculinity and Identity, The 'I' of the Tiger*, London: Routledge.

Woodward, S. (2005) 'Looking Good, Feeling Right: Personal Aesthetics of the Self', in S. Kuchler and D. Miller, *Clothing as Material Culture*, Oxford: Berg.

Woolf, N. (1991) *The Beauty Myth: How Images of Beauty Are Used Against Women*, New York: Anchor.

Woolf, V. (1938) *Three Guineas*, Harmondsworth: Penguin.

Woollett, A., Marshall, H., Nicolson, P. and Dosanjh-Matwala, N. (1994). 'Asian Women's Ethnic Identity: The Impact of Gender and Context in Accounts of Women Bringing Up Children in East London', in K.K Bhavnani and A. Phoenix (eds), *Shifting Identities, Shifting Racisms: A Feminism and Psychology Reader*, London: Sage.

Wright, E. (1997) 'Thoroughly Postmodern Feminist Criticism', in S. Kemp and J. Squires (eds), *Feminisms*, Oxford: Oxford University Press.

WWC (Women and Work Commission) (2006) *Shaping a Fairer Future*, London, Department of Trade and Industry.

Yeates, N. (2005) 'A Global Political Economy of Care', *Social Policy and Society*, 4 (2): 227–34.

Yip, A. (2004) 'Negotiating Space with Family and Kin in Identity Construction: the Narratives of British Non-Heterosexual Muslims', *Sociological Review*, 52(3): 336–50.

Youdell, D. (2004) 'Engineering Education Markets, Constituting Schools, and Subjectivating Students: The Bureaucratic, Institutional, and Classroom Dimensions of Educational Triage', *Journal of Education Policy*, 19 (4): 407–32.

Youdell, D. (2005) 'Flirting and Working? The Commensurability of Popular Desirable Hetero-Femininity and Institutionally Acceptable Student-Hood', paper presented at *ESRC seminar series: Girls and Education 3–16*, Cardiff University, November.

Young, I.M. (1990) *Justice and the Politics of Difference*, Princeton, NJ: Princeton University Press.

Young, I.M. (2005) *On Female Body Experience: 'Throwing Like a Girl' and Other Essays*, Oxford: Oxford University Press.

Young, L. (1995) *Fear of the Dark: Race, Gender and Sexuality in the Cinema*, London: Routledge.

Younger, M. and Warrington, M. (2003) 'Raising Boys' Achievement', DfES Research Report RR636 (http://www.standards.dfes.gov.uk/genderandachievement/pdf/HomertonReport-final.pdf?version=1, accessed June 2005).

Zylinska, J. (2005) *The Ethics of Cultural Studies*, London: Continuum.

# Author Index

# Subject Index

CPSIA information can be obtained at www.ICGtesting.com
Printed in the USA
LVOW06s1612180713

343558LV00014B/1245/P